PEARSON EDEXCEL INTERNATIONAL GCSE (9–1)

INFORMATION AND COMMUNICATION TECHNOLOGY

Student Book

Pete Bell

Published by Pearson Education Limited, 80 Strand, London, WC2R 0RL.

www.pearsonglobalschools.com

Copies of official specifications for all Pearson qualifications may be found on the website: https://qualifications.pearson.com

Text © Pearson Education Limited 2017
Edited by Fleur Frederick, Unber Sheikh and Andrew Lowe
Designed by Cobalt id
Typeset and illustrated by Tech-Set Ltd, Gateshead, UK
Cover design by Pearson Education Limited
Picture research by Frances Topp
Cover photo © Getty Images: hadynyah
Inside front cover: **Shutterstock.com:** Dmitry Lobanov

The rights of Pete Bell to be identified as author of this work have been asserted by him in accordance with the Copyright, Designs and Patents Act 1988.

First published 2017

25
14

British Library Cataloguing in Publication Data
A catalogue record for this book is available from the British Library

ISBN 978 0 435 18893 1

Copyright notice
All rights reserved. No part of this publication may be reproduced in any form or by any means (including photocopying or storing it in any medium by electronic means and whether or not transiently or incidentally to some other use of this publication) without the written permission of the copyright owner, except in accordance with the provisions of the Copyright, Designs and Patents Act 1988 or under the terms of a licence issued by the Copyright Licensing Agency, 5th Floor, Shackleton House, 4 Battlebridge Lane, London, SE1 2HX (www.cla.co.uk). Applications for the copyright owner's written permission should be addressed to the publisher.

Printed in Italy by L.E.G.O. S.p.A. Lavis (TN)

Picture Credits
The author and publisher would like to thank the following individuals and organisations for permission to reproduce photographs:

(Key: b-bottom; c-centre; l-left; r-right; t-top)

123RF.com: 147tr, Adamgolabek 159tr, Alphaspirit 182tr, Marcel Braendli 130b, **Alexander Spatari:** 186, 234, 244t, 245, 246, 251, 252, 253, 255b, 258, 259, 260, 261; fotokostic 187t, Christos Georghiou 240cr, Antonio Guilem 120t, Shawn Hempel 24br, Igor Klimov 32cr, lightwave 127tr, Nataliia 276tr, stockbroker 133b, Algirdas Urbonavicius 40t, Maksym Yemelyanov 26l; **Alamy Stock Photo:** 23t, 248t, Ian Allenden 30tl, Art Directors & TRIP 35b, Blend Images 239b, Aleksey Boldin 171c, Chih-Chung Johnny Chang 22cl, B Christopher 72cr, 160b, CoverSpot Photography 85c, Directphoto Collection 116t, Estock 107cl, Eyre 76bl, Mike Goldwater 157c, David J. Green 37r, H. Mark Weidman Photography 72b, Bengt Hultqvist 210l (insert), D. Hurst 14t, Image Source 170r, Isle of Man 51c, Wilawan Khasawong 6t, Dzmitry Kliapitski 8cl, Jason Knott 309t, Daniel Krasoń 19b, Richard Levine 255tl, Lyubomir Levterov 32bl, Oleksiy Maksymenko 32cl, Mauritius Images 21bl, NetPics 118r, North Wind Picture Archives 109t, Paul Paladin 5c, Malcolm Park 209c, Mehul Patel 22b, Reuters 19t, Reuters / Arnd Wiegmann 28bl, Reuters / Tobias Schwarz 28br, Thomas Rey 60b, Alex Segre 29br, Richard Sheppard 152t, SJA Photo 24t, Jochen Tack 12c, Hugh Threlfall 11bl, Alexander Vedmed 74bl, Paul Velgos 29l, Wavebreakmedia Ltd PH85 24cr, Xinhua 25t, Zoonar / Igor Poleshchuk 59t; **CUI Inc:** 37l; **Doro:** 8tr; **Getty Images:** Andrew Aitchison 129cl, Bagi1998 24cl, Bloomberg / David Paul Morris 13c, Bloomberg / Simon Dawson 154t, Menno Boermans 72cl, Jessica Durrant 166c, ESA 52bl, Future Publishing 12t, Johnkellerman 30tr, Stuart Kinlough 2c, 64c, 94c, 180c, 200c, Zero Liew 23c, Peter Macdiarmid 129tl, Per Makitalo 36br, Matejmo 96tr, Official Windows Magazine 15tr, Scanrail 5t, Science Photo Library 18b, Stocktrek Images 73tr, TomekD76 30c, Alvis Upitis 27b, Wachiwit 21tr; **Gold GMT:** 8tl; **Michel Grandjean:** Grandjean, Martin (2014). "La connaissance est un réseau". Les Cahiers du Numérique 10 (3): 37-54 (DOI 10.3166 / LCN.10.3.37-54). 115tr; **NASA:** Tim Copra 52br; **National Archives:** Crown Copyright 117tr; **Pearson Education:**

Lord and Leverett 161l, 162l, Naki Kouyioumtzis 187; **Science Photo Library Ltd:** Phanie / Svidineenko 37b; **Shutterstock.com:** 145r, Africa Studio 6c, Alisafarov 177r, Ambient Ideas 208tr, Antun Hirsman 199, Asharkyu 34c, AstroStar 17b, Aviemil 210l (backspace), Sven Bannuscher 209t, Bbernard 115tl, Joe Besure 69tl, Sinisa Bobic 210l (tab), Alexey Boldin 22tl, Simon Bratt 85b, Burnel1 33bc, Cigdem 202tr, Cristovao 168tr, Andrea Danti 27l, Dgbomb 70r, Matus Duda 31b, Maksym Dykha 33t, Esbobeldijk 33b, Fonzales 190b, fotoscool 116, Georgejmclittle 169, Kaspars Grinvalds 9t, Antonio Guillem 121tl, Hanohiki 79tr, Harvepino 4tr, Hoperan 176tr, Icons vector 149l, Improvize 86cl, Chamnong Inthasaro 72t, Brian A Jackson 7c, Jocic 33cr, Russell Johnson 23b, Chris Johnsson 13t, JUN3 210l(del key), Anan Kaewkhammul 183bc, Karynav 239t, Igor Kyrlytsya 21tl, Lexaarts 71tl, Linn Currie 161c, 162c, Lobke Peers 226r, Ivan Martynyuk 84tl, Mikhail Mishchenko 307tr, Monkey Business Images 127bl, Nobeastsofierce 29bl, Nuclearist 132t, Francesco Ocello 157tl, Photobank Gallery 66tr, Pinkyone 225, 226l, Tatiana Popova 179l, Pressmaster 127br, Ra2studio 151b, Ronstik 262r, s4svisuals 105, Sari ONeal 10, Sashkin 84c, Sayasouk 170l, singh_lens 128, Slava2009 243b, 244b, Stocksnapper 44l, Syda Productions 32br, Tam_odin 210l (shift), Tanuha2001 42t, Tavizta 209l (caps lock), The Loupe Project. 210r (keyboard), UrbanImages 161r, 162r, Vasiliy Torzhinskiy 111c, wavebreakmedia 127tl, Peter Wollinga 133r, You can more 6b, Vlada Zhi 133t; **SuperStock:** 36t, 121c, All Canada Photos / OleksiyMaksymenko 15l, Marka / Danilo Donadoni 33cl; **Ushahidi Inc:** 130tr

Figures
Figures on page 134 and page 136 Facebook, https://en.facebookbrand.com/, Facebook © 2016, Facebook is a trademark of Facebook, Inc.

Screenshots
Screenshot on page 48 reprinted with permission from Adobe Systems Incorporated; Screenshots on page 55 and 104 from Twitter: Twitter, Tweet and Twitter Bird Logo are trademarks of Twitter, Inc. or its affiliates; Screenshot on page 87 © 2015 Google Inc. All rights reserved. Google and the Google Logo are registered trademarks of Google Inc.; Screenshot on page 134 Facebook © 2016, Facebook is a trademark of Facebook, Inc.; Screenshot on page 143 with permission from Tumblr; Screenshot on page 161 from Cats Protection website, with permission; Screenshot on page 185 from https://soundation.com/user/mrbell/track/igcse_sound used with permission; Screenshots on page 188 and page 189 Pearson Education Ltd; Screenshots on pages 203, 209, 211, 212, 213, 214, 215, 217, 218, 219, 222, 224, 227, 228, 242, 256, 303 courtesy of LibreOffice: "LibreOffice" and "The Document Foundation" are registered trademarks of their corresponding registered owners or are in actual use as trademarks in one or more countries; Screenshot on page 263 from KompoZer used with permission.

All other images © Pearson Education

Endorsement statement
In order to ensure that this resource offers high-quality support for the associated Pearson qualification, it has been through a review process by the awarding body. This process confirms that this resource fully covers the teaching and learning content of the specification or part of a specification at which it is aimed. It also confirms that it demonstrates an appropriate balance between the development of subject skills, knowledge and understanding, in addition to preparation for assessment.

Endorsement does not cover any guidance on assessment activities or processes (e.g. practice questions or advice on how to answer assessment questions), included in the resource nor does it prescribe any particular approach to the teaching or delivery of a related course.

While the publishers have made every attempt to ensure that advice on the qualification and its assessment is accurate, the official specification and associated assessment guidance materials are the only authoritative source of information and should always be referred to for definitive guidance.

Pearson examiners have not contributed to any sections in this resource relevant to examination papers for which they have responsibility.

Examiners will not use endorsed resources as a source of material for any assessment set by Pearson. Endorsement of a resource does not mean that the resource is required to achieve this Pearson qualification, nor does it mean that it is the only suitable material available to support the qualification, and any resource lists produced by the awarding body shall include this and other appropriate resources.

ABOUT THIS BOOK	vi
ASSESSMENT OVERVIEW	viii
UNIT 1: DIGITAL DEVICES	2
UNIT 2: CONNECTIVITY	64
UNIT 3: OPERATING ONLINE	94
UNIT 4: ONLINE GOODS AND SERVICES	166
UNIT 5: APPLYING INFORMATION AND COMMUNICATION TECHNOLOGY	180
UNIT 6: SOFTWARE SKILLS	200
ANSWERS TO END-OF-CHAPTER QUESTIONS	334
GLOSSARY	340
INDEX	348

UNIT 1
DIGITAL DEVICES

CHAPTER 1: DIGITAL DEVICES	4
CHAPTER 2: SOFTWARE	42
CHAPTER 3: MEMORY AND PROCESSORS	59

UNIT 2
CONNECTIVITY

CHAPTER 4: DIGITAL COMMUNICATION	66
CHAPTER 5: NETWORKS	79

UNIT 3
OPERATING ONLINE

CHAPTER 6: RISKS TO DATA AND PERSONAL INFORMATION	96
CHAPTER 7: IMPACT OF THE INTERNET	109
CHAPTER 8: ONLINE COMMUNITIES	132
CHAPTER 9: THE IMPLICATIONS OF DIGITAL TECHNOLOGIES	147
CHAPTER 10: ONLINE INFORMATION	159

UNIT 4
ONLINE GOODS AND SERVICES

CHAPTER 11: ONLINE SERVICES	168
CHAPTER 12: THE CLOUD	176

COURSE STRUCTURE v

UNIT 5
APPLYING INFORMATION AND COMMUNICATION TECHNOLOGY

CHAPTER 13: APPLYING ICT — 182

UNIT 6
SOFTWARE SKILLS

CHAPTER 14: FILE MANAGEMENT — 202
CHAPTER 15: WORD PROCESSING — 208
CHAPTER 16: GRAPHICS — 239
CHAPTER 17: PRESENTATION — 248
CHAPTER 18: WEB AUTHORING — 262
CHAPTER 19: SPREADSHEETS — 276
CHAPTER 20: DATABASE MANAGEMENT — 307

ANSWERS TO END-OF-CHAPTER QUESTIONS — 334
GLOSSARY — 340
INDEX — 348

ABOUT THIS BOOK

This book is written for students following the Pearson Edexcel International GCSE (9–1) Information and Communication Technology (ICT) specification and covers both years of the course. The specification and sample assessment materials for ICT can be found on the Pearson Qualifications website.

In each unit of this book, information is interspersed with activities in order to put learning into practice and *Chapter Questions* help assess understanding in preparation for the exam. Other features such as *Did you know*? and *Hint* boxes help to expand knowledge and reinforce learning.

The language throughout this textbook has been reviewed by a language specialist to ensure it is written in a clear and accessible style, with both advanced general and ICT-specific terminology highlighted subject specific vocabulary is also defined in the glossary at the back of the book.

EXTRA RESOURCES

Downloadable interactive practice activities are provided as part of your Activebook. They are marked with this symbol in the student book and can be downloaded by clicking on this icon within the Activebook.

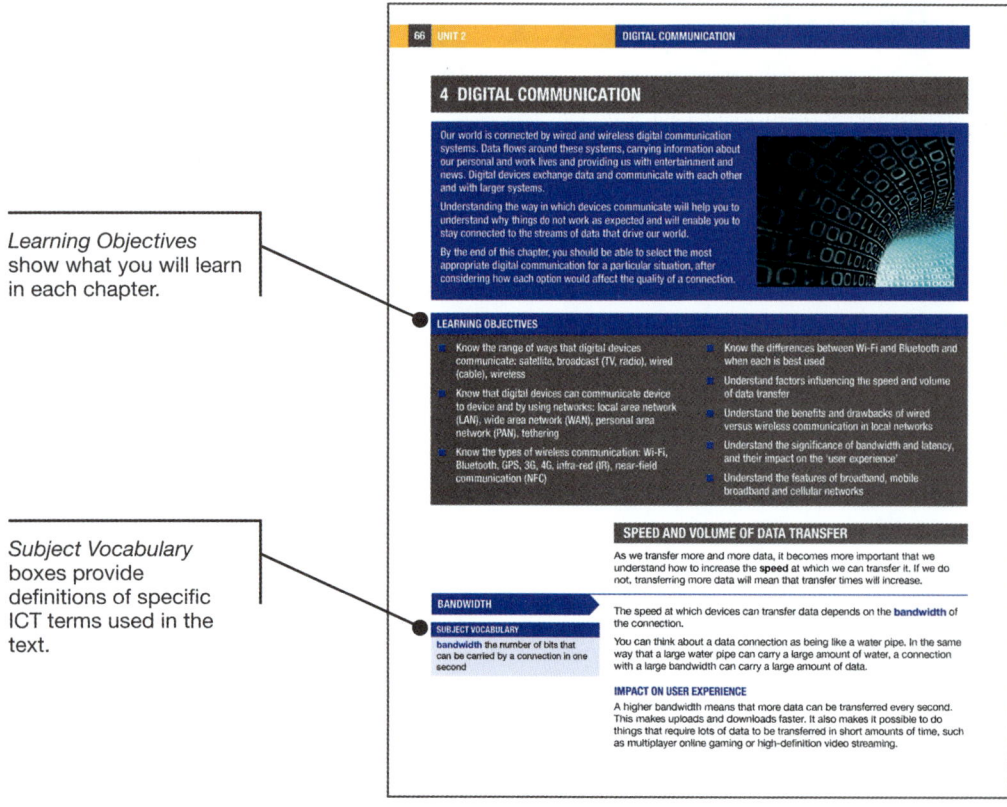

Learning Objectives show what you will learn in each chapter.

Subject Vocabulary boxes provide definitions of specific ICT terms used in the text.

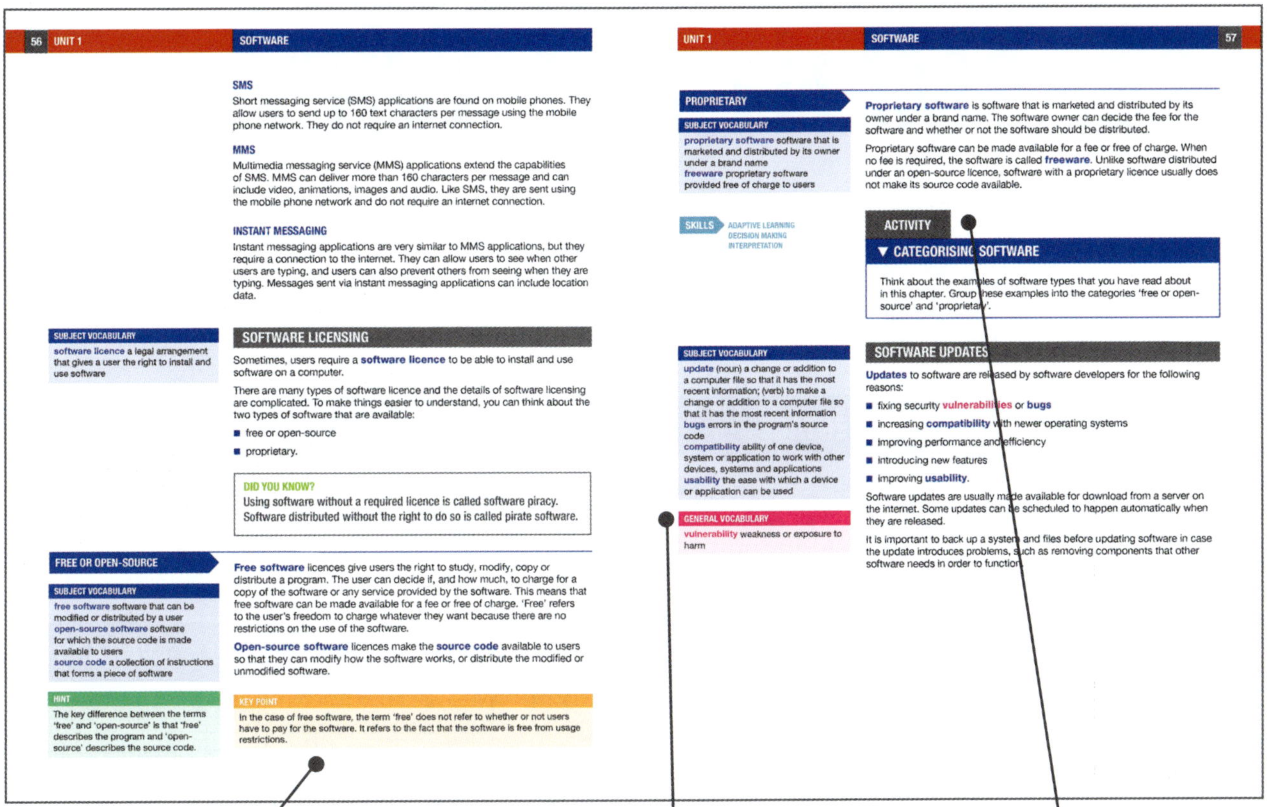

56 UNIT 1 SOFTWARE

SMS
Short messaging service (SMS) applications are found on mobile phones. They allow users to send up to 160 text characters per message using the mobile phone network. They do not require an internet connection.

MMS
Multimedia messaging service (MMS) applications extend the capabilities of SMS. MMS can deliver more than 160 characters per message and can include video, animations, images and audio. Like SMS, they are sent using the mobile phone network and do not require an internet connection.

INSTANT MESSAGING
Instant messaging applications are very similar to MMS applications, but they require a connection to the internet. They can allow users to see when other users are typing, and users can also prevent others from seeing when they are typing. Messages sent via instant messaging applications can include location data.

SUBJECT VOCABULARY
software licence a legal arrangement that gives a user the right to install and use software

SOFTWARE LICENSING
Sometimes, users require a **software licence** to be able to install and use software on a computer.
There are many types of software licence and the details of software licensing are complicated. To make things easier to understand, you can think about the two types of software that are available:
- free or open-source
- proprietary.

DID YOU KNOW?
Using software without a required licence is called software piracy. Software distributed without the right to do so is called pirate software.

FREE OR OPEN-SOURCE
SUBJECT VOCABULARY
free software software that can be modified or distributed by a user
open-source software software for which the source code is made available to users
source code a collection of instructions that forms a piece of software

Free software licences give users the right to study, modify, copy or distribute a program. The user can decide if, and how much, to charge for a copy of the software or any service provided by the software. This means that free software can be made available for a fee or free of charge. 'Free' refers to the user's freedom to charge whatever they want because there are no restrictions on the use of the software.
Open-source software licences make the **source code** available to users so that they can modify how the software works, or distribute the modified or unmodified software.

HINT
The key difference between the terms 'free' and 'open-source' is that 'free' describes the program and 'open-source' describes the source code.

KEY POINT
In the case of free software, the term 'free' does not refer to whether or not users have to pay for the software. It refers to the fact that the software is free from usage restrictions.

UNIT 1 SOFTWARE 57

PROPRIETARY
SUBJECT VOCABULARY
proprietary software software that is marketed and distributed by its owner under a brand name
freeware proprietary software provided free of charge to users

Proprietary software is software that is marketed and distributed by its owner under a brand name. The software owner can decide the fee for the software and whether or not the software should be distributed.
Proprietary software can be made available for a fee or free of charge. When no fee is required, the software is called **freeware**. Unlike software distributed under an open-source licence, software with a proprietary licence usually does not make its source code available.

SKILLS ADAPTIVE LEARNING, DECISION MAKING, INTERPRETATION

ACTIVITY
▼ CATEGORISING SOFTWARE
Think about the examples of software types that you have read about in this chapter. Group these examples into the categories 'free or open-source' and 'proprietary'.

SUBJECT VOCABULARY
update (noun) a change or addition to a computer file so that it has the most recent information; (verb) to make a change or addition to a computer file so that it has the most recent information
bugs errors in the program's source code
compatibility ability of one device, system or application to work with other devices, systems and applications
usability the ease with which a device or application can be used

GENERAL VOCABULARY
vulnerability weakness or exposure to harm

SOFTWARE UPDATES
Updates to software are released by software developers for the following reasons:
- fixing security **vulnerabilities** or **bugs**
- increasing **compatibility** with newer operating systems
- improving performance and efficiency
- introducing new features
- improving **usability**.

Software updates are usually made available for download from a server on the internet. Some updates can be scheduled to happen automatically when they are released.
It is important to back up a system and files before updating software in case the update introduces problems, such as removing components that other software needs in order to function.

Key Point boxes summarise the essentials.

General Vocabulary boxes provide definitions of the general terms used in the text

Activities provide exercises to help deepen your understanding of a topic.

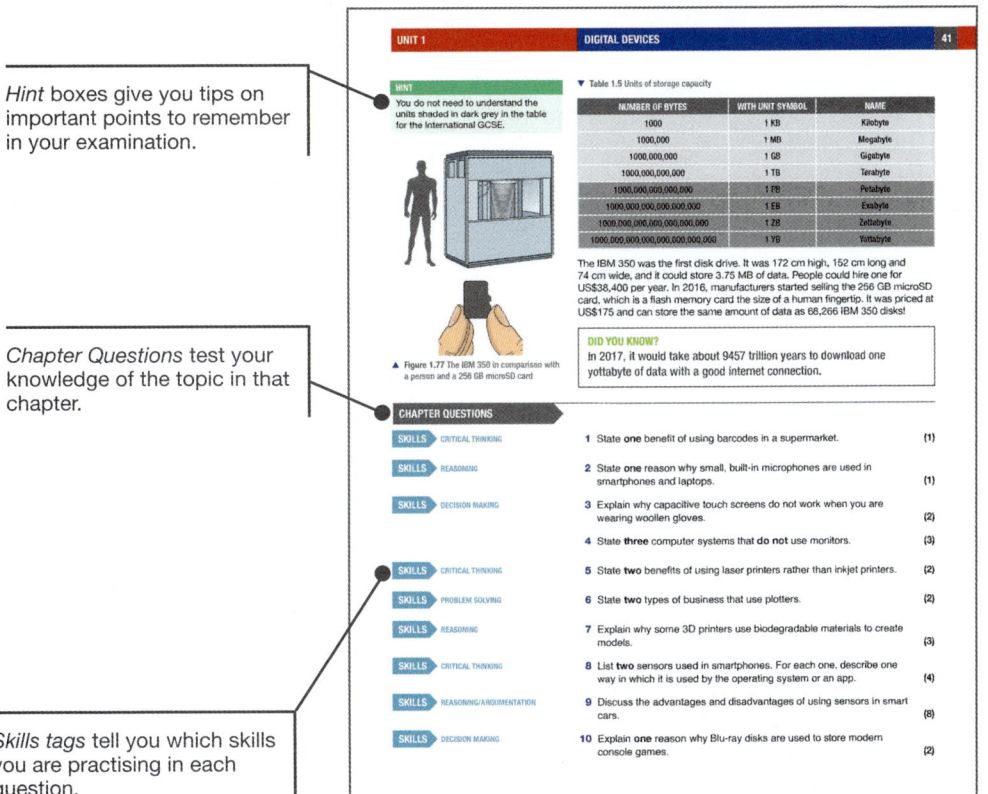

Hint boxes give you tips on important points to remember in your examination.

Chapter Questions test your knowledge of the topic in that chapter.

Skills tags tell you which skills you are practising in each question.

UNIT 1 DIGITAL DEVICES 41

HINT
You do not need to understand the units shaded in dark grey in the table for the International GCSE.

▲ Figure 1.77 The IBM 350 in comparison with a person and a 256 GB microSD card

▼ Table 1.5 Units of storage capacity

NUMBER OF BYTES	WITH UNIT SYMBOL	NAME
1000	1 KB	Kilobyte
1000,000	1 MB	Megabyte
1000,000,000	1 GB	Gigabyte
1000,000,000,000	1 TB	Terabyte
1000,000,000,000,000	1 PB	Petabyte
1000,000,000,000,000,000	1 EB	Exabyte
1000,000,000,000,000,000,000	1 ZB	Zettabyte
1000,000,000,000,000,000,000,000	1 YB	Yottabyte

The IBM 350 was the first disk drive. It was 172 cm high, 152 cm long and 74 cm wide, and it could store 3.75 MB of data. People could hire one for US$38,400 per year. In 2016, manufacturers started selling the 256 GB microSD card, which is a flash memory card the size of a human fingertip. It was priced at US$175 and can store the same amount of data as 68,266 IBM 350 disks!

DID YOU KNOW?
In 2017, it would take about 9457 trillion years to download one yottabyte of data with a good internet connection.

CHAPTER QUESTIONS

SKILLS CRITICAL THINKING
1 State **one** benefit of using barcodes in a supermarket. (1)

SKILLS REASONING
2 State **one** reason why small, built-in microphones are used in smartphones and laptops. (1)

SKILLS DECISION MAKING
3 Explain why capacitive touch screens do not work when you are wearing woollen gloves. (2)

4 State **three** computer systems that **do not** use monitors. (3)

SKILLS CRITICAL THINKING
5 State **two** benefits of using laser printers rather than inkjet printers. (2)

SKILLS PROBLEM SOLVING
6 State **two** types of business that use plotters. (2)

SKILLS REASONING
7 Explain why some 3D printers use biodegradable materials to create models. (3)

SKILLS CRITICAL THINKING
8 List **two** sensors used in smartphones. For each one, describe one way in which it is used by the operating system or an app. (4)

SKILLS REASONING/ARGUMENTATION
9 Discuss the advantages and disadvantages of using sensors in smart cars. (8)

SKILLS DECISION MAKING
10 Explain **one** reason why Blu-ray disks are used to store modern console games. (2)

ASSESSMENT OVERVIEW

The following tables give an overview of the assessment for the Edexcel International GCSE in Information and Communication Technology.

We recommend that you study this information closely to help ensure that you are fully prepared for this course and know exactly what to expect in the assessment.

PAPER 1	PERCENTAGE	MARK	TIME	AVAILABILITY
Written examination paper Paper code 4IT1/01 Externally set and assessed by Edexcel	50%	100	1 hour and 30 minutes	June examination series First assessment May/June 2019

PAPER 2	PERCENTAGE	MARK	TIME	AVAILABILITY
Practical examination paper Paper code 4IT1/02 Externally set and assessed by Edexcel	50%	100	3 hours	June examination series First assessment May/June 2019

ASSESSMENT OBJECTIVES AND WEIGHTINGS

ASSESSMENT OBJECTIVE	DESCRIPTION	% IN INTERNATIONAL GCSE
AO1	Demonstrate knowledge and understanding of Information and Communication Technology (ICT)	25-27%
AO2	Apply knowledge, understanding and skills to produce ICTbased solutions	46-52%
AO3	Analyse, evaluate, make reasoned judgements and present conclusions*	24-26%

* Students will be required to demonstrate approximately 15% analysis and 10% evaluation.

RELATIONSHIP OF ASSESSMENT OBJECTIVES TO UNITS

UNIT NUMBER	ASSESSMENT OBJECTIVE		
	AO1	AO2	AO3
Paper 1	20-23%	14-16%	13-14%
Paper 2	5-6%	34-36%	10-11%
Total for International GCSE	25-27%	46-52%	24-26%

PAPER 1	PERCENTAGE	MARK
Written paper Paper code 4IT1/01	**Structure** Paper 1 assesses 50% of the total ICT qualification. The examination comprises a mixture of multiple-choice, short- and long-answer questions.	Total number of marks available: 100
PAPER 2	**PERCENTAGE**	**MARK**
Practical paper Paper code 4IT1/02	**Structure** Paper 2 assesses 50% of the total ICT qualification. There are two sections in the paper – both are required. There is no optional element to the practical examination.	Total number of marks available: 100

| DIGITAL DEVICES 04 | SOFTWARE 42 | MEMORY AND PROCESSORS 59 |

UNIT 1
DIGITAL DEVICES

Assessment Objective 1

Demonstrate knowledge and understanding of Information and Communication Technology (ICT)

Assessment Objective 2

Apply knowledge, understanding and skills to produce ICT based solutions

Assessment Objective 3

Analyse, evaluate, make reasoned judgments and present conclusions

In this unit, you will learn about the features, purpose and use of a range of digital devices and the software that can be used with them. Understanding the rapid developments in the features and functionality of digital devices will help you to understand their current and possible future uses by individuals, organisations and society.

1 DIGITAL DEVICES

Digital devices are pieces of hardware that use computers or microcontrollers, and they are found everywhere in our digital world. They enhance and support how we live our lives every day. They can connect and work together to give us the data we need, when and where we need it.

Digital devices are always developing. This changes the way in which they are used by individuals, organisations and local, national and global societies.

LEARNING OBJECTIVES

- Be aware that mainframe computers are used for complex processing tasks and microprocessors are embedded in products such as washing machines
- Understand that laptop and desktop computers are types of personal computers. Some laptops are used as desktop replacements
- Know about types of mobile phones; smartphones and specialist phones and how they connect to the network (SIM)
- Know about tablet devices
- Be able to describe the purpose and use of other digital devices such as:
  - cameras and camcorders
  - games consoles
  - home entertainment systems
  - media players
- Know about navigation aids and how they are used
- Understand the terms 'multifunctional' (e.g. mobile phones that include a camera, have limited game playing functionality and GPS) and 'convergence' (e.g. functionality of smartphones and tablet devices becomes more similar) in the context of digital devices
- Understand features of digital devices: portability, performance, storage, user interface, connectivity, media support, energy consumption, expansion capability, security features
- Be able to discuss the features of identified digital devices

- Be able to identify digital devices and associated peripheral devices that meet particular needs, including accessibility
- Know about types of output peripheral such as monitor (screen size, resolution), printer (laser, inkjet, 3D), plotter, data projector, speaker, control device and when they would be used
- Know about types of input peripheral such as keyboard, mouse, tracker ball, joystick, graphics tablet, scanner, digital camera, webcam, microphone, touch screen, OMR reader, OCR reader, bar code scanner, biometric scanner, magnetic stripe reader, chip and pin, sensor and when they would be used
- Be able to differentiate between storage devices and the media used to store data
- Know the characteristics of hard disk drives (HDD), solid state drives (SSD), optical disk drives, flash memory drives
- Know that storage devices can be internal or external
- Know about types of storage media such as hard disks, optical disks (CD, DVD, Blu-ray), flash memory devices, magnetic tape
- Know that storage media can be recordable / write once (R) and rewritable (R/W)
- Understand the terms describing the capacity of storage such as bit, byte and multiples of these (kbytes, mbytes, gbytes, tbytes) (using 1KB = 1000 bytes)

UNIT 1 DIGITAL DEVICES

TYPES OF DIGITAL DEVICES

There are many types of digital devices. They range from very powerful **mainframe computers**, used by large organisations for complex processing tasks such as statistical analysis and bulk data processing, to **microprocessors** used to control washing machines, televisions and other household appliances. Examples of the devices you will consider include personal computers, digital cameras and home entertainment systems.

SUBJECT VOCABULARY

mainframe computer a large, powerful computer that can do a lot of complicated jobs quickly and can be used by a lot of people at the same time

microprocessor the device that controls what a computer does; it takes data as input, does something with it and provides output

▲ Figure 1.1 A mainframe computer

▲ Figure 1.2 A microprocessor

SKILLS
CRITICAL THINKING
INTERPRETATION
COMMUNICATION

ACTIVITY

▼ DIGITAL DEVICES

1 Research the difference between a mainframe computer, a server and a supercomputer.

2 Create a list of the digital devices in your home that use microprocessors.

PERSONAL COMPUTERS

Personal computers (PCs) are common in homes and offices. They come in many different shapes and sizes, such as desktops and laptops.

SUBJECT VOCABULARY

upgrade to make a computer better and able to do more things

peripheral device equipment that is connected to a computer and used with it

DESKTOPS

Desktops have more space for components than laptops and often provide users with the option to **upgrade** them or add additional components. A desktop computer usually needs to have **peripheral devices** connected to it, such as a monitor, a printer, a mouse and a keyboard. For more information about peripheral devices, see pages 19, 20 and 32.

▲ Figure 1.3 A desktop computer

Some desktops are 'all-in-one'. This means that they combine the monitor with the PC hardware, as shown in Figure 1.4.

▲ Figure 1.4 An all-in-one computer

LAPTOPS

Laptops include a keyboard, a screen, a track pad (see page 23) and a rechargeable battery. Having these features means that they can be taken away from the desk, which makes them an example of a **portable** device.

GENERAL VOCABULARY

portable easy to carry or move

▲ Figure 1.5 A laptop computer

Some laptops are called 'desktop replacements'. These tend to be larger than other laptops, as well as having a bigger and better-quality screen and higher performance levels.

SUBJECT VOCABULARY

embedded computing computing hardware that is fixed into position and carries out a specialist task

physical computing interactive systems that can sense and respond to the world around them

SINGLE-BOARD COMPUTERS

Single-board computers (SBCs) are affordable computers used in education, **embedded computing** projects and **physical computing** projects. The Raspberry Pi Zero (see Figure 1.6) is an example of an SBC. The unit itself costs very little and uses a cheap microSD card as its storage.

▲ **Figure 1.6** The Raspberry Pi Zero (top) and its microSD card (top left)

MOBILE PHONES

Mobile phones use a SIM card to connect to a mobile phone network. SIM stands for subscriber identity module, and a SIM card is used to identify the subscriber to a mobile phone network.

DID YOU KNOW?
Sri Lanka has more mobile phones than people. In 2015, for every 100 Sri Lankan citizens there were 113 mobile phones.

▲ **Figure 1.7** The SIM card from a mobile phone

SUBJECT VOCABULARY
user the person who uses a computer system

SPECIALIST PHONES

Some mobile phones have specialist features to provide **users** with functions that meet particular user needs. For example, some phones have an emergency button that is linked to a list of emergency contacts. When this button is pressed, the phone will call each person on the list until someone answers.

SKILLS CRITICAL THINKING
PERSONAL AND SOCIAL RESPONSIBILITY
COMMUNICATION
INTERPERSONAL SKILLS

ACTIVITY

▼ **EMERGENCY BUTTON**

Discuss which groups of people could need a phone with an emergency button. How would this phone meet their needs?

GENERAL VOCABULARY
accessibility a measure of how easy something is to use, especially by people with disabilities

Other phones meet users' **accessibility** needs. Examples include the Alto 2 'talking phone', shown in Figure 1.8, which is a specialist mobile phone for blind and partially sighted people. It meets its users' needs because every feature and function is spoken aloud. Other phones provide fewer, larger buttons and connections for hearing aids.

SUBJECT VOCABULARY

Wi-Fi (wireless fidelity) a way of connecting computers or other electronic machines to a network or the internet by using radio signals rather than wires

games console an electronic device that is used for playing computerised video games on a screen

application a program that allows a user to perform a task; applications are often called apps

virtual keyboard a keyboard displayed on and used via a touch screen

▲ Figure 1.10 A virtual keyboard

SKILLS CRITICAL THINKING
INTERPRETATION
COMMUNICATION

▲ Figure 1.8 The Alto 2 'talking phone' reads the names of contacts and text messages aloud to its user

▲ Figure 1.9 Some mobile phones use tactile keypads, which are more responsive than other keypads, and give the user a choice of on-screen text size and colours

SMARTPHONES

Smartphones are small computers with **Wi-Fi** and mobile phone connectivity to allow them to make phone calls and access the internet. They also include features of other devices such as cameras, media players and hand-held **games consoles**. They have a more advanced operating system than other mobile phones. **Applications** (or apps) can be downloaded onto the smartphone, which allow users to customise their smartphones with entertainment, educational and business features. Most smartphones use a touch screen to allow users to input information. A **virtual keyboard** is used to enter text, numbers and other characters.

Because they combine so many features, smartphones use more power than other types of mobile phone. This means that they have a shorter battery life and need to be charged more regularly than other mobile phones.

ACTIVITY

▼ SMARTPHONES AND MOBILE PHONES

1 Research which smartphone features use the most power.
2 Make a list of activities for which a standard mobile phone would be more suitable than a smartphone.

SKILLS CRITICAL THINKING
PERSONAL AND SOCIAL RESPONSIBILITY

ACTIVITY

▼ ACCESSIBILITY

The Royal National Institute of Blind People is a UK organisation that supports people with sight impairments. Do an internet search for the key terms 'RNIB mobile phone accessibility' to visit the RNIB's website, which will give you lots of information about the accessibility features of mobile phones and smartphones.

Watch the video on the RNIB's website about the accessibility features of major smartphones and make a list of the features mentioned. Which features did you already know about?

| UNIT 1 | DIGITAL DEVICES | 9 |

TABLETS

Tablet devices or tablets are bigger than smartphones, but have similar features. For example, a tablet device has a touch screen, apps and Wi-Fi connectivity to provide access to the internet. Some tablet devices have SIM card slots to allow internet connectivity using the mobile phone network, so that they can be online when they are not within range of a Wi-Fi signal.

▲ **Figure 1.11** A tablet device

CAMERAS AND CAMCORDERS

Digital cameras and camcorders use light sensors to capture images formed by light passing through the device's lens. Traditionally, cameras are used to capture still images and camcorders are used to capture moving images. However, most digital cameras can now film moving images and most camcorders can photograph still images.

> **DID YOU KNOW?**
> Moving images (movies) are simply a sequence of images called 'frames'. Figure 1.12 shows how the frame rate affects the quality of a movie.

6 frames per second
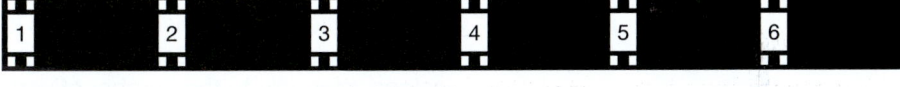

24 frames per second

◀──────── 1 second ────────▶

▲ **Figure 1.12** High frame rates produce smooth results, whereas low frame rates can produce results that appear to stutter or jump

The quality of the image captured by the camera depends on the quality of the lens, the image processor and the resolution of the sensor.

- A good lens allows light to travel through it without introducing any defects. It also allows the user to choose how much light can travel through it, which affects the final image.
- A good image processor can **compensate** for poor lighting conditions.
- Digital images are made up of small dots called **pixels**. Better-quality sensors can capture more detail and produce images with a greater number of pixels. The sensor resolution of a camera is expressed as the number of pixels that can be captured, as shown in Table 1.1. Some cameras use more than one sensor, each dedicated to a different colour or wavelength of light.

> **GENERAL VOCABULARY**
> **compensate** to reduce or correct a negative effect

> **SUBJECT VOCABULARY**
> **pixel** a small dot that helps to make up an image

SUBJECT VOCABULARY

resolution the number of pixels used by a screen to display an image

pixelated an effect that creates an unclear image consisting of large individual pixels that are visible to the human eye

▲ Figure 1.13 The area of the image with the leaf becomes **pixelated** when enlarged

▼ Table 1.1 Maximum display size at different **resolutions**

Resolution (number of pixels)	Maximum display size of image (in pixels, width × height) before pixelation occurs
1.3 megapixel (1.3 million pixels)	1280 × 960
2 megapixel	1600 × 1200
3 megapixel	2048 × 1536
4 megapixel	2272 × 1704
8 megapixel and above	2560 × 1920

HOME ENTERTAINMENT SYSTEMS

TELEVISIONS

Televisions display still and moving images on a screen. The quality of the image is set by the number of pixels that are used to display the image. This is referred to as the screen's resolution. High definition (HD) television screens contain a larger number of pixels, which means that they have a higher resolution than standard definition televisions.

The resolution of a television in pixels is stated as horizontal pixels × vertical pixels. Often, television manufacturers do not specify the number of horizontal pixels and instead refer only to the number of vertical pixels. For example, a resolution of 1280 × 720 is often stated as 720p and 1920 × 1080 is stated as 1080p.

Ultra High Definition (UHD) television screens are sometimes referred to as 4K or 8K because they have a horizontal resolution of approximately 4,000 or 8,000 pixels. 8K screens make each pixel impossible to tell apart even when users are close to the screen.

▲ Figure 1.14 Comparison chart showing different screen resolutions

UNIT 1 DIGITAL DEVICES

SKILLS
CRITICAL THINKING
COMMUNICATION
SELF-DIRECTION
INTERPERSONAL SKILLS

SUBJECT VOCABULARY

stream play a file on your computer while it is being downloaded from the internet, rather than saving it as a file and then playing it

smart the ability of a device to use data from sensors to perform a programmed action independently; smart devices are often also able to connect to the internet

ACTIVITY

▼ **TYPES OF TELEVISION**

1. Research the cost of HD, 4K and 8K televisions.
2. Research the types of content that is broadcast or available to buy in each resolution. How easy would it be to **stream** content in each resolution?
3. Estimate how far you sit from your television when watching television at home, then research how close to the screen a user must be in order to notice the quality of the three different resolutions.
4. Discuss whether it is worth paying the extra cost for 4K and 8K televisions in order to watch television. Do you think there is any point in creating 16K screens for home use?

For the production of sound, most televisions come with built-in speakers. However, these are often small and of limited quality because the screen is usually very thin. Most modern televisions can be connected to an external sound system to improve their sound quality.

Smart televisions use apps and can download and stream content from the internet.

SOUND SYSTEMS

Sound systems can produce loud, rich sound using high-quality speakers and amplifiers. Some speakers contain built-in amplifiers.

Sound systems can play music from CDs or from local storage. They can usually be connected to personal devices like smartphones, **media players** and tablet devices using wired connections like **USB** or wireless connections like **Bluetooth**. They can also be connected to a local network via Wi-Fi to play music that is stored on connected devices. Some sound systems can also connect to the internet to play music stored online.

SUBJECT VOCABULARY

media player an electronic device that can store and play digital music and videos and show digital photographs

USB (Universal Serial Bus) a standard for wired connectivity that can also supply electric power

Bluetooth wireless connectivity that allows devices to connect over short distances

set-top box (STB) a device that sends video and audio received from a broadcaster to a television

PERSONAL VIDEO RECORDERS

A personal video recorder (PVR) is a device that records broadcasted content so that it can be watched at a later date.

Some devices fall into multiple categories. For example, some satellite television devices contain both a **set-top box (STB)** and a PVR.

BLU-RAY AND DVD PLAYERS

Blu-ray and DVD players connect to televisions in order to play films and other content that is stored on DVD or Blu-ray disks (see page 39 for more on Blu-ray media). Blu-ray players will usually play DVD disks, but DVD players will not play Blu-ray disks.

Blu-ray disks can store HD movies, which have higher-quality picture and sound. Newer 4K Ultra HD Blu-ray players can play 4K content on 4K televisions.

▲ Figure 1.15 A Blu-ray player

GAMES CONSOLES

▲ Figure 1.16 How many games consoles have you tried?

Games consoles are designed to enable users to play video games on a television screen. Games are provided on disks or as downloads from the internet. They use controllers, which are often wireless, to control the characters, vehicles and/or objects in the game.

Some consoles use motion sensors to allow the player to control the game with gestures and body movements. Other games use virtual reality controllers and headsets to immerse the player in a realistic gaming experience, where their own movements in the real world are replicated by an **avatar** in the virtual world of the game.

> **SUBJECT VOCABULARY**
>
> **avatar** a figure that represents a person in a computer game or other virtual environment

▲ Figure 1.17 Have you played any virtual reality games?

SKILLS
CRITICAL THINKING
PERSONAL AND SOCIAL RESPONSIBILITY
COMMUNICATION
INTERPERSONAL SKILLS

ACTIVITY

▼ **VIDEO GAMES**

Discuss the age ratings of popular games. Do you think these age ratings are appropriate? Do you think age ratings are necessary? Explain the reasons for your answer.

Modern games consoles are multifunctional (see page 15). They may have apps and connectivity that provide access to local networks and the internet as well as the option to play movies and music. Some consoles also have disk drives to play films and other content on DVD, Blu-ray or 4K Ultra HD Blu-ray media.

| UNIT 1 | DIGITAL DEVICES | 13 |

▲ Figure 1.18 Consoles can often do more than just play games

Handheld versions of games consoles provide mobile gaming. Handheld consoles have a built-in screen and less storage than a full-size console. This means that the games that can be played on these devices often have reduced image and sound quality, reduced game complexity and limited storylines in order to reduce the amount of **data** that needs to be stored.

SUBJECT VOCABULARY
data values that represent information

MEDIA PLAYERS

DID YOU KNOW?
Network attached storage (NAS) devices often have media streaming capabilities built in.

Media players provide video and audio content to a television. This content could be streamed directly from the internet or accessed from networked or local storage. Media players can be connected to a television directly or using a wired or wireless network. They are controlled using a remote control or, in some cases, a smartphone app. Some media players offer output in 4K.

▲ Figure 1.19 Have you used any other examples of media players?

SKILLS CRITICAL THINKING
COMMUNICATION
INTERPERSONAL SKILLS

DID YOU KNOW?
A Raspberry Pi Zero single-board computer and free software can be used as a media player. This makes it a very affordable alternative to a television and media player, or a smart television.

SUBJECT VOCABULARY
flash memory a form of storage that stores data as electrical charges held in tiny electrical cells

ACTIVITY

▼ **SMART TELEVISIONS**

Smart televisions have the streaming and networking functions of a media player built in. Do you think that smart televisions are going to replace media players? Discuss your reasons for thinking that this may or may not happen.

Personal media players are compact, portable devices with local storage to hold media files for playback. They are useful when travelling or exercising due to their small size and long battery life. They often use solid state **flash memory** storage (see page 62), which is not affected by being moved or shaken.

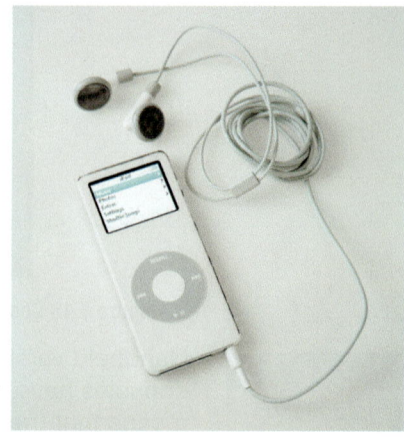

▲ Figure 1.20 Personal media players are portable so they need to function while on the move

NAVIGATION AIDS

Navigation aids (such as Sat-Nav) can calculate the best route between two or more locations and can provide updates to the route if it is not followed accurately. They are commonly used in cars, delivery vans and ships. They provide visual prompts and alerts to help drivers take the correct route, such as by taking a particular turning. Specialist devices with audio alerts and waterproof and shockproof cases are available for walkers, cyclists and runners.

SUBJECT VOCABULARY

GPS the Global Positioning System that uses radio signals from satellites to show your exact position on the Earth on a special piece of equipment

Navigation aids use information from **GPS** satellites to determine the exact location of the device on Earth. Navigation aids also use orientation sensors to know which way the device is currently pointing, and the device will display the user's position and orientation on a map. Maps are either stored permanently on the device or downloaded from the internet when they are needed.

DID YOU KNOW?

GPS satellites orbit more than 20km above Earth. They are accurate to within 5 metres.

GPS does not need internet connectivity in order to work. However, navigation aids need internet connectivity in order to update map data.

Smartphones are now replacing specialist in-car navigation aids. There are many navigation apps for smartphones which have a range of features.

HOME AUTOMATION DEVICES AND SMART ASSISTANTS

One type of emerging technology is a group of devices that can be used to create smart homes. For example, home automation devices can connect a range of digital devices which sense and control functions in the home, such as temperature and lighting. These functions can be controlled from apps on smartphones or the internet.

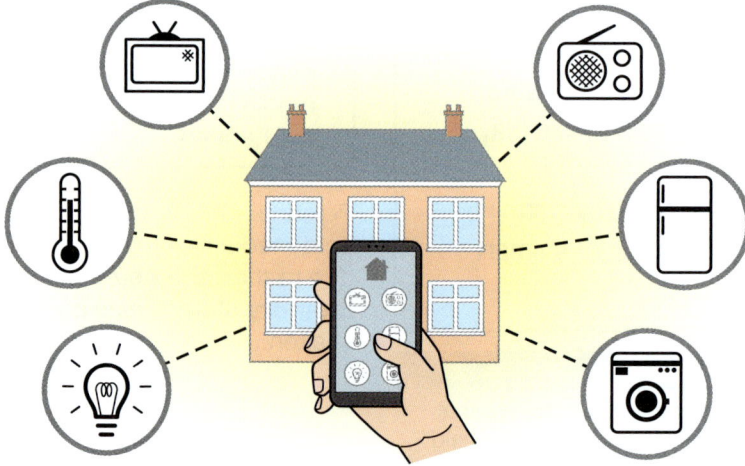

▲ Figure 1.21 Home automation devices can connect digital devices to control functions in the home

MULTIFUNCTIONAL DEVICES AND CONVERGENCE

SUBJECT VOCABULARY

multifunctional device a device that can perform a range of different functions

SKILLS SELF-DIRECTION

A smartphone is a type of mobile phone, which means that its primary function is to make phone calls. It can also be used to take photographs or to function as a navigation aid, fitness tracker, music player or handheld games console. Because a smartphone can perform such a range of different functions, it is classed as a **multifunctional device**.

ACTIVITY

▼ MULTIFUNCTIONAL DEVICES

Identify another example of a multifunctional device. What is its primary function? What else can it do?

SUBJECT VOCABULARY

convergence when the designs of devices change so that they become similar to one another

As they develop, devices like smartphones often adopt technologies and features from other types of device. This is called **convergence**.

▲ Figure 1.22 Some laptops now have touch screens that can flip 360 degrees, allowing them to operate as tablet devices

Convergence blurs the distinction between different types of device. For example, smartphones and tablet devices are very similar. They are different in that a smartphone has mobile phone network connectivity and is smaller than a tablet device. However, newer smartphones are getting bigger to look more like tablets (and are known as 'phablets'), while tablet devices can now connect to mobile phone networks. Similarly, most smartphones have digital cameras, while some digital cameras have Wi-Fi and mobile phone network connectivity.

▲ Figure 1.23 Some tablet devices come with attachable keyboards, allowing them to operate as laptop computers

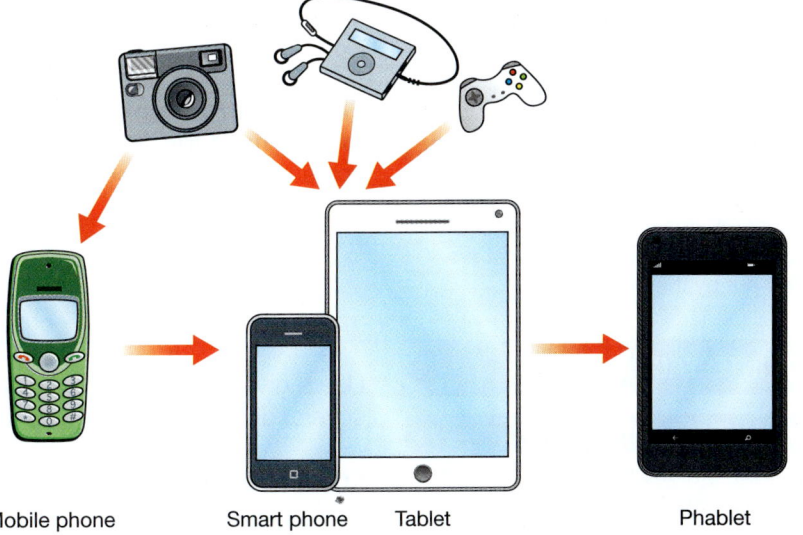

▲ Figure 1.24 As devices develop, their features often converge

UNIT 1 — DIGITAL DEVICES

SKILLS › SELF-DIRECTION

ACTIVITY

▼ **CONVERGING DEVICES**

Research the differences and similarities between smartphones, tablet devices and touch screen laptops.

FEATURES OF DIGITAL DEVICES

SUBJECT VOCABULARY

connectivity a device's ability to connect to networks and other devices

The digital devices that you use have a number of features, such as portability, performance and **connectivity**. Different devices will have different features.

PORTABILITY

For a device to be portable, it needs to be easy to carry and move around. This means that the portability of a device is directly related to its size and weight. For some devices, such as a television or a desktop computer, portability is unlikely to be a priority.

PERFORMANCE

SUBJECT VOCABULARY

processor one or more Central Processing Units (CPUs) that carry out software instructions

RAM Random Access Memory, which is the memory in a computer system that is used for running software

virtual memory storage used by the processor once the space in RAM has run out

A high-performance device performs its job or tasks quickly. The speed at which a device performs is determined by the speed at which it can carry out instructions from its software. Software instructions are carried out by the **processor**, which means that a faster processor will increase performance (see page 62).

Instructions are loaded into the processor from **RAM**, which means that faster RAM will also allow instructions to be loaded into the processor more quickly. RAM holds all software instructions to be carried out, so more RAM will allow the system to have more programs running at the same time. In addition, because instructions are loaded into RAM from storage, such as a hard disk (see page 39), faster storage will enable faster loading of instructions to RAM.

When the space in RAM runs out, storage is used as an overflow, and this is known as **virtual memory** (see page 60). This means that fast storage means faster access to instructions in virtual memory.

The software itself can also be written in an efficient way that makes the most of the processor's capabilities. Inefficient software can slow down the whole system and therefore has an impact on a device's performance.

STORAGE

SUBJECT VOCABULARY

file a collection of data that represents a document, image, database or similar

program a set of instructions that are carried out by the processor

Files and **programs** are stored in storage. More available storage allows users to store more files and programs. Storage speed also affects performance, as you saw in the previous section.

USER INTERFACE

SUBJECT VOCABULARY

user interface the system that allows a user to interact with a device

Users give commands to a device through the **user interface**. There are several different types of user interface.

COMMAND LINE INTERFACE (CLI)

When using a command line interface, users enter text instructions and the computer system provides results or feedback as text. This type of interface is often found on older systems or for devices with limited storage because it requires little memory.

Commands have to be typed precisely because the interface only recognises certain commands. There is usually a help menu for users that lists and explains the acceptable commands.

▲ Figure 1.25 A command line interface

MENU-DRIVEN INTERFACE

This type of interface displays a list of options as a menu. Selecting one of these options will either trigger a command or display another menu with further options to choose from.

Menu-driven interfaces are easier to use than command line interfaces, but can take more time as you have to go through the menu structure each time you want to carry out a command, rather than typing the command directly into the system.

This type of interface is used in many devices including ATMs (cash machines in banking), televisions and older mobile phones.

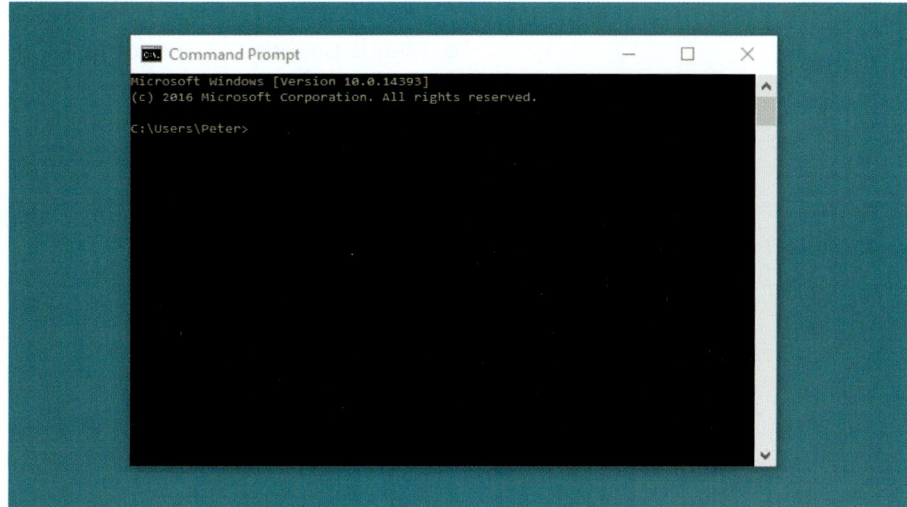

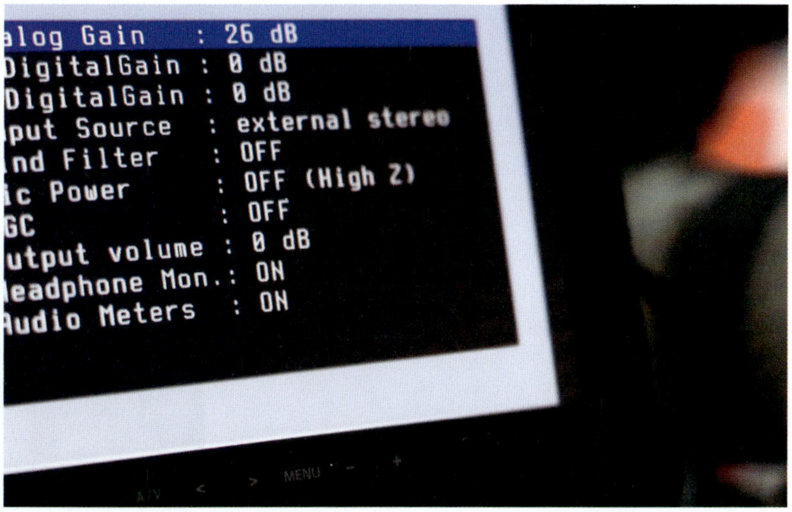

▲ Figure 1.26 A menu-driven interface for a monitor

GRAPHICAL USER INTERFACE (GUI)

A graphical user interface is controlled by a pointer on the screen and uses a screen made up of windows, icons and menus.

- Windows are areas of the screen that are dedicated to applications or operating system tasks.
- Icons are small images that represent an application. They can be selected with the pointer to open the application.
- Menus provide options for tasks relating to the operating system or open application.

This is the easiest type of interface to use, but it takes up more memory and storage than a command line or menu-driven interface.

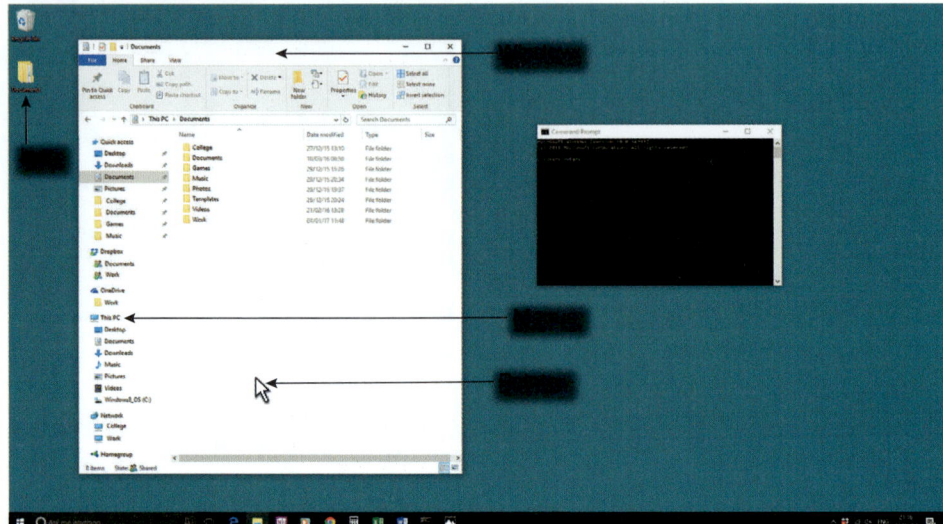

▲ Figure 1.27 A graphical user interface uses windows, icons, menus and pointers (WIMP)

VOICE INTERFACE

A voice interface allows the user to give spoken commands to a device. The device has voice recognition software which matches the spoken words against a library of words to find a match. To save storage on the device, the library of words is often stored online, so these devices usually require internet access.

The disadvantage of using a voice interface is that sometimes the software cannot find a match or returns an incorrect match, which produces unwanted results. For this reason, voice interfaces sometimes check the instruction with the user before searching for a match. Some voice interfaces use the results of this confirmation to 'learn' the voice of their user and improve future matches.

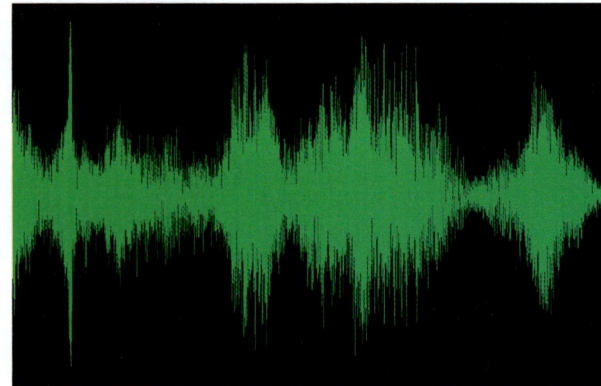

▲ Figure 1.28 Voice interfaces compare the spoken commands to a library of matched words

The advantage of voice interfaces is that hands-free operation is possible. This means that they are often used in vehicles in order to improve road safety.

▲ Figure 1.29 Some voice interface devices can control home entertainment systems, appliances and systems such as lighting and heating

GESTURE INTERFACE

This type of interface allows the user to control the device by swiping their finger or fingers across the screen, or by pinching their fingers together to zoom in or out. This type of interface is commonly found on devices with touch screens.

CONNECTIVITY

SUBJECT VOCABULARY

back up to make a copy of information stored on a computer in case the original is lost or damaged

Devices can share data by connecting to each other using wired or wireless connectivity. Connectivity can be used to update software, **back up** files or play media from one device on another. Different connectivity types provide different speeds of data transfer and levels of convenience. Wired connectivity is usually faster and more reliable, but introduces additional cost, mess, inconvenience and safety risks such as tripping, especially for young children.

You will learn more about connectivity types in *Unit 2 Connectivity* (pages 71–76).

MEDIA SUPPORT

SUBJECT VOCABULARY

media items such as memory cards and CD-ROMs that make information available to people and devices

Different devices can read data from and write data to different types of **media**. Examples of media include SD and microSD flash memory cards, and DVD. If devices do not have built-in (native) media, adapters can usually be connected to provide connectivity to an external device into which the media can be inserted.

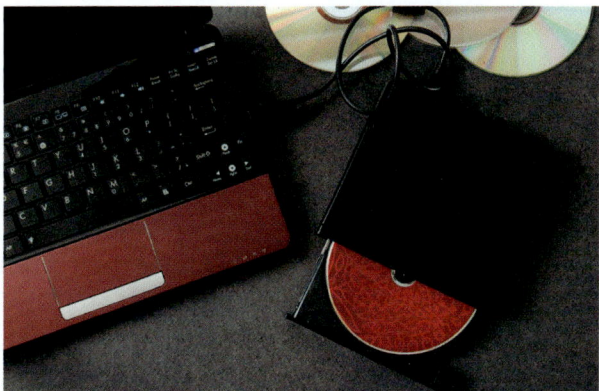

▲ Figure 1.30 Some laptops are too thin to incorporate an optical disk drive, so an adapter is required to connect an external drive

ENERGY CONSUMPTION

Digital devices require electricity to work. One benefit of lower energy consumption in mobile devices is a longer battery life. Due to the rising cost of energy and pressure from customers and governments to be more environmentally responsible, manufacturers are creating digital devices that consume less energy. The aim of this is to save their customers money and demonstrate social responsibility, such as by reducing environmental damage.

You will learn more about sustainability in *Unit 3 Operating online* (page 153)

> **DID YOU KNOW?**
> Computers can generate a lot of heat. This means that a large proportion of the energy consumed in data centres is used to cool the computers.

SKILLS SELF-DIRECTION
PERSONAL AND SOCIAL RESPONSIBILITY

ACTIVITY

▼ **TECHNOLOGY AND THE ENVIRONMENT**

Visit environment.google in order to research the steps that Google™ has taken to make its activities more environmentally responsible. You could also watch Google's video, *Story of Send*.

EXPANSION CAPABILITY

Some PCs allow users to install additional components. Some smartphones and tablet devices have expansion slots to allow them to make use of flash memory cards (see page 19). Systems can also be expanded using ports such as USB ports. These allow the user to connect extra devices called peripheral devices (pages 21–41).

SECURITY FEATURES

The data stored on digital devices may be private, valuable or both. This means that devices need to have security features to keep their users' data safe.

SOFTWARE SECURITY

To prevent unauthorised access to data, digital devices have a range of software security features to ensure that the person trying to use the device is allowed to do so.

The operating systems of many devices can be set so that, when the device is turned on, the user must enter a password or personal identification number (PIN) before the device can be used. Another common security setting **locks** the device's screen or keyboard if it has not been used for a specified period of time, after which the password or PIN will be required to unlock it again. Some devices are set so that, if an incorrect password or PIN is entered, the user must wait a set amount of time before trying again. Such systems may even **wipe** the data after only a few failed attempts. This prevents criminals from freely guessing thousands of combinations in order to break into the device or system.

The longer and more complex a password is, the better it is. Pattern PINs are used by some smartphone operating systems, and they allow the user to set a swipe pattern between a group of points. A four-digit pattern PIN is more secure than a four-digit PIN, because it has 389,112 possible combinations, whereas the four-digit PIN has 10,000 possible combinations.

SUBJECT VOCABULARY

lock to make a device inactive so that it requires a password or PIN to reactivate it
wipe to delete data from a device or drive

> **DID YOU KNOW?**
> A four-digit PIN only has 10,000 possible combinations (0000–9999). A six-digit PIN is much more secure, with 1 million possible combinations.

▲ Figure 1.32 Entry screen for a pattern PIN

> **KEY POINT**
>
> Do you think your password or PIN is secure enough? If not, you should change it now.

SKILLS — CRITICAL THINKING
INTELLECTUAL INTEREST AND CURIOSITY

▲ Figure 1.33 A Kensington security lock in use

▲ Figure 1.31 A smartphone's lock screen

Some devices use biometric scanners, such as Apple® Touch ID®[1], to provide authorised users access to data on that device (see page 27 for more about biometric scanners).

You will learn more about passwords, PINs and other ways to secure data in *Unit 3 Operating online* (page 100).

PHYSICAL SECURITY

Physical security to prevent theft is also important. Many devices use security slots which can have locks attached to secure them to furniture. Some attach to specialist slots. Others connect to a port on the device with special screws used to secure the locks in place. Figure 1.33 shows an example of a security lock.

ACTIVITY

▼ DRONES AND SECURITY

1 Search for and watch these three videos online:
   - TU Delft – Ambulance Drone'
   - Drone Racing: First Person View (FPV) Lateline
   - Amazon® Prime Air's First Custom Delivery

   How do the features of these drones allow them to perform their function?

2 Search for 'Eagles drones Dutch Police' and read an online news article about how police are responding to the negative use of these devices.

TYPES OF PERIPHERAL DEVICES

Peripheral devices are devices that can be connected to a computer, such as a PC or tablet device. Peripherals can be connected inside or outside a computer and can be grouped into three types (see Figure 1.34):

- input
- output
- storage.

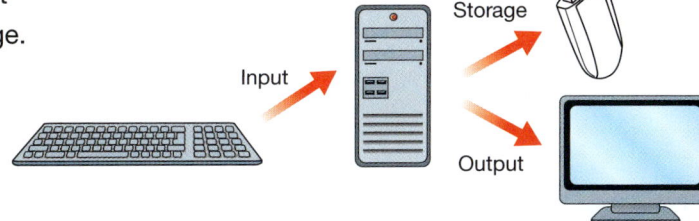

[1] TOUCH ID® IS A TRADEMARK OF APPLE INC., REGISTERED IN THE U.S. AND OTHER COUNTRIES

▲ Figure 1.34 Data is input from devices such as keyboards and processed by a computer, and the results can then be sent to output devices such as screens

SKILLS EXECUTIVE FUNCTION
CREATIVITY
COMMUNICATION
COLLABORATION
RESPONSIBILITY

ACTIVITY

▼ THE CHARACTERISTICS OF PERIPHERAL DEVICES

Create posters that include the characteristics and uses of a range of peripheral devices. You could split the work between members of your class so that some of you investigate input peripherals, some investigate output peripherals and some investigate storage peripherals.

INPUT

Input peripherals are devices that send data to the computer. They allow the user to control the computer or store data captured from sources outside the system.

KEYBOARDS

Keyboards use buttons known as keys, which users press to input text or to interact with software. Keyboards send data to the computer either using a wired or wireless connection. Different types of keyboards are used for different operating systems, languages and functions, as shown in Figure 1.35.

▲ Figure 1.35 Different layouts are provided for different operating systems or language requirements

Combinations of key presses allow the user to access common software commands called **shortcuts**. Some people learn to touch-type, which is a method of typing without needing to look at the keys. This increases the speed at which these people can input data.

SUBJECT VOCABULARY

shortcut a combination of key presses used to access common software commands quickly

▲ Figure 1.36 This is an example of a keyboard used with specialist video software; the keys are **mapped** to specialist commands

SUBJECT VOCABULARY

mapped linked

UNIT 1 — DIGITAL DEVICES

SKILLS ▸ PROBLEM SOLVING

DID YOU KNOW?
The layout of keys on a standard QWERTY keyboard comes from the layout of keys on a typewriter. The most commonly used letters were spread out, to reduce the number of times the metal typewriter hammers hit each other.

SUBJECT VOCABULARY
pointer an on-screen indicator used to select displayed objects

ACTIVITY

▼ KEYBOARD SHORTCUTS

Choose a piece of software and look up three keyboard shortcuts that you could use to complete common tasks more quickly.

POINTING DEVICES

A **pointer** is used on a screen to select displayed objects. There are several types of device that allow you to control a pointer.

- **Mouse:** A mouse uses an optical sensor to recognise the movement of the device. Its sensitivity can be affected by the surface upon which it is placed. Some mice use roller balls to control the movement of the pointer.

▲ Figure 1.38 Have you used a roller ball before?

- **Tracker ball:** A tracker ball is rolled to move the pointer. It does not have buttons to press.

▲ Figure 1.39 Tracker balls are often used in installations like the kiosk shown here

- **Track pad:** The track pad surface senses finger movements, touches and presses.

▲ Figure 1.40 Track pads are often built into laptop computers to save space

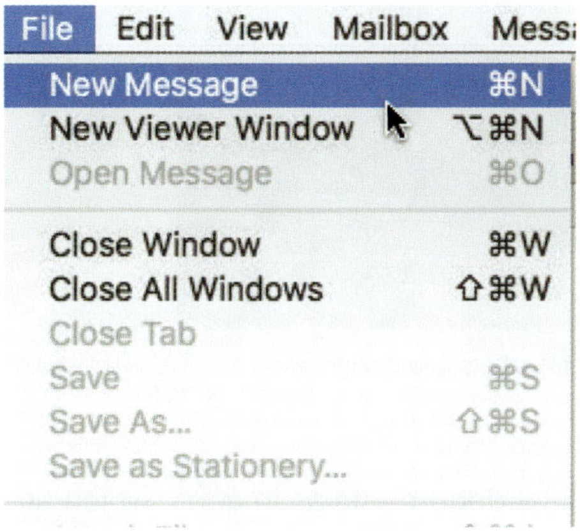

▲ Figure 1.37 An arrow is often used as the pointer

24 UNIT 1 — DIGITAL DEVICES

> **SUBJECT VOCABULARY**
> **sprites** on-screen graphics in a computer game, used to represent characters, vehicles and objects

- **Joystick:** Joysticks are commonly used on games controllers to move **sprites** around the game.

▲ Figure 1.41 Have you used a joystick like this one?

- **Graphics tablet:** A graphics tablet is a flat pad that is used with a **stylus**. Users use the stylus to draw or write on the graphics tablet. These devices are often used by digital artists and designers.

> **SUBJECT VOCABULARY**
> **stylus** a pen-shaped device

▲ Figure 1.42 Graphics tablets are often used by digital artists and designers

SCANNER (INCLUDING OCR AND OMR)

Scanners use light sensors to record physical documents as images, which are then saved as files to the computer.

Software allows scanners to read **characters** on the document and store the result in a text file. This is known as Optical Character Recognition (OCR).

Optical Mark Recognition (OMR) software can also be used with scanners to detect simple marks on a document. A common use for OMR is for recognising and recording responses to multiple choice tests.

▲ Figure 1.43 An OMR multiple choice response sheet

> **GENERAL VOCABULARY**
> **characters** printed or written letters and symbols

BARCODE SCANNER

A **barcode** is a pattern of lines and gaps that can be read by barcode scanners, which detect the width of lines and gaps in a barcode. Barcodes are often used on parcels, so that they can be tracked, and on items for sale in shops. The barcode represents letters and numbers which are used to identify the item.

> **SUBJECT VOCABULARY**
> **barcode** a pattern of lines and gaps that can be read by a device

There are two types of barcode:
- linear
- matrix.

▶ Figure 1.44 Linear barcode used to identify a parcel

Matrix codes are also known as QR codes. They are newer than linear barcodes and have some advantages over linear barcodes, such as:

- they can hold much more information than linear barcodes
- they can be scanned from any angle.

In South Korea, a supermarket company wanted to open a new shop, but there was no space left on the high street. Instead, the company created a 'virtual store' by putting posters of their supermarket shelves in a subway station, as shown in Figure 1.45. Every item pictured on the shelves had its own QR code that shoppers could scan. This allowed people to shop while they were travelling to work in the morning, knowing that their shopping would be delivered to their home that evening.

> **DID YOU KNOW?**
> There are apps for smartphones and tablet devices that use the device's camera to read barcodes and QR codes. There are also websites that allow users to create barcodes and QR codes.

▲ Figure 1.45 A Virtual Subway Store in South Korea

SKILLS EXECUTIVE FUNCTION
RESPONSIBILITY
CO-OPERATION

SUBJECT VOCABULARY

plain text text that is not specially formatted

ACTIVITY

▼ MATRIX CODES

Visit a website to create a QR code for a **plain text** message. Ask a friend to scan it to reveal the message you have left for them.

WEBCAM

Webcams are specialised cameras. They are generally lower quality than camcorders, and may have built-in microphones to capture sound. They can be used as security cameras and can stream images or video to the internet.

SKILLS CRITICAL THINKING
INTELLECTUAL INTEREST AND CURIOSITY

ACTIVITY

▼ USING WEBCAMS

Webcam footage can be used for a variety of purposes. For example, if you do an internet search for 'Bondi Beach webcam', you will be able to see live footage from Bondi Beach in Australia, which can be used to check the conditions for surfing at the beach.

Find out about any webcams in your local country or local area. What are they being used for? Who would be interested in the footage?

SUBJECT VOCABULARY

diaphragm a thin round object, especially in a telephone or loudspeaker, that is moved by sound or that moves when it produces sound

analogue representing information with continuously variable electrical signals that digital signals approximate

sound card a device built into or added into a computer to allow it to playback and record audio

VoIP Voice over Internet Protocol, which is the technology that allows people to use broadband internet connections to speak to other people, rather than using a conventional telephone

MICROPHONE

A microphone is used to capture sound. It uses a **diaphragm** which moves when air hits it. This movement produces an **analogue** electrical signal. A microphone converts the electrical signal to a digital signal with its **sound card**, which acts as an analogue-to-digital converter.

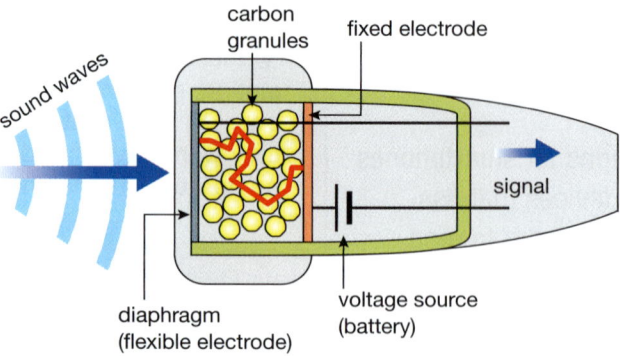

▲ Figure 1.46 Sound waves hitting a microphone and being converted to an electrical signal

Small, low-quality microphones are often built into computers and are used for voice recognition, recording speech or allowing **VoIP** calls using software such as Skype©. Higher quality microphones are often used by recording artists and can be connected to a sound card's audio input port.

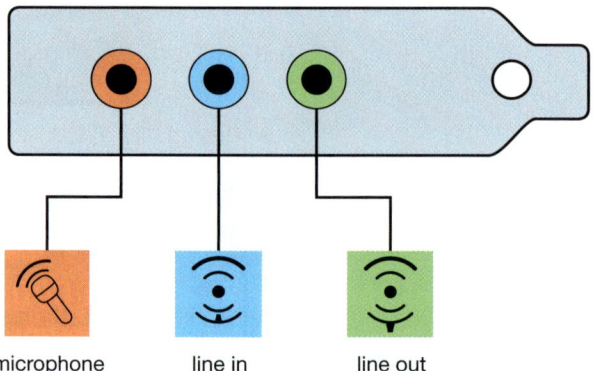

▲ Figure 1.47 A microphone can be plugged into a port on the sound card

▲ Figure 1.48 This headset contains a microphone and headphone speakers

HINT

Microphones can often be included in other devices, such as the headset in Figure 1.48. The headset itself is not a type of peripheral device, but a piece of equipment for combining a microphone and headphone speakers. Try to provide specific examples of peripheral devices when answering questions in the exam.

DID YOU KNOW?

Microphones are often used in order to make devices and technology accessible to people with disabilities, as they provide access for people who are unable to input data using a mouse and keyboard.

TOUCH SCREEN

Touch screens are used in many devices, including smartphones, tablet devices, laptops and desktop computers. There are two types of touch screen:

- resistive
- capacitive.

HINT

Do not confuse accessibility (increasing people's ability to access devices and technologies) with usability (making devices more efficient and satisfying to use).

UNIT 1 — DIGITAL DEVICES

GENERAL VOCABULARY

capacitive able to hold an electrical charge
conductive able to conduct electricity

When a user presses on a **resistive** screen, the pressure causes two layers underneath the screen to touch and make a connection. Resistive touch screens are more durable than capacitive touch screens, but are harder to read because more layers reflect more light. In addition, they can only recognise one touch at a time, so they are not suitable for multi-touch applications.

Under the glass of a **capacitive** screen, there is a layer of **capacitive** material. When a user touches the screen, a small amount of charge flows away from their finger because humans are **conductive**. The change in electrical charge is measured precisely: the closer the finger is to the charged areas, the more current flows away. This allows the computer to calculate the precise location at which the screen was touched. Capacitive touch screens are often used in smartphones.

BIOMETRIC SCANNER

If you have watched a spy film, you may have seen a biometric scanner being used. Biometric scanners work by measuring part of the unique physical characteristics of a user, often multiple times, until a suitable average result is produced. This average result is then stored and future samples are compared against it in order to check whether the person being scanned is the authorised user. This allows the information to be updated so that the saved sample is perfected.

Four examples of biometric scanners are as follows.

- **Fingerprint recognition:** These scanners read the patterns of arches, loops and whorls in a human fingerprint. Fingerprints are unique to each individual person, which makes them a useful method of identification, but fingerprints can be obscured, damaged or changed, such as by injury or disease.

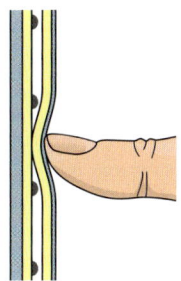

▲ Figure 1.49 A resistive touch screen

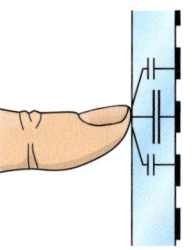

▲ Figure 1.50 A capacitive touch screen

▲ Figure 1.51 A fingerprint scanner detects unique patterns in your fingerprints

Arch Loop Whorl

▲ Figure 1.52 Examples of different types of fingerprint patterns

- **Facial recognition:** These scanners identify the structure of a human face in order to identify an individual.

▲ Figure 1.53 Surveillance scanners are also used by some government agencies to recognise number plates, models and colours of vehicles

- **Voice recognition:** These scanners require a microphone to capture the voice. They then compare the voice print against a saved original and check to see whether the two prints match. (See page 26 for more information about microphones.)

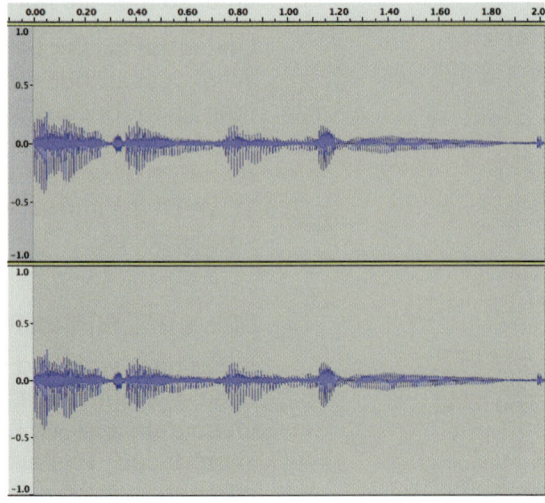

▲ Figure 1.54 Voice recognition software compares a voice print with a stored original and checks for a match

- **Iris recognition:** Like fingerprints, the human iris has a unique pattern, though an iris scan is approximately 120 times more detailed than a fingerprint. This means that iris recognition is 120 times more reliable when identifying people.

> **GENERAL VOCABULARY**
>
> **iris** the round, coloured part of an eye

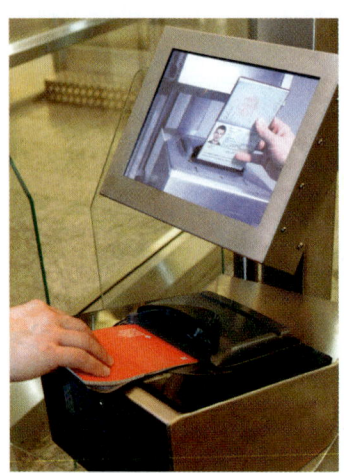 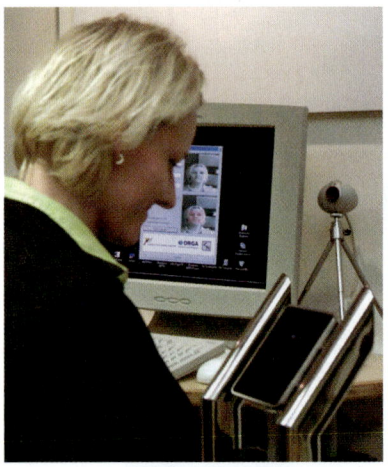

▲ Figure 1.55 Some passports now contain a chip that holds biometric data about the passport holder that is compared with the results of biometric scans carried out at airports

▼ Table 1.2 Advantages and disadvantages of using biometric scanners

ADVANTAGES	DISADVANTAGES
Easier for users than passwords because biometric data cannot be forgotten	Cause privacy and security concerns because detailed personal information is stored electronically
More difficult to trick or confuse biometric scanners than some other methods	Possible to trick or confuse them
Can speed up transactions	Expensive to make and buy
Are not restricted by language barriers	Make some people feel uncomfortable

UNIT 1 — DIGITAL DEVICES

SKILLS
- CRITICAL THINKING
- COMMUNICATION
- INTERPRETATION
- ADAPTIVE LEARNING
- EXECUTIVE FUNCTION
- PERSONAL AND SOCIAL RESPONSIBILITY
- INITIATIVE
- COMMUNICATION
- COLLABORATION
- CO-OPERATION
- INTERPERSONAL SKILLS
- RESPONSIBILITY

ACTIVITY

▼ USING BIOMETRIC SCANNERS

1. Use the internet to do some research and create a table that compares the advantages and disadvantages of each method of biometric scanning (see *Unit 6 Software skills* (page 308) for more information about creating tables).
2. Create a survey to ask other people how they would feel about using each type of biometric scanner. What are their concerns?
3. What affects the reliability of each type of biometric scanner? Discuss your research findings and your thoughts with your teacher and the rest of your class.
4. What other factors could be considered when choosing a biometric security system?

CARD READERS

Card readers are used to read data stored on a card that is carried by a user. The data can be used to unlock doors, access secure areas, make payments or track people, parcels and even pet animals.

Cards can carry data using three methods. Each method needs a specialist type of reader.

- **Magnetic strip:** This is the least secure method as the data on the magnetic strip can easily be stolen by criminals who put the card through a card reader without the card owner's knowledge.
- **Programmable chip:** Data on a programmable chip is only readable when a correct PIN is entered into the reader. In 2005, the UK introduced the chip and PIN system, which reduced certain types of **fraud** by 67%.

▲ **Figure 1.56** Magnetic strip reader being used to unlock a door

SKILLS
- PERSONAL AND SOCIAL RESPONSIBILITY
- INTERPERSONAL SKILLS

ACTIVITY

▼ FRAUD

In the UK, online fraud rose 79% in the first three years after the country switched to the chip and PIN system. Discuss why this may have happened.

GENERAL VOCABULARY

fraud deceiving other people for criminal reasons

▲ **Figure 1.57** Examples of cards using chip and PIN

- **Radio Frequency Identification (RFID) and Near Field Communication (NFC):** RFID is a short-range wireless communication method, and Near Field Communication (NFC) is a branch of RFID. RFID tags are cheap and small and they can be included in a variety of objects such as cards, key fobs and smartphones. They contain a unique identification number (ID) that is linked to records in a database. For example, the first image in Figure 1.58 shows a traveller using a prepaid travel card. A unique ID stored on the card links to account information stored in a database. You will learn more about databases in Unit 6 Software skills (page 307).

▲ Figure 1.58 RFID tags can be included in a variety of objects

SENSORS

Sensors are used to input data about the physical environment. They can automatically input data without the need for human action. Their output is then processed by a computer. Sensors are one of the main features of smart devices such as smartphones and smart environments such as **smart homes**.

> **SUBJECT VOCABULARY**
>
> **sensor** an input peripheral that inputs data about the physical environment
>
> **smart home** a home equipped with devices that can connect to the internet and be controlled remotely by a computer or smartphone app

▲ Figure 1.59 (Left to right) motion sensor, **proximity** sensor, temperature sensor and button sensor; the red item at the top is a light sensor and the red item at the bottom is a UV sensor

> **GENERAL VOCABULARY**
>
> **proximity** how close something is relative to something else

The use of sensors has many benefits, such as:

- they can be placed in remote or dangerous places
- they can monitor continually
- they remove the possibility of human error
- they can sense things that people cannot (such as small changes in pressure or gas levels)
- the data is easily (sometimes automatically) converted to a digital form.

There are many different types of sensor to allow for the monitoring of a range of environmental factors. Some of these factors are:

- light
- moisture and humidity
- temperature
- proximity and distance
- motion and movement (such as Passive Infrared (PIR) sensors)
- pressure.

SKILLS — CRITICAL THINKING, INTELLECTUAL INTEREST AND CURIOSITY

ACTIVITY

▼ USING SENSORS

1 For each environmental factor listed above, state one remote and one dangerous environment where a sensor could be used.

2 Research the appliances in modern smart homes that can use sensors. For each one, describe how sensors are used.

3 Research how sensors can help to prevent air traffic accidents. Can you find any instances where they may have caused accidents?

▲ Figure 1.60 Sensors are used in aircraft and data from them are displayed to the flight crew on instruments in the cockpit

OUTPUT

Output peripherals are connected to a computer and output the results of the computer's processing in various forms, including:

- electronic display
- printed text
- video
- audio
- tactile (touch) forms.

MONITOR

Monitors allow users to see the output from the computer on an electronic display. Features of monitors include:

- screen size, which is measured diagonally
- resolution, which is measured in pixels (see pages 9–10 for information about pixels and screen resolutions)
- energy efficiency measures, such as going into a low-power standby mode if no input is detected.

Some monitors also use touch screen technology (see page pages 26–27 for more information about touch screens).

▲ **Figure 1.61** Monitors have evolved over time to provide better quality and more features

SKILLS COMMUNICATION
EXECUTIVE FUNCTION

ACTIVITY

▼ **USING MONITORS**

1. Discuss the different uses for monitors.
2. Create a table of the uses for monitors with different sizes and resolutions (see *Unit 6 Software skills* (pages 220–223) for more information about creating tables).

PRINTER

There are three types of standard printer: dot matrix, inkjet and laser.

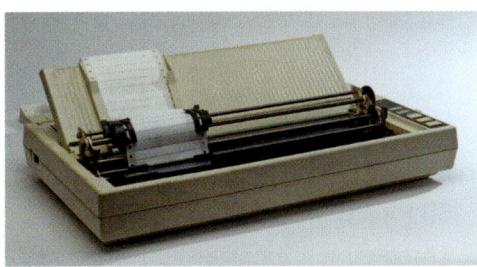

▲ Figure 1.62 Laser (top left), inkjet (right) and dot matrix (bottom left) printers

GENERAL VOCABULARY

carbon copy a copy of a document made using carbon paper (paper coated in a coloured substance that leaves traces on clean paper)

- **Dot matrix:** These printers are sometimes called 'impact' printers. This is because the print is made by hitting or 'impacting' the paper through a ribbon of ink, and this process is very noisy. The paper often has a number of **carbon copy** layers so it can make several copies of the same document as it prints it.

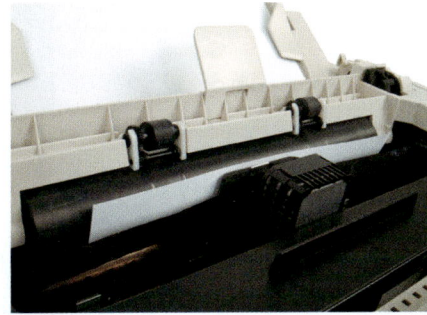

▲ Figure 1.63 A dot matrix printer

- **Inkjet printers:** These printers use cartridges containing different coloured ink. Black ink is held in a one cartridge, while the colour cartridge is often split into three colours: cyan, magenta and yellow. Tiny dots of these inks are sprayed onto the paper to form images or text.

DID YOU KNOW?

Many cartridges can be refilled to save money and protect the environment.

▲ Figure 1.64 Cartridges used in an inkjet printer

UNIT 1 — DIGITAL DEVICES

SUBJECT VOCABULARY

discharge remove the electrical charge from something
toner a type of ink

- **Laser printers:** These printers contain a rotating cylinder or drum that holds an electrical charge. A laser is used to **discharge** certain points on the drum and 'draw' an image. Electrically charged **toner** is attracted to those points on the drum and is heated onto paper that is passed over the drum.

▼ Table 1.3 Comparing printer types

	SPEED	PRINTER COST	COST PER COPY	COLOUR PRINTING	QUALITY	EXAMPLES OF WHERE IT IS USED
Dot matrix	Slowest	Cheap	Low	Rare	Low	When multiple copies are required.
Inkjet	Fast	Medium	High	Yes	High	Home printing and photographs
Laser	Fastest	Expensive	Medium	Yes	Highest	High-volume printing, often used in offices

3D PRINTER

Three-dimensional (3D) printers create real-life versions of digital models. These printers work by adding layers of heated material from the bottom of the model all the way to the top. 3D-printed models take a long time to create.

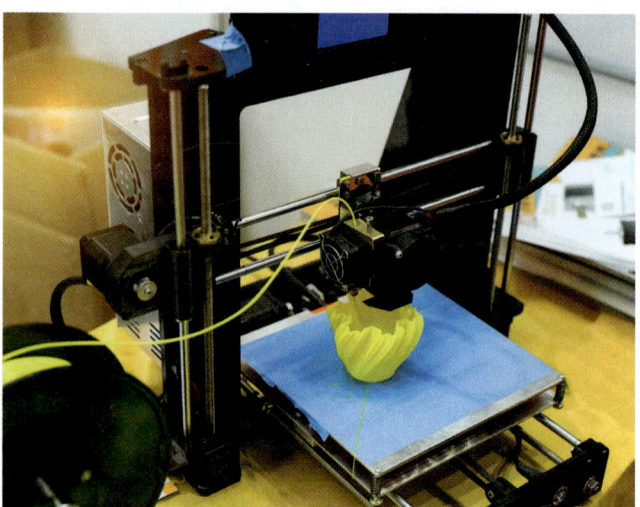

▲ Figure 1.65 A 3D printer

SKILLS INTELLECTUAL INTEREST AND CURIOSITY

ACTIVITY

▼ USING 3D PRINTERS

Find a video online that shows a 3D printer in action.

3D printers are often used to create complex items, sometimes with working parts. Some of these items could not be assembled in any other way. Examples of 3D-printed items include aeroplane parts, artificial limbs, prototype models of cars and even food such as pasta and chocolate.

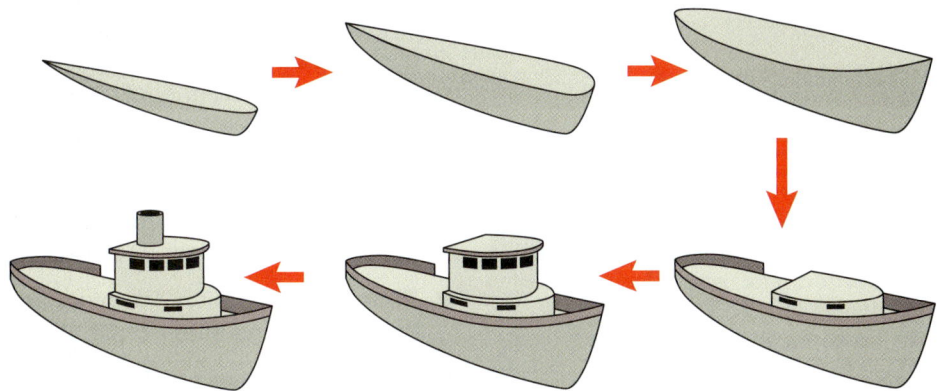

▲ Figure 1.66 Stages of building a 3D-printed model

SKILLS   INTELLECTUAL INTEREST AND CURIOSITY
PERSONAL AND SOCIAL RESPONSIBILITY
ETHICS
COMMUNICATION
REASONING/ARGUMENTATION

ACTIVITY

▼ **TECHNOLOGY AND ETHICS**

1 In 2013, someone published the plans for a 3D-printed gun online. Discuss the impact of this.

2 Write notes to support two opposing arguments. One argument should support the wide availability of 3D printers, and the other should argue against the wide availability of these printers. You could then use your notes to debate this topic in your class.

PLOTTER

▲ Figure 1.67 A plotter

> **DID YOU KNOW?**
> Plotters can also use a cutter attachment instead of the pen attachment to cut vinyl. This can be used to create stickers or images to go on printed clothing.

Plotters are used by a variety of professionals, including product designers, architects, engineers and **cartographers**. The plotter draws high-quality images created in Computer Aided Design (CAD) software onto large sheets of paper. It does this by moving a pen across the paper to draw the lines, and the pen can be raised away from and lowered onto the sheet of paper. Some plotters can also roll the paper backwards and forwards.

GENERAL VOCABULARY

cartographers people who draw and produce maps

DATA PROJECTOR

Data projectors are used for home entertainment, such as watching television or playing games, and for giving presentations in classrooms and business meetings. They have the following features.

- **Light bulbs:** These bulbs can have various brightness levels (measured in lumens) and are expensive to replace.
- **Resolution:** Like monitors, they use different quality screens (see page 9–10 for more about screen resolutions).
- **Zoom functionality:** The projected image can be made larger by enlarging the image using either **optical zoom** or **digital zoom**.
- **Portability:** Some smaller and lighter projectors are available, and these are easier to move around.

> **SUBJECT VOCABULARY**
>
> **optical zoom** focusing a lens in order to zoom in on an object
>
> **digital zoom** enlarging part of an image to produce the effect of zooming in

▲ Figure 1.68 Data projectors are used to project a large image (or film) onto screens

SKILLS ADAPTABILITY SELF-DIRECTION

ACTIVITY

▼ TYPES OF PROJECTOR

1. Do some online research to find an appropriate projector for:
   - use in a classroom
   - a home entertainment system
   - a person travelling on business.
2. For each projector that you identify, find out how long its light bulbs last (on average) and how much the replacement bulbs cost.

SPEAKER

Speakers allow a computer to output sound. Speakers often come in pairs to provide **stereo sound**. Multiple speakers are commonly used to provide **surround sound** in home entertainment systems. These speakers need a special amplifier that can deliver different levels of sound to each speaker to provide **spatial awareness**.

> **SUBJECT VOCABULARY**
>
> **stereo sound** sound that comes from two sides (left and right)
>
> **surround sound** sound that comes from four or more sides, used so that sounds from a film or television programme come from all around the viewer as they would in real life
>
> **GENERAL VOCABULARY**
>
> **spatial awareness** the impression of a realistic space

▲ Figure 1.69 A pair of speakers is required for stereo sound because one is used for the left side and one is used for the right side

UNIT 1 — DIGITAL DEVICES

SKILLS SELF-DIRECTION, PROBLEM SOLVING

SUBJECT VOCABULARY

mono sound sound that comes from a single speaker

SKILLS ADADPTIVE LEARNING

ACTIVITY

▼ DIFFERENT TYPES OF SOUND

Do some research to find out when **mono sound** may be most appropriate. When might listeners prefer stereo sound?

A single speaker is usually used to provide low-quality audio feedback to a user. These speakers are often small and low-quality, and are often found in alert systems such as alarms and buzzers.

ACTIVITY

▼ USING LOW-QUALITY SPEAKERS

Think of the appliances and devices in your home that use low-quality speakers (you might want to start in the kitchen!).

CONTROL DEVICE

Control devices are also known as actuators, and they are components of a system that make something happen in the real physical world. These devices are often mechanical. Examples of actuators include:

- valves
- pistons
- heaters
- coolers
- motors.

▲ **Figure 1.70** A piezoelectric 'piezo' speaker used in a watch

▲ **Figure 1.71** Robots use actuators that are powered in many ways such as electricity, chemicals and compressed air

DID YOU KNOW?

Nanorobots are made up of tiny sensors and actuators that are capable of assisting a surgeon by carrying out very precise medical procedures.

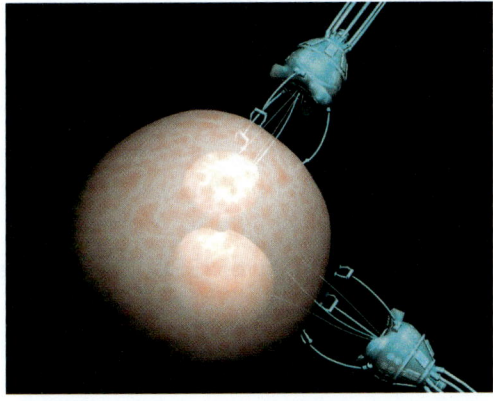

▲ **Figure 1.72** Nanorobots allow doctors to make smaller incisions or cuts and more precise movements than they could if they used their own hands

SECONDARY STORAGE (STORAGE)

GENERAL VOCABULARY

volatile likely to change, especially quickly or unpredictably

HINT

People often confuse storage and memory. You must know the difference between these terms, including what they do and the ways in which they are used.

SUBJECT VOCABULARY

virtual memory space on a computer for storing instructions and programs until they are needed or being used
motherboard the circuit in a computer with connectors to which other components connect

Secondary storage is often referred to as 'storage'. However, it should not be confused with primary storage or main memory, which are terms sometimes used to refer to Random Access Memory (RAM) or Read Only Memory (ROM). You will learn more about RAM and ROM on pages 59–61. Secondary storage is non-**volatile**, which means it will not lose data when the system's power is turned off.

Secondary storage is used for:

- storing a document for future use
- storing an application, ready to be loaded into RAM when the user opens the application
- **virtual memory** (see page 60).

DEVICES

Storage devices are used to store data or software that is used in a computer system.

Storage devices can be either internal or external. Internal drives connect directly to the computer's **motherboard**. External devices are connected to the computer's motherboard through the different ports and adapters on the computer's exterior.

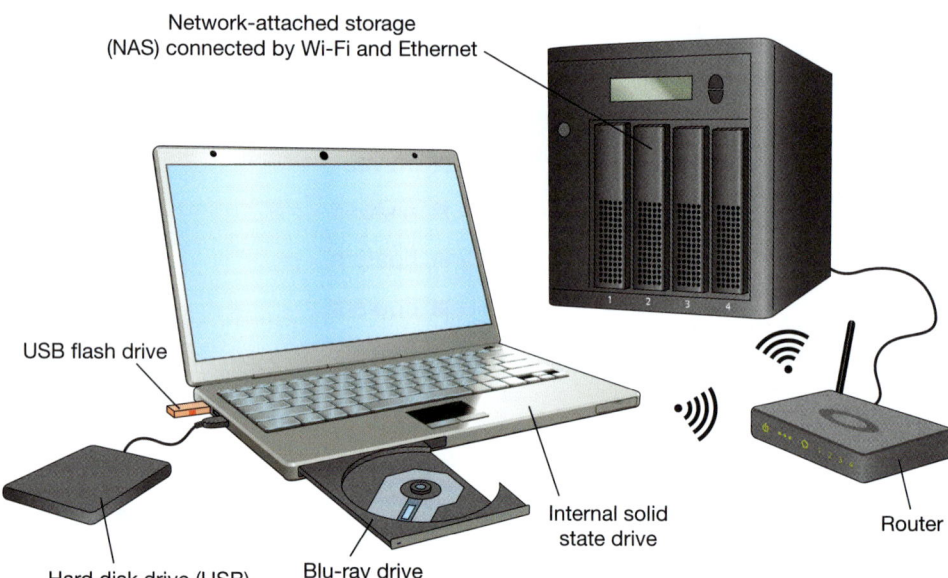

▲ Figure 1.73 Storage can be internal or external

There are different types of storage device.

- Hard disk drives (HDD) contain hard disk media. The drives provide a connection from the disk to the motherboard, either directly or using a wireless adapter like Wi-Fi or a wired port like USB.
- Solid state drives (SSD, often referred to as flash drives) contain flash memory media. They are otherwise identical to hard disk drives.
- Optical disk drives contain optical disk media. Newer drives are often compatible with older media. For example, a disk drive that can read Blu-ray media can also read DVD and CD media. This is known as **backwards compatibility**.

HINT

You must know the difference between a storage device and storage media. Remember: a storage device *contains* the storage media and *accesses* the data stored on it. For example:
1. flash memory is the media used to store data, whereas a USB drive is used to contain the flash media so that it can be read by the computer after it is plugged into a USB port
2. a DVD disk is the media used to store data, whereas a DVD drive reads the data on the DVD disk.

SUBJECT VOCABULARY

backwards compatibility the ability to be used with older technology without having to be specially adapted

UNIT 1 — DIGITAL DEVICES

GENERAL VOCABULARY

concentric (of circles or circular objects) sharing the same central point
spindle a rod around which something spins

SUBJECT VOCABULARY

platters circular plates
read/write head the part of a disk drive that passes across (or floats) the platters on a very thin layer of gas above the platters
seek time the time it takes for a read/write head to locate the area on the disk where the data to be read is stored

DID YOU KNOW?

The gap between the platter and the read/write head is only a few nanometers wide. This means that a dust particle or even a smoke particle could cause a collision between the platter and the read/write head. To prevent this, hard drives use filters in their ventilation systems or are built as sealed units.

HINT

If a read/write head crashes into a platter, it can cause damage to data and the platter. This would not happen with a solid state drive.

DID YOU KNOW?

Optical media layers deteriorate (get worse) over time, so they have to be stored carefully to prevent data loss.

DID YOU KNOW?

Blu-ray disks get their name from the colour of laser used. The laser light is actually a violet colour, but perhaps 'violet-ray' was not considered a good enough name.

MEDIA

Hard disks

Hard disks are made up of many **concentric platters**. These platters make up a cylinder that spins on a central **spindle**. A **read/write head** moves on an arm across tracks on the platter. The amount of time that it takes the read/write head to access data on the tracks is determined by how fast the cylinder of platters spins and how fast the read/write head is moved across the tracks. When reading, a read/write head changes the magnetic field into electrical current. When writing, it transforms electrical current into a magnetic field.

Typical spin speeds are 5400 revolutions per minute (rpm) or 7200 rpm.

The average **seek time** for a read/write head is 4–15 milliseconds (ms).

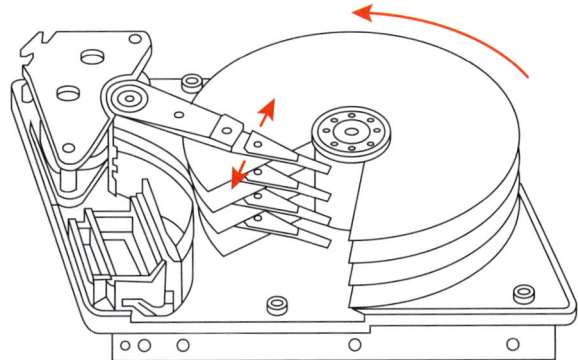

▲ Figure 1.74 Read/write heads move across a hard disk platter to access data as the cylinder spins

Optical media

Types of optical media include CDs, DVDs and Blu-ray disks.

- **CDs** can store up to 700 MB of data. The data is written to the disk using a laser, which writes data to a plastic layer beneath layers of aluminium and acrylic.
- **DVDs** look very much like CDs. Data is written to DVDs using a shorter wavelength of red laser light, which allows DVDs to store more data. They can store 4.7 GB on a single-sided, single-layer disk. Double-sided, dual-layer disks can store as much as 18 GB.
- **Blu-ray** disks are similar to CDs and DVDs, but use a scratch-protection coating. Violet laser light is used to store data at greater density than the red laser light used in DVDs. They can store 25 GB on a single-sided disk, and double-sided disks can store 50 GB.

All optical media is recordable and is known as CD-R, DVD-R or BD-R. Some CDs and DVDs can be rewritten (CD-RW, DVD-RW), and some Blu-ray media can be written then erased and rewritten (BD-RE).

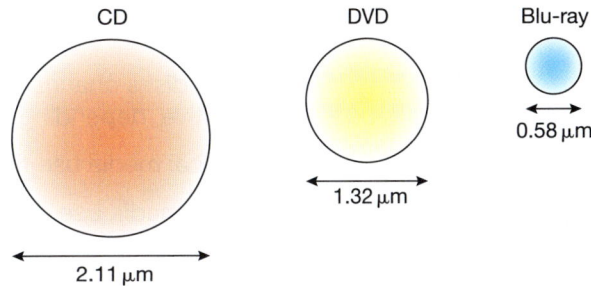

▲ Figure 1.75 Comparison of various lasers used to store data on optical media

> **DID YOU KNOW?**
> One explanation of why flash memory is so-called is that each cell is flashed (flooded) with electrons, forcing it to hold its charge. One other explanation for the name is that data is written very quickly (or, in colloquial English, 'in a flash').

Flash media

Flash media are more energy-efficient than hard disks as they do not have moving parts. For the same reason, they are also less likely to fail when they are moved around. This makes them suitable for use in portable devices.

Magnetic tape

Magnetic tape was originally designed to record sound, but it is now also used to store data.

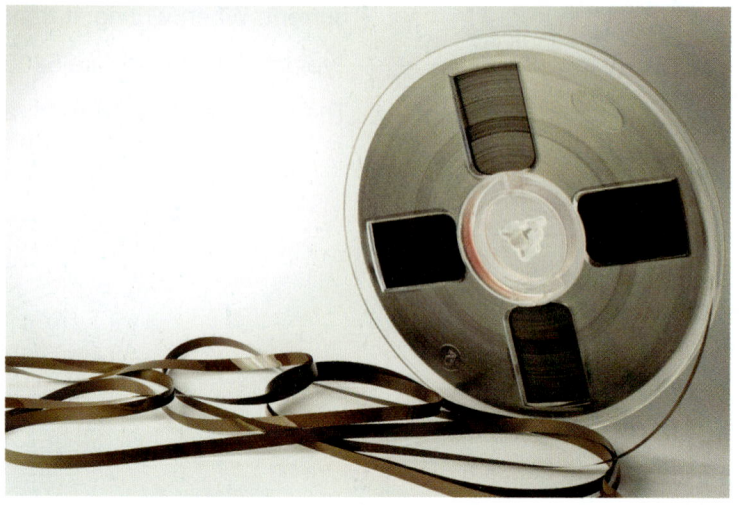

▲ Figure 1.76 Magnetic tape is mainly used for backing up data in large organisations

▼ Table 1.4 Comparing types of media

	HARD DISK	FLASH MEDIA	OPTICAL MEDIA	MAGNETIC TAPE
DATA ACCESS SPEED	Fast	Fastest	Slow	Slowest
MAXIMUM CAPACITY	Varies, up to 128 GB	Varies, up to many TB	CD 700 MB DVD 18 GB Blu-ray 50 GB	Varies, up to 185 TB
COST PER GB	High	Very high	Medium	Low
USE	Servers, personal computers, backups	Laptops, mobile devices	Multimedia (music, games and films), file backups	Whole system backups and archives
PORTABILITY	Not suitable	Yes	Not suitable	Not suitable

> **SUBJECT VOCABULARY**
> **data access speed** how quickly data can be read from or written to media
> **capacity** the amount of data that can be stored on media
> **bit** (**bi**nary dig**it**) a single unit of information with a value of either 0 or 1; eight bits equal one byte

Storage media store data in binary form. This means that each **bit** of data holds one of two values: 0 or 1. Different media types interpret 0 or 1 differently.

- Hard disks change the magnetic charge of a platter to either negative or positive, depending on whether the value is 0 or 1.
- Optical media use tiny bumps on the disk's surface to represent 0 and 1.
- Flash media use different levels of electrical charge, held in tiny individual cells, to represent 0 or 1.
- Magnetic tape changes the magnetic charge of the tape to either negative or positive, depending on whether the value is 0 or 1.

> **DID YOU KNOW?**
> The 'bi' in '**bi**nary' comes from the Latin for 'two'.

UNIT 1 — DIGITAL DEVICES

> **HINT**
> You do not need to understand the units shaded in dark grey in the table for the International GCSE.

▼ Table 1.5 Units of storage capacity

NUMBER OF BYTES	WITH UNIT SYMBOL	NAME
1000	1 KB	Kilobyte
1000,000	1 MB	Megabyte
1000,000,000	1 GB	Gigabyte
1000,000,000,000	1 TB	Terabyte
1000,000,000,000,000	1 PB	Petabyte
1000,000,000,000,000,000	1 EB	Exabyte
1000,000,000,000,000,000,000	1 ZB	Zettabyte
1000,000,000,000,000,000,000,000	1 YB	Yottabyte

The IBM 350 was the first disk drive. It was 172 cm high, 152 cm long and 74 cm wide, and it could store 3.75 MB of data. People could hire one for US$38,400 per year. In 2016, manufacturers started selling the 256 GB microSD card, which is a flash memory card the size of a human fingertip. It was priced at US$175 and can store the same amount of data as 68,266 IBM 350 disks!

> **DID YOU KNOW?**
> In 2017, it would take about 9457 trillion years to download one yottabyte of data with a good internet connection.

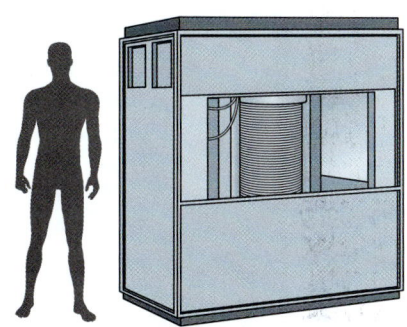
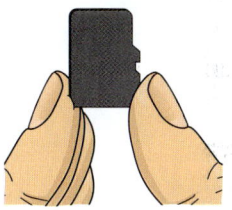

▲ Figure 1.77 The IBM 350 in comparison with a person and a 256 GB microSD card

CHAPTER QUESTIONS

SKILLS — CRITICAL THINKING
1 State **one** benefit of using barcodes in a supermarket. (1)

SKILLS — REASONING
2 State **one** reason why small, built-in microphones are used in smartphones and laptops. (1)

SKILLS — DECISION MAKING
3 Explain why capacitive touch screens do not work when you are wearing woollen gloves. (2)

4 State **three** computer systems that **do not** use monitors. (3)

SKILLS — CRITICAL THINKING
5 State **two** benefits of using laser printers rather than inkjet printers. (2)

SKILLS — PROBLEM SOLVING
6 State **two** types of business that use plotters. (2)

SKILLS — REASONING
7 Explain why some 3D printers use biodegradable materials to create models. (3)

SKILLS — CRITICAL THINKING
8 List **two** sensors used in smartphones. For each one, describe one way in which it is used by the operating system or an app. (4)

SKILLS — REASONING/ARGUMENTATION
9 Discuss the advantages and disadvantages of using sensors in smart cars. (8)

SKILLS — DECISION MAKING
10 Explain **one** reason why Blu-ray disks are used to store modern console games. (2)

2 SOFTWARE

The programs that run on a computer are called software. Programs are instructions that are carried out or executed by the computer's processor, which provides other instructions for the rest of the computer.

Some computers can only run one program at a time, while others can run multiple programs at the same time. Some computers are single purpose, which means that they are only able to run one piece of software (for example, the software used to control a microwave). Other computers are general purpose, which means that they are able to carry out a range of tasks (for example, the software used in a tablet computer).

There are two basic groups of software: system software and application software.

LEARNING OBJECTIVES

- Be able to identify the purpose of systems software and applications software
- Know about operating systems and system software tools such as utilities
- Know about the role/function of the operating system, including basic knowledge of:
  - single user and network
  - memory management
  - resource management
  - security
  - print spooling
- Know about software applications (apps), including office-productivity tools, web authoring, image and sound editing, presentation software, control software, project management software
- Know about software licensing types (free/open source and proprietary software)
- Understand that the purpose of communication software is to provide remote access to systems and to exchange files and messages in text, images, audio and/or video formats between different computers or users
- Know why software is updated, how it is done and possible risks to data/systems
- Understand that settings of ICT systems can be configured to meet the accessibility needs of individuals
- Be able to justify choices made in identifying and configuring hardware and software

SYSTEM SOFTWARE

Programs that are designed to maintain or operate the computer system are known as system software.

UTILITY SOFTWARE

Utility software is one form of system software, which carries out configuration and maintenance tasks.

BACKUP

Backup utilities create a copy of files and programs. Backups can be set to run automatically (usually at a time when the system is not in use) or can be started by a user.

You will learn more about backups in *Unit 3 Operating online* (pages 104–105).

> **SUBJECT VOCABULARY**
>
> **utility software** (also known as utilities) system software that carries out configuration and maintenance tasks

DEFRAGMENTATION

As data is stored to hard disk, some systems spread it across the disk wherever there is free space. This means that sometimes data is **fragmented** and stored out of order or out of sequence.

GENERAL VOCABULARY

fragmented broken into pieces

▲ **Figure 2.1** Data is sometimes stored in the nearest free space, which results in data getting out of sequence. This is an illustrative example.

Data from the same file may be spread over multiple locations on a platter, on different platters in the cylinder or sometimes even on different disks. When these files are loaded, data has to be retrieved from these multiple locations. The read/write head of the hard drive has to find this data, which takes extra time and slows down the process of loading the files.

To avoid this and to speed up the system, disk defragmentation utilities reorder the fragments of data so that they are stored as close to each other as possible.

▲ **Figure 2.2** Defragmentation puts the data back in order so that the read/write head does not have to search the disk for fragments of data. This is an illustrative example.

Defragmentation utilities are usually set to run automatically, but they can also be started by a user.

SKILLS EXECUTIVE FUNCTION
INTELLECTUAL INTEREST AND CURIOSITY
SELF-DIRECTION

ACTIVITY

▼ DEFRAGMENTATION

1 Run a defragmenter analysis on your system. When was the analysis last run? How fragmented was the data last time the analysis ran?
2 Research the need for defragmentation on SSDs.

COMPRESSION

Compression utilities reduce the original size of a file or set of files.

Where there are repeated patterns of data, rather than storing every repeated instance, only the first instance of the data is stored, alongside how many times it is repeated. For example, in Figure 2.4, there were eight instances of a, six instances of b and two instances of c in the original file. This data can be compressed to be stored as 'a8b6c2', which reduces the amount of storage needed.

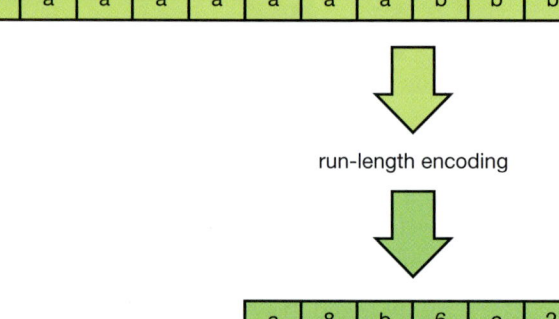

▲ Figure 2.3 Data can be compressed to remove unnecessary use of code or space in the file. This is an illustrative example.

▲ Figure 2.4 Run Length Encoding is one method of data compression

The resulting compressed file is not usually readable by the original application. Compression utilities also have the ability to **decompress** (extract) the data from a compressed file so it can be read by the original application again.

FORMATTING

Disk formatting prepares storage media such as a hard disk drive or USB flash drive for its first use. If a disk has already been used, then formatting it will make all of the data on the disk unreadable by normal applications.

DID YOU KNOW?
Different operating systems require disks to be formatted in certain ways in order to perform specialist tasks. Disks can also be formatted in a way that makes them compatible with all operating systems.

SUBJECT VOCABULARY

decompress extract data from a compressed file so that it can be read

Disk formatting utilities make this process easy for users by providing them with the option to choose the file system, file unit sizes and the name of the disk. Perhaps most importantly, they make sure that the user really wants to format the disk.

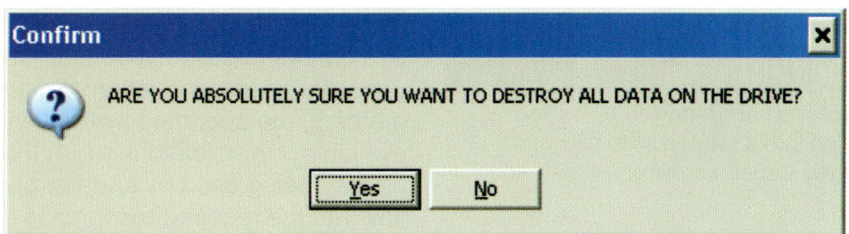

▲ Figure 2.5 Accidentally formatting the wrong disk could result in the unwanted loss of data

> **DID YOU KNOW?**
> Formatting a disk will not erase the data completely and it can still be recovered using specialist tools, but there are some utilities which will overwrite the data so that files cannot be recovered.

OPERATING SYSTEMS

The operating system (OS) allows the user to control and manage the computer's hardware.

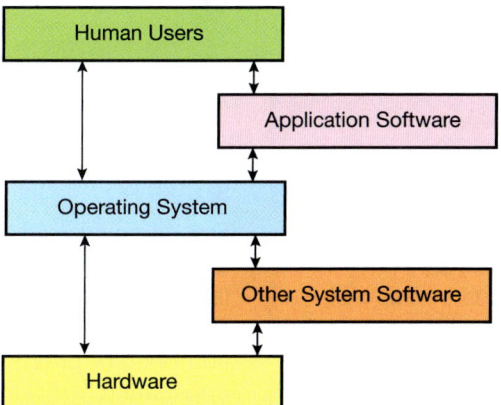

▲ Figure 2.6 The operating system lets the user control the hardware, either directly or by using applications software or system software

GENERAL VOCABULARY

customise to change something in order to make it more suitable for a particular user or to make it look special or different from things of a similar type

Single-user operating systems only allow for a general user and do not provide the option to **customise** the user interface for different users. They are often found in household appliances.

Network operating systems have additional functionality, including:
- sending requests to a server when users log in with their username and password
- separating user accounts and ensuring that users cannot access each other's files
- providing access to network storage and shared resources such as networked printers.

MEMORY MANAGEMENT

The operating system allocates the required amount of memory (RAM) to one or more applications. When the application no longer requires the memory space, the operating system makes the space available for other applications to use.

The operating system also handles the creation of virtual memory. See page 60 for more information about virtual memory.

RESOURCE MANAGEMENT

System resources include internal components, such as the processor and **graphics card**, and external devices, such as printers. As well as allocating memory, the operating system ensures that system resources are made available to applications when they are required. If a system resource is already being used by another application, then the operating system may say that the required resource is in use and place the additional request in a queue. For some resources, such as printers, the operating system can tell the user when the resource becomes available.

> **SUBJECT VOCABULARY**
>
> **graphics card** a device built into or added into a computer to allow it to display visual graphics

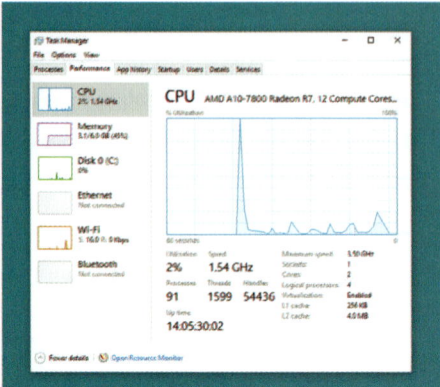 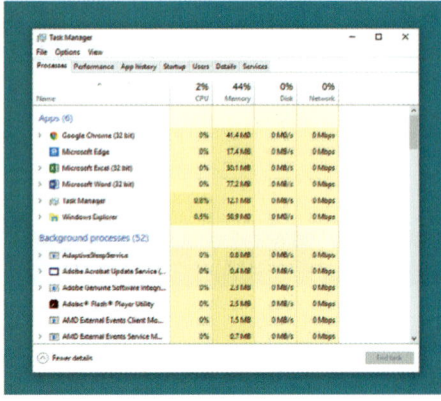

▲ Figure 2.7 Information about the use of memory and resources is provided by utility software

SECURITY

Operating systems can give users secure access to a computer's storage and other hardware through usernames and passwords, biometric scanning (see pages 27–28) or personal access cards. This process is called **authentication**. Operating systems can provide software **firewalls** to authorise or prevent network data from remotely accessing a service or application.

> **SUBJECT VOCABULARY**
>
> **authentication** the process of confirming that a user is permitted to access certain files, hardware and software
>
> **firewall** a system (hardware or software) that protects a computer network from being used or looked at by people who do not have permission to do so

PRINT SPOOLING

During large print jobs, the computer will have the pages ready for the printer faster than the printer can produce them. The operating system keeps each page in a queue ready for printing. This process is called **print spooling**.

> **SUBJECT VOCABULARY**
>
> **print spooling** the process of keeping pages queued in order, ready to be printed by a printer

APPLICATION SOFTWARE

Software applications (apps) allow users to produce a digital product, such as a presentation or image, or carry out specific tasks that are not related to the operating system.

Apps are usually downloaded from servers on the internet. Some devices, like smartphones and tablets, use operating systems that provide access to app stores. Some of these only make apps available to users after the store has checked the quality of the app and has ensured that the app does not include code that will harm a user's device or data. Apps can also be installed from storage media like DVDs.

You will learn more about online software in *Unit 4 Online goods and services* (178–179).

UNIT 1   SOFTWARE   47

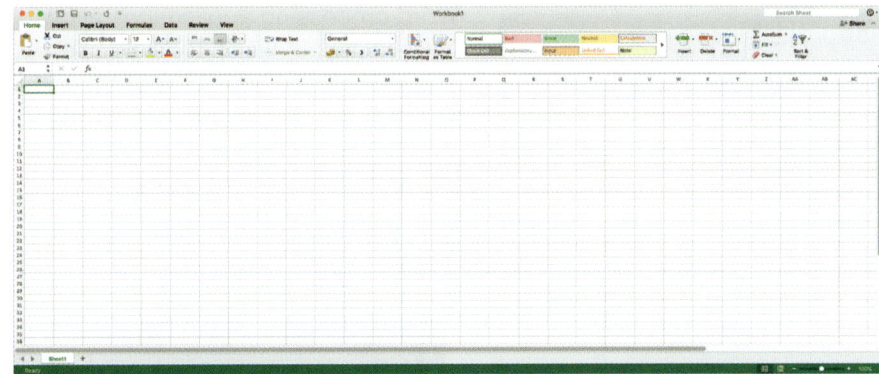

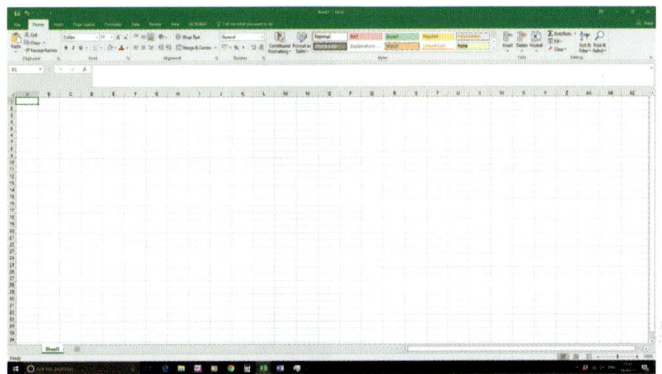

▲ **Figure 2.8** Some developers provide versions of their apps for different types of computer and operating systems. The top window shows the Apple macOS version whilst the bottom window shows the Microsoft® Windows version.

> **HINT**
>
> When you are writing about application software in your exam, you should refer to the application by its type rather than by a particular name. For example, use the term 'word processing software' rather than the brand name Microsoft® Word.

You need to be able to identify the type of software that meets specific needs. Each type of application software has particular features that make it suitable to perform a particular function. Sometimes more than one type of application can complete the task, but you should consider which one is most suitable.

OFFICE PRODUCTIVITY SOFTWARE

> **SUBJECT VOCABULARY**
>
> **application suite** a collection of application software that share the same look and user interface; often, they can share data between each other and share some functionality
>
> **hyperlink** a link that can be clicked in order to go to another location (often a web page on the internet)

Office productivity software is any application that can carry out work-related tasks. They are often available as an **application suite**.

WORD PROCESSING

Word processing software lets users create documents that mostly include words, but also some images. They can also include tables, **hyperlinks**, equations, simple drawings and shapes and charts. An example of word processing software is Writer from the LibreOffice application suite.

Word processors are a good choice of application for creating:

- letters
- reports
- essays
- books (for example, this book was written using word processing software).

Some word processing applications allow people to work together on a document. Comments can be added to the text so that others can understand the writer's intention and give feedback. The software can also track any changes made to the document, giving others the option to accept or reject those changes.

SUBJECT VOCABULARY

font the size and style of text

Word processing applications allow users to change the **font** and provide different layout views to allow users to position text and images on the page. They usually come with spelling and grammar checking tools that identify errors in the text as the user types.

DESKTOP PUBLISHING (DTP)

DTP software has many similar features to those in word processing software. The main difference is the way in which the software allows users to work with complicated page layouts. An example of DTP software is Adobe® InDesign®[2].

▲ **Figure 2.9** Page layouts in DTP software help the designer to see what the final version will look like when printed

SPREADSHEET

Spreadsheet applications are used to do calculations. Users can use and create formulae and functions to perform automatic calculations on values that can be entered and changed later. These features allow spreadsheets to be used to model financial scenarios and answer 'what if?' questions, such as '**What** would the cost per ticket be **if** I changed the maximum number of staff required at my event?'.

▲ **Figure 2.10** Two scenarios from a financial model

Venue	Gold			1	=VLOOKUP(C11,$L$3:$R$5,5)
Catering package	Gold			1	=VLOOKUP(C12,$L$3:$R$5,3)
Entertainment	Bronze			3	=VLOOKUP(C13,$L$3:$R$5,4)
Decorations	Silver			2	=VLOOKUP(C14,$L$3:$R$5,6)
Transport	Gold			1	=VLOOKUP(C15,$L$3:$R$5,7)
Number of Staff required					=ROUNDUP(D5/10,0)
Ticket price needed					=(G14-J14)/D5
Meets requirements?					=IF(D19>D8,"No","Yes")

▲ **Figure 2.11** Formulae and functions are used for calculations that are carried out automatically when values change

[2] ADOBE AND ADOBE INDESIGN ARE EITHER REGISTERED TRADEMARKS OR TRADEMARKS OF ADOBE SYSTEMS INCORPORATED IN THE UNITED STATES AND/OR OTHER COUNTRIES

An example of spreadsheet software is Microsoft® Excel®.

You will learn more about spreadsheets in *Unit 5 Applying Information and Communication Technology* (page 185) and *Unit 6 Software skills* (page 276).

DATABASE

Database management systems (DBMS) are used to enter, edit and search data. Some systems can also produce reports that dynamically display real-time changes to the data as it updates.

DBMS software features include:

- data entry forms so that users can input data
- query editors so that users can select all data that meets certain criteria
- report builders so that users can display data in a more readable format.

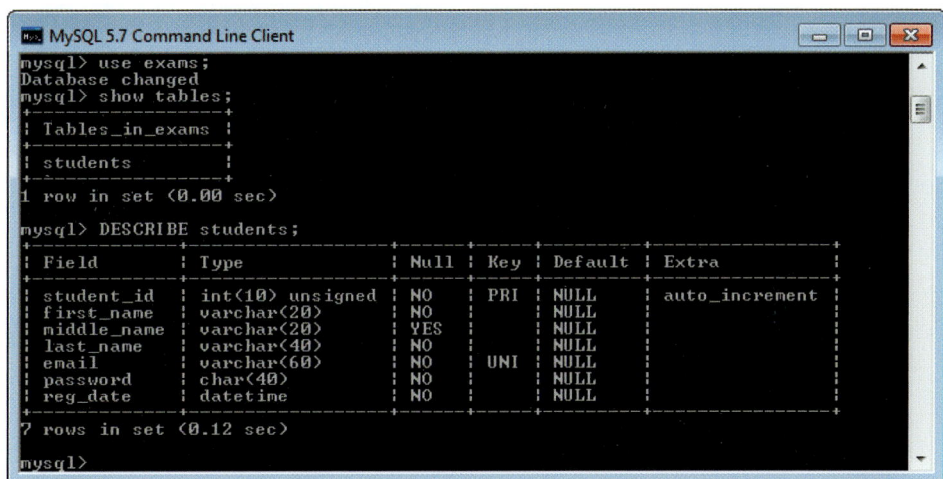

▲ Figure 2.12 This DBMS software uses a command line interface and contains fewer features

▲ Figure 2.13 A report from a database

An example of DBMS software is Oracle® MySQL.

You will learn more about databases in *Unit 6 Software skills* (pages 307–333).

WEB AUTHORING

SUBJECT VOCABULARY

Hypertext Markup Language (HTML) a computing language read by web browser software
intranet a computer network used for exchanging or seeing information within a company
web server a computer that stores web pages and sends them to other devices that request them (often using web browser software)

Web authoring software lets users create web pages that include text and images. The pages are output as **Hypertext Markup Language** (HTML). HTML is read by web browser software such as Google® Chrome™[3], Microsoft® Edge or Mozilla® Firefox®[4]. Web browsers translate HTML into pages that people can see and read. Web pages can be linked together to create a website for people to view on an **intranet** or on a **web server** on the internet.

You will learn more about web browsers on page 55 and in *Unit 2 Connectivity* (page 87).

Although some people prefer to create or customise web pages by writing their own HTML, some applications will allow users to produce complex websites with little or no experience of HTML coding. These applications are sometimes called 'What You See Is What You Get' (WYSIWYG) editors, because the published page will look very similar to the page that the user edits in the web authoring application. An example of web authoring software is Adobe® Dreamweaver®[5].

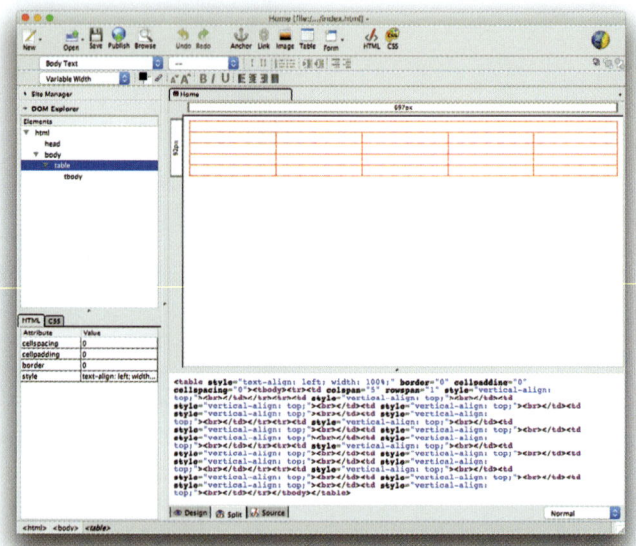

▲ Figure 2.14 Some web authoring software can display the code and design views one after the other

IMAGE EDITING

SUBJECT VOCABULARY

bitmap a computer image that is stored or printed as an arrangement of bits
vector graphic a graphical image made up of points and lines

Image editing applications let users create and change **bitmap** images, such as digital photographs, or **vector graphics**, such as drawings or logos.

GRAPHICS EDITORS

Graphics editing applications allow users to create or edit vector graphics. An example of graphics editing software is Serif® Affinity Designer[6]. Features of graphics editors include:

- vectorising images (that is, converting or tracing bitmap graphics to vector graphics)
- layers (that is, having the ability to place some graphics on top of others)
- adding text
- adding or drawing shapes and lines
- resizing, aligning or moving shapes and lines
- altering the colour of shapes, lines and fill areas.

3 © 2015 GOOGLE INC. ALL RIGHTS RESERVED. GOOGLE® CHROME™ IS A TRADEMARK OF GOOGLE INC
4 MOZILLA FIREFOX IS A TRADEMARK OF THE MOZILLA FOUNDATION
5 ADOBE AND ADOBE INDESIGN ARE EITHER REGISTERED TRADEMARKS OR REGISTERED TRADEMARKS OF ADOBE SYSTEMS INCORPORATED IN THE UNITED STATES AND/OR OTHER COUNTRIES
6 "SERIF" AND "AFFINITY" ARE BOTH REGISTERED TRADEMARKS OF SERIF EUROPE LTD

UNIT 1   SOFTWARE   51

PHOTO EDITORS

These allow users to edit and enhance digital photographs and images. An example of photo editing software is GNU Image Manipulation Program (GIMP). Features of photo editors include:

- adjusting brightness and contrast
- resizing the image
- altering sharpness and blurring
- applying filters and effects such as distortion
- red-eye removal
- **cropping**.

> **SUBJECT VOCABULARY**
>
> **cropping** using a photo editor to remove the edges of an image

> **SKILLS** INTELLECTUAL INTEREST AND CURIOSITY
> ETHICS
> COMMUNICATION
> INTERPERSONAL SKILLS

ACTIVITY

▼ EDITING IMAGES

Go to the website of the cosmetics company, Dove, and search for the key terms 'evolution video' to find the video *Evolution*, which is about the way in which the beauty industry uses image editing applications. Watch the video, then discuss the impact that image editing applications can have on society.

▲ **Figure 2.15** There are many photo editing apps available for smartphones; finished images can be stored to local storage or shared online

SOUND EDITING

Sound editing software allows users to edit audio files or to join together different audio files in order to create multitrack music or soundtracks for video. An example of sound editing software is Audacity®. Features of this software include:

- cut and join audio clips
- **mute** and **solo** some audio tracks
- alter volume levels for individual tracks
- change **tempo**

> **SUBJECT VOCABULARY**
>
> **mute** silence an audio track
> **solo** only play one particular audio track
> **tempo** the speed at which a track is played

GENERAL VOCABULARY

reverberation prolonging a sound

SUBJECT VOCABULARY

normalisation increasing the average volume of a piece of audio to a defined maximum level

- frequency equalisation (changing the levels of high and low pitch frequencies)
- add effects like **reverberation**
- apply audio processing:
  - reverse
  - noise reduction
  - **normalisation**
  - fade the volume in, so that it gets louder, or out, so that it gets quieter.

PRESENTATION SOFTWARE

SUBJECT VOCABULARY

slide a single page of a presentation
pathway the sequence of or route through a series of slides

Presentation software allows users to create engaging multimedia content, including images, text, animation and video. This content can be placed on **slides** or **pathways** that are used to illustrate and support the spoken content of a talk given to an audience. An example of presentation software is Prezi™[7].

Some applications allow users to practise timings and add narration that automatically plays back on the appropriate slides. These slides can be set to advance automatically after a set period of time, or on command from the presenter. Notes can be added to the presentation to remind and prompt the presenter to speak about specific points during the presentation.

CONTROL APPLICATIONS

Control applications are used to make something happen in the physical environment. This type of software is often used to automate the movement of control devices or actuators, such as motors. See page 37 for more information about actuators.

▲ Figure 2.16 Astronauts on the International Space Station use control software to move a robotic arm into position in order to capture a supply capsule

Control software takes input from one or more sensor(s), makes a decision based on the input value and then outputs something, such as a command, as a result.

[7] PREZI IS A TRADEMARK OF PREZI, INC. ALL RIGHTS RESERVED.

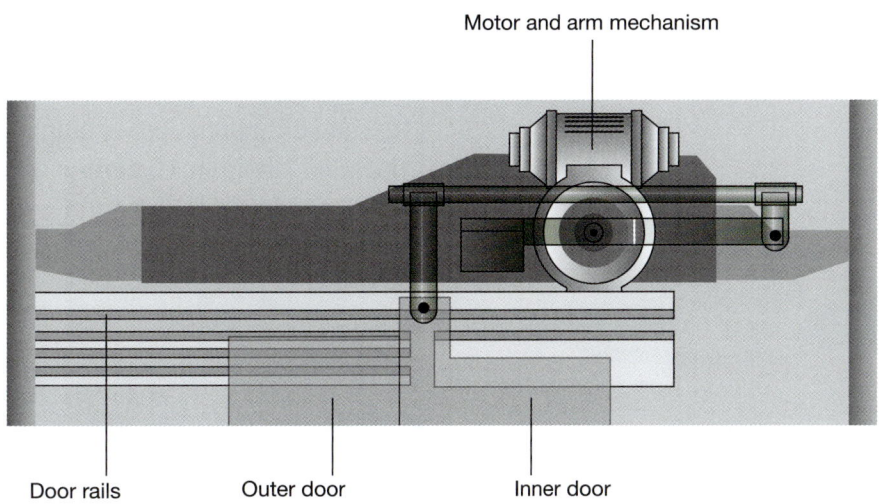

▲ **Figure 2.17** Lift doors are opened and closed automatically by control software when a sensor detects that the lift is level with the floor and has stopped

Control software is often used in engineering, vehicles and building control systems. However, a developing group of control applications is in the area of home automation systems, where devices can be monitored and controlled using a smartphone app.

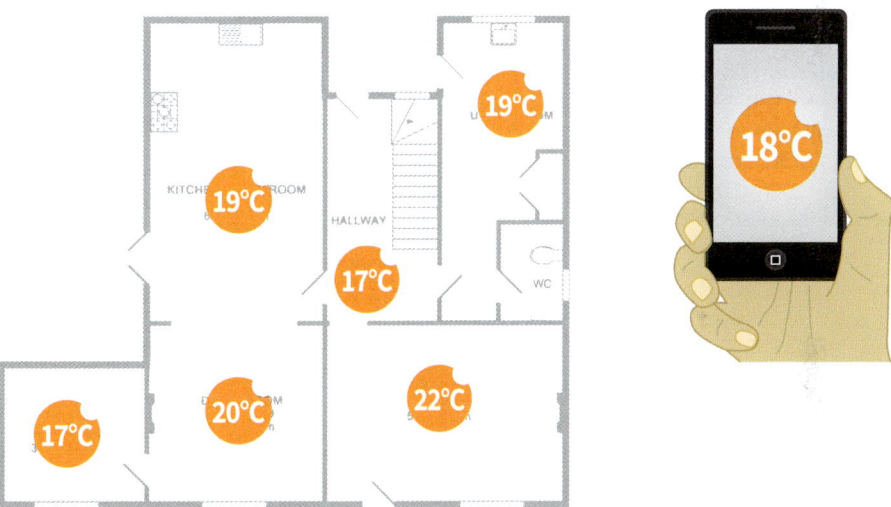

▲ **Figure 2.18** Smartphone apps can be used to control home heating and cooling systems

SKILLS — ADAPTIVE LEARNING
INTELLECTUAL INTEREST AND CURIOSITY
COMMUNICATION

ACTIVITY

▼ REMOTE CONTROL

1 Discuss the objects in your home that you think could be connected to the internet in order to be switched on or controlled remotely.

2 Now discuss potential ways in which you could automatically control these connected things in your home based on changes in the environment that are detected by remote sensors or sensors in a smartphone. See Figure 2.19 and the Did you know? feature for some examples.

> **DID YOU KNOW?**
> Some smartphone apps can control internet-connected devices in certain situations. For example, if the smartphone calculates that its location is within 10 metres of a garage door, it will send an instruction via the internet to the garage door motors to turn on and open the door.

SKILLS — INTELLECTUAL INTEREST AND CURIOSITY / CONTINUOUS LEARNING

ACTIVITY

▼ THE INTERNET OF THINGS

Do some research to find out what is meant by the term, 'the internet of things'.

Control applications are often created by programmers rather than general users and they are not as easy to modify as other application software.

PROJECT MANAGEMENT

GENERAL VOCABULARY

timeline a linear graphical representation of events and the time and order in which they occur

critical path the shortest time a project will take to complete (if no problems or failures are experienced)

milestone a time or date by which a task must be completed

Project management applications are used to help plan and track the individual tasks in a project, so that project managers can make the most efficient use of the available resources. Some tasks cannot be started until a previous task is completed or has been partly completed, so it is important for a project manager to see which tasks are dependent on others. When all of these dependent tasks are combined together into a **timeline**, it is easy for the project manager to see the **critical path**. These applications can also be used to set **milestones**.

Project management applications can be used to allocate tasks to individual people or groups of people. They often provide the option for individuals or groups of people to be allocated to more than one task. Some project management applications also provide tools for tracking the costs and arranging for resources to be delivered on time.

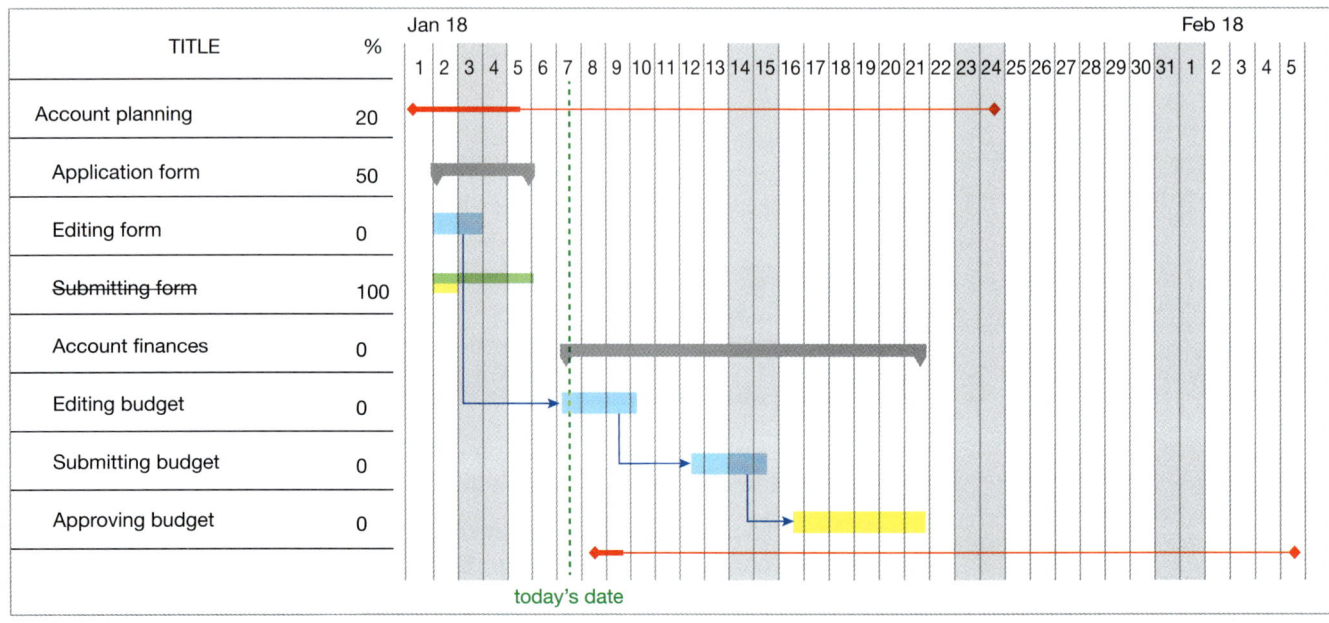

▲ Figure 2.19 Gantt charts are often used to visualise the timelines and milestones for the individual tasks in a project

UNIT 1   SOFTWARE

COMMUNICATION SOFTWARE

Communication software provides remote access to systems and allows users to contact people using the internet. It can be used to send files and messages as text, images, audio and video.

WEB BROWSERS

Web browsers allow users to view web pages and websites created in web authoring software and hosted on servers that are connected to the internet. These servers may be in another country. Different browsers have different features and compatibility with file types used on the World Wide Web.

Browsers also allow users to access other systems that use the internet but are not on the World Wide Web, such as **file transfer protocol** (FTP) servers.

> **SUBJECT VOCABULARY**
>
> **file transfer protocol** (FTP) a method of exchanging data and files across a network

EMAIL

Emails can be sent and received by software installed on a computer. This locally installed software acts as a client to an email server (see page 89 for more information about the client-server model). In addition, it often stores or uses a database of contacts, which is sometimes available as another application.

As well as locally installed applications, users can access email through webmail software, which they reach through a web browser. Webmail is an example of a web application that is hosted on a web server and accessed using an internet connection. Some webmail applications allow users to store emails offline for access when they do not have an internet connection.

Email applications often provide features such as labels to help organise emails and **filters**.

> **SUBJECT VOCABULARY**
>
> **filter** a computer program that only allows certain types of information to pass through it

SOCIAL MEDIA

Social media can be accessed through a web browser or by using locally installed apps.

▲ **Figure 2.20** Social media companies give access to their services through their web pages

Some apps provide access to multiple social media accounts. App developers create apps that people can download and install on their digital devices. TweetDeck is an example of communication software used with social media.

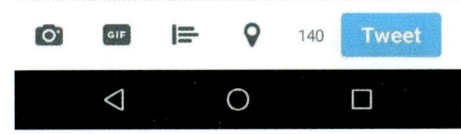

▲ **Figure 2.21** Apps are available for mobile devices as well as PCs

SMS

Short messaging service (SMS) applications are found on mobile phones. They allow users to send up to 160 text characters per message using the mobile phone network. They do not require an internet connection.

MMS

Multimedia messaging service (MMS) applications extend the capabilities of SMS. MMS can deliver more than 160 characters per message and can include video, animations, images and audio. Like SMS, they are sent using the mobile phone network and do not require an internet connection.

INSTANT MESSAGING

Instant messaging applications are very similar to MMS applications, but they require a connection to the internet. They can allow users to see when other users are typing, and users can also prevent others from seeing when they are typing. Messages sent via instant messaging applications can include location data.

SOFTWARE LICENSING

> **SUBJECT VOCABULARY**
>
> **software licence** a legal arrangement that gives a user the right to install and use software

Sometimes, users require a **software licence** to be able to install and use software on a computer.

There are many types of software licence and the details of software licensing are complicated. To make things easier to understand, you can think about the two types of software that are available:

- free or open-source
- proprietary.

> **DID YOU KNOW?**
> Using software without a required licence is called software piracy. Software distributed without the right to do so is called pirate software.

FREE OR OPEN-SOURCE

> **SUBJECT VOCABULARY**
>
> **free software** software that can be modified or distributed by a user
> **open-source software** software for which the source code is made available to users
> **source code** a collection of instructions that forms a piece of software

Free software licences give users the right to study, modify, copy or distribute a program. The user can decide if, and how much, to charge for a copy of the software or any service provided by the software. This means that free software can be made available for a fee or free of charge. 'Free' refers to the user's freedom to charge whatever they want because there are no restrictions on the use of the software.

Open-source software licences make the **source code** available to users so that they can modify how the software works, or distribute the modified or unmodified software.

> **HINT**
> The key difference between the terms 'free' and 'open-source' is that 'free' describes the program and 'open-source' describes the source code.

> **KEY POINT**
> In the case of free software, the term 'free' does not refer to whether or not users have to pay for the software. It refers to the fact that the software is free from usage restrictions.

UNIT 1 — SOFTWARE

PROPRIETARY

SUBJECT VOCABULARY

proprietary software software that is marketed and distributed by its owner under a brand name
freeware proprietary software provided free of charge to users

SKILLS ADAPTIVE LEARNING, DECISION MAKING, INTERPRETATION

Proprietary software is software that is marketed and distributed by its owner under a brand name. The software owner can decide the fee for the software and whether or not the software should be distributed.

Proprietary software can be made available for a fee or free of charge. When no fee is required, the software is called **freeware**. Unlike software distributed under an open-source licence, software with a proprietary licence usually does not make its source code available.

ACTIVITY

▼ **CATEGORISING SOFTWARE**

Think about the examples of software types that you have read about in this chapter. Group these examples into the categories 'free or open-source' and 'proprietary'.

SOFTWARE UPDATES

SUBJECT VOCABULARY

update (noun) a change or addition to a computer file so that it has the most recent information; (verb) to make a change or addition to a computer file so that it has the most recent information
bugs errors in the program's source code
compatibility ability of one device, system or application to work with other devices, systems and applications
usability the ease with which a device or application can be used

GENERAL VOCABULARY

vulnerability weakness or exposure to harm

Updates to software are released by software developers for the following reasons:

- fixing security **vulnerabilities** or **bugs**
- increasing **compatibility** with newer operating systems
- improving performance and efficiency
- introducing new features
- improving **usability**.

Software updates are usually made available for download from a server on the internet. Some updates can be scheduled to happen automatically when they are released.

It is important to back up a system and files before updating software in case the update introduces problems, such as removing components that other software needs in order to function.

CHAPTER QUESTIONS

SKILLS — ADAPTIVE LEARNING

SKILLS — INTERPRETATION

SKILLS — REASONING

SKILLS — REASONING

SKILLS — INTERPRETATION

SKILLS — INTERPRETATION

SKILLS — CRITICAL THINKING, REASONING, COMMUNICATION, PRODUCTIVITY

SKILLS — PROBLEM SOLVING

SKILLS — REASONING

1 State what is meant by the term 'application software'. (1)

2 State **three** types of utility software. (3)

3 Describe the role of the operating system. (2)

4 Explain why utility software allows the user to schedule backup processes. (2)

5 Explain the benefit of using compression utilities to archive files. (2)

6 Describe how presentation software can help a presenter to give a talk. (2)

7 Describe **one** use of control software in a relevant industry. (2)

8 Discuss why a building company might use project management software. (8)

9 State **three** types of service provided by communication software. (3)

10 State **two** reasons for updating software. (2)

3 MEMORY AND PROCESSORS

Memory is used to store instructions. The processor executes those instructions. Both of these parts of the computer system have a big impact on the performance of the system. Specifically, they affect the speed at which software can be loaded and the speed at which software tasks can be completed

LEARNING OBJECTIVES

- Know that RAM stands for Random Access Memory and that ROM stands for Read Only Memory
- Be able to describe the characteristics of RAM and ROM, the differences between them and the impact on the user of the size of ROM/RAM
- Be able to describe the characteristics and uses of flash memory
- Understand the function of the processing unit (CPU)
- Know how the speed of a processor is measured

MEMORY

Memory can be accessed faster than secondary storage. Memory is used to store instructions so that the processor can fetch the instructions quickly in order to process them.

There are three types of memory that you need to know about:

- Random Access Memory (RAM)
- Read Only Memory (ROM)
- Flash memory.

RANDOM ACCESS MEMORY (RAM)

Software is loaded into RAM from a computer's secondary storage. The processor then fetches software instructions from memory and executes them.

HINT

- Two examples of secondary storage are hard disks and SSDs (see page 38).
- Memory is often called main memory or primary storage, and storage is often called secondary storage.

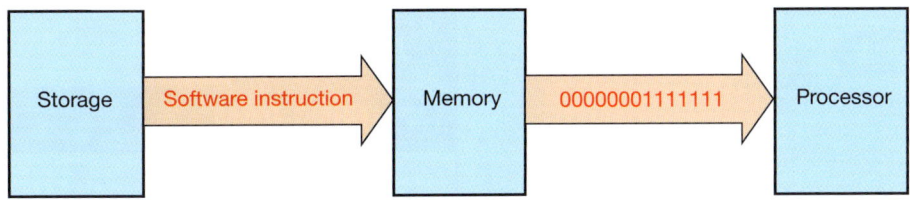

▲ **Figure 3.1** Processors fetch software instructions from memory. The processor then decodes and executes the instructions

RAM is **volatile**, meaning that it cannot store data when it has no power. This means that, if you turn off your computer's power, any data held in RAM will be lost.

IMPACT OF THE SIZE OF RAM ON THE USER

RAM is used to store programs that are in use. The more RAM that is available, the more programs can run at the same time. This is important when you need to use many files or programs at the same time.

When the computer system does not have enough space in RAM, the operating system creates virtual memory by using an area of secondary storage. Secondary storage is much slower than RAM, so the user will notice a big decrease in system performance when the processor has to access instructions from virtual memory. When a solid state drive (SSD) is used as secondary storage, data is swapped to and from the SSD quickly and frequently. Although SSDs have faster access times than hard disk drives, this constant swapping can greatly reduce the performance of the SSD.

When programs or files are closed, they are removed from RAM. As space in RAM becomes available, active programs are moved into RAM from virtual memory, and this will improve the performance of those programs.

A user can add more RAM to a system, but only up to the maximum supported by the computer and operating system. Adding more RAM can improve the performance of a computer system when the user is using multiple files or programs at the same time. It can also be useful to increase the amount of RAM when programs are updated, as the updates often include more complex features that require the use of more memory.

▲ Figure 3.2 A user can increase the amount of RAM using RAM slots on a motherboard

SKILLS INTELLECTUAL INTEREST AND CURIOSITY
REASONING

ACTIVITY

▼ USING RAM

1. Choose two operating systems. Research the maximum amount of RAM that can be installed for each one.
2. Research the cost of 4 GB of RAM today. What would that have cost last year? Investigate the price over the last five years and look at the price trend. What do you notice?

UNIT 1 — MEMORY AND PROCESSORS

READ ONLY MEMORY (ROM)

ROM stores data permanently. Unlike RAM, ROM is **non-volatile**, meaning that data is not lost when the power is turned off. ROM is used in computer systems that store only one programme (single purpose computers), such as calculators, digital watches and washing machines. General purpose computers, such as home PCs and laptops, also use ROM to **boot** the system and load the operating system from secondary storage.

SUBJECT VOCABULARY

boot start up

- ROM is generally used to refer to memory that cannot be changed after manufacture. Its full name is Mask Programmed Read Only Memory.
- PROM stands for **Programmable** Read Only Memory. It is manufactured with the ability to be written to, but it can only be written to **once**.

Although the computer system cannot swap instructions in and out of ROM, it is possible to change the contents of some types of ROM so that the data on it can be updated. These types of ROM are called:

- EPROM (**Erasable Programmable** Read Only Memory)
- EEPROM (**Electrically Erasable Programmable** Read Only Memory).

The contents of EPROM and EEPROM can be erased and then rewritten to. Data stored in EPROM can be erased by exposing it to strong ultraviolet (UV) light. Data stored in EEPROM is erased by applying a voltage to one of the pins on the ROM chip. This means that you do not have to remove the ROM chip to erase the contents of EEPROM.

EEPROM later developed into flash memory (see pages 13 and 62 for more information about flash memory).

SUBJECT VOCABULARY

firmware a type of software that controls a hardware device

The process of erasing and rewriting the contents of EPROM or EEPROM is used when updating the **firmware** for a device (see page 57 for more information about software updates).

SKILLS — INTELLECTUAL INTEREST AND CURIOSITY

ACTIVITY

▼ USING DIFFERENT TYPES OF ROM

- List five digital devices that use PROM that do not need to be edited.
- List five digital devices that use EPROM or EEPROM that can be edited.

DIFFERENCES BETWEEN RAM AND ROM

▼ Table 3.1 Comparing the characteristics of RAM and ROM

	RAM	ROM (all types)
STORES DATA WHEN POWER OFF?	No (volatile)	Yes (non-volatile)
CAN SWAP INSTRUCTIONS IN AND OUT?	Yes	No
ACCESSIBLE IN ANY ORDER?	Yes	Yes
INTENDED TO STORE…	Temporary data	Permanent data
CAN BE UPGRADED?	Yes	No

FLASH MEMORY

Flash memory is a type of EEPROM. Like other types of ROM, it is **non-volatile**. It does not have any moving parts, so it has a fast access time and low power consumption. Because of its low power consumption, flash memory is used in the SSDs that are used in portable devices, such as laptop computers, as these devices often rely on internal batteries for their power. Flash memory is often used as removable storage in USB drives and SD cards.

PROCESSORS

A processor is made up of one or more Central Processing Units (CPUs). These carry out software instructions. In processors that are made up of more than one CPU, each CPU is referred to as a core. For example, in a quad-core processor, four cores are working during each **processor cycle**. This means that it can do up to four times as much work as a single-core processor.

> **SUBJECT VOCABULARY**
>
> **processor cycle** the process of fetching a program instruction from memory, decoding the actions required by the instruction and then executing those actions

> **DID YOU KNOW?**
>
> In multi-core processors, each core can run more slowly than in a single-core processor. This saves energy and produces less heat, which means that the processor requires less cooling. This makes the computer quieter as the fan does not have to cool the system. Reducing the amount of time in which the fan is running also reduces the amount of energy that the system uses, making the system more environmentally friendly and further increasing the battery life of mobile devices.

Processor speed is measured in **clock cycles per second**. This is the number of times per second the processor can carry out one or more instructions. Clock cycles are measured in units called hertz (Hz), kilohertz (kHz), megahertz (MHz) and gigahertz (GHz).

> **SUBJECT VOCABULARY**
>
> **clock cycles per second** used to measure processor speed; the number of times per second the processor can carry out one or more instructions

▼ Table 3.2 Measuring clock cycles

Name	Abbreviation	Clock cycles per second
Hertz	Hz	1
Kilohertz	kHz	1000
Megahertz	MHz	1000,000
Gigahertz	GHz	1000,000,000

Although clock cycles measure processing speed, there are other factors that affect how much work a processor can do in a given time. A user should also consider the amount of work that a CPU can do in each clock cycle. Different processors can carry out more instructions per core in each cycle.

UNIT 1 | MEMORY AND PROCESSORS | 63

SKILLS REASONING
        ADAPTIVE LEARNING

ACTIVITY

▼ WORKING AT DIFFERENT SPEEDS

It can be useful to think of processing speeds in relation to people or machinery working.

1. Two people are each moving a large pile of sand from one place to another by hand.
   - Person A can move 100 portions every hour.
   - Person B can move 10 portions every hour.

   Who will finish first: Person A or Person B?

2. Now imagine that Person A uses a spoon to move each portion and Person B uses a digger to move each portion. Who will finish first now?

3. Now Person C is also trying to move their own pile of sand. They are using a digger at the same rate as Person B, but Person C's digger has four buckets (a 'quad-core digger'!). Who will finish first now?

▲ Figure 3.3 The fastest does not always finish first

HINT

When thinking about the scenario in Question 2, consider that Person A moves more times per hour, but Person B moves more sand each time they move.

CHAPTER QUESTIONS

1. State what is meant by 'ROM'. (1)

2. State what is meant by 'RAM'. (1)

SKILLS REASONING

3. Explain why increasing the amount of RAM in a system improves the user experience. (3)

SKILLS INTERPRETATION

4. Describe what virtual memory is and why it is used. (2)

SKILLS INTERPRETATION

5. List **three** characteristics of RAM that make it different to ROM. (3)

SKILLS REASONING

6. Explain **two** reasons why the characteristics of flash memory make it suitable for use as secondary storage in smartphones. (4)

SKILLS INTERPRETATION

7. Which **one** of these describes the term 'clock cycle'? (1)

   A The number of times per second that a processor can carry out instructions.

   B The number of instructions that a processor can carry out each second.

   C The number of times that a processor can load instructions for processing.

   D The number of times that each process repeats in a processor.

DIGITAL COMMUNICATION 66   **NETWORKS 79**

UNIT 2 CONNECTIVITY

Assessment Objective 1
Demonstrate knowledge and understanding of Information and Communication Technology (ICT)

Assessment Objective 2
Apply knowledge, understanding and skills to produce ICT based solutions

Assessment Objective 3
Analyse, evaluate, make reasoned judgments and present conclusions

In this unit, you will learn about the ways in which digital devices exchange data and communicate with each other and with larger systems supporting online organisations. Understanding which technology to use in a particular context, and knowing how to do so securely, are increasingly important because of people's growing need to connect from everywhere.

4 DIGITAL COMMUNICATION

Our world is connected by wired and wireless digital communication systems. Data flows around these systems, carrying information about our personal and work lives and providing us with entertainment and news. Digital devices exchange data and communicate with each other and with larger systems.

Understanding the way in which devices communicate will help you to understand why things do not work as expected and will enable you to stay connected to the streams of data that drive our world.

By the end of this chapter, you should be able to select the most appropriate digital communication for a particular situation, after considering how each option would affect the quality of a connection.

LEARNING OBJECTIVES

- Know the range of ways that digital devices communicate: satellite, broadcast (TV, radio), wired (cable), wireless
- Know that digital devices can communicate device to device and by using networks: local area network (LAN), wide area network (WAN), personal area network (PAN), tethering
- Know the types of wireless communication: Wi-Fi, Bluetooth, GPS, 3G, 4G, infra-red (IR), near-field communication (NFC)
- Know the differences between Wi-Fi and Bluetooth and when each is best used
- Understand factors influencing the speed and volume of data transfer
- Understand the benefits and drawbacks of wired versus wireless communication in local networks
- Understand the significance of bandwidth and latency, and their impact on the 'user experience'
- Understand the features of broadband, mobile broadband and cellular networks

SPEED AND VOLUME OF DATA TRANSFER

As we transfer more and more data, it becomes more important that we understand how to increase the **speed** at which we can transfer it. If we do not, transferring more data will mean that transfer times will increase.

BANDWIDTH

SUBJECT VOCABULARY

bandwidth the number of bits that can be carried by a connection in one second

The speed at which devices can transfer data depends on the **bandwidth** of the connection.

You can think about a data connection as being like a water pipe. In the same way that a large water pipe can carry a large amount of water, a connection with a large bandwidth can carry a large amount of data.

IMPACT ON USER EXPERIENCE

A higher bandwidth means that more data can be transferred every second. This makes uploads and downloads faster. It also makes it possible to do things that require lots of data to be transferred in short amounts of time, such as multiplayer online gaming or high-definition video streaming.

UNIT 2 — DIGITAL COMMUNICATION

▲ Figure 4.1 Binary data is stored within and transferred between digital devices

SUBJECT VOCABULARY

buffer an area of memory used to temporarily store data, especially when streaming video

When streaming video, all of the data does not need to be downloaded before playback can start. Instead, a portion of the video data is stored temporarily in an area of memory called a **buffer**. The video will not start until there is enough data in the buffer to play a few seconds of video. While those few seconds are playing, more data is downloaded to fill up the buffer. If the buffer is empty, there is no more video to play and it will pause until more data is downloaded. To avoid the buffer becoming empty, data must be constantly downloaded into the buffer, filling it up at a rate faster than it is emptied.

Imagine a glass of water being repeatedly filled up from a big bottle. The bottle is like the full video data file and the glass is like the buffer that holds the data ready to be used.

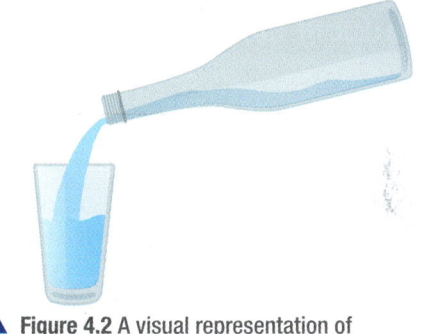

▲ Figure 4.2 A visual representation of streaming

LATENCY

SUBJECT VOCABULARY

latency the amount of time it takes to send data between devices
domain the name used to identify a web server

As well as bandwidth, the speed of data transfer also depends on **latency**. Latency is the delay in the time it takes to send data between devices. If you think again about a data connection acting like a water pipe, latency is the average time that it takes for a drop of water to flow through the pipe.

You can identify latency by 'pinging' a **domain**. When you ping a domain, you send a packet of data to a server and the packet of data is immediately returned by the server to the originating device. The 'ping time' is the amount of time it takes for the packet of data to make the return trip.

SKILLS — INTELLECTUAL INTEREST AND CURIOSITY
EXECUTIVE FUNCTION
REASONING
PROBLEM SOLVING

ACTIVITY

▼ PINGING DOMAINS

Using a command line interface (Terminal in MacOS and Linux or Command Prompt in Windows), type 'ping [domain]' to ping the following domains:

- gov.au (by typing 'ping gov.au')
- newsfirst.lk
- gov.uk

Note the ping time for each domain. Why are they different?

SKILLS > INTELLECTUAL INTEREST AND CURIOSITY

ACTIVITY

▼ SPEED TESTING

Carry out a speed test on the internet connections of a fixed line broadband device, such as a laptop or PC, and a mobile broadband device, such as a smartphone.

IMPACT ON USER EXPERIENCE

In online gaming, the game will play smoothly if the bandwidth is adequate. However, if the latency is high, events in the game will **lag** and the game will not seem responsive to the player's commands. When watching live television, high latency will result in a delay between the real-time events and the video being received for playback.

GENERAL VOCABULARY
lag move slowly or fail to keep up

FACTORS THAT AFFECT SPEED AND VOLUME OF DATA TRANSFER

When devices transfer data, they can be affected by many factors that stop bits from reaching their destination. These bits then have to be sent again, which slows the overall data transfer rate.

TRANSFER METHOD

Wireless methods have to work on a limited number of **frequencies**. In comparison, copper cable can carry more frequencies than wireless methods. This means that cabled methods can have more bandwidth available to them than wireless methods.

SUBJECT VOCABULARY
frequency the waveband at which a radio signal is transmitted

HINT
Some older wired methods have less bandwidth than newer wireless methods.

INTERFERENCE

Other electromagnetic signals disrupt or interfere with wired and wireless signals. For example, interference can be caused by signals from wireless devices, wireless routers and appliances emitting electromagnetic fields like fridges and microwave ovens. Cabled connections can be **shielded** from this interference by having the wires wrapped in a thin layer of metal.

GENERAL VOCABULARY
shielded protected

BLOCKAGES

Walls and furniture reduce the strength of wireless signals. This reduces the available bandwidth.

DISTANCE

The strength of a wired or wireless signal is reduced as the distance that it has to travel increases.

DEVICE-TO-DEVICE COMMUNICATION

Devices can connect directly to each other using wired or wireless methods. This is called device-to-device communication. Table 4.1 shows some examples of device-to-device communication.

SUBJECT VOCABULARY

minijack a plug and socket widely used for analogue audio signals in portable devices

HDMI (High-Definition Multimedia Interface) used to transmit video and audio data

▲ Figure 4.3 Device-to-device communication

▼ Table 4.1 Examples of device-to-device communication

DEVICE 1	DEVICE 2	CONNECTION BETWEEN DEVICES 1 AND 2	USE
Temperature sensor	Air conditioner	Wired	To turn on the air conditioning when the temperature is too high
Smartphone	Headphones	**Minijack**	To play music from the smartphone on the headphones
Laptop	External hard drive	USB	To transfer files
Camcorder	Monitor	**HDMI**	To operate as a security camera
Games controller	Games console	Bluetooth	To control a game

NETWORK COMMUNICATION

When two or more computers are connected, a network is created. There are four major types of network.

LOCAL AREA NETWORK (LAN)

A LAN is a network that connects digital devices that are in a small geographical area, like a building or group of buildings that are close to each other.

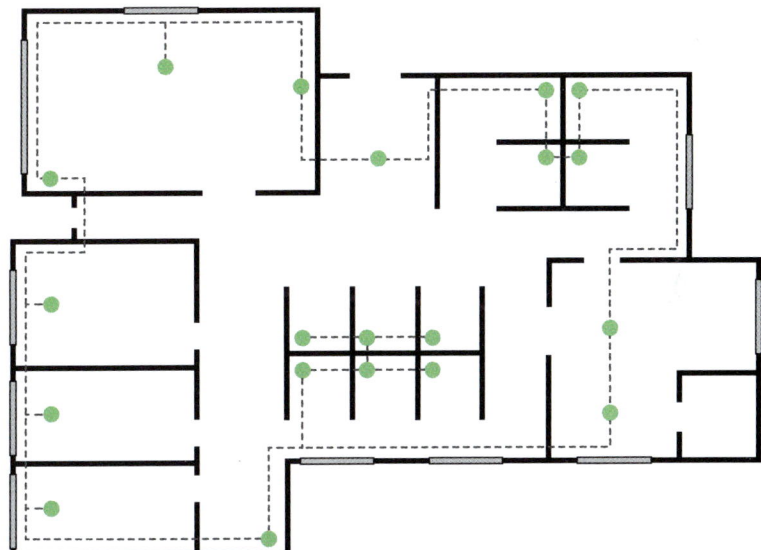

▲ Figure 4.4 LANs are found in homes, schools and office buildings

WIDE AREA NETWORK (WAN)

A WAN is a network that is spread over a large geographical area. WANs are often used to connect different buildings owned by national and international businesses, law enforcement agencies, health and education organisations and government departments. Some organisations launch their own satellites to provide connectivity for their own global WANs.

WANs often use connectivity provided by a third-party telecommunications company, often linking LANs together through the internet. Because of their wider reach, WANs often have slower transfer speeds than LANs.

> **DID YOU KNOW?**
> The internet is the largest example of a WAN.

▲ Figure 4.5 The internet is the largest example of a WAN

PERSONAL AREA NETWORK (PAN)

A PAN is a group of connected devices that are all near an individual user. For example, a user could connect their smartwatch to their smartphone, which is connected to their laptop and home cinema speaker system. Devices in a PAN can either be connected to each other directly or connected through access points (see page 84 for more information about access points).

When a PAN only uses wireless connectivity, it can also be referred to as a WPAN (**W**ireless **P**ersonal **A**rea **N**etwork). However, the general term PAN is more commonly used to refer to all types of PAN.

TETHERING

SUBJECT VOCABULARY

tethering connecting a host device that uses a mobile broadband connection with other devices so that they can use the host's broadband connection

Tethering is the process of connecting a host device, such as a smartphone or a tablet device, that uses a mobile broadband connection with one or more other devices. This enables the other device or devices to share the host device's broadband connection.

▲ Figure 4.6 Devices can be tethered using wired or wireless connectivity

SUBJECT VOCABULARY

service agreement contract

Mobile phone network providers can enable or disable tethering as part of the **service agreement**. Some network providers charge more for this feature to be enabled.

THE WAYS IN WHICH DIGITAL DEVICES COMMUNICATE

The methods that digital devices use to share data and some common uses of these methods are shown in Table 4.2.

▼ Table 4.2 Ways in which digital devices communicate and their common uses

Method	Technology	Use
Satellite	Radio waves	GPS, television, telephone, military
Broadcast	Radio waves	Television shows, radio shows
Wired	Electrical signal	Networking, connecting peripherals
Wireless	Radio waves	Networking, connecting peripherals

SATELLITE COMMUNICATION

▲ Figure 4.7 A communication satellite

Satellites transmit data to and receive data from digital devices. Digital devices use antennae to receive the radio signals that satellites transmit.

The benefit of satellite communication is that the number of satellites means that the system is always available. It also cannot be affected by power shortages. The drawback is that satellite signals do not pass through solid objects. This means that they will not work in areas with tall buildings or in tunnels. Signals can also be affected by atmospheric weather conditions such as heavy snow or rain.

GPS

Satellite communications are used for GPS. Navigation aids make use of GPS signals to calculate the exact location of a device. GPS signals are sent from a network of 24 satellites orbiting the Earth. At any one time, a device will be within view of approximately 12 of these satellites. However, a view of only four satellites is required to calculate an accurate location, as illustrated in Figure 4.8.

For more information about navigation aids, see *Unit 1 Digital devices* (page 14)

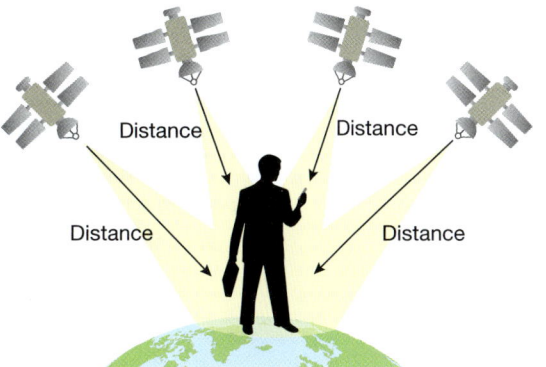

▲ Figure 4.8 Only four satellites need to be in view to get an accurate location of a device using a GPS signal

TELEVISION

Digital Video Broadcasting (DVB) is the internationally accepted standard method of broadcasting digital television. DVB-S (Digital Video Broadcasting – Satellite) is one example of DVB. A video signal from the broadcaster is transmitted using a large antenna on Earth to one or more satellites, which then broadcast the signal back down to Earth. A satellite television viewer will have an antenna installed, and this receives the signal and sends it to a set-top box. The set-top box decodes the signal and converts it so that it is ready to be sent to a television. Some televisions have decoders installed, so the antenna can be connected directly to the television rather than requiring a set-top box to decode the signal first.

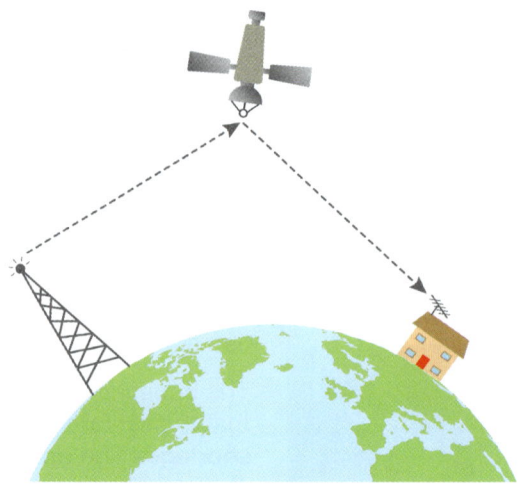

▲ Figure 4.9 DVB-S (Digital Video Broadcasting – Satellite)

DVB-S2 and DVB-S2X are newer digital broadcasting standards. They provide more functionality, such as High Definition Television (HDTV), interactive services and internet access.

TELEPHONE

Satellite communication is also used to allow people in remote areas to place voice calls using satellite telephones.

▲ Figure 4.10 A receiving antenna with a set-top box

▲ Figure 4.11 Satellite telephones use antennae to transmit data to (and receive data from) one or more satellites

▲ Figure 4.12 Satellite phones are used in remote areas

MILITARY

The military in many countries use satellites for communication systems, such as the Global Command and Control System.

▲ Figure 4.13 The Global Command and Control System provides military communication

BROADCAST COMMUNICATION

ANALOGUE TELEVISION AND RADIO

Transmitters broadcast television and radio signals that are received by a viewer's antenna. This antenna sends a signal through a wire to the television or radio receiver, which converts it into images and audio.

> **DID YOU KNOW?**
> In some countries, analogue signals have been switched off and only digital signals are now broadcast. In January 2017, Norway became the first country to begin switching off the transmissions from its national FM radio stations.

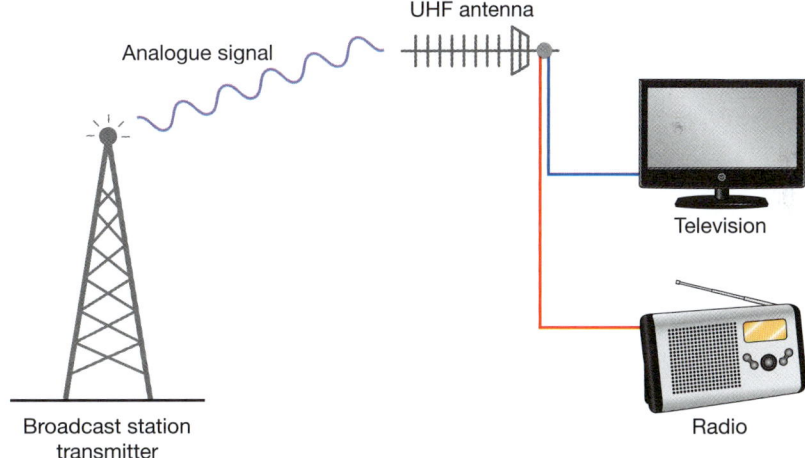

▲ Figure 4.14 An analogue signal is received by an antenna and fed to different devices

DIGITAL TELEVISION

DVB-T (Digital Video Broadcasting – **Terrestrial**) is a method of DVB where the transmitters are based on Earth, rather than in orbit as they are in DVB-S. To receive digital television broadcasts transmitted by DVB-T, viewers can use the same antenna that they use to receive analogue broadcasts. They do not need a special antenna.

DVB-T2 is a newer standard that provides more functionality, such as High Definition Television (HDTV) and interactive services.

> **GENERAL VOCABULARY**
> **terrestrial** on the Earth

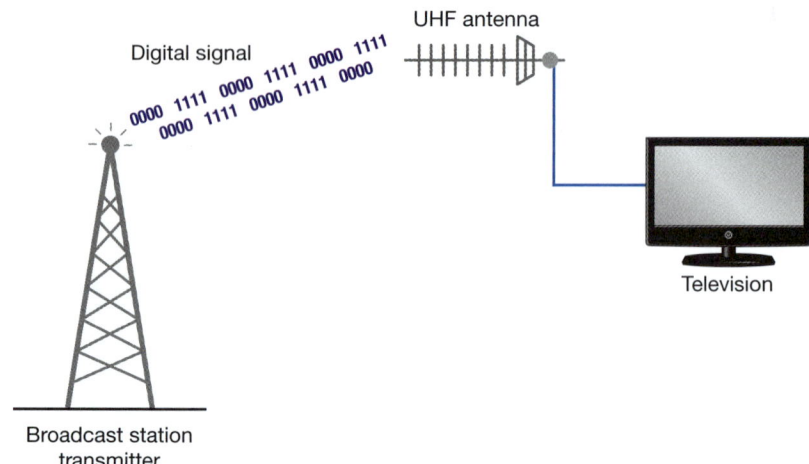

▲ **Figure 4.15** Some televisions have decoders installed, so the antenna can be connected directly to the television rather than requiring a set-top box to decode the signal first

DIGITAL RADIO

DAB (Digital Audio Broadcasting) is used in Europe and the Asia Pacific region. It is broadcast in the same way as DVB. DAB provides more radio stations and can also carry text data that DAB receivers can display. The text data can include the time, name of the station and details of the music being played.

WIRED COMMUNICATION

SUBJECT VOCABULARY

Ethernet a network connectivity standard that provides a way for computers to communicate

Devices can use cables to communicate with each other via a wired connection. There are many different types of wired connection. Some are used for many different purposes, such as USB. Others are only used to meet one particular need, such as **Ethernet**.

Some of the uses for different wired connection types are given in Table 4.3.

▼ Table 4.3 Common wired connection types and their uses

CONNECTION TYPE	USE
HDMI	Digital video connections
S/PDIF	Digital audio connections
Minijack	Personal headphones
USB	Storage transfer
Ethernet	Networking

USB is a very common connection type. USB has been through a number of revisions, and each revision allows faster data transfer speeds. This development of standards is common with all types of connectivity. This progress is made necessary as digital devices become more complex in their features and functionality.

Ethernet allows a user to connect to wired networks. As Ethernet technology develops, the speed at which data can be transferred between devices is improved. Ethernet cables can be 100 metres long before the signals they carry start to lose quality.

▲ **Figure 4.16** An Ethernet connection

UNIT 2 — DIGITAL COMMUNICATION

WIRELESS COMMUNICATION

HINT
The terms 'Wi-Fi' and 'internet access' are often used incorrectly to mean the same thing. Wi-Fi allows you to wirelessly connect to a network. That network may or may not be connected to the internet. For more information about networks, see pages 79–93.

Devices can also use wireless connectivity to communicate with each other. Just as with wired communication, there are many different types of wireless connection.

> **DID YOU KNOW?**
> A laser transmitter in New Mexico, USA is used to beam a wireless signal 384,400 km to a satellite orbiting the moon. It can carry 19.44 megabits of data per second, which is more than enough to stream live television.

WI-FI
Wi-Fi is used in home and office networks. Some companies provide Wi-Fi access in towns and cities. Wi-Fi is a wireless technology used to connect devices to a network. That network can itself then be connected to the internet, so that devices connected to the Wi-Fi network can connect to the internet.

Wi-Fi uses the IEEE 802.11 specification of standards for wireless communication. The specification is revised regularly to take account of improvements in technology. Each revision to the specification is given a different letter or pair of letters at the end. The first version was IEEE 802.11**a**. Each revision of the technology improves the speed at which data can be transferred and increases the distance over which devices can connect.

SKILLS — SELF-DIRECTION

ACTIVITY
▼ **DIFFERENT REVISIONS OF WI-FI**

Do some research to compare the different revisions of Wi-Fi. How do their speeds and range differ?

BLUETOOTH
Bluetooth is a type of wireless connectivity that lets devices connect over short distances. It cannot carry as much data as Wi-Fi. Bluetooth devices need to be **paired** with each other before they can communicate.

Bluetooth can be used to transfer small files between devices. It is used to connect devices such as smartphones and laptops to peripherals such as portable speakers, headphones, earphones, keyboards and mice.

SUBJECT VOCABULARY
pair connect two devices (usually only with each other)

▼ Table 4.4 Comparing Wi-Fi and Bluetooth

	WI-FI	BLUETOOTH
Range	Long ✓	Short ✗
Bandwidth	High ✓	Low ✗
Power	High ✗	Low ✓
Security	High ✓	Low ✗
Can connect multiple devices simultaneously	Yes ✓	Limited ✗ (usually have to be paired)

> **DID YOU KNOW?**
> Wi-Fi Direct is an alternative to Bluetooth. It is a low-power version of Wi-Fi that can connect two devices directly over a short range.

3G AND 4G

3G and 4G are sometimes referred to as mobile broadband. They are used to provide internet access to mobile devices such as smartphones and tablet devices when a Wi-Fi signal is not available. The G stands for 'generation', meaning that 4G is the fourth generation of mobile broadband technology. Future generations of the technology are planned to improve the speed and availability of the signal.

SKILLS SELF-DIRECTION
INTELLECTUAL INTEREST AND CURIOSITY

ACTIVITY

▼ **3G AND 4G**

1. Compare the speeds, costs and availability of 3G and 4G in your location.
2. Research the next generation of this technology.

HINT

3G or 4G is **not** the same as Wi-Fi. 3G and 4G connectivity is provided by mobile phone companies. Some people say they 'have Wi-Fi' when they mean that they have a mobile broadband connection.

INFRA-RED (IR)

Infra-red signals cannot carry much data and only have a short range. Transmitters must have a clear line of sight to receivers, because this allows the signal to travel in a straight line between them without being blocked by solid objects like walls. The signal is also affected by sunlight. It is often used in remote-control devices such as television remote controls.

SUBJECT VOCABULARY

infra-red a type of electromagnetic radiation with a longer frequency than that of visible light

NEAR-FIELD COMMUNICATION (NFC)

NFC uses close proximity RFID (Radio Frequency Identification) chips. NFC is used in smartphones, payment cards and travel cards.

For more information about NFC and RFID chips, see *Unit 1 Digital devices* (page 30).

SKILLS SELF-DIRECTION

ACTIVITY

▼ **COMPARING WIRELESS CONNECTIONS**

Complete Table 4.5 by identifying the technology used by each type of wireless connection and some common uses for that type of connection.

▼ Table 4.5 Wireless connections: technology and uses

METHOD	TECHNOLOGY	USE
Wi-Fi	Radio waves	Home and office networks
Bluetooth		
3G and 4G		
Infra-red		
NFC		

▲ **Figure 4.17** Infra-red is commonly used by remote controls to transmit signals

BENEFITS AND DRAWBACKS OF WIRED vs WIRELESS

The World Health Organization (WHO) says that current research findings suggest that exposure to wireless signals does not cause health issues. However, it also says that further long-term research about the effects on children using mobile phones for more than 10 years is necessary. This is because symptoms may take a long time to appear and young people are most vulnerable to radiation.

> **DID YOU KNOW?**
> The wavelength of Wi-Fi (12 cm) is at least 300,000 times longer than the wavelength of light (400–700 nanometres). The WHO generally considers anything above the wavelength of light to be harmless to humans.

KEY POINT

The International Agency for Research on Cancer is part of the WHO. It classifies Wi-Fi as a possible human **carcinogen**. However, many things are possibly carcinogenic. For example, Wi-Fi shares this classification with coffee, carpentry, foam cups and pickled vegetables.

GENERAL VOCABULARY

carcinogen a substance that can cause cancer

▼ Table 4.6 Comparing wired and wireless connectivity

	WIRED	WIRELESS
COST	Cables are cheap if purchasing for a small number of devices	• No need to buy cables • May need a wireless access point for multiple connections
SAFETY	Risk of tripping over cables	None (though some people are worried about the effects of radiation)
SPEED	Faster than wireless	Slower than wired
STABILITY	Less affected by interference than wireless	Affected by interference and obstacles
PORTABILITY	• Not portable as limited by connecting cables • May need signal booster if connection is more than 100 metres long	Portable within signal range
MESS	Can look untidy if lots of cables are used	Tidy
SECURITY	Most secure	Less secure than wired connection because it is easier to intercept a wireless signal
MAINTENANCE	Using cables and ports continuously over a long period of time may damage them	None

HINT

Cellular network is another name for a mobile phone network.

SUBJECT VOCABULARY

Internet Service Provider (ISP) a company that provides customers with access to the internet

fibre optic cable a cable that sends data using light signals

copper cable a cable that sends data using electrical signals, which are conducted through copper wires

BROADBAND, MOBILE BROADBAND AND CELLULAR NETWORKS

Broadband networks provide fast access to the internet through a connection to an **Internet Service Provider** (ISP). They use the **fibre optic cable** or **copper cable** network. You will learn more about fibre optic cables on page 84.

Mobile broadband provides high-speed wireless connectivity using 3G or 4G technology to connect to the mobile phone network, which acts as the user's ISP.

CHAPTER QUESTIONS

SKILLS REASONING

1 a Explain **one** reason why some games console controllers use Bluetooth rather than infra-red to connect to the console. **(1)**

   b State **one** way in which using infra-red in games console controllers could affect the experience of the person playing the game. **(1)**

SKILLS INTERPRETATION

2 Describe how video streaming works. **(3)**

SKILLS REASONING

3 Explain why streaming is more convenient for the user than downloading. **(3)**

SKILLS PROBLEM SOLVING

4 State **three** types of wired connection. **(3)**

SKILLS INTERPRETATION

5 Which **one** of these best describes the internet? **(1)**

   A LAN
   B WAN
   C PAN
   D VLAN

SKILLS REASONING

6 Explain why global games companies use games servers in multiple countries to ensure that the experience of users is not negatively affected when playing online games. **(3)**

5 NETWORKS

A network is created when two or more computers are connected together. Using a network, a computer can communicate with others and share resources such as hardware, software and data. It does this by sending data in a packet, which is a unit of data packaged together so that it can travel across a network.

The first network was created in 1960 by a commercial airline when it connected two mainframe computers together in order to speed up its reservation system. In 1962, researchers at the Advanced Research Projects Agency (ARPA) developed a project called the 'Intergalactic Computer Network'. In 1969, computers at four universities in the USA were connected, which created the ARPANET. This is considered to have been the predecessor of the internet.

LEARNING OBJECTIVES

- Know about network operating systems and how devices are identified on a network: device name, internet protocol (IP) and machine address code (MAC)
- Understand the function of components of wired and wireless systems: cable, wireless access point, router, gateway, booster, server
- Know the role of these for connecting to and using the internet:
  - web browser
  - ISP
  - search engine
  - filter software
- Know about peer-to-peer and client-server networks
- Know about the role of servers in a client-server network
- Understand the benefits of using local area network:
  - shared peripherals
  - shared data
  - flexible access
  - media streaming
  - communication
  - shared access to the internet
- Understand the benefits of using a client-server network:
  - control of user access rights
  - centralised administration
  - centralised backup
  - shared software
  - shared storage and file access
  - roaming profiles (hotdesk)
- Know about and understand the use of logins and passwords, firewalls, WEP/WPA, encryption, VPN, file access rights, transaction logs and backups
- Be able to select suitable methods of securing data for a particular context

SUBJECT VOCABULARY

protocols rules that allow the exchange and transmission of data between devices

REQUIREMENTS FOR CONNECTING TO NETWORKS

In order to connect to a network, computers need to fulfil certain requirements so that they all operate using standard **protocols**.

NETWORK OPERATING SYSTEMS

GENERAL VOCABULARY

stand-alone capable of functioning on its own, such as a stand-alone computer working on its own without being part of a network

A network operating system allows a computer to communicate on a network. It provides additional functionality to a **stand-alone** operating system, including:

- passing usernames and passwords to a server for checking when a user logs in
- separating user accounts and ensuring that users cannot access each other's files
- providing access to network storage and shared resources such as networked printers.

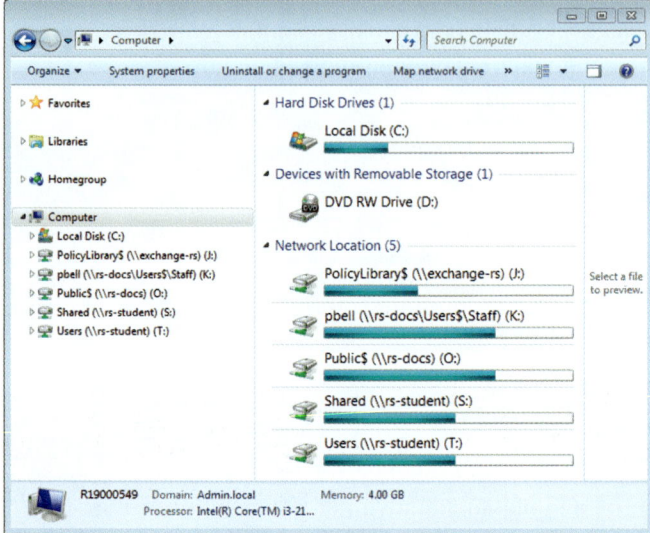

▲ **Figure 5.1** Network operating systems provide access to shared storage that is available on the network

SKILLS CRITICAL THINKING
EXECUTIVE FUNCTION

ACTIVITY

▼ **COMPARING OPERATING SYSTEMS**

Create a table to compare the features of a network operating system to a stand-alone operating system.

HOW DEVICES ARE IDENTIFIED ON A NETWORK

There are three methods used to identify devices on a network:

- Internet Protocol (IP)
- MAC address
- device name.

SUBJECT VOCABULARY

IP address a unique address that networked devices use to send data to each other

INTERNET PROTOCOL (IP)

An **IP address** is a unique address that networked devices use to send data to each other. Each piece of data that is sent across a network carries the IP address of the destination, so that each device in the network knows where to send it.

SUBJECT VOCABULARY

hexadecimal a base-16 number system that uses the numbers 0–9 and the letters A–F

network administrator a person who manages an organisation's network

DID YOU KNOW?

IPv4 can store over 4 billion addresses. It was developed because of the huge growth in the number of devices that were being connected.

GENERAL VOCABULARY

dynamically in a way that is open to change

Dynamic Host Configuration Protocol (DHCP) server a networked computer that automatically assigns an IP address to other computers when they join the network

SKILLS INTELLECTUAL INTEREST AND CURIOSITY
CRITICAL THINKING
REASONING
COMMUNICATION
INTERPERSONAL SKILLS

IP addresses are made up groups of numbers. There are two main versions of IP in use.

- **IPv4** uses four groups of up to three numbers separated by full stops (for example, 192.168.1.1).
- **IPv6** uses eight groups of four **hexadecimal** numbers separated by colons (for example, 2001:0db8:0000:0042:0000:8a2e:0370:7334).

IP addresses can either be assigned by a **network administrator** or allocated **dynamically** by a server running **Dynamic Host Configuration Protocol** (DHCP).

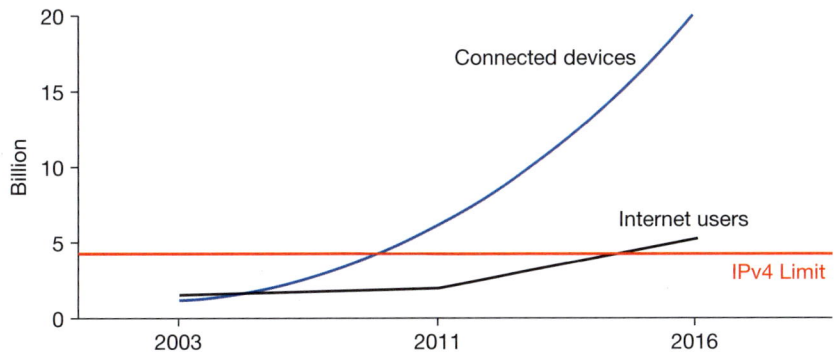

▲ Figure 5.2 IPv4 can hold 4,294,967,296 possible addresses

ACTIVITY

▼ IP ADDRESSES

1 Research the maximum number of addresses that can be provided by IPv6.
2 Discuss why the number of connected devices is growing at a faster rate than the number of internet users.

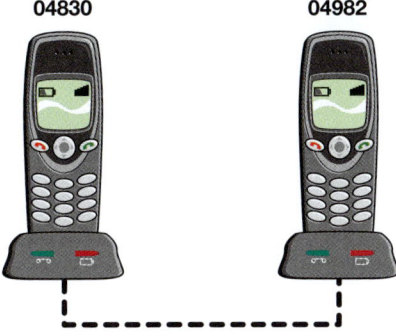

▲ Figure 5.3 When you make a telephone call, you dial a number that identifies the destination telephone

Asgiriya International Cricket Stadium, Kandy 20000, Sri Lanka

IP address (220.247.227.202).

▲ Figure 5.4 When you post a letter, you write the address on the letter so that every part of the postal system knows where to send it

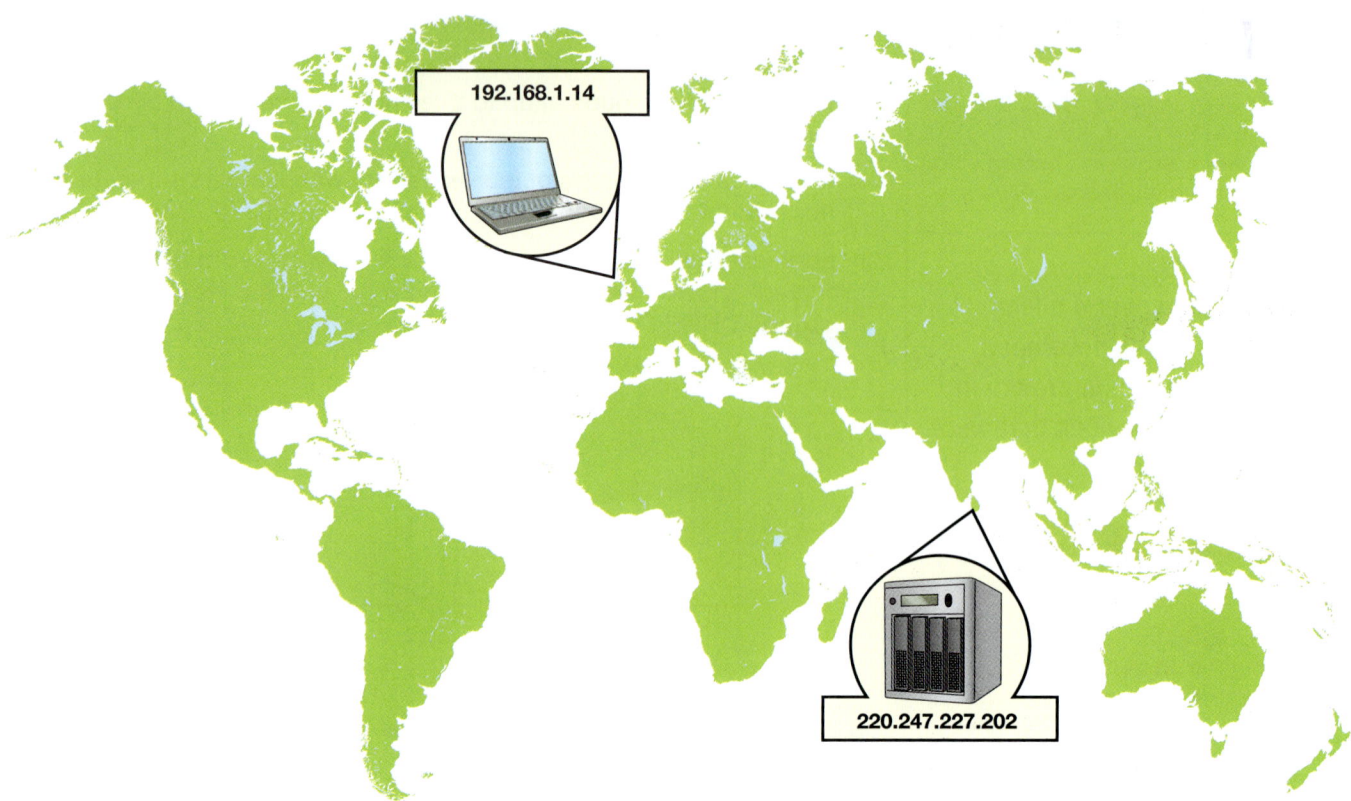

▲ Figure 5.5 When sending data, devices include the destination address of the data, just like in the telephone or postal system

GENERAL VOCABULARY

universally unique the only one of its kind in the world

SUBJECT VOCABULARY

identifier a group of letters, numbers, or symbols that a computer has been programmed to recognise and uses to process information

MAC ADDRESS

Unlike IP addresses, which can be dynamically allocated by users or servers, media access control (MAC) addresses are **universally unique identifiers** given to the network interface card (NIC). MAC addresses are used in devices connected to local area networks (LANs) using Ethernet, Bluetooth or Wi-Fi.

MAC addresses are assigned by the NIC manufacturer and are generally considered to be fixed addresses.

A MAC address is usually made up of six pairs of characters. The first three pairs identify the manufacturer and the remaining pairs are assigned by the manufacturer to uniquely identify the device. Figure 5.6 is an example of a MAC address.

▲ Figure 5.6 A MAC address

SKILLS SELF-DIRECTION
PROBLEM SOLVING

ACTIVITY

▼ USING MAC ADDRESSES

Using the internet and other resources, find out which manufacturer made the device with the MAC address in Figure 5.6.

UNIT 2   NETWORKS

SUBJECT VOCABULARY

hotspot a place in a public building where there is a computer system with an access point, which allows people in the building with a wireless computer or Bluetooth mobile phone to connect to a service such as the internet

▼ Table 5.1 Uses of MAC addresses

USE	EXAMPLE
Restricting or allowing access to a network	MAC address filtering checks the MAC address of devices attempting to gain access to a network and only grants access to devices with specified MAC addresses
Identifying a device on a network	Some Wi-Fi hotspots only provide free access for a certain length of time, and they identify a device using its MAC address in order to work out whether it is trying to access the hotspot for longer than the permitted time
Tracking a device	Some companies and organisations track devices (and therefore their users) by checking which wireless access points have been accessed by specific MAC address
Assigning 'static' or 'fixed' IP addresses	Each time a device connects to a network, it is identified by a DHCP server (usually using its MAC) and given the same IP address as before

SKILLS   INTELLECTUAL INTEREST AND CURIOSITY
CRITICAL THINKING
REASONING
COMMUNICATION
INTERPERSONAL SKILLS
PERSONAL AND SOCIAL RESPONSIBILITY

ACTIVITY

▼ SPOOFING

MAC addresses can be changed through a process called spoofing, which means using the MAC address of another device. Discuss how spoofing would affect each of the uses listed in Table 5.1.

DEVICE NAME

A device name is a descriptive name that helps users to identify computers on a network. Device names are not used by computers to communicate with each other as they are not always unique. This means that they could cause conflicts if data was sent to more than one device with the same name for processing.

You can change a device name using tools in the device's operating system.

SKILLS   ADAPTABILITY

ACTIVITY

▼ IDENTIFYING DEVICES ON YOUR NETWORK

Identify the name, an IP address and the MAC address of a device on a network that you use.

COMPONENTS OF WIRED AND WIRELESS SYSTEMS

Wired and wireless systems can be made up of a variety of components.

CABLE

SUBJECT VOCABULARY

Mbit/s the amount of data that can be transferred per second, measured in Megabits (1 Mb = 1 million bits)

Gbit/s the amount of data that can be transferred per second, measured in Gigabits (1 Gb = 1,000,000,000 bits)

Cables are used to connect devices in a wired network. In homes and small businesses, Cat5e cables are used for Ethernet connections. These cables are able to transfer data at 10 **Mbit/s**, 100 Mbit/s or 1 **Gbit/s**. Cat5e cable connects devices through their NICs. The device's NIC allows the computer to exchange data with other networked computers and contains LEDs that signal network activity.

Cat6 cables can be used to transfer data at 10 Gbit/s. These are more expensive than Cat5e cables and are usually only used by businesses.

▲ **Figure 5.7** Cat5e cable is used to connect devices through their NICs

DID YOU KNOW?
400 Gbit/s Ethernet is expected to be available by late 2017.

DID YOU KNOW?
The speed of a network is limited by its slowest part. For example, if a network uses 10 Gbit/s cables and its internet connection speed is 100Mbit/s, then the internet connection is the slowest part of the network. This means that the 10 Gbit/s cables will not speed up the internet download speeds. The cables will only be transferring data at 1/100 of their maximum.

Fibre optic cables are flexible fibres. Each fibre optic cable contains a glass thread that bounces light signals between two devices faster and further than is possible with wire cables. Fibre optic cables can now carry data at 40 Gbit/s over many kilometres without affecting signal quality.

Fibre optic cables are expensive. This means that they are used by telecommunications companies and by organisations that need very fast data transfer speeds, such as science and engineering laboratories, hospitals, banks, schools and universities.

▲ **Figure 5.8** Fibre optic cable is capable of very high transfer speeds

WIRELESS ACCESS POINT

A wireless access point allows devices with Wi-Fi connectivity to connect to a wired network. They are often built into other hardware, such as routers (see page 85), but they are also available as stand-alone devices that connect to a wired network using Ethernet cables.

▲ **Figure 5.9** Wireless access points can be used in a small business to provide Wi-Fi access to wireless devices in a network

SWITCH

SUBJECT VOCABULARY
port a socket into which cables and devices can be plugged

A switch connects devices on a network. It has **ports**, each of which can be connected to a device using a cable. Connecting a wireless access point to a switch via a cable gives wireless devices access to the wired network. The switch makes sure that data sent from any device gets to the correct device on the network. For example, when printing a document, a laptop will send data that includes the printer's IP address to the switch and the switch then sends the data to the connected printer.

UNIT 2 NETWORKS

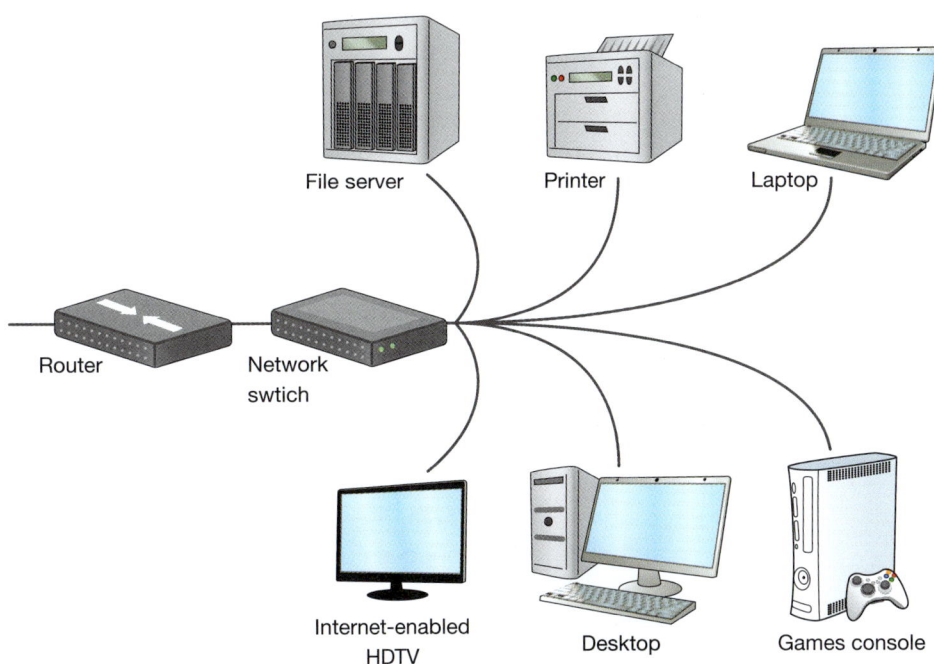

▲ **Figure 5.10** A switch allows multiple devices to send data to each other

▲ **Figure 5.11** A switch

GATEWAY

A gateway connects two different types of network. For example, a LAN is connected to a WAN using a gateway.

ROUTER

A router stores the addresses of all devices that are connected to it so that it can forward network traffic to its destination using the quickest route.

Most routers used in homes include a switch and a wireless access point. They also act as gateways, connecting the LAN to the internet, which is a type of WAN. Home routers are dynamically allocated an IP address by the internet service provider (ISP).

▲ **Figure 5.12** This router has a four-port switch; the last (grey) port on the right is used to connect the router to a WAN (in this case, the internet)

BOOSTER

A booster is used to amplify the signal in a network so that its range can be extended. For homes and offices, wired Ethernet connections often have a maximum range of 100 m. Wireless signals have limited range, too. Boosters can be used for both wired and wireless connections.

Wireless access points can be set to repeater mode in order to act as boosters for Wi-Fi signals, as shown in Figure 5.9.

SERVER

A server is a computer that shares its resources with connected devices. Computers connected to a server are known as **clients**. Resources that can be shared by one or more servers include printers, storage and applications.

> **SUBJECT VOCABULARY**
>
> **client** a computer connected to a server

AUTHENTICATION SERVER

An authentication server checks usernames and passwords. When a user successfully logs in, the client receives an electronic certificate that it can then use to access various resources, including applications and storage.

PRINT SERVER

A print server manages multiple printers at a time, dealing with print requests from client computers and adding jobs to a queue so that individual printers are not overloaded with requests. Print servers can also monitor and process print requests, making sure that users or departments can be invoiced for the jobs that they send to the printers.

FILE SERVER

File servers allow users to access shared and private storage.

APPLICATION SERVER

Application servers provide clients with access to applications that can be run directly from the server.

> **HINT**
>
> A single computer can be used to perform multiple server functions. Performing multiple roles will affect a computer's performance. Its ability to perform multiple roles will depend on its resources, especially its memory and processor.

▲ **Figure 5.13** Servers are often more powerful than clients, with lots of memory and fast processors to enable them to process multiple requests for their resources

WEB SERVER

Web servers process requests for data made via **Hypertext Transfer Protocol (HTTP)**. Together, all of the content stored on all web servers is known as the World Wide Web. Client computers often access web servers from outside the LAN to which the server is connected.

You will learn more about the difference between the internet and the World Wide Web in *Unit 3 Operating online* (page 110).

> **SUBJECT VOCABULARY**
>
> **Hypertext Transfer Protocol (HTTP)** a set of standards that control how computer documents that are written in HTML connect to each other

> **DID YOU KNOW?**
>
> HTTP was developed in 1989 by Sir Tim Berners-Lee as a way of sharing information with colleagues. He is credited with inventing the World Wide Web.

CONNECTING TO AND USING THE INTERNET

In order to access the online services provided by servers and data centres, users must have a connection to the internet. Users also need software that allows them to use and work with the services effectively and safely.

INTERNET SERVICE PROVIDER (ISP)

SUBJECT VOCABULARY

telecommunications infrastructure the networks of hardware facilities, owned by private and public organisations, that are used to transfer data

To connect to the internet, users need to subscribe to an ISP. ISPs provide connections to the **telecommunications infrastructure** that forms the framework for the internet. ISPs provide access via mobile telephone networks and landline telephone networks. Commercial ISPs charge subscription fees for access to the internet. Some ISPs provide free access as part of community schemes, which aim to provide internet access to groups of residents who either do not have or do not want access to commercial ISPs.

WEB BROWSER

A web browser is a type of software application used to request and display information stored on web servers. Examples of web browsers are Mozilla Firefox, Google Chrome, Internet Explorer® or Microsoft Edge, Opera[8], and Safari®[9].

▶ Figure 5.14 Web browsers have versions available for mobile devices

SEARCH ENGINE

A search engine provides users with a way to find information in web pages stored on web servers. Users enter keywords that describe the information they want to find. The search engine then compares the keywords with those in its database of web pages and returns the results that are the closest match to the given keywords.

▲ Figure 5.15 A search engine

---

8 OPERA IS A TRADEMARK OF OPERA SOFTWARE A
9 SAFARI® IS A TRADEMARK OF APPLE INC., REGISTERED IN THE U.S. AND OTHER COUNTRIES

> **HINT**
> Many people confuse search engines with web browsers. A search engine allows users to search and find information using keywords. A web browser is an application that users can use to view online content. Users can use a web browser to access a search engine.

> **DID YOU KNOW?**
> Some search engines allow users to search for information by uploading an image that represents the information they are looking for. The web browser then compares the image against a database of pages that include similar images and returns the results that are the closest matches.

You will learn more about search engines in *Unit 3 Operating online* (page 160–163).

FILTER SOFTWARE

SUBJECT VOCABULARY

URL (uniform resource locator) a website address
blacklist a list of unacceptable URLs
whitelist a list of acceptable URLs

Filter software prevents users from accessing inappropriate information. When a user tries to access a web page, the address (**URL**) and/or the contents of the web page are compared against two lists of URLs and keywords stored in the filter software's database. The two lists are the **blacklist** and the **whitelist**.

- If the results match anything in the blacklist, the user will be prevented from viewing the web page.
- If the result matches anything in the whitelist, then the user will be allowed to view the web page.
- If the result does not match anything in either the blacklist or the whitelist, the user will be allowed to view the information.

Administrators can add URLs to the blacklist and whitelist. The blacklist can be updated during software updates.

Filter software can help schools and parents to protect children from accessing disturbing or age-inappropriate content.

LOCAL AREA NETWORKS (LANS)

A LAN is a network contained to a small area, such as a home or office network (see page 69 for more information about LANs). Computers in a network can be connected using one of two different models:

- peer-to-peer
- client-server.

PEER-TO-PEER NETWORKS

Computers in a peer-to-peer network share their resources with other computers in the network, but they do not access servers. Figure 5.16 is an example of a peer-to-peer network.

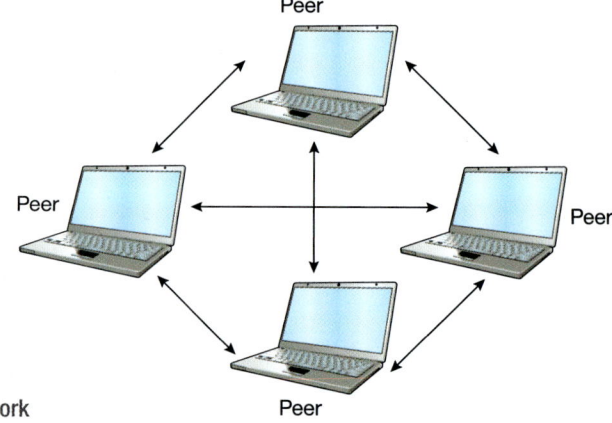

▶ Figure 5.16 A peer-to-peer network

CLIENT-SERVER NETWORKS

Some networks use servers (see page 86). A network that uses servers and clients is called a client-server network. Figure 5.17 is an example of a client-server network.

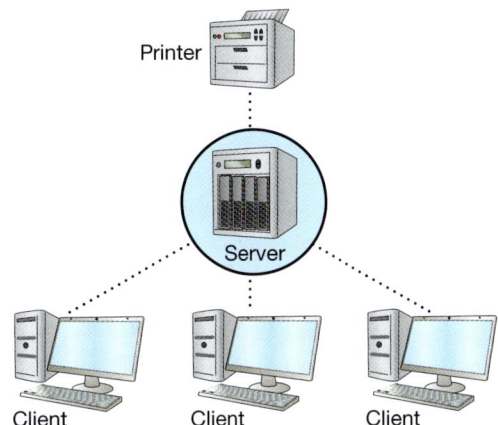

▲ Figure 5.17 A client-server network

BENEFITS OF USING LANS

Connecting computers using a LAN provides a range of benefits. These include:

- access to shared peripherals
- access to shared storage and data
- flexible access (that is, being able to access peripherals, storage and data from any connected device)
- media streaming (including movies, music and gaming)
- communication (that is, being able to send messages and files to others on the network)
- shared access to the internet.

SKILLS INTELLECTUAL INTEREST AND CURIOSITY
ADAPTABILITY
SELF-DIRECTION

ACTIVITY

▼ LAN PARTIES

What is a 'LAN party'? Use the internet to find out and write your own definition of the term.

BENEFITS OF USING CLIENT-SERVER NETWORKS

There are several benefits of using client-server networks that are not available when using a peer-to-peer network.

- **Control of user access rights:** Users, or groups of users, can be given access to some resources (such as storage or printers) and restricted from accessing others.
- **Centralised administration:** Resources and user accounts can be managed by an individual, or individual group of servers and administrators. This ensures that support can be provided by people who have an overview of the network and avoids inexperienced users creating problems for themselves or others.
- **Centralised backup:** User data is protected from loss because backups can be automated for all users. This makes it more likely that backups will happen than if individual users were asked to complete backups themselves.

- **Shared software:** Application servers (see page 86) can provide access to shared software. Some servers can provide access to operating systems.
- **Shared storage and file access:** The amount of storage available to users can be managed centrally. Sharing storage means that users can make files available to others. File permissions can be set for individual files, folders or drives, allowing users to either read only or read and write to different files.
- **Roaming profiles:** This is the ability to log into any computer in an office and see your settings and files. This allows users to access data, applications, mail and printers from any client, enabling them to work from anywhere where there is a client.

> **HINT**
> You learned about sharing software, storage and file access in *Unit 1 Digital devices* (pages 4–63).

SECURING DATA ON NETWORKS

Security prevents unauthorised users from accessing network resources and data.

LOGINS AND PASSWORDS

> **SUBJECT VOCABULARY**
> **login** user or account information, such as a user name or account name
> **authenticate** confirm that the user is who they say they are

Users log in to computers on a network to access centrally managed resources. Without the correct **login** details, users cannot access the network or its resources.

Passwords are used to **authenticate** a user to the network. An authentication server can be used to manage the authentication of a user to a range of network resource and services. This means that, once a user has been authenticated, they do not have to log in each time they access a resource or service.

See page 86 for more information about authentication servers. You will learn more about passwords in *Unit 3 Operating online* (page 100).

FIREWALLS

A firewall is used at the gateway to a network. It controls the network traffic to and from a network, particularly the traffic from the internet. Firewalls prevent unauthorised users from accessing network devices and resources, such as storage. Firewalls are available as hardware and software, which can be installed on computers to prevent attacks from within a network.

ENCRYPTION

Encryption is the process of encoding, scrambling or jumbling data so that unauthorised users are prevented from being able to understand it.

> **SKILLS** INTELLECTUAL INTEREST AND CURIOSITY
> CREATIVITY
> ADAPTABILITY
> SELF-DIRECTION
> COMMUNICATION

> **ACTIVITY**
>
> ▼ **ANCIENT ENCRYPTION**
>
> Research how a tool called a scytale was used by Spartans to encrypt messages. Create your own scytale and then use it to produce an encrypted message.

> **SUBJECT VOCABULARY**
> **cipher** a code

One method used to encrypt text is called a Caesar **cipher**. This method shifts each letter to the left by a set number of places. The number of places by which the letters have been shifted is known as the key.

Figure 5.18 shows an example of using a Caesar cipher. The top row is the original alphabet. The bottom row shows the alphabet after applying a Caesar cipher with a shift of four places. The example shows how the original letter F is encrypted to B.

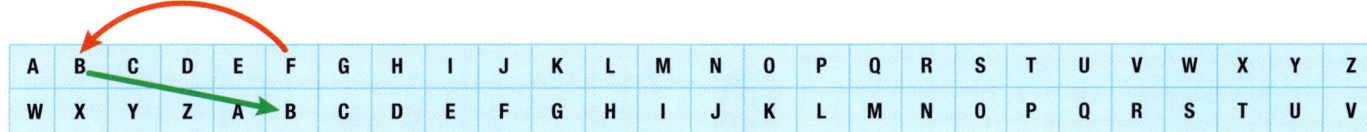

▲ **Figure 5.18** Once you know the key, it is easy to decrypt the message

SKILLS ▸ PROBLEM SOLVING
INTELLECTUAL INTEREST AND CURIOSITY

ACTIVITY
▼ DECRYPTING A MESSAGE

Using Figure 5.18, decrypt this message: WHWJ PQNEJC. When you have decrypted it, you will find that it is a person's name. Research the importance of this person's work during the Second World War.

SKILLS ▸ PROBLEM SOLVING
INTELLECTUAL INTEREST AND CURIOSITY
ADAPTABILITY
CO-OPERATION
RESPONSIBILITY

ACTIVITY
▼ ENCRYPTING A MESSAGE

1. The following is a message encrypted with a Caesar cipher. The shift is 16.
CEIJBO XQHCBUII
Decipher the message to give the original text.

2. Use a new Caesar cipher key to create an encoded message for a classmate. Do not include spaces between words, because this makes it harder to decrypt the message. Give them the encrypted message and see whether they can decrypt it and tell you the key.

A Caesar cipher is quite easy to crack, but most modern encryption is much more secure. There are two types of encryption:

- symmetric key encryption
- public key encryption.

SYMMETRIC KEY ENCRYPTION
Symmetric key encryption uses the same key at both ends of the process, meaning that the same key is used to encrypt and decrypt the data.

PUBLIC KEY ENCRYPTION
Public key encryption uses two mathematically related keys called a key pair. One key is used to encrypt the data and a different key is used to decrypt it.

A computer shares a public key with other computers that want to send it encrypted data. This public key is mathematically related to a private key, which is not shared.

Figure 5.19 shows an example of public key encryption. If Farooq wants to send Iyabode an encrypted message, Farooq uses Iyabode's public key to encrypt the data. The data is then sent to Iyabode, who uses her private key to decrypt the message.

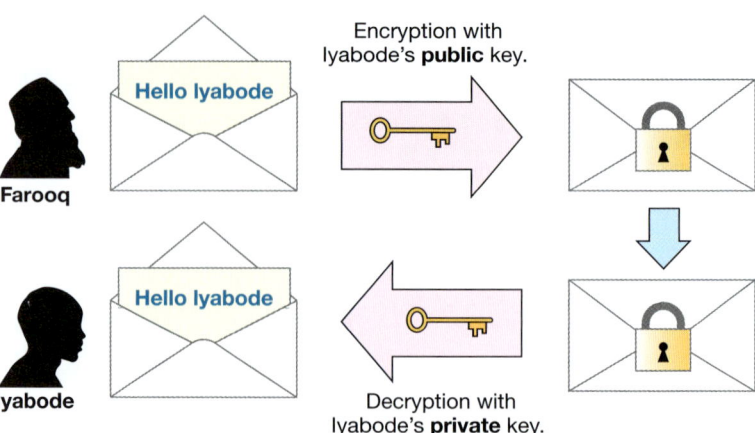

▲ **Figure 5.19** Farooq first sends Iyabode a request to send a secure message, then Iyabode shares her public key with Farooq

Although Farooq's message won't be secure, because the public key is published, anyone who receives the message will not be able to understand it without Iyabode's private key.

WIRELESS ENCRYPTION PROTOCOL (WEP)

It is easier to intercept data in a wireless network than in a wired network. Wireless Encryption Protocol (WEP) is used to secure the wireless transfer of data. It is the least secure wireless data encryption method. This is because every device on the wireless network uses the same key for every transfer. This means that if an **eavesdropper** studies enough **packets**, they can identify the key, and this provides them with unlimited access to all data from every device on the wireless network.

> **DID YOU KNOW?**
> Experts tested the strength of WEP by examining 10,000 packets in less than a minute. Having done this, they then took less than 3 seconds to identify the WEP encryption key used to encrypt the packets.

WI-FI PROTECTED ACCESS (WPA)

Wi-Fi Protected Access (WPA) is a security protocol designed to provide better encryption than WEP. WPA generates a new key for each device on the wireless network. New keys are also provided for each packet of data that is sent.

VIRTUAL PRIVATE NETWORK (VPN)

A VPN provides access to a private LAN from a remote location. The connection to the LAN is created using the infrastructure of a public network like the internet. Data sent using a VPN is encrypted so that it is secure if it is intercepted. An individual might use a VPN to:

- access their employer's network when working from home
- access computers in a different geographical location, perhaps to avoid the local restrictions on access to web content (such as due to censorship or **geolocation rights management**)
- make secure payments
- prevent surveillance of and access to their web activity.

HINT
A key is not the same as a password.

SUBJECT VOCABULARY

eavesdropper an unauthorised person or piece of software that intercepts data from a private communication
packet a unit of data packaged to travel across a network

SUBJECT VOCABULARY

geolocation rights management the use of a user's location to block access to services online; for example, a television channel might only allow users in their own country to watch their shows online

UNIT 2 — NETWORKS

> **DID YOU KNOW?**
> Mobile, desktop and browser apps are available to make it easy for users to change their network settings so that they can use VPNs.

FILE ACCESS RIGHTS

File access rights are also known as file permissions. They can be set for individual files, folders or drives, and they ensure that users are either allowed to read only or allowed to read and write to the file, folder or drive.

TRANSACTION LOGS

SUBJECT VOCABULARY
log a record of events
transaction the exchange of data

All network activity can be recorded in a **log** file. Although this does not directly secure network data, a **transaction** log can help to identify which computers and network devices have been accessed. This can allow administrators to identify any unusual activity that might be a threat to data security.

BACKUPS

A backup is a copy of one or more files. The backup or backups are usually stored on a different storage device to the original file.

For more information about backups, see *Unit 1 Digital devices* (page 42) and *Unit 3 Operating online* (pages 104–105).

CHAPTER QUESTIONS

SKILLS ▸ PROBLEM SOLVING

1. Which **one** of these connects a LAN to a WAN? (1)
   - A Switch
   - B Gateway
   - C Modem
   - D Server

SKILLS ▸ DECISION MAKING

2. Explain why public key encryption is more secure than symmetric key encryption. (2)

SKILLS ▸ PROBLEM SOLVING

3. State which security device controls the traffic entering a network. (1)

SKILLS ▸ PROBLEM SOLVING

4. State **two** methods by which devices are identified to each other on a network. (2)

SKILLS ▸ REASONING

5. Explain why IPv6 was used to replace IPv4. (2)

SKILLS ▸ PROBLEM SOLVING

6. State **two** uses for a VPN. (2)

SKILLS ▸ REASONING / PROBLEM SOLVING

7. State the reason why a booster is used in a network. (1)

SKILLS ▸ INTERPRETATION

8. Describe how encryption secures data. (3)

SKILLS ▸ PROBLEM SOLVING

9. List **three** methods of securing data on networks. (3)

SKILLS ▸ DECISION MAKING

10. State **three** benefits to users of using a local area network. (3)

SKILLS ▸ ADAPTIVE LEARNING / EXECUTIVE FUNCTION / ADAPTABILITY / COMMUNICATION

11. Draw and label a network diagram for a home that includes:
    - two smartphones
    - one tablet device
    - two desktop PCs
    - internet access. (8)

RISKS TO DATA AND PERSONAL INFORMATION 96   IMPACT OF THE INTERNET 109   ONLINE COMMUNITIES 132
IMPLICATIONS OF DIGITAL TECHNOLOGIES 147   ONLINE INFORMATION 159

UNIT 3
OPERATING ONLINE

Assessment Objective 1
Demonstrate knowledge and understanding of Information and Communication Technology (ICT)

Assessment Objective 2
Apply knowledge, understanding and skills to produce ICT based solutions

Assessment Objective 3
Analyse, evaluate, make reasoned judgments and present conclusions

In this unit, you will learn about the impact of the use of digital devices on individuals, organisations and society, as well as the risks of operating online to individuals and organisations. The digital world offers great opportunities to those who can access it. However, it is important to appreciate that not everyone has access to it and that those people who do have access must manage the risks of using powerful and developing technologies.

6 RISKS TO DATA AND PERSONAL INFORMATION

Huge amounts of data are transmitted and stored digitally, and a lot of this data contains personal or financial information. Because of this, digital systems are targeted by criminals who try to access data so that they can use it to commit fraud or identity theft.

You need to be aware of the risks to your data when operating online. You also need to know about the methods that are used to secure data in order to prevent unauthorised access and use.

LEARNING OBJECTIVES

- Be aware of risks to data and information:
  - unauthorised access
  - deliberate damage by malware
  - accidental deletion
  - theft of personal data: phishing, pharming
- Know about methods available to secure data and personal information online:
  - firewalls
  - encryption
  - passwords, PIN, biometrics, CAPTCHA tests, security questions
  - anti-malware, anti-virus, anti-adware, anti-spyware
  - access rights, file permissions
  - secure websites
  - not opening email attachments or following web links
  - backup procedures
- Know about online payment systems: third party payment systems such as PayPal, bank cards, contactless cards using NFC – and how payments are protected: VeriSign, HTTPS

RISKS TO DATA AND INFORMATION

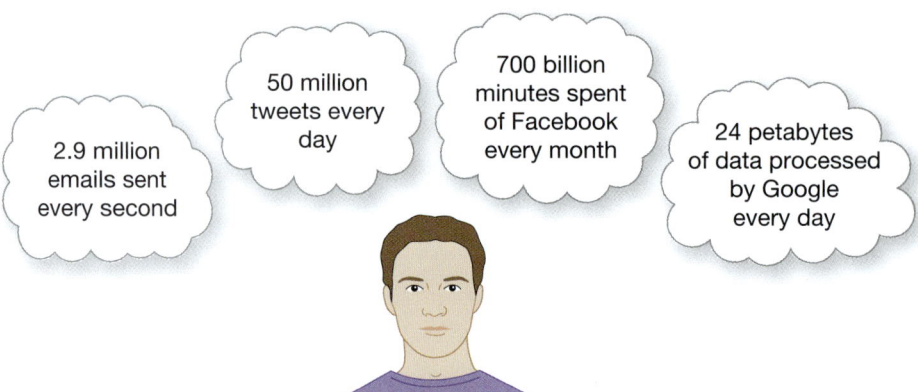

▲ Figure 6.1 The amount of data communicated online in order to carry personal and financial information is almost unimaginable

UNIT 3 — RISKS TO DATA AND PERSONAL INFORMATION

UNAUTHORISED ACCESS

Access to networks by users who are not permitted to access them is called unauthorised access.

Unauthorised users can attempt to gain access to networks directly by themselves. Alternatively, they may create software that runs thousands of times per second on devices, inputting multiple login details in order to attempt to gain access to networks with poor security.

> **DID YOU KNOW?**
> In 2012, a survey showed that 31% of people store financial data on their PC.

SUBJECT VOCABULARY

malware (**mal**icious soft**ware**) software that is created with the intention to do harm

Sometimes, devices on a network can be targeted by unauthorised users in order to be used as botnets. Botnets are groups of computers that have their resources used for harmful purposes, such as running and spreading **malware**.

DELIBERATE DAMAGE BY MALWARE

Malware can show messages, play sounds, delete files or reprogram systems to perform tasks that will harm the system and the connected hardware.

SKILLS INTELLECTUAL INTEREST AND CURIOSITY
PERSONAL AND SOCIAL RESPONSIBILITY
SELF-DIRECTION
CRITICAL THINKING
COMMUNICATION
INTERPERSONAL SKILLS

ACTIVITY

▼ **THE IMPACT OF MALWARE**

Research Stuxnet malware and the damage that it caused to nuclear facilities in Iran. Discuss your findings with your class.

Some malware (known as **ransomware**) threatens to delete a user's files or places restrictions on a user's access to software or resources until money is paid, usually to an anonymous account. These messages are usually very threatening and distressing for users. They are often written in a way that makes the user believe that they must pay quickly. This puts pressure on the user to act before they have time to think clearly about the threat and how to manage it.

▲ Figure 6.2 Ransomware

ACCIDENTAL DELETION

Users can sometimes delete files or even the entire contents of a drive by mistake. This can happen if:

- they press a key on a keyboard by accident
- they format media on the wrong storage device
- their device loses power unexpectedly.

THEFT OF PERSONAL DATA

Criminals use a number of methods to steal personal data.

SUBJECT VOCABULARY

phishing the criminal activity of sending emails or having a website that is intended to trick someone into giving away personal information such as their bank account number or their computer password; this information is then used to get money or goods

PHISHING

Phishing is a technique used by criminals to get personal information and payment details from users. It involves sending large numbers of messages that appear to be from real organisations, such as shops, banks or charities. Phishing messages are often sent as emails. These emails ask the user to provide their information by replying to the message or following a hyperlink that opens a webpage into which the user is asked to type their personal details.

```
Compliments of the season

I am the Head of Corporate Investment at Investments and
Securities Dubai.

I do have an authorisation of a client who is an African
leader with difficult political position to seek for
individuals with financial management understanding to
handle his wealth devoid of his name.

If you have experiences or projects in need of funding do
let us have a description of your experiences alongside your
address and business name so we can discuss a lot more.

Sincerely

Mukhtar Hassan
```

▲ Figure 6.3 Some phishing emails are less believable than others; the email address can be a giveaway as to the authenticity of the sender

Sometimes, phishing messages are highly customised or personalised and are targeted at a smaller number of particular users. This technique has become known as spear phishing.

> **DID YOU KNOW?**
> The threat from spear phishing grew by 55% between 2014 and 2015.

> **DID YOU KNOW?**
> SMS phishing is sometimes referred to as smishing.

Phishing messages can also be sent via SMS or instant message apps so that users open the fake webpage in a mobile browser. Users may not realise that the webpage is fake, particularly if they have never seen the company's real webpage in a mobile browser. As a result, they might type in their username and password details and reveal this personal data to the criminals.

PHARMING

Like phishing, pharming is a technique used by criminals to gain personal information and payment details from users. Criminals create fake versions of trusted websites to trick users into entering their login details, which are then used by the criminals to access users' accounts.

There are two main methods by which users are directed to a pharming site.

- **Internet traffic** going to the real website is redirected to the fake website, so that users think they are visiting the real thing. Criminals do this by altering the **domain name servers** to make internet traffic go to their fake site. They can also use malware to redirect web requests.

- Often, the URL of a pharming website is designed to be very similar to the URL of the real website. This means that if a user misspells the URL when typing it into the address bar of their web browser, they could go to the pharming site by mistake. For example, if the URL of a real bank is http://moneybank.lk and the criminals create a website with the URL http://moneybamk.lk, it could be easy for the user to make a mistake and arrive at the fake website.

▲ Figure 6.4 A fake **webform**, linked from an SMS message and opened in a mobile browser

SUBJECT VOCABULARY

webform a data entry form on a web page
internet traffic data transferred between computers connected to the internet
domain name server a computer connected to the internet that translates domain names, such as pearson.com, into IP addresses

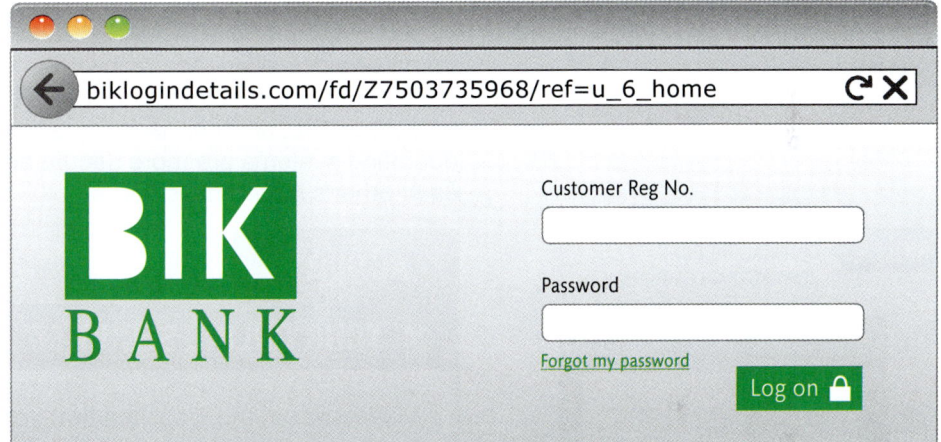

▲ Figure 6.5 Users should always check the URL of websites that they visit to make sure that they are not fake websites

METHODS TO SECURE DATA AND PERSONAL INFORMATION ONLINE

Much of the data transmitted online is sensitive and valuable, and it is important to protect that data from unauthorised access. There are several different methods used to secure data and personal information.

FIREWALLS

Firewalls control the data travelling into and out of a network. They examine the network addresses and ports of the data. They then compare those details to a list of rules that can be changed by network administrators. The list of rules determines what traffic should be allowed to travel into and out of the network. In this way, firewalls can prevent unauthorised access to a network and protect the network from malware. See *Unit 2 Connectivity* (page 90) for more information about firewalls.

ENCRYPTION

Encryption uses a key to scramble data into an unreadable form. If encrypted data is intercepted on the network, it is useless unless the interceptor has or can identify the key. See *Unit 2 Connectivity* (page 90) for more information about encryption.

PASSWORDS, PINS AND BIOMETRICS

Passwords, PINs and biometrics are used online to authenticate a user so that they can access an online system, such as webmail or an online bank account. See *Unit 1 Digital devices* (pages 20–21 and 27–28) for more information about passwords, PINs and biometrics.

Users should make sure that their password is:

- more than eight characters long
- a mix of letters, numbers and symbols
- a mix of uppercase and lowercase letters
- made up of random characters (that is, not common words, names or dates)
- changed frequently
- something that they have not used before.

When entering a password or a PIN, the characters are often **masked** so that anyone watching the screen cannot see what is typed.

Some services allow the password to be remembered. This is not recommended for multiple users of computers with stand-alone operating systems, as it may mean that another user can access someone else's accounts. Network operating systems are more secure and will not allow different users to see each other's stored passwords.

> **DID YOU KNOW?**
> '123456', '12345678', and 'password' were the three most commonly used passwords in the USA and Western Europe in 2015.

SUBJECT VOCABULARY
masked hidden

SKILLS CRITICAL THINKING, CONTINUOUS LEARNING

ACTIVITY

▼ YOUR ONLINE SECURITY

Make a list of the websites that you use that require a password. List up to 10 websites, then answer the following questions.

- Do you use the same password for each website?
- Do any of those sites contain sensitive data?
- Have you changed your password recently? If not, do it as soon as possible.

▲ Figure 6.6 Passwords can be masked

CAPTCHA TESTS AND SECURITY QUESTIONS

When users create an online account, they may be given a test called a **CAPTCHA** test. CAPTCHA tests are used to make sure that data is entered by a human and not by an automatic software program known as a bot or web robot.

SUBJECT VOCABULARY
CAPTCHA a computer program or system that can identify whether a user is a human or a computer
bot a computer program that can interact with systems or users

> **DID YOU KNOW?**
> CAPTCHA stands for Completely Automated Public Turing Test To Tell Computers and Humans Apart.

Some CAPTCHA tests work by asking users to enter a randomly generated series of letters and numbers that are displayed on the screen. Automatic software cannot read the letters displayed, or enter them into the required field, so this is used to distinguish human users from bots.

▲ Figure 6.7 Image identification CAPTCHA tests are another way of checking that users are human

▲ Figure 6.8 CAPTCHA tests can play audio versions for users who cannot read the text

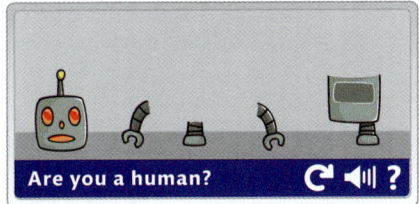

▲ Figure 6.9 CAPTCHA tests can ask users to complete more challenging tasks

reCAPTCHA tests work in the same way as CAPTCHA tests, but they use extracts of text from scanned books or a selection of images that share common features. When a user solves a reCAPTCHA test, their solution is used to help digitise books and annotate images. This helps to make more books available online and improves the information provided in online maps and other services.

SKILLS ADAPTABILITY

ACTIVITY

▼ HUMAN VERSUS COMPUTER

Can you read the text better than the computer in Figure 6.10?

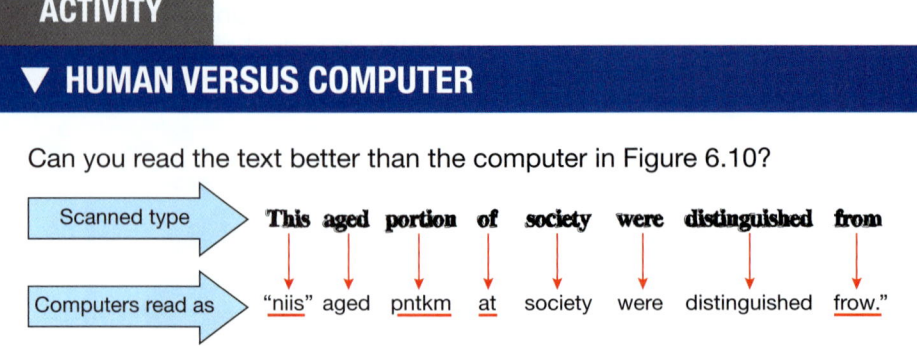

▲ Figure 6.10 Computers find it difficult to interpret scanned text from books but humans can read the text much more easily, which means that using humans to interpret scanned text produces more accurate outcomes

SKILLS INTELLECTUAL INTEREST AND CURIOSITY
CRITICAL THINKING
PERSONAL AND SOCIAL RESPONSIBILITY

ACTIVITY

▼ reCAPTCHA

Investigate reCAPTCHA tests. Discuss whether you think it is right for companies to use these tests to help translate text and classify information, or whether you think companies are exploiting internet users as unpaid labour.

ANTI-MALWARE

SUBJECT VOCABULARY

real time processing data within milliseconds of it being input and making the output available almost immediately
virus malware that uses networks to spread to connected devices
virus definitions sequences of code that are found in computer viruses
quarantine isolate a suspected virus in a protected area of storage where it cannot harm other files

Anti-malware prevents malware from accessing or operating on computers. It scans computer files in **real time** and allows users to scan files, folders, disks or whole systems.

ANTI-VIRUS

A **virus** is malware that uses networks to spread to connected devices. Viruses are spread via communication software such as email or web browsers or by being loaded into a computer's memory from external storage such as USB flash drives. Viruses often look like normal files. However, they have unique **virus definitions** that can be identified by anti-virus software.

Anti-virus software constantly checks files that are downloaded and loaded by a computer for signs of virus definitions. If the anti-virus software finds a match, it **quarantines** the file so that it cannot be run.

▲ Figure 6.11 A virus checker can quarantine an infected file so that it cannot infect other files

Anti-virus software has to be updated regularly because virus code can be changed, either automatically or by the developers of the virus. There is a constant battle between people who create the threats to data and people who create software to protect data.

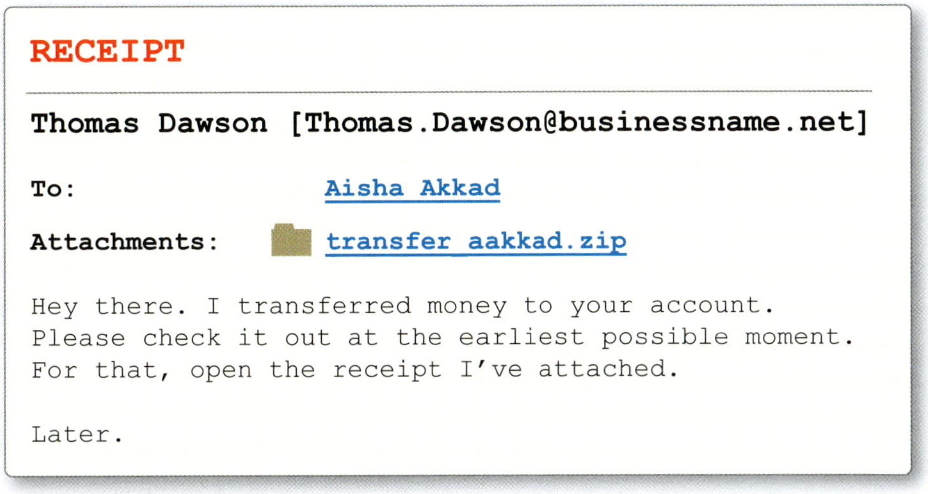

```
RECEIPT

Thomas Dawson [Thomas.Dawson@businessname.net]

To:            Aisha Akkad
Attachments:   transfer aakkad.zip

Hey there. I transferred money to your account.
Please check it out at the earliest possible moment.
For that, open the receipt I've attached.

Later.
```

▲ Figure 6.12 Viruses are often spread by email

SKILLS — PERSONAL AND SOCIAL RESPONSIBILITY / CRITICAL THINKING

ACTIVITY

▼ **STAYING ALERT**

Identify the items in the email in Figure 6.12 that might alert the user to the fact that opening the attachment may carry a risk.

Anti-virus utilities are often combined with software that protects against adware and spyware (see the next sections on anti-adware and anti-spyware). For this reason, anti-virus software is often known more generally as anti-malware.

ANTI-ADWARE

Adware displays unwanted adverts to users. Anti-adware software detects, quarantines and removes adware.

ANTI-SPYWARE

Spyware secretly monitors and records computer data and user input. For example, a keylogger is a type of spyware that monitors and records actions such as key presses or mouse movements. Criminals can then analyse this information to identify a user's passwords for websites, or financial data such as credit card numbers and security codes.

Anti-spyware software detects, quarantines and removes spyware.

SUBJECT VOCABULARY

adware software that displays unwanted adverts
spyware software that monitors and records data and user input

DID YOU KNOW?
Each day, 230 new keyloggers are discovered.

ACCESS RIGHTS AND FILE PERMISSIONS

SUBJECT VOCABULARY

permissions authorisation settings that provide the ability for a user or users to access files, folders or drives

Permissions can be set for access to files, folders or drives, allowing users to read only or read and write to the file.

SECURE WEBSITES

SUBJECT VOCABULARY

Hypertext Transfer Protocol Secure (HTTPS) a secure form of HTTP
payment server a computer that authorises financial transactions

Hypertext Transfer Protocol (HTTP) is used to exchange data between a web server and a client (that is, a computer that is accessing the web server). However, data transferred using HTTP is not secure, so **Hypertext Transfer Protocol Secure** (HTTPS) was developed. HTTPS authenticates **payment servers** and provides encryption using Secure Socket Layer (SSL) and, more recently, Transport Layer Security (TLS).

HTTPS keeps communications private and provides security for users' online accounts. Web browsers often show that a website is secure by displaying a green padlock in the address bar.

▲ Figure 6.13 A green padlock is used by most browsers to indicate that a website is secure

> **DID YOU KNOW?**
> In 2016, experts reported that 75% of all **legitimate websites** had serious security problems.

SUBJECT VOCABULARY

legitimate website a website that is operated legally

EMAIL ATTACHMENTS AND WEB LINKS

HINT

Hover over a link to see its URL.

SUBJECT VOCABULARY

executable file a computer file that can be run as a program
hover over use the mouse to position the cursor on an object on a computer screen without clicking on the object

Users should always be careful when opening email attachments or hyperlinks in emails and other messages. This is because some are fake and designed to steal users' personal information (see page 98). Users should ensure that their anti-malware software is up to date and be especially careful if:

- they do not recognise the sender
- the text is general, impersonal or irrelevant to the user
- the text contains spelling or grammatical errors
- the attached file is an **executable file** such as an .exe or .zip file
- the text contains a message telling the user to do something immediately
- the user does not recognise the URL.

BACKUP PROCEDURES

> **DID YOU KNOW?**
> There are three types of backup.
> 1. A **full backup** creates a copy of all files.
> 2. A **differential backup** creates a copy of all files that have changed since the last full backup.
> 3. An **incremental backup** saves a copy of only the files that have changed since the last full or incremental backup.

Backups create one or more copies of data. A backup is usually stored to an external storage device. This makes the data more secure, because the backup files will be safe even if the original storage device fails or is damaged, lost or stolen.

Backups can also be saved to online storage. This means that a copy of the data is held in two different geographical locations. Backing up to online storage can be slower because the process uses an internet connection.

Users need to decide how many files to back up and how often they should back them up. More regular backups will require more storage space. However, less frequent backups may result in a loss of data (for example, if that data has not been backed up recently).

Loss of files or damage to files can be caused by:
- theft
- malware
- flooding or fire
- power cuts.

See *Unit 1 Digital devices* (page 42) for information on backup utilities.

Good ideas for backup procedures are as follows.
- Set automatic backups.
- Do not use optical media because they deteriorate over time and are fragile.

UNIT 3 — RISKS TO DATA AND PERSONAL INFORMATION

- Schedule backups for late in the evening when users will not be using the data that is being backed up in order to avoid conflicts.
- Create more than one copy.
- Keep one copy of a folder containing important files backed up using online storage.
- Store copies at multiple locations.
- Store important data in a fireproof **safe**.

GENERAL VOCABULARY

safe a strong metal box or cupboard with special locks to contain money and valuable things

SKILLS — SELF-DIRECTION

ACTIVITY
▼ DATA SECURITY
Read through the list of ideas for creating a thorough backup procedure. Discuss how each idea will help to keep data secure.

SKILLS — INTERPRETATION

ACTIVITY
▼ RAID BACKUP STORAGE
Research RAID backup storage. Why is RAID 1 backup storage better for data security than RAID 0 backup storage?

HINT

Never put humans in charge of creating backups because they will forget. An automatic system is more reliable.

ONLINE PAYMENT SYSTEMS

People can pay for goods and services online using various payment systems. These systems send payment details across networks to computers that process the payments.

DID YOU KNOW?

About 85% of payments around the world are still made in cash.

▲ Figure 6.14 Many countries are moving quickly towards a **cashless society**

GENERAL VOCABULARY

cashless society a society in which people pay for goods and services using methods other than cash

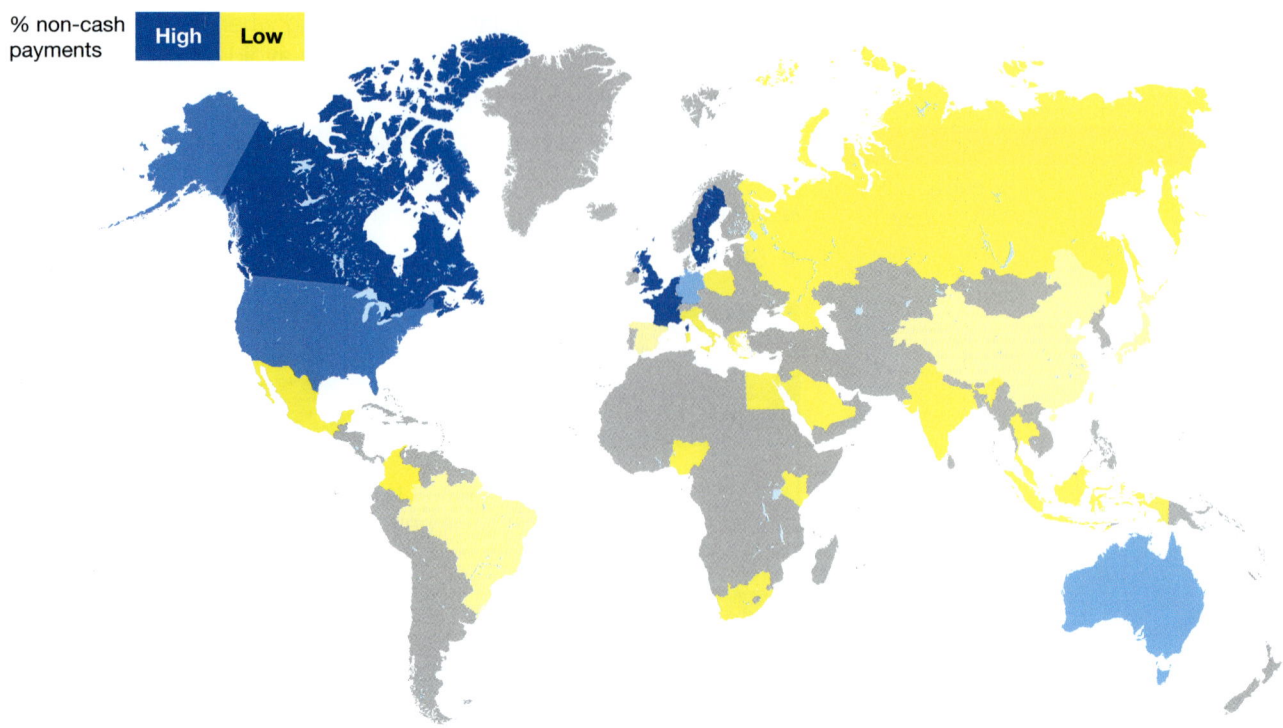

▲ **Figure 6.15** The percentage of people using non-cash payments differs in different countries around the world

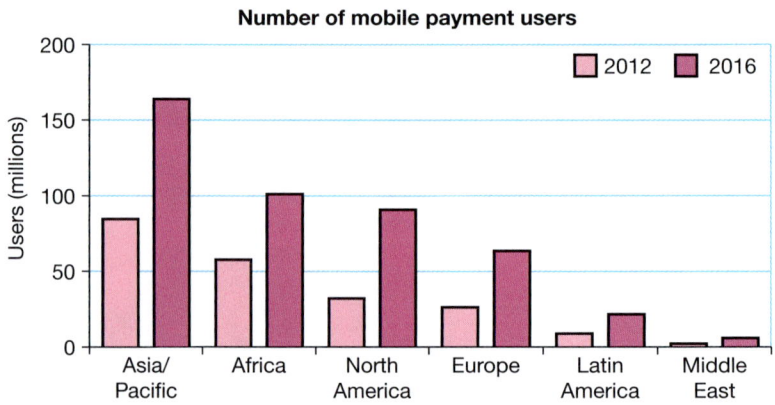

▲ **Figure 6.16** Mobile payments are a growing area

ONLINE THIRD-PARTY PAYMENT PROCESSORS

SUBJECT VOCABULARY

payment processor a computer that authorises financial transactions

Online third-party **payment processors** like PayPal or Skrill allow users to create an account so that they can send and receive money using email accounts for identification. Users can also use systems that link with online shopping applications, which can make shopping easier and faster.

BANK CARDS

GENERAL VOCABULARY

expiry date the date after which something can no longer be used

Bank cards allow customers to pay for goods and services online and in shops. When paying online, you usually need to enter the:

- card number
- **expiry date** (and sometimes the start date) of the card
- name on the card
- three- or four-digit card security code (CSC).

UNIT 3
RISKS TO DATA AND PERSONAL INFORMATION

> **HINT**
> - The card security code is often called a card verification code (CVC) or card verification value (CVV).
> - The card number is not the same as the bank account number.

▲ Figure 6.17 A bank card contains a number of security and identifying features

▲ Figure 6.18 Systems are used to authenticate people using payment cards online

When a user chooses to use a card online, they are sometimes asked to authenticate the payment by entering a password using a secure system. These systems are used by financial organisations such as Mastercard®[10], which operates the Mastercard SecureCode® system.

CONTACTLESS CARDS USING NFC

SUBJECT VOCABULARY

reader a piece of electronic equipment that can read information that is stored or recorded somewhere, for example, on a card

contactless users can use a contactless debit card or credit card to pay for things by waving it over a machine, without using a pin number

Near field communication (NFC) is used in payment cards to allow the transfer of payment data. The payment does not require a PIN or any form of user-authentication. If a card **reader** is in range and requesting payment, then the **contactless** card will take payment up to a maximum amount. This amount is limited, so that any people using card readers or apps to commit fraud can only steal a small amount.

NFC cards can be wrapped in foil to prevent the very weak signal from being intercepted by criminals. See *Unit 1 Digital devices* (page 30) for more information about the uses of NFC.

SUBJECT VOCABULARY

smartwatch a watch that provides data connectivity and often uses sensors to provide feedback to the device about its environment

▲ Figure 6.19 Criminals can use card readers or apps on NFC-enabled devices such as smartphones and **smartwatches** in order to commit fraud

10 MASTERCARD® IS A REGISTERED TRADEMARK OF MASTERCARD INTERNATIONAL, INC.

PROTECTING ONLINE PAYMENTS USING HTTPS

See page 104 for more information about secure websites and the use of HTTPS.

SKILLS EXECUTIVE FUNCTION / COMMUNICATION

ACTIVITY

▼ **RISKS TO DATA**

Produce a fact sheet for other students at your school or college. The fact sheet should help to increase their awareness of the risks to their data and the methods that they can use to reduce those risks.

CHAPTER QUESTIONS

SKILLS PROBLEM SOLVING

1 Which **one** of these is used to control internet traffic entering a network? (1)
   A Server
   B Backup
   C Firewall
   D Encryption

SKILLS INTERPRETATION

2 Explain why CAPTCHA tests work. (2)

3 State the purpose of pharming and phishing. (1)

SKILLS PROBLEM SOLVING

4 List **three** pieces of data from a bank card that a user is asked to enter when making an online payment. (3)

SKILLS INTERPRETATION

5 Describe **one** way in which incremental backup differs from differential backup. (2)

SKILLS INTERPRETATION

6 Describe how encryption secures data on a network. (2)

SKILLS PROBLEM SOLVING

7 State **two** methods used by an online system to authenticate a user. (2)

SKILLS PROBLEM SOLVING / PERSONAL AND SOCIAL RESPONSIBILITY

8 State **two** methods used by criminals to get users to visit fake sites. (2)

SKILLS INTERPRETATION / COMMUNICATION

9 Explain **one** disadvantage of using online storage for backups rather than local storage.

(2)

7 IMPACT OF THE INTERNET

The invention of printing allowed books to be reproduced quickly and accurately, without the errors caused by copying texts by hand. These inventions enabled the sharing and discussion of a wider range of ideas and information. This led to an increase in knowledge and literacy throughout the world, enabling faster and more reliable academic progress.

Like printing, the internet is one of the most important technological developments in human history. It has had positive and negative effects on individuals, organisations and society as a whole. It enables us to communicate by sharing text, images, video, music and software, to travel all over the world and into outer space, and to distribute and consume goods and services from many different countries.

LEARNING OBJECTIVES

- Know about the impact on employment, such as new job opportunities as the nature of a job changes, new skills requirements, potential job loss
- Understand the impact on working practices, including collaborative working and flexible or mobile working
- Know that the internet gives better access to information and services, new ways of learning, wider range of entertainment and leisure opportunities
- Know about social impacts such as:
  - reduced social interaction
  - increases in cyberbullying
  - reduced physical activity
- Understand how to stay safe online
- Understand how the availability of digital devices and the internet enables individuals to work from home
- Know the benefits and drawbacks of working from home for individuals and organisations
- Understand positive impacts: improved communication, access to global markets and workforce, changes in the way information is managed and used
- Understand negative impacts: security issues, risk of hacking, greater competition
- Understand the impact on society of the ability of individuals to have less-restricted access to networks at any time
- Know about the gap between information rich and information poor
- Understand the causes and implications of unequal access to ICT (locally, globally)
- Know about the impact on individuals and communities of limited or no access to digital technologies
- Understand the impact of changes in ways of socialising

THE INTERNET

The internet is not the same thing as the World Wide Web. The internet is the **inter**connected **net**work of computers that provides many online services to users. The World Wide Web is just one use of the internet.

Protocols are used by applications to transfer data across the internet. These protocols include:

- IMAP (**i**nternet **m**essage **a**ccess **p**rotocol) for email
- FTP (**f**ile **t**ransfer **p**rotocol) for sending files
- SSH (**s**ecure **sh**ell) for secure remote logins
- VoIP (**v**oice **o**ver **i**nternet **p**rotocol), used for voice call services like Skype
- XMPP (**ex**tensible **m**essaging **p**resence **p**rotocol), used for messaging services like WhatsApp
- HTTP (**h**yper**t**ext **t**ransfer **p**rotocol), used for the World Wide Web.

SUBJECT VOCABULARY
protocols rules that allow the exchange and transmission of data between devices

KEY POINT
The internet is connected devices. The World Wide Web is connected content.

IMPACT OF THE INTERNET ON INDIVIDUALS

The internet has changed how people live and work, giving them greater access to information and services.

INFORMATION AND SERVICES

The internet improves users with access to information from news, sport and weather services. Information can spread on the internet within seconds, which means that users have access to the latest news, sport and weather. This ensures that individuals can be up-to-date at all times.

Before the internet, two of the most important channels through which people could access these services were television or radio. These channels have some disadvantages solved by the internet, but they also have some advantages over the internet. These are shown in Table 7.1.

▼ Table 7.1 The impact of the internet on individuals' access to information services

TELEVISION AND RADIO		INTERNET
Only broadcast at certain times	→	Available all the time
Only a few channels	→	Millions of channels
Content decided by editors	→	Not always edited
Only available within range of a transmitter	→	Access from anywhere with a connection
Limited access to news from other countries	→	More open access, though some content is geo-restricted
Held to enforceable standards	→	Not always held to enforceable standards

SKILLS
INTERPRETATION
CRITICAL THINKING
REASONING

GENERAL VOCABULARY
beneficial resulting in good

ACTIVITY

▼ **ADVANTAGES AND DISADVANTAGES OF THE INTERNET**

For each of the changes in Table 7.1, decide whether you think the impact of the internet has been **beneficial** or not. Explain each of your decisions.

UNIT 3 — IMPACT OF THE INTERNET

As well as access to news, sport and weather information, users can also use the internet to:

- access booking systems for travel, leisure and entertainment
- do their shopping and banking
- study using virtual learning environments (VLEs), with online support from teachers and other students.

The internet has also provided a wider range of entertainment, with more entertainment providers giving access to **on-demand** services, movie and music streaming, downloads and gaming services. You will learn more about these online services in *Unit 4 Online goods and services* (pages 168–175).

Individuals can also add content to webpages. This has had an enormous impact on the way in which information is distributed around the world. It can be used to share information about serious issues and also for entertainment.

GENERAL VOCABULARY

on-demand whenever required (for example, catch-up television services)

KEY POINT

The development of online **interactivity**, which allowed users not only to read webpages but also to add information to them, became known as Web 2.0. It changed the way in which people communicated.

SUBJECT VOCABULARY

meme a photo, a piece of video, a joke or similar content that spreads quickly on the internet

interactivity the ability of a computer to respond to input

▲ Figure 7.1 **Memes** have amused millions of people

SKILLS — INTELLECTUAL INTEREST AND CURIOSITY

ACTIVITY

▼ **MEMES**

Research the story behind 'success kid'. Who is he? Why did this image become so popular? How have some companies used this image?

SKILLS — INITIATIVE, SELF-DIRECTION

ACTIVITY

▼ **THE INTERNET IN YOUR LIFE**

Write a paragraph on how the internet influences a typical day in your life.

EMPLOYMENT

The internet has had an impact on individuals' employment, often requiring people to learn new skills so they can change the way they work.

SKILL REQUIREMENTS

Many employers now require employees to use the internet for work, meaning that employees need to learn new skills. For example, journalists used to write articles using a word processor and submit them to their editor for publication. Now the journalists are often also required to post and update their stories on social media, write blogs, send broadcasts from their smartphones and interact with their audience. In addition, they must be able to react quickly to stories, which means that their typing and proofreading skills must be of a good standard to allow them to post a story quickly and without mistakes.

Similarly, modern teachers must be familiar with the information and services available on the internet so that they can teach their students about them. They must also be able to help their students manage the risks that they face in the online world.

NEW JOB OPPORTUNITIES AS THE NATURE OF JOBS CHANGES

As the internet changes the work that people do, this provides new job opportunities. For example, a plumber is no longer limited to installing and repairing pipework. Homeowners are now purchasing smart systems that can be controlled from digital devices using the internet. This means that plumbers have opportunities to extend their skills to include these new technologies in their work. No matter whether an individual is a plumber, a teacher or a journalist, they will be able to find more employment opportunities if they are able to offer modern services.

As the nature of jobs changes and the use of the internet at work grows, skilled workers are needed to support this development. People are required to train and advise unskilled workers and to create the digital devices and software that workers use. Other people are needed to install and maintain the systems that they use.

SKILLS CRITICAL THINKING, REASONING, INTERPRETATION, ADAPTIVE LEARNING, COMMUNICATION

ACTIVITY

▼ TECHNOLOGY AND JOBS

1 Complete Table 7.2. The first job has been done for you as an example. For each job, add a way in which the internet has changed that job, suggest a new skill to meet the change, and identify a new job opportunity for someone who could support the new skill. Now add a job of your choice in the last row, then complete the rest of the row.

▼ Table 7.2 The impact of the internet on employment

JOB	NATURE OF CHANGE	NEW SKILL	JOB OPPORTUNITY IN SUPPORTING THIS SKILL
Photographer	Clients want immediate access to photos	Uploading and sharing files online	Maintaining and updating servers
Medical scientist			
Teacher			

2 Use the example of the photographer given in Table 7.2 to explain how the internet has led to the creation of new jobs.

UNIT 3 — IMPACT OF THE INTERNET

JOB LOSSES

If employees do not keep updating their skills in the use of the internet, they may not have the skills required to carry out new work. If they are not willing or able to retrain, they could lose their jobs.

WORKING PRACTICES

Working practices are the ways in which people carry out the tasks that are part of their jobs.

GENERAL VOCABULARY

collaborative working working together

COLLABORATIVE WORKING

The internet enables people to connect with one another in real-time. This means that the process of sharing work between employees is more efficient. This kind of **collaborative working** allows work to be done more quickly or done 24 hours a day.

Collaborative working allows work to be split into a number of individual tasks, each of which can be done by a different employee. This has benefits and drawbacks.

- **Benefits**
  - Each employee can focus on one task.
  - Employees become experts in their area through (narrow) experience or training.

- **Drawbacks**
  - Employees do not share their skills and expertise.
  - Employees have reduced understanding of the whole project.

Collaborative working also allows more than one person to work on a task at the same time. This also has benefits and drawbacks.

- **Benefits**
  - Expertise is shared.
  - Employees can check each other's work.

- **Drawbacks**
  - It can be difficult for lots of people to agree.
  - It can be difficult to co-ordinate the work of many employees.

FLEXIBLE WORKING

Flexible working is a way of working that suits an employee's needs. For example, it allows employees to decide the hours that they work or enables them to work from home. This is possible because employees can use the internet to access systems from anywhere with an internet connection at any time of day.

Flexible working has benefits, but it also has drawbacks.

- **Benefits**
  - Employees can work at a time of day that is right for them and take breaks whenever they need to.
  - Employees can fit their work around their family life.

- **Drawbacks**
  - Employees do not meet face to face as much, which can reduce their understanding of each other and their employer.
  - Employees may not manage their work effectively, which could affect their home life or cause exhaustion.

The flexibility provided by the internet also enables employees to work when they are travelling. For example, mobile working allows employees to work on their way to and from the office. It also allows employees who work on the move, such as repair engineers and salespeople, to access to up-to-date data when **on-site** or at a client's location. This also has benefits and drawbacks.

- **Benefits**
  - Employees can access up-to-date information.
  - Employees can work from anywhere with an internet connection.

- **Drawbacks**
  - Employees could become exhausted if they work longer hours than expected when travelling.
  - They may not have access to the same facilities or resources as employees who only work in one place.

> **GENERAL VOCABULARY**
>
> **on-site** at a particular place of work or a place where something is being built (rather than away from that place)

SOCIAL IMPACT

The internet has had a huge impact on the way in which people socialise, particularly thanks to the rise of social media sites such as Facebook® and Twitter®. In November 2016, Facebook had 1.79 billion monthly active users spending 50 minutes per day using its various services. If Facebook was a country, this would have meant that it had the biggest population of any country on the planet.

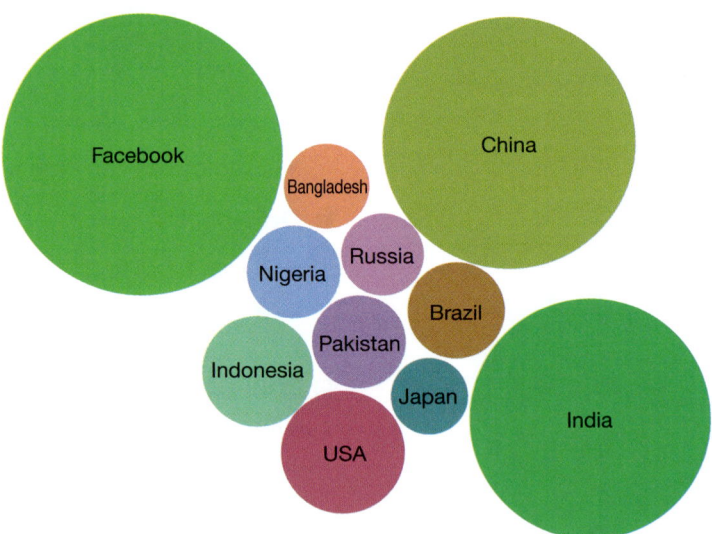

▲ Figure 7.2 The 'population' of Facebook compared with some of the world's countries

SOCIAL INTERACTION

Humans are naturally social, which means that we require **social interaction** with others. Humans feel a need to connect with each other and to participate actively in the world around us. The internet allows humans to communicate with any other connected person on the planet, through online gaming, video, instant messaging, social networking and online spaces for work and learning.

> **GENERAL VOCABULARY**
>
> **social interaction** communication with and reaction to others

UNIT 3 — IMPACT OF THE INTERNET

▲ Figure 7.3 Society is a network of people and the internet is a network of devices

▲ Figure 7.4 Some people argue that it is not how you socialise that is important, whereas others are concerned that socialising online is isolating us from reality and affecting our ability to form real relationships

Some people are concerned that our increasing use of virtual environments is replacing face-to-face social interaction. They believe that this is damaging people's ability to talk to each other and understand each other's emotions.

The effects of developing social skills in virtual environments rather than physical environments is now being studied and debated by psychologists and experts in child behaviour. There is particular concern about the effect on young children failing to interact with others face-to-face during the period in which they develop their ability to understand emotions. However, other people argue that being able to connect with more people and information is a good thing. They say that it is not important whether we do this via the internet or face-to-face.

The internet gives users access to a wider community, which can make people more aware of other cultures and societies and can broaden their view of the world. However, some people ask whether socialising online is a good thing. They argue that that we tend to connect with people who think like us or, worse, with people suggested to us by **social network applications**. You will learn more about these applications on pages 133–138.

SUBJECT VOCABULARY

social network applications software that allows social interaction and the creation of links between users based on shared characteristics and interests

SKILLS ▶ INTELLECTUAL INTEREST AND CURIOSITY

ACTIVITY

▼ FILTER BUBBLES

Carry out an internet search using the key terms 'Eli Pariser TED talk' to find a video of the author Eli Pariser discussing the concept of 'filter bubbles'. He explores how the code behind websites decides the content that users see online and the connections that users make with others.

DID YOU KNOW?

In some countries, three- and four-year-old children spend an average of eight hours and 18 minutes online each week.

CYBERBULLYING

Cyberbullying is the term used to describe the use of the internet to send text, images or multimedia in order to upset or embarrass someone. Bullying exists offline, but online bullying can be equally upsetting or even more distressing than offline bullying. Online bullies may use hurtful messages or distribute upsetting images of their victims that the bully may even have edited. Bullies can also isolate their victims by preventing them from participating in online events or discussions, which makes them feel upset and lonely.

Bullies who use the internet often hide their identity, making the experience even worse for their victim. However, most online communication is easily monitored and it is often possible to find the bullies by identifying the device which they used. See *Unit 2 Connectivity* (pages 69–70) for more information about identifying devices on a network.

SUBJECT VOCABULARY

cyberbullying using the internet to send text, images or multimedia in order to upset or embarrass someone

One other factor that makes cyberbullying different and possibly more damaging than in-person bullying is that, on the internet, information can spread very quickly and to more people. This can make the victim feel worse.

PHYSICAL ACTIVITY

Access to online goods and services means that people do not have to leave the comfort of their homes to shop, go to the bank or even go to school. It has reduced the need to travel, and this reduced need for physical activity as part of daily life could have negative effects on people's health and wellbeing.

However, some people would argue that access to some location-based games, such as Pokémon Go, promotes physical activity. They also argue that the ability to join online communities aimed at fitness motivates people to exercise, as users enjoy the encouragement that they can get from other members of the community.

> **HINT**
>
> When thinking about issues, it is often good to consider both sides of a discussion. When answering extended questions in the examination, consider whether a balanced response is appropriate. If it is, show that you understand the benefits and drawbacks of the issue that you are discussing.

▲ Figure 7.5 Some uses of the internet encourage users to be physically active

SKILLS LEADERSHIP
SELF-PRESENTATION
ASSERTIVE COMMUNICATION
PERSEVERANCE

ACTIVITY

▼ **DEBATING THE IMPACT OF THE INTERNET**

Prepare for and take part in a class debate on the topic: 'the internet has had a positive impact on individuals'.

STAYING SAFE ONLINE

▲ Figure 7.6 Governments in many countries have launched online campaigns to help young people stay safe when using the internet

UNIT 3 — IMPACT OF THE INTERNET

SKILLS — INTELLECTUAL INTEREST AND CURIOSITY
INTERPRETATION
PERSONAL AND SOCIAL RESPONSIBILITY

ACTIVITY

▼ STAYING SAFE ON THE INTERNET

Carry out an internet search using the key terms 'CEOP Jigsaw video' to find a video aimed at helping 8–10-year-olds stay safe online. What are the key messages of the video?

To stay safe when using the internet, users should follow three main rules:

- **zip it**
- block it
- **flag** it.

GENERAL VOCABULARY

zip it a colloquialism used to tell someone to say nothing about a particular subject, or to be quiet
flag to make a mark against some information to show that it is important

ZIP IT — Keep your personal stuff private and think about what you say and do online.

BLOCK IT — Block people who send nasty messages and don't open unknown links and attachments.

FLAG IT — Flag up with someone you trust if anything upsets you or if someone asks to meet you offline.

▲ Figure 7.7 Follow these rules to help you stay safe online

ZIP IT

Keep your personal information private and do not share it with strangers. This includes being careful about what personal information you share online. Examples of personal information you should not share include your:

- location
- school name
- phone number
- real name
- photos
- mailing address or email address.

You can use **privacy settings** on social networks to stop strangers from viewing your profile. You should also use a strong password that you change regularly and never give it to anyone, even your friends.

SUBJECT VOCABULARY

privacy settings a method that allows users to control who can see information from their online profiles

BLOCK IT

Always block **offensive** messages or friend requests from strangers on social networking sites. Do not open suspicious attachments or links, and you can use safe search filters to reduce the chance of seeing **age-inappropriate content**.

GENERAL VOCABULARY

offensive very rude or insulting and likely to upset people
age-inappropriate content materials (such as text, images, video and animations) that are not suitable for a particular age group
grooming creating an emotional connection with someone with the intention of making them less cautious, making it easier to do them harm

FLAG IT

You should always tell an adult if something online upsets you or if someone you don't know requests to meet you. Users can also report **grooming** behaviour to national crime agencies.

IMPACT OF THE INTERNET

The Virtual Global Taskforce is an international organisation that tries to protect young people online. Its Report Abuse button (see Figure 7.8) can be found on many social media sites.

▲ Figure 7.8 Many websites provide the Report Abuse button, which links people to online support

DIGITAL FOOTPRINT

Your **digital footprint** is the **impression** that you leave online. Much of what you share online can be recorded forever, either on archive sites or as backups.

ACTIVITY

▼ THE INTERNET ARCHIVE

Go online and search for the 'Internet Archive' to see what sort of content is made available on their website.

Content can be easily viewed by people whom you did not expect to see it. It can also be copied and shared easily, which means that it could become available to more people than you expect.

Ask yourself the following questions before sharing content online.

- Would I show this to my parents or grandparents?
- When I am looking for a job in the future, what will employers think if they see this?
- Could people **misinterpret** this, either now or in the future?
- Am I happy for this to be shared by people that I don't know?

You can minimise your digital footprint by:

- closing your old social media accounts and requesting that all archive data is deleted
- searching for your own name online and see what information about you is publicly available
- asking website owners to remove old content that is out of date, irrelevant or false
- reading the terms and conditions when you create online accounts, because some services still have rights over your data even after you close your account.

SUBJECT VOCABULARY

digital footprint all the data that a user creates online, which is recorded and stored

GENERAL VOCABULARY

impression a mark

SKILLS ▶ INTELLECTUAL INTEREST AND CURIOSITY

KEY POINT

Always consider that the things you post online now may not be the same as your views in the future.

GENERAL VOCABULARY

misinterpret to misunderstand the correct meaning of facts or of something that someone says or does

UNIT 3   IMPACT OF THE INTERNET   119

SKILLS
ADAPTABILITY
PERSONAL AND SOCIAL RESPONSIBILITY
EXECUTIVE FUNCTION
CREATIVITY

ACTIVITY

▼ GUIDELINES FOR ONLINE SAFETY

Create a leaflet for students in your school that explains how they can stay safe online. It should contain no more than 200 words and use no more than four images.

ONLINE WORKING FROM HOME

Before the internet existed, offices were seen as necessary to provide a central location for people to discuss business and collect, distribute and file paperwork. Offices also allowed employees to be supervised by their managers.

SKILLS
INTELLECTUAL INTEREST AND CURIOSITY
ADAPTIVE LEARNING

ACTIVITY

▼ CHANGING OFFICE ENVIRONMENTS

Carry out an internet search using the key terms 'Brazil movie Ministry of Information' to find a clip set in the Ministry of Information in Terry Gilliam's movie, *Brazil*. Compare this to a modern office environment. What is the same? What has changed?

Many businesses have established processes and procedures, including set working hours, such as 09.00–17.00, and scheduled meetings. Many organisations also require their employees to work within one or more central offices. Historically, this was logical because employees could only access computer systems in a centralised office space. Later, employees could use LANs to access shared storage and resources, but still had to be within the office in order to do so. See *Unit 2 Connectivity* (page 69) for more information about LANs.

However, this has changed. As computer systems became cheaper and more powerful, they began to be used in people's homes. Many modern digital devices can run a range of software and can be used to access the internet, online systems and applications. People can use digital devices provided by their employer, or even their own devices to connect to the internet and work from home.

KEY POINT

Connected digital devices have led to the availability of a decentralised, distributed approach. For some types of organisation, this has meant that the traditional office is no longer the most appropriate or productive environment for its employees.

Unlike the traditional central office, the internet is decentralised, which means that it is not controlled by any one individual or organisation. Using the internet to work from home has benefits and drawbacks for organisations and their employees.

DID YOU KNOW?
An average office worker spends a total of about 80,000 hours in an office during his/her career.

BENEFITS OF WORKING FROM HOME

▲ **Figure 7.9** Working from home can have benefits for both individuals and organisations

Benefits to individuals

- No need to travel to work:
  - reduces stress caused by traffic, public transport delays and overcrowded transport
  - saves money
  - makes people feel as though they are helping the environment by reducing travel emissions.
- Can spend more time working or resting, because they spend less time travelling to work.
- No need to wear a uniform or business clothes, which reduces cost.
- Can work at a time to suit them.
- Can work on tasks for longer periods of time without distractions from colleagues or scheduled meetings.
- Can work in a comfortable environment.
- Can organise work around social or family commitments.

Benefits to organisations

- Can attract a talented, motivated workforce.
- Can employ people who are located anywhere because they do not need to travel.
- Do not need to buy or rent office space or furniture for employees.
- Workers do not have to commute, so will not be delayed getting to work by weather or transport issues.
- Workers may work more effectively at home.

SKILLS INTELLECTUAL INTEREST AND CURIOSITY

ACTIVITY

▼ **EFFICIENT WAYS OF WORKING**

Carry out an internet search using the key terms 'Jason Fried TED talk' to watch Jason Fried talk about why offices are not the best places to get work done.

DRAWBACKS OF WORKING FROM HOME

▲ Figure 7.10 Working from home can also have drawbacks for both individuals and organisations

SKILLS PROBLEM SOLVING

Drawbacks to individuals

- May be distractions at home, such as family and leisure activities.
- Suffer from a lack of social interaction with colleagues.
- Feel disconnected from the company.

Drawbacks to organisations

- May be concerns about data security.
- May be more difficult to manage and support employees who are not in the office.
- Employees working at home might not work as hard.
- Can be complicated to organise payments and permissions for workers in different countries.

ACTIVITY

▼ HOW TO IMPROVE WORKING FROM HOME

For each of the drawbacks that you have just read, suggest solutions that would make working from home better for individuals and organisations.

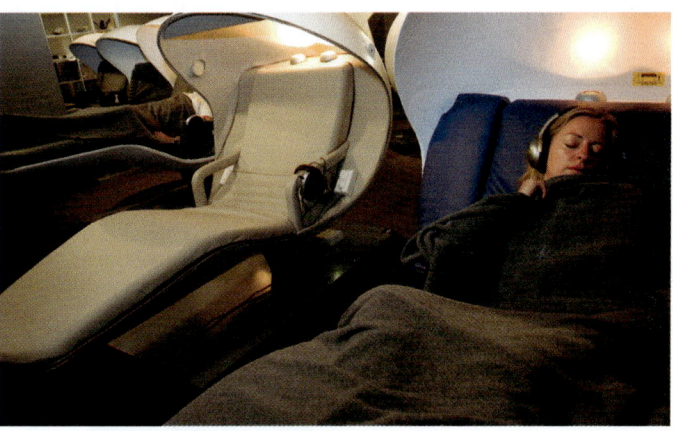

▲ Figure 7.11 Some organisations like Google™ provide **perks** like sleep pods at their offices to encourage their employees to feel more at home in the office

GENERAL VOCABULARY

perks something provided to employees by their employer in addition to their wages, such as goods, meals, or a car

SKILLS INTERPRETATION
EXECUTIVE FUNCTION
ADAPTABILITY
PRODUCTIVITY
COMMUNICATION

ACTIVITY

▼ PERSPECTIVES ON WORKING FROM HOME

1. Write a letter or email from an employee asking their employer to let them work from home. Explain how the internet makes it possible to work from home.

2. Write a reply from the employer that explains the benefits and drawbacks for the organisation and the employee. Your reply should finish with a decision on whether or not the employer is going to let the employee work from home.

IMPACT OF THE INTERNET ON ORGANISATIONS

The internet has had a significant impact on organisations as well as on individuals. Many of its effects on organisations have been positive, but some have been negative.

POSITIVE IMPACTS

SUBJECT VOCABULARY

in-video advertising advertisements that appear within online videos
viral marketing a type of advertising used by internet companies in which computer users pass on advertising messages or images through email, sometimes without realising that they are doing so
cookies information that a website stores on a user's computer so that the website recognises the user when they use it again
profile compilation of personal information about an individual

GENERAL VOCABULARY

corporate communication the process of providing information about a company for its employees or for its customers and the public, so that they know what the company is trying to achieve and have a good opinion of the company

SKILLS INTELLECTUAL INTEREST AND CURIOSITY

IMPROVED COMMUNICATION

Organisations can communicate and interact with their customers and employees more easily and in real-time using email, instant messaging and social media. They can provide up-to-date information about the development, pricing and availability of their products and services. Organisations can also publish live information online, allowing people to follow the organisation's activities. Figure 7.12 shows how a charity might use internet services to communicate with different groups.

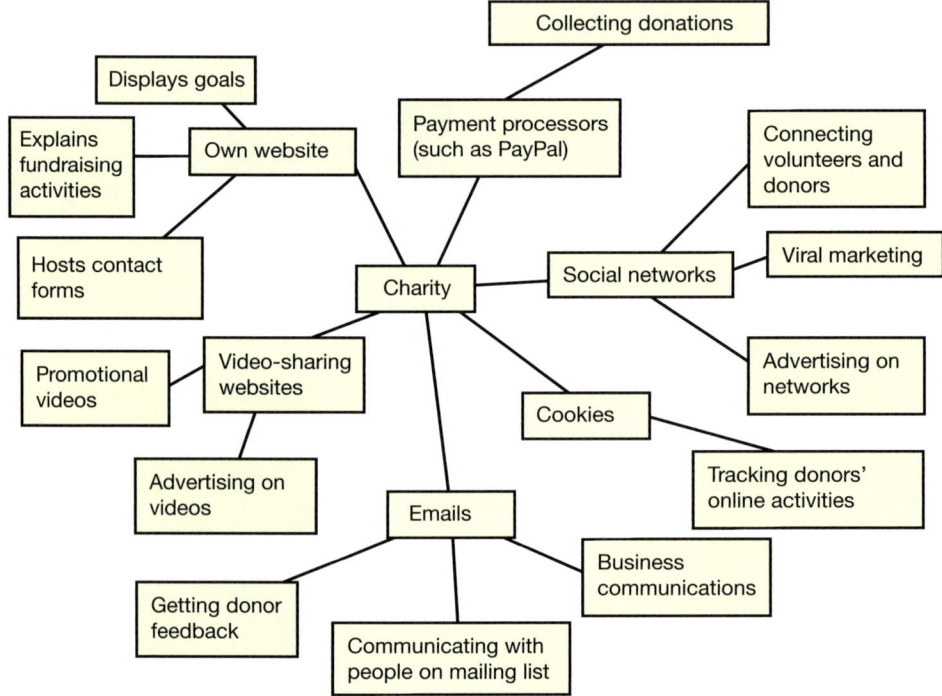

▲ Figure 7.12 A charity can use many internet services to communicate with different groups of people

ACTIVITY

▼ **SOCIAL MEDIA AND POLITICS**

Investigate some of the ways in which political organisations have used social media to communicate with voters during recent campaigns.

ACCESS TO GLOBAL MARKETS

The internet has made it easier for organisations to advertise and sell to customers in countries around the world. Producers of digital content are now able to sell their products online without having to create physical packaging and can avoid postage charges. In addition, the internet has also ensured that manufacturers have easier access to businesses that produce materials and parts and can communicate more easily with them.

ACCESS TO GLOBAL WORKFORCE

Thanks to the internet, organisations can employ people in other countries. This allows organisations to be more selective when hiring employees, because they do not just have to employ people who live within travelling distance of the organisation's offices. This means that the organisation can make use of different skills and time zones. For example, Figure 7.13 shows how three teams in three different time zones can cover all 24 hours in one day by working three shifts of eight hours (3 × 8 = 24). The organisation may also be able to reduce its costs because people in some countries will accept lower wages than in other countries.

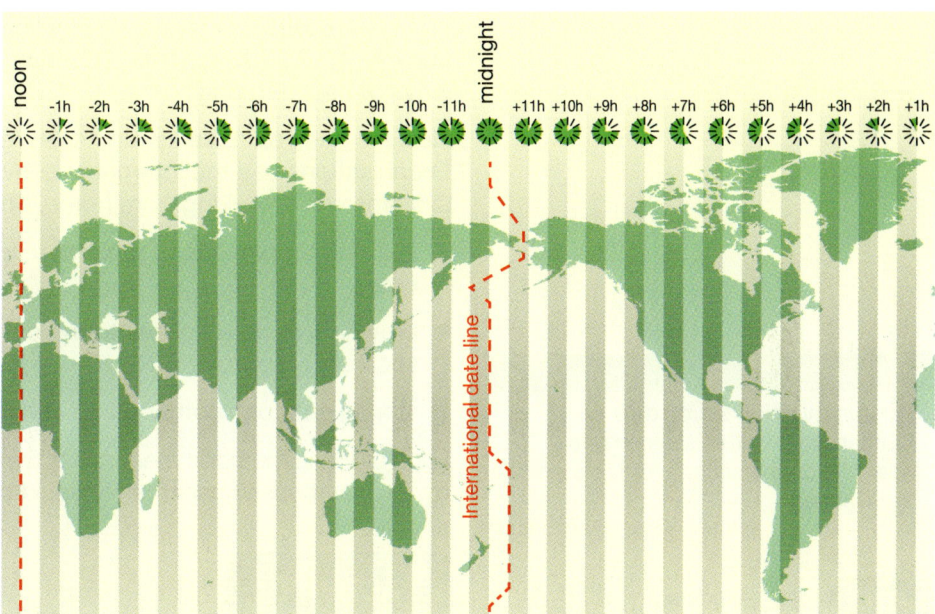

▲ Figure 7.13 Companies often use teams in different time zones in order to provide 24-hour customer support, with all employees working in daylight hours in their local area

SKILLS ANALYSIS
        PROBLEM SOLVING

ACTIVITY

▼ USING DIFFERENT TIME ZONES

A company employs people in your country from 09.00 until 17.00. Find two other countries in which it could employ people to work the same times of day while still ensuring that the company provides 24-hour customer support.

HOW INFORMATION IS MANAGED AND USED

Organisations can make use of **big data** to understand the behaviour of their customers, improve the customer experience and make their processes more efficient.

For example, a computer game retailer could use data gathered from analysing social media posts, web browsing patterns, movie ratings and current game sales in order to predict which game will sell best in six months' time. The retailer can then make sure that they buy enough stock of the game in order to meet demand, and avoid buying too much stock of any games that they predict will not be popular.

SUBJECT VOCABULARY

big data the analysis of huge quantities of data collected from many sources (such as smartphones, online applications, social media and payment systems) in order to find patterns of behaviour and interactions

Another example is the use of weather data from hundreds of thousands of sensors, smartphones and aircraft. Processing this data allows organisations to understand how different types of weather can affect their services. For example, supermarkets can use the data to change the number of products or staff they will need. Energy suppliers can use it to calculate how many people will need heating. Governments can use it to predict and warn people of extreme weather events, which could protect property and save lives.

NEGATIVE IMPACTS

SECURITY ISSUES

The data stored by organisations is often private and valuable. If data is stored in a central location, it can be physically secured by walls, locks, alarms and security guards. None of these methods is totally safe, but they are all good ways of securing data.

However, as you have already seen, employees often work from home. Organisations use the internet to provide their employees with access to their systems while working from home. They do so using three methods:

- allowing employees to transfer a copy of the organisation's data to home via email
- providing remote access to the data stored in the organisation's building, such as by using a VPN
- storing data on another company's servers and providing access to that data.

Each of these methods means that the data is more vulnerable to being accessed by an unauthorised user than it would be if it remained in a central location.

HINT
If an organisation stores data on another organisation's servers, it must rely on the security of the other organisation.

SKILLS INTERPRETATION ADAPTABILITY

▲ Figure 7.14 As soon as data leaves a secure building, it becomes much less secure

ACTIVITY

▼ PRIVATE AND VALUABLE DATA

Complete Table 7.3 by providing examples of private or valuable data stored by the types of organisation listed in the table. When you have finished, add your own choice of organisation in the bottom row and identify examples of private or valuable data that it holds.

▼ Table 7.3 Organisations that hold private or valuable data

ORGANISATION	EXAMPLES OF PRIVATE OR VALUABLE DATA
Banks	
Hospitals	
Online retailers	
Schools	

There are three main ways in which unauthorised users can gain access to systems.

- Authorised users reveal their login details, either intentionally or unintentionally, such as by losing paper copies of their login details, saving their login details to a computer that they lose, being pressured into telling someone their details or having passwords which are easy to guess. Organisations

UNIT 3 — IMPACT OF THE INTERNET

GENERAL VOCABULARY

accountable when someone is held responsible for the effects of their actions and must be willing to explain or be criticised for their actions

SUBJECT VOCABULARY

hacking accessing a system using malicious methods

HINT

Hacking is not the same as stealing someone's password. Hacking is when the unauthorised and authorised users use different methods to access the same system.

have policies that help employees to understand and manage these risks. Policies like these make employees **accountable** for their actions, which means that they are more likely to act responsibly.

- Unauthorised users intercept the data, either as it is transferred over the internet from the organisation to the employee's computer or as it is transferred within the employee's LAN after it has been transferred via the internet (WAN). Organisations often use encryption to secure data when it is transferred using the internet, which protects data even if it is intercepted. See *Unit 2 Connectivity* (page 90) for more information about encryption.

- Unauthorised users **hack** into the organisation's systems. To prevent access to their systems from the internet, organisations use authentication, firewalls and intrusion detection systems. See *Unit 2 Connectivity* (page 90) for more information about firewalls.

GREATER COMPETITION

In the past, organisations usually competed with other organisations in their local area or their own country. However, the use of the internet means that organisations must now compete in a global marketplace. In some industries, there are more organisations with which to compete. Large organisations can also become less attractive to customers because they may be less flexible than small online businesses.

Some types of organisation and even whole industries have been put at risk due to the way in which the internet has provided new channels for the trade and distribution of goods and services. There are many examples of this.

- Music and film retailers have been threatened by the increased use of online downloads and streaming.
- DVD rental companies have had to deal with similar challenges, as more people now watch films online.
- Record labels have been threatened by the fact that independent artists can publish and distribute their music online.
- Estate agents have lost business as individuals advertise their properties online.
- Newspaper publishers and television broadcasters have had to adapt because individuals have a greater choice and more convenient access to news and information services online.
- Postal services have been negatively affected by people's ability to send messages and digital media instantly.

IMPACT OF THE INTERNET ON SOCIETY

The development of the internet has affected many aspects of society and people's lives.

THE CAUSES OF UNEQUAL ACCESS TO ICT

SUBJECT VOCABULARY

digital divide the gap between people who have access to digital devices and the internet and people who do not

In 2016, approximately 46% of the world's population had access to the internet. Access to information and communication technology (ICT) is not equal. The difference between those with technology and those without is often referred to as the **digital divide**.

UNIT 3

IMPACT OF THE INTERNET

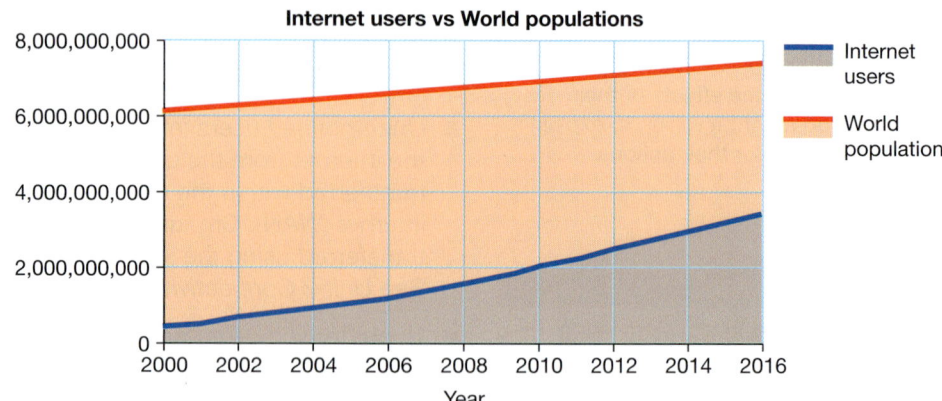

▲ Figure 7.15 Although more people are able to access the internet than ever before, it is still not available to all

In Figure 7.16, countries that are coloured green have high percentages of people who access the internet. Countries that are coloured red have low percentages of people who access the internet.

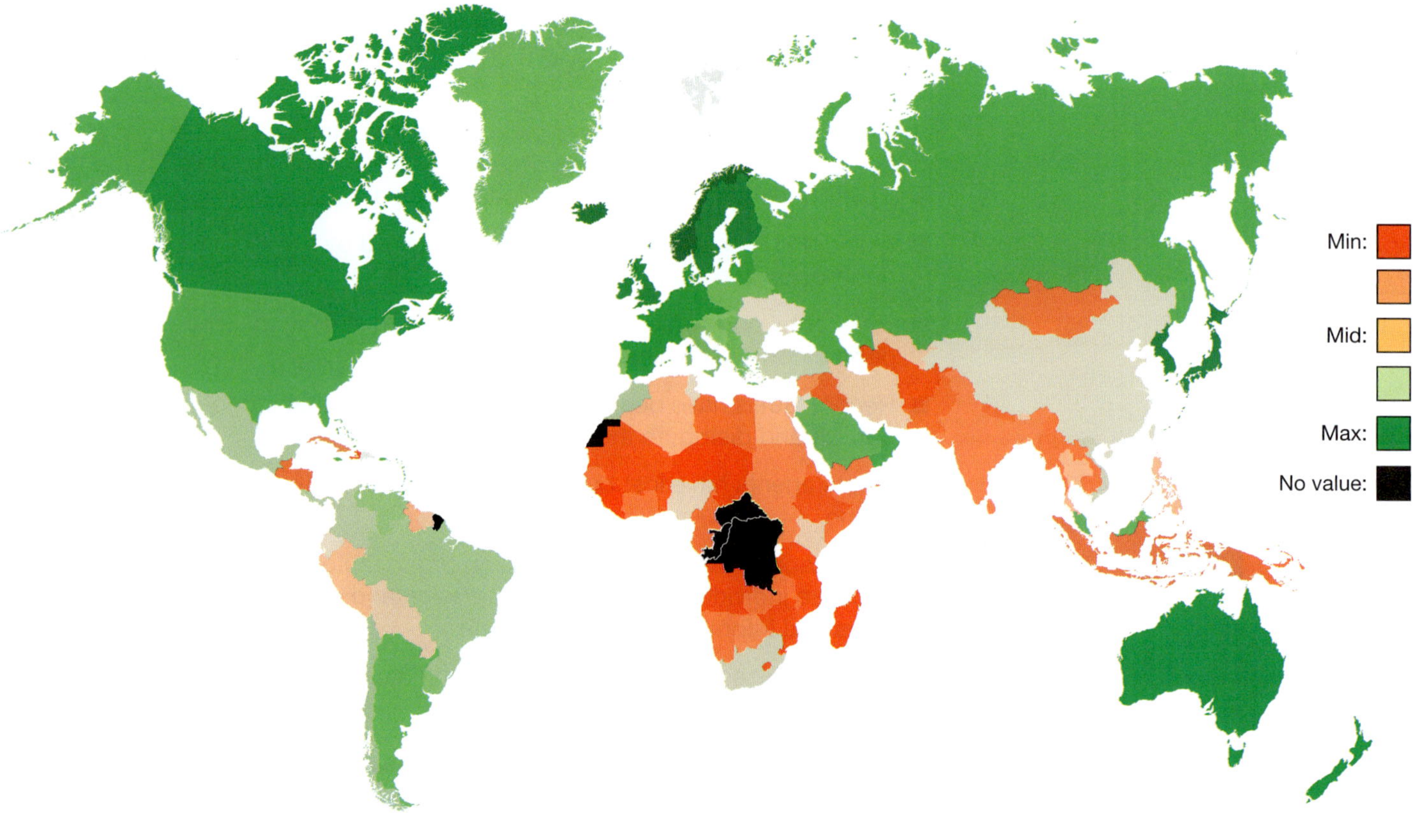

▲ Figure 7.16 Lots of people in many regions of the world use the internet, but the proportion of internet users is smaller in Africa and South Asia

SKILLS CRITICAL THINKING
EXECUTIVE FUNCTION
COMMUNICATION

ACTIVITY

▼ THE DIGITAL DIVIDE

Create a mind map that highlights the causes and effects of the digital divide and its impact on society.

IMPACT OF THE INTERNET

> **KEY POINT**
> The digital divide is not just about access to the internet. It also relates to access to television, telephones and a wide range of digital devices.

People's access to ICT can be affected by a number of factors.

- **Economy and infrastructure:** Countries with advanced economies can afford to invest in the infrastructure required to provide access to networks and the internet. In countries with emerging and developing economies, governments may prioritise other needs, such as food and healthcare, rather than access to digital technologies.

▲ Figure 7.17 There is a close relationship between people's income and their access to technology

> **KEY POINT**
> Although the proportion of people with access to technology is higher in richer economies, national wealth is not the only factor that determines access to ICT.

> **DID YOU KNOW?**
> Some people believe that governments prevent people from accessing ICT in order to control their citizens rather than to protect them. In 2016, the United Nations criticised the way in which some governments deliberately blocked or disrupted their citizens' internet access.

- **Location:** People may not be able to access online systems in remote locations. For example, in rural areas or locations where wireless signals or cabling cannot reach, such as heavily forested and mountainous areas.
- **Politics:** Governments that want to control access to information can either prevent or reduce access to the internet for their citizens. Some governments do not allow people to visit certain websites or content from other countries. Other governments have banned people from using satellite receivers so that they cannot access television or radio broadcasts from countries with cultural influences they disagree with.
- **Religion:** Some religions ban access to certain technologies. For example, Old Order Amish communities in the United States of America do not use radio, television or the internet.
- **Disability**: If digital devices are not designed to be **inclusive**, people with disabilities can find accessing technology more difficult and may have to rely on adaptations to be able to use ICT.
- **Social factors:** In every region of the world, social factors such as age, gender, education and income affect people's ability to access ICT.

> **GENERAL VOCABULARY**
> **inclusive** making sure that all individuals and sections of society are included in or have access to something

UNIT 3 — IMPACT OF THE INTERNET

SKILLS
- CRITICAL THINKING
- REASONING
- INTERPRETATION
- PERSONAL AND SOCIAL RESPONSIBILITY

ACTIVITY

▼ CAUSES OF REDUCED INTERNET ACCESS

Do some research into the cause of reduced internet access for each of the social factors listed on page 127, then use your findings to complete Table 7.4.

▼ Table 7.4 Causes of reduced internet access

FACTOR	REDUCED ACCESS FOR	CAUSES
Age	Older people	
Education	People with a lower level of education	
Income	People with lower income	
Gender	Female users	

▲ Figure 7.18 In many countries, women are less likely than men to access the internet or to own a smartphone.

THE IMPACT OF LIMITED OR NO ACCESS TO DIGITAL TECHNOLOGIES

If an individual or community has limited or no access to digital technologies, they have less access to communication with other people. This makes them more isolated and can reduce their understanding of different cultures. It also reduces the availability of:

- goods and services, affecting people's ability to find bargains and good deals
- entertainment, reducing people's access to popular culture
- education, reducing people's employment opportunities.

However, some people argue that limited or no access to digital technologies builds stronger communities, because it increases the amount of time that people within the community spend with each other in person.

THE IMPACT OF LESS RESTRICTED ACCESS TO NETWORKS

GENERAL VOCABULARY

media mass communication such as broadcasting, publishing and the internet

Less restricted access to networks has had an impact on a number of elements of society. For example, one key element of society is the **media**. Before the internet, if an individual person wanted to broadcast a message, they had to own or be able to persuade a media organisation to broadcast it, or they had to go into the street and start shouting! However, the internet has caused a shift in power, because social media and video streaming services like YouTube® have enabled people to broadcast their own messages and interact with global audiences.

Online content is still controlled to an extent by moderators, who enforce the service owners' policies on what kinds of content should be published. What users see online is also determined by the programs that control what stories and videos are promoted to their reading lists and viewing lists. These decisions can be based upon users' browsing history or the browsing history of friends linked to their online profiles. In some cases, these decisions depend on whether individuals and organisations have paid to promote their information to users.

SUBJECT VOCABULARY

user-generated created by the individuals who use the service

User-generated reference sites such as Wikipedia have challenged society's ideas about expertise. This is because truth, knowledge and accuracy are no longer checked by a limited number of experts or editors. Instead, ordinary people can now put information online that may or may not be true.

The development of the internet has created billionaires. At the same time, it also provides millions of volunteers with further opportunities to work for free for good causes.

The use of the internet has also had an impact on law enforcement. For example, in 2011, riots spread across parts of England. The spread of the riots was linked with the use of mobile phone networks to spread messages through social media and instant messaging services, which helped the rioters to organise themselves and avoid the police.

▲ Figure 7.19 The internet gave citizens the ability to spread information about the 2011 riots in England

However, the police also used networks. For example, they used the network of CCTV cameras to record the actions of rioters. In the days after the riots, footage captured on smartphones was uploaded to photo blogging websites and spread through social media, and communities helped identify those responsible for the damage caused during the riots. To help them gather information about the phones that were used to organise the riots, the police also asked phone companies to provide information about the phones' owners, where calls were made from, and lists of calls made to and from the phones.

▲ Figure 7.20 By 10am on the morning after the third day of rioting, the tag #riotcleanup was the top trending tag in the UK and second worldwide

Although it was claimed that the police in England were not prepared to keep up with the use of social networks during the riots, they have since developed their use of appropriate technologies and methods to monitor these communication methods. The internet was also used by citizens to organise clean-up events, proving that social media can be used for positive purposes.

SUBJECT VOCABULARY

digital humanitarian movement a group of people working together using ICT to promote human welfare

The **digital humanitarian movement** is an excellent example of socially responsible use of the internet. For example, in 2007, there was civil unrest and tribal violence in Kenya, and traditional media struggled to cover the events. A blogger called Ory Okolloh co-founded a website called Ushahidi, which is Swahili for 'witness'. The website provided people with the ability to record and map incidents of attacks that were happening during the crisis. By giving them a voice, Ushahidi put the Kenyan authorities under pressure to act to reduce the attacks on Kenyan citizens.

> **SUBJECT VOCABULARY**
>
> **crowd-mapped** data provided by many individuals, forming a 'crowd', which is then superimposed on a map using geolocation information from users' data submissions

Since 2007, Ushahidi has been used to track and report thousands of human rights violations. It also helped people to map victims of the 2010 earthquakes in Haiti and the 2015 earthquakes in Nepal, ensuring that emergency teams and humanitarian organisations were aware of when and where people needed help.

▲ Figure 7.21 A **crowd-mapped** crisis zone during the Japanese tsunami in 2011

THE GAP BETWEEN INFORMATION RICH AND INFORMATION POOR

As a result of the growth of the internet, a divide has been created between people who have access to online information, and people who do not. This divide is often referred to as the information gap.

> **SUBJECT VOCABULARY**
>
> **information rich** people with good access to information provided by communication technologies
>
> **information poor** people with limited access to information provided by communication technologies

People who are **information rich** have good access to information. This improves their level of education and enhances their ability to make decisions. In comparison, people who are **information poor** have reduced access to information, which decreases their education and reduces their ability to make decisions.

The information gap existed before the internet, because some people had more access than others to information from television, newspapers and books. However, the development of the internet has widened the gap because it has increased the amount of information that is available to people online and that is unavailable to people without internet access.

People who do not have access to the internet do have some alternatives to increase their access to information. For example, mobile networks can be used to provide access to SMS so that farmers in remote areas can communicate with buyers to make sure that they get a fair price for their produce. SMS messages can also provide farmers with weather forecast updates so that they can prepare for and protect their farms from bad weather.

▲ Figure 7.22 Farmers in remote areas can connect to networks using SMS so that they have more information

> **HINT**
>
> SMS messages are often called text messages or texts.

However, mobile text message services do not provide as much access to services and information as the internet can. With the internet, people have greater access to communication, news, entertainment, goods, banking and other services like tax and applications for driving licences.

UNIT 3   IMPACT OF THE INTERNET

THE IMPACT OF THE INTERNET ON CHANGES IN WAYS OF SOCIALISING

As people increase their use of the internet, they spend more time in the virtual world than the real world. The internet has arguably affected the way that people think and their ability to form relationships with others.

People can use the internet in order to connect with people around the world whom they have never met. However, it can also cause people to become isolated from their own families and local communities because they spend most of their time looking at the screens of their digital devices. For example, having friends' and family's **status updates** sent directly to you means that you no longer have to ask them what they are doing. Some people have argued that social media makes friendship meaningless, because on social media even complete strangers can be labelled 'friends'.

SUBJECT VOCABULARY

status update a message or post that a user adds to their own social media page to inform others of something that they consider important enough to share

CHAPTER QUESTIONS

SKILLS REASONING

1 Which **one** of these activities is only possible when using the internet? (1)

   A Television
   B Radio
   C Streaming
   D Mobile telephone calls

SKILLS INTERPRETATION

2 State **two** benefits to employees of working from home. (2)

SKILLS INTERPRETATION

3 State **two** drawbacks to organisations of employees working from home. (2)

SKILLS DECISION MAKING

4 Explain **one** reason why the use of the internet may affect the ability of individuals to interact with other people face-to-face. (3)

SKILLS REASONING

5 Explain **one** reason why cyberbullying can be more distressing than in-person bullying. (2)

6 State what is meant by the term 'collaborative working'. (1)

SKILLS REASONING

7 State **three** factors that affect unequal access to ICT. (3)

SKILLS REASONING

8 State **three** examples of services that are not available to those with limited or no access to digital technologies. (3)

SKILLS INTERPRETATION

9 Describe **two** ways in which greater access to networks has affected society. (4)

SKILLS INTERPRETATION

10 Describe the effect of the internet on the information gap. (2)

SKILLS PRODUCTIVITY REASONING

11 Discuss the impact of the internet on how individuals socialise. (8)

SKILLS INTERPRETATION DECISION MAKING

12 Describe **two** ways in which individuals can stay safe online. (4)

SKILLS INTERPRETATION

13 Explain why organisations' use of the internet increases the risk to data security. (3)

8 ONLINE COMMUNITIES

People use online communities to socialise, share information, play games, work, learn and create. In this chapter, you will consider the functions of different types of communities, the features that provide these functions, how communities are used to reach global audiences and how community members can be protected from online risks.

LEARNING OBJECTIVES

- Understand key features of online communities:
  - social networking
  - online gaming
  - online work spaces
  - virtual learning environments (VLE)
  - user-generated reference sites: wikis, websites, forums
  - user-generated content: video sharing sites, blogs, websites
  - social bookmarking

- Know the functions and target audience of different forms of online communities

- Understand the ways in which online communities are used to communicate and collaborate on a global scale

- Be aware of the purpose of responsible use and acceptable behaviour policies

- Understand how to stay safe online: cyber bullying, anonymity of others (misrepresentation), disclosure of personal information/location

SUBJECT VOCABULARY

online community a group of people with a shared common interest who communicate online
member someone who is part of an online community

KEY POINT

All online communities allow users to interact with other people.

SOCIAL NETWORKING COMMUNITIES

FEATURES AND FUNCTIONS OF DIFFERENT ONLINE COMMUNITIES

Each type of **online community** has:

- a **function**, which is what it does for people who use it
- **features**, which enable (or allow it to achieve) its function.

Different online communities provide different features that their **members** can use to interact with each other. Features that provide the function of one type of community now could be used for other types of community in the future, because the internet and its uses are always evolving.

Social networking is the practice of forming groups in a society. This is something that humans have been doing for a long time before the invention of the computer. However, the internet has provided new ways for us to form social networks. Examples of online social networking communities include Facebook, Baidu® and Twitter.

UNIT 3 — ONLINE COMMUNITIES

GENERAL VOCABULARY

professional someone who works in a job that needs special education and training, such as a doctor, lawyer or architect

DID YOU KNOW?
Members of social networking communities typically only interact with five or six friends on a daily basis.

SUBJECT VOCABULARY

profile a collection of information about a user

DID YOU KNOW?
Some people compete to see how many 'friends' they can have on social networks. The maximum number of people with whom you can maintain stable relationships is approximately 150. This is known as the Dunbar number. This is true for humans and also for most primates, such as chimpanzees and orangutan.

SKILLS DECISION MAKING
EXECUTIVE FUNCTION
PERSONAL AND SOCIAL RESPONSIBILITY

THE FUNCTION OF SOCIAL NETWORKING COMMUNITIES

Online social network communities allow members to connect through shared interests or relationships.

These communities include **professional** networks such as LinkedIn® and personal networks such as Facebook. These different types of network started out with separate functions. However, just like the convergence of different types of digital device (see *Unit 1 Digital devices*, page 15), the features and use of different types of social network are starting to mix together. For example, some personal networks such as Facebook and Twitter are used by professionals and businesses as well as for personal relationships.

FEATURES THAT ENABLE THE FUNCTION OF SOCIAL NETWORKING COMMUNITIES
Profiles

When you create an account with a social networking community, you can add information about yourself. Some services allow members to decide which information should be made public, which information should only be visible to certain people and which information should not be visible to anyone. A collection of user information is known as a **profile**.

Profiles can be personalised by members and they can include:

- biographical details such as name, gender, date of birth, location and language
- an 'about you' or short description of the user
- details about the user's work and education
- travel history
- family details such as relationship status, family members and pets
- contact information such as telephone number, email address and website
- profile and background images, colour schemes and designs.

Martin Chan

▲ Figure 8.1 What profiles have you created online?

ACTIVITY

▼ **PUBLIC AND PRIVATE INFORMATION**

Design your own profile for a professional social networking community. Consider what information you would make public and what you would choose to keep private.

Friend, follow and connect

Different social networking communities have similar features that allow users to add someone to their social network. These can be known by many different names such as friend, follow and connect.

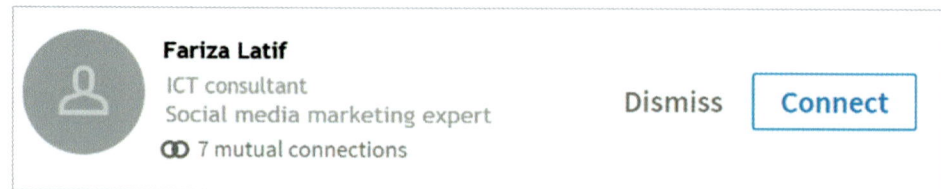

▲ Figure 8.2 Examples of buttons on social media networks that allow users to add people to their networks

Some communities allow their members to restrict other users' access to their full profile until the other users request to add them to their network. Other communities allow totally unrestricted access. For more information about staying safe online, see pages 143–145.

Stream, wall and timeline

A user's stream, wall or timeline is the place where the **posts** from members' friends appear.

> **SUBJECT VOCABULARY**
>
> **post** (noun) a message sent to an internet discussion group so that all members of the group can read it

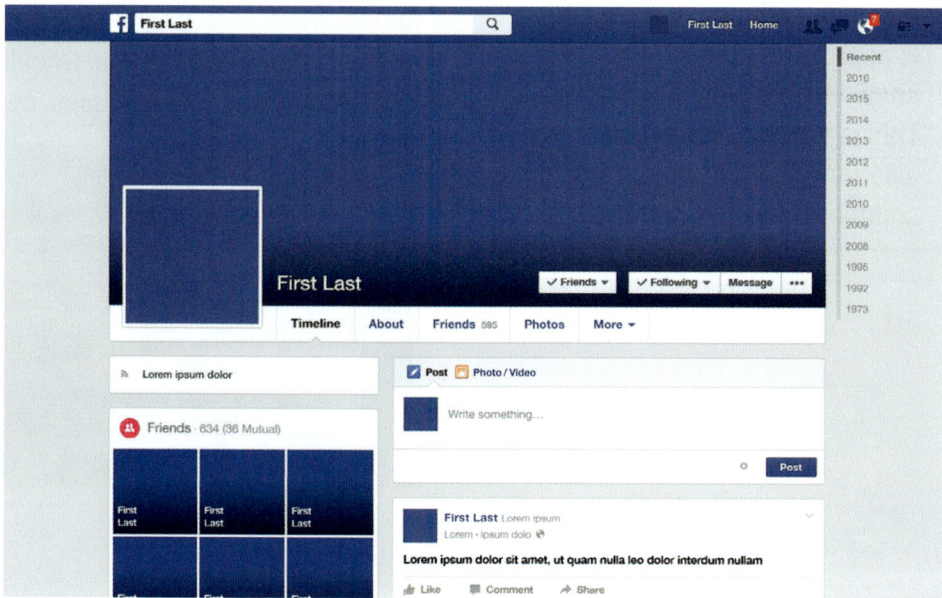

▲ Figure 8.3 An example of a Facebook wall

The development of the wall or timeline has changed how people communicate online, as it ensures that information is brought straight to the user rather than making the user look for information.

Status updates and posts

Members of a social networking community can either send a message to other members in their network or send it publicly to all members of the community. Some communities allow members to select sub-groups of members within their network that will be able to see their message.

SUBJECT VOCABULARY

post (verb) to put a message or computer document on the internet so that other people can see it

targeted marketing advertising that is matched to internet users based on their attributes, such as their age group or their gender, or their internet browsing history

KEY POINT

The use of targeted marketing has made some people consider the cost of social networking communities. They are often free to use, but does this mean that they are really free of charge? The answer to this question depends on the value that you put on your own personal information and the way in which it can be traded.

GENERAL VOCABULARY

promote publicise

GENERAL VOCABULARY

categorise to put things into groups or categories according to the type of thing that they are

SUBJECT VOCABULARY

tag a label that you can add to a post
connections people or accounts to whom a user is connected

Social networks are powerful marketing tools because they contain a huge amount of information that people **post** about themselves. The owners of the social networking community can store this information in a database and analyse it. They can then sell this information to advertisers, because this gives the advertisers the ability to specifically target relevant sponsored posts to matched members. The ability to match members to advertisements is called **targeted marketing**.

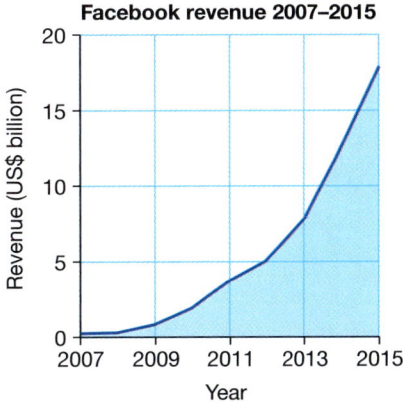

▲ **Figure 8.4** Selling the use of members' personal information for targeted marketing is a key part of Facebook's revenue, and helped the business to earn almost US $18 billion in 2015

Members can also pay a fee to **promote** their posts. This feature is often used by organisations for marketing purposes and allows them to make their posts available to more members of the community. Targeted marketing allows members of some communities to target their promotions at other members with particular profiles, such as a particular age group or gender, so that the promoted posts appear at the top of those members' streams.

Some posts are known as sponsored posts. These posts appear at the top of all members' streams and do not use their profile data in order to target members with relevant profiles.

Groups, lists and circles

Social networking communities usually allow members to create named groups, lists or circles of members. Users' posts can then be made visible only to members of one or more of those groups. For example, a member could use this to keep posts for family separate from posts for work. Organisations can also use this so that smaller teams of people can communicate with each other effectively without sending information to everyone in the entire organisation.

Tags

Tags allow members to **categorise** the content that they create and post on social networking communities. Other members can then search for content using the tags that were added to the content when it was posted.

User suggestions

Social networking communities suggest other members that users might want to connect with. They often do this by analysing a user's interests and the interests of people within that user's social network, then matches them to friends of existing **connections**.

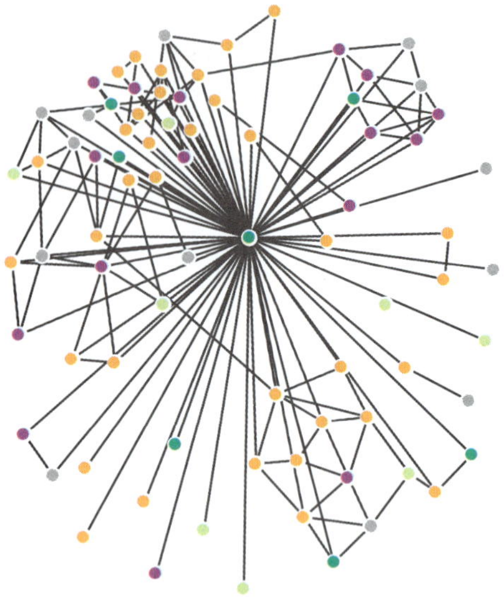

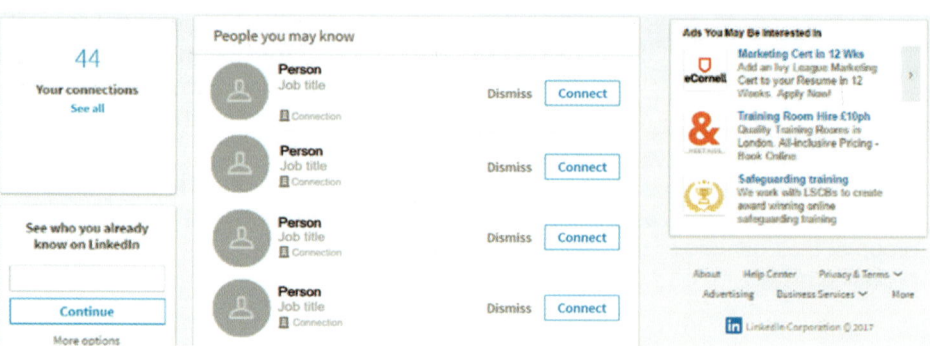

▲ Figure 8.6 An example of a 'Do you know?' web page on a social networking community

Reactions, ratings, likes, upvotes and downvotes

Social networking communities have features that enable users to show their reactions to posts by other people, such as liking them or finding them funny. These features also allow users to recommend posts to other members of their community.

Downvotes are used on some social networking communities to show that users dislike a post. However, some people think that downvotes send a negative message, which is something that social networking communities usually try to avoid.

▲ Figure 8.7 Examples of buttons that allow users to interact with a post using likes, reactions and ratings

Share

Share functionality allows members of a social networking community to repeat other members' posts to the community. This makes the original posts available to more people. When a post is shared widely on the internet and spreads far beyond its creator's original social network, people describe this as 'viral' or 'going viral'.

▲ Figure 8.8 Examples of buttons that allow users to share content

Comments and quotes

Social networking communities provide different ways for members to write comments about other members' posts. This functionality allows members to have online conversations and to communicate with each other.

▲ Figure 8.9 Examples of buttons that allow users to comment on content

---

▲ Figure 8.5 A social network map that shows the connections between members in a professional network; each **cluster** represents members who work in one particular industry

GENERAL VOCABULARY

cluster a group of things that are arranged very close together

SUBJECT VOCABULARY

viral something that is circulated widely by being shared through networks to large numbers of internet users

Third-party integration

Many websites now include direct links to social networking sites so that people can easily share the information provided on the third-party website.

SKILLS ADAPTIVE LEARNING

> **ACTIVITY**
>
> ▼ **FEATURES OF SOCIAL MEDIA NETWORKING SITES**
>
> Identify and label the following features of social networking sites on the post shown in Figure 8.10.
> - Tag
> - Share
> - Like
> - Connect

▲ Figure 8.10 A post

ADDITIONAL FEATURES OF SOCIAL NETWORKING COMMUNITIES

Add content to posts

Allowing members to add content such as photographs, videos and URLs to their posts means that members can share their experiences in different ways. This feature usually allows users to **preview** the content before they post it.

Private or direct messages

Most social networking communities allow their members to send private messages to each other, rather than having to post messages publicly.

Notifications

Notifications tell members about new activities within a social networking community. They help keep members involved with the rest of the community.

▲ Figure 8.11 Examples of notification icons

GENERAL VOCABULARY

preview see a document, page or film before it is produced in its final form and published

SUBJECT VOCABULARY

notification an alert that tells a user about a new interaction or new content within a social networking community

Analytics

Many social network communities also allow their members to see information about how other people have reacted to their posts. This type of **analytics** service helps individuals and organisations to identify their most effective communications so that they can increase the size of their networks and gain new followers.

The size and activity of the social networking community is also important. As more members engage with the community, organisations are more likely to pay to promote their posts on that community as it provides them with a bigger market.

> **SUBJECT VOCABULARY**
>
> **analytics** information that results from the analysis of data

▲ **Figure 8.12** Examples of analytics services that are available on social networking communities

ONLINE GAMING COMMUNITIES

Examples of online gaming include PlayStation Network, Xbox Live, Steam©[10] and **Massively Multiplayer Online Role-playing Games** (MMORPGs).

THE FUNCTION OF ONLINE GAMING COMMUNITIES

Online gaming communities exist in order to allow members of the community to play **multiplayer games** together.

FEATURES THAT ENABLE THE FUNCTION OF ONLINE GAMING COMMUNITIES

The features that support the function of online gaming communities include:

- links to social media
- user profiles
- information that allows users to find out how to complete games
- **experience points** that can be tracked and displayed on a user's profile. This enables other users to choose to compete against other players based on their levels of experience, making competitions more or less challenging.
- discussion boards and **forums** that allow members to discuss **tactics**
- statuses that allow users to see if other members are online
- notifications about what is happening in the game.

> **SUBJECT VOCABULARY**
>
> **Massively Multiplayer Online Role-playing Game** (MMORPG) an online video game that allows large numbers of people to play together
>
> **multiplayer games** games that are played by more than one person, usually online
>
> **experience points** credits earned by a user for completing one part of a game
>
> **forum** a website or web page where users can post comments and information and reply to other users' comments
>
> **GENERAL VOCABULARY**
>
> **tactics** the methods used to achieve a goal

[10] ©2016 VALVE CORPORATION. STEAM AND THE STEAM LOGO ARE TRADEMARKS AND/OR REGISTERED TRADEMARKS OF VALVE CORPORATION IN THE U.S. AND/OR OTHER COUNTRIES. ALL RIGHTS RESERVED.

UNIT 3 — ONLINE COMMUNITIES

ONLINE WORK SPACES

Examples of online work spaces include Adobe® Connect™ [11], Slack®, Microsoft SharePoint® and Workplace by Facebook.

THE FUNCTION OF ONLINE WORK SPACES

Online work spaces exist so that members of the community can collaborate together for the purposes of work.

FEATURES THAT ENABLE THE FUNCTION OF ONLINE WORK SPACES

The features that support the function of online work spaces include:

- **cloud storage** and web applications that allow members to work on documents through web browsers
- comments that can be left on documents for other users to see and reply to
- enabling documents to be edited at the same time by two or more members, which allows users to develop the documents together
- messaging systems so that members can discuss the work
- shared calendars so users can see each other's diaries and arrange meetings
- shared **contact lists**
- **chat rooms** to allow discussion of work
- systems for booking resources such as ICT equipment, meeting rooms and transport
- virtual meeting spaces with the ability for members to:
  - give and watch presentations
  - speak to each other using VoIP
  - use video conferencing tools.

> **SUBJECT VOCABULARY**
>
> **cloud storage** storage provided by servers that are connected to the internet
>
> **contact list** a virtual address book that allows users to quickly access the contact details of friends and colleagues
>
> **chat room** a place on the internet where users can write messages to other people and receive messages back from them immediately

VIRTUAL LEARNING ENVIRONMENTS

Examples of **virtual learning environments** (VLEs) include Pearson Active Teach, Google Classroom™ [12], Moodle™, Schoology® and Blackboard®.

THE FUNCTION OF VLES

VLEs are used to allow students and teachers to use learning and assessment materials.

FEATURES THAT ENABLE THE FUNCTION OF VLES

The features that support the function of VLEs are very similar to those found in online work spaces. In addition, many VLEs look like and work in a similar way to social networking communities, but they do not aim to connect users with people outside their network.

Features of VLEs include:

- a wall or timeline similar to those on social networking communities that contains posts by teachers and students
- a notice board for announcements about the course
- the ability to share audio, video, web links or files
- quizzes or multiple choice tests that are often graded automatically
- tools for submitting assignments

> **SUBJECT VOCABULARY**
>
> **virtual learning environments** (VLEs) websites that contain teaching and learning tools

[11] ADOBE® CONNECT™ IS A REGISTERED TRADEMARK OF ADOBE SYSTEMS INCORPORATED IN THE UNITED STATES AND/OR OTHER COUNTRIES

[12] GOOGLE CLASSROOM IS A TRADEMARK OF GOOGLE INC. USE OF THIS TRADEMARK IS SUBJECT TO GOOGLE BRAND PERMISSIONS

SUBJECT VOCABULARY

moderate decide whether content is appropriate; moderators decide whether posts should be removed or posted at all

single sign on (SSO) a system that allows users to log in once to access a number of related websites and systems

gradebook a virtual method of recording students' scores on assignments and tests

- communication tools, with posts usually **moderated** by the teacher:
  - forums for discussions
  - chat rooms
  - wikis
  - blogs
- third-party integration, such as social networking features.

VLEs also have the following additional features.

- **Log-in system:** This is often linked to the school or college's information management systems so that students are logged in automatically if they are already registered on their institution's network. This is known as **single sign on**.
- **Document editors:** These allow teachers to create and edit documents that students can use and sometimes collaborate on with their teachers.
- **Gradebooks:** These allow teachers and students to monitor progress through course materials and assignments.
- **Access statistics:** These allow teachers to track how frequently students access and use the VLE's facilities.

USER-GENERATED REFERENCE SITES

User-generated reference sites are information websites created and maintained by communities of members.

SUBJECT VOCABULARY

wiki a website or database that is developed by a number of collaborating users, all of whom can add and edit content

WIKIS

A **wiki** is a website or database that is developed by a number of collaborating users, all of whom can add and edit content. Examples include the online encyclopaedia, Wikipedia, and the online music database, Discogs.

The function of wikis

The function of a wiki is to allow members of the community to collaborate in order to build and edit web pages.

Features that enable the function of wikis

The features that enable the function of wikis include:

- member accounts, which allow users to track which edits have been made by which members of the community
- an edit button, which takes editors to a text editor so that they can edit the content
- structured language, which allows members to format web pages or add links to other content
- search tools.

DID YOU KNOW?
'Wiki' is a Hawaiian word that means 'fast'.

SKILLS ADAPTIVE LEARNING, EXECUTIVE FUNCTION

ACTIVITY

▼ USING WIKIS

1. Carry out an internet search using the keywords 'video Wikipedia contributes free knowledge' to find and watch Wikipedia's video, *How Wikipedia Contributes to Free Knowledge*.

2. Work with your teacher to set up your own class wiki using free online resources accessible through a search engine.

UNIT 3 — ONLINE COMMUNITIES

FORUMS

An online forum is a website or web page where users can post comments and information and reply to other users' comments. Forums are also known as bulletin boards or message boards. Examples of forums include Yahoo!® Google Groups™ [13], Stack Overflow®, Quora® and The Student Room®.

The function of forums

Forums provide members of the community with online spaces for structured discussions. Posts on the forum are arranged in topics or **threads**.

Features that enable the function of forums

The features that enable the function of a forum include:

- groups, allowing members in one group to have different levels of access or rights to members in other groups
- moderators, who are members who have the right to allow or block posts or members
- administrators, who are members with the same privileges as moderators plus some additional rights, such as being able to promote members to be moderators and **demote** moderators
- posts, which are messages sent by members to the group
- threads, which are topics for conversation, with replies usually arranged and sorted by date or topic
- sticky notes or stickies, which are threads kept at the top of the list of threads to make them easily accessible to members
- ratings, which allow members of the community to rate other members' posts and enable members to see how helpful or genuine the posts are
- private or direct message functions, which allow members of the community to send private messages to each other; sometimes these can also be seen by moderators or administrators.

Many forums also include a number of **safety features**.

- **Word or URL censoring:** When posts are submitted to a forum, they are scanned (usually automatically by software) for inappropriate words and URLs. If any are found, the post is rejected automatically or sent to moderators to check.

- **Ignore or block:** These are safety features that **mute** members or stop them from being able to access the forum. These are often applied across the whole forum by moderators or administrators.

- **Rules and responsible or acceptable use policies:** These tell members what they can and cannot do on the forum. If members break the rules, then moderators or administrators can send them a warning via private message or block them from the forum.

- **Report or flag a user or post:** This feature allows members to tell moderators if other members have broken the rules of the forum.

USER-GENERATED CONTENT

User-generated content is content available online that has been made by users of a particular site or service.

VIDEO-SHARING AND PHOTO-SHARING SITES

Examples of sites where users can share their videos and photographs include Vimeo®, Flickr®, 500px, Giphy® and YouTube®.

SUBJECT VOCABULARY

thread a series of messages concerning the same subject, written by members of an internet discussion group

GENERAL VOCABULARY

demote make someone a lower rank or remove their privileges
mute silence someone or something

---

[13] GOOGLE GROUPS™ IS A TRADEMARK OF GOOGLE INC. USE OF THIS TRADEMARK IS SUBJECT TO GOOGLE BRAND PERMISSIONS.

The function of video-sharing and photo-sharing sites

These sites allow people to access and share content created and uploaded by members of the community.

Features that enable the function of video-sharing and photo-sharing sites

The features that enable the function of video- and photo-sharing sites include:

- user accounts and profiles
- content management systems, which allow users to add content to a page or to edit content on a page
- tags to categorise shared content
- ratings, which allow users to rate shared videos and photographs
- comments, which allow people to discuss the photographs and videos that have been shared
- third-party integration such as social networking features, which allows users to share and react to uploaded videos or photographs on social networking sites.

BLOGS AND VLOGS

A **blog** is a website or web page that is updated regularly, often written like a diary or a series of articles. A **vlog** is a video blog. Examples of blog and vlog communities include Weibo®, Wordpress®, Tumblr® and YouTube.

The function of blogs and vlogs

Blog and vlog communities allow people to create online diaries of events or articles. They are very similar to wikis, but they usually contain additional features and more integration with social networking sites.

> **HINT**
>
> Individual blogs or vlogs are only called communities if two or more authors collaborate to create and update them, or if they allow interaction between the **blogger** and their readers.

Features that enable the function of blogs and vlogs

The features that enable the function of blogs and vlogs include:

- user accounts and profiles
- text editors, which allow bloggers to write and edit their content online
- upload tools for adding videos and photographs
- tags
- ratings
- comments
- third-party integration such as social networking features, which allows users to share and react to the blog or vlog.

SUBJECT VOCABULARY

blog (short for we**b** **log**) a website or web page that is updated regularly, often written like a diary or a series of articles
vlog (short for **v**ideo **log**) a video blog
blogger someone who creates or maintains a blog

SKILLS ADAPTIVE LEARNING
EXECUTIVE FUNCTION
COMMUNICATION

ACTIVITY

▼ **USING BLOGS**

Create a free account with a blogging community and write a blog diary of your week. Read the section on how to stay safe online first.

SOCIAL BOOKMARKING SITES

SUBJECT VOCABULARY

social bookmarking using tags to categorise web documents and URLs so that other people can find content by using the tags in a search

KEY POINT

Many online communities share similar features. For example, some online work spaces provide **social bookmarking** features and social networks provide features also used on forums and gaming communities. Most types of community also provide ways for their users to stay safe online.

Social bookmarking sites allow users to categorise and share web documents and URLs so that other people can access them. Examples include Pinterest®, Digg®, Pocket™, reddit® and StumbleUpon®.

THE FUNCTION OF SOCIAL BOOKMARKING SITES

Social bookmarking sites exist to allow people to share web documents and URLs with each other.

FEATURES THAT ENABLE THE FUNCTION OF SOCIAL BOOKMARKING SITES

The features that enable the function of social bookmarking sites include:
- social networking features to connect users with each other
- third-party integration such as social networking features, which allows users to share and react to content on social bookmarking sites directly from websites using buttons
- tags to organise and categorise URLs
- user accounts.

THE USE OF ONLINE COMMUNITIES FOR COMMUNICATION AND COLLABORATION ON A GLOBAL SCALE

Because of the global reach of the internet, online communities are accessed by members from all over the world. Many communities have translation tools to provide wider access to their content and services.

DID YOU KNOW?
Wikipedia is available in 292 languages. Most of the work to translate the content is done by community members.

Bar chart: Distribution of internet users by region:
- Asia: 48.4%
- Americas (North & South): 21.8%
- Europe: 19%
- Africa: 9.8%
- Oceania: 1%

▲ Figure 8.13 Distribution of 2.7 billion internet users by region in 2013

HOW TO STAY SAFE ONLINE

Most online communities have features that help members of the community to stay safe online. For more information about staying safe online, see pages 116–119.

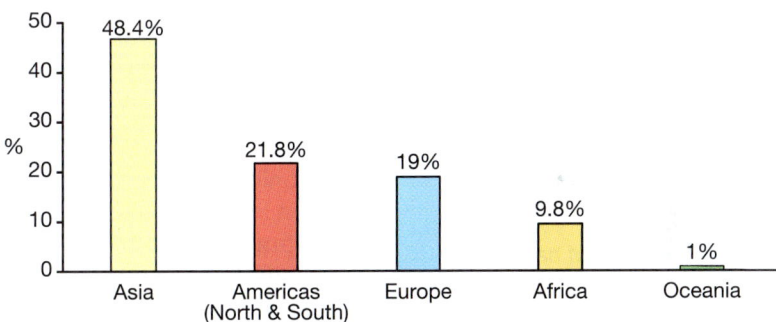

▲ Figure 8.14 Most online communities allow their members to report users who break the rules of the community. This is an example from Tumblr

ANONYMITY OF OTHERS AND MISREPRESENTATION

Members of online communities can choose to stay **anonymous** online. **Anonymity** can protect users, but it also means that some users can **misrepresent** themselves by pretending to be someone that they are not.

SKILLS PERSONAL AND SOCIAL RESPONSIBILITY
COMMUNICATION
SELF-PRESENTATION

ACTIVITY

▼ **MISREPRESENTATION**

Carry out an internet search using the key terms 'NCA CEOP Command – Who Are You Really Talking To Online?' to find the video uploaded by CEOP about misrepresentation. Discuss the video's message with your teacher and the rest of your class.

KEY POINT

Make sure you know who you are talking to online. If you get to know someone online, never arrange to meet them **in person** on your own. If someone asks you to meet them, tell an adult whom you trust.

GENERAL VOCABULARY

anonymous unidentified and unnamed
anonymity the state of being anonymous; when other people do not know who you are or what your name is
misrepresentation pretending to be someone or something that you are not
in person face-to-face; in the real world

DISCLOSURE OF PERSONAL INFORMATION OR LOCATION

GENERAL VOCABULARY

disclose make information known to other people
grooming pretending to befriend someone (often a child or young adult) with the intention of harming or abusing that person

SUBJECT VOCABULARY

geotag (verb) to add location data to a piece of content

It can be dangerous to **disclose** too much personal information online. For example, people could use this information for the purposes of **grooming** or to locate the person or their friends and family. In some cases, location data can be given away, either on purpose or by accident, by uploading **geotagged** photographs to photo-sharing sites.

Many online community apps for mobile devices enable users to include their location in their posts. This information is provided by GPS data, or calculated from data provided by the user's Wi-Fi access point or ISP data. If this feature is activated, then any member of the community can find out exactly where that person is.

To reduce the risk, online safety organisations advise individuals to think carefully about how much of their personal information they want to make public, and not to post publicly any images containing information about their location. It is also recommended that users check and update their privacy settings regularly, so that only people that they know in the real world can access their personal information online. Finally, members of online communities should report anyone who they think may be misrepresenting themselves or who is acting in a way that puts members of the community at risk.

SKILLS PERSONAL AND SOCIAL RESPONSIBILITY
COMMUNICATION
INTERPERSONAL SKILLS
INTERPRETATION
ADAPTIVE LEARNING

ACTIVITY

▼ **DISCLOSING PERSONAL INFORMATION**

Look at the social network profile shown in Figure 8.15. Analyse how the information provided in this profile could be used by criminals. How do you think this boy should change his profile in order to keep himself safe online? Discuss your ideas as a class.

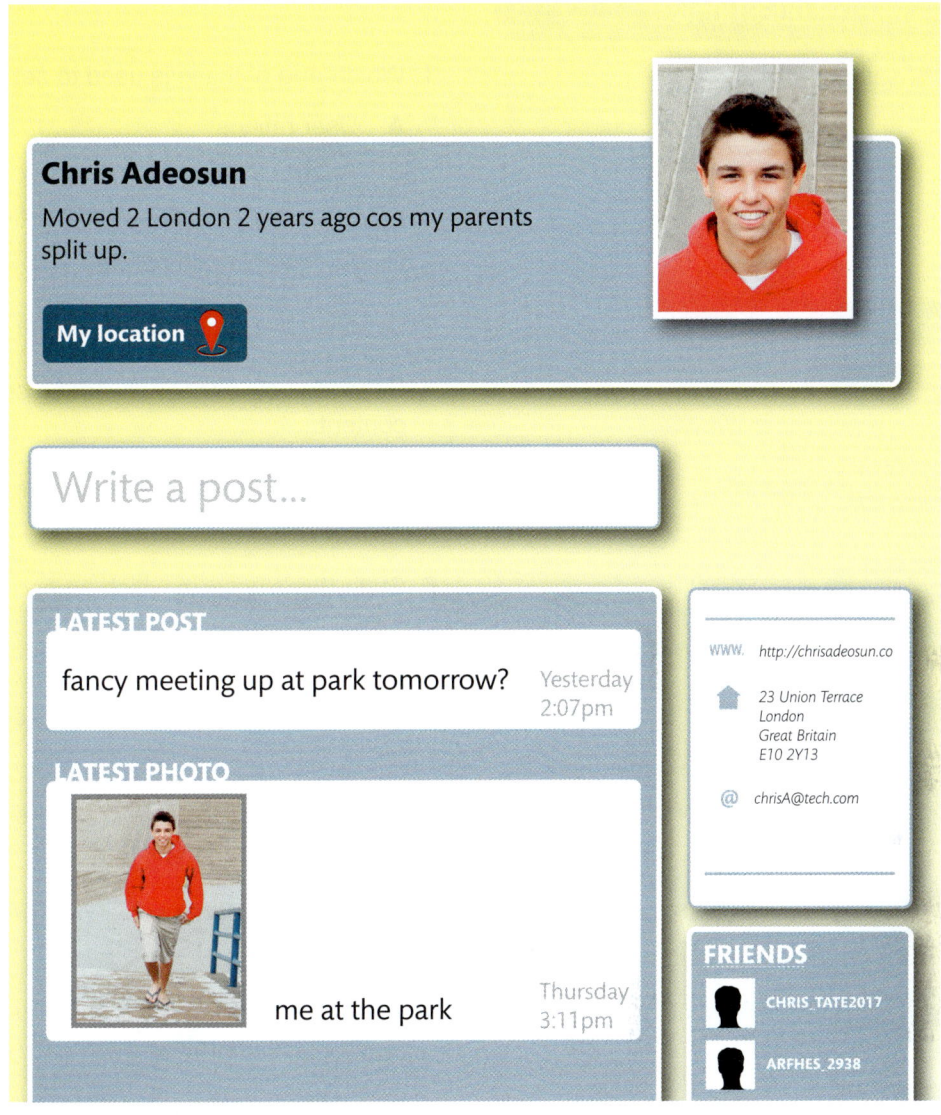

▲ **Figure 8.15** A social network profile

SKILLS PERSONAL AND SOCIAL RESPONSIBILITY
ETHICS
COMMUNICATION

ACTIVITY

▼ FAKE SOCIAL MEDIA PROFILES

How do you think you could spot a fake social media profile? Discuss this with your teacher and the rest of your class. Produce some short guidelines to help students at your school or college ensure that they do not talk to people who are misrepresenting themselves online.

CYBERBULLYING

Cyberbullying is the term used to describe the use of the internet to send text or images in order to upset or embarrass someone. For more information about cyberbullying, see page 115.

CHAPTER QUESTIONS

SKILLS PROBLEM SOLVING

1 Which **one** of these is used to set the rules for an online community? (1)
   A User ratings
   B Analytics
   C Features that allow commenting and sharing
   D Acceptable use policies

SKILLS INTERPRETATION

2 Describe the use of tags in online communities. (2)

SKILLS INTERPRETATION

3 Describe how social networking services benefit from members sharing content. (4)

SKILLS REASONING

4 Explain why some online communities have administrators and moderators. (3)

SKILLS PROBLEM SOLVING

5 State **three** ways in which a user can personalise their online profile. (3)

SKILLS PROBLEM SOLVING

6 State the function of social bookmarking (1)

SKILLS REASONING

7 Explain why online work spaces could benefit a large international organisation. (3)

SKILLS INTERPRETATION

8 Describe how social networking sites are able to make suggestions to members about people that they may want to connect with. (2)

SKILLS INTERPRETATION

9 Describe how some social networking sites are able to decide which advertisements to show to different members. (2)

SKILLS PROBLEM SOLVING

10 State **four** ways in which students can use the features of VLEs to support their learning. (4)

SKILLS PROBLEM SOLVING

11 State **three** examples of interactions that social network users can have with a member's post. (3)

SKILLS REASONING
DECISION MAKING
PERSONAL AND SOCIAL RESPONSIBILITY

12 Discuss the factors that users of social networking sites should consider when sharing personal information. (8)

9 IMPLICATIONS OF DIGITAL TECHNOLOGIES

Digital technologies are incredibly powerful tools. Their implications and how they are used will determine whether their use helps to build a better society. The use of digital technologies has changed the way in which people share and use information, images, music and films. It has introduced new challenges relating to protecting the rights of individuals while also protecting communities from harm. It forces society to rethink and question the concepts of ownership, privacy, identity, censorship and control. It can provide new ways of improving people's health and safety, while at the same time it can put people's health and safety at risk. It also helps people to understand and control their impact on the environment, but also creates new ways in which people can damage the environment.

LEARNING OBJECTIVES

- Know about data protection, the legal requirements of those storing data about individuals and an individual's legal rights
- Understand how copyright legislation affects the use of digital information and media
- Understand that individuals' movements and communications can be monitored
- Be aware of safe and responsible practice when using ICT
- Understand sustainability issues and ways of mitigating the environmental impact of digital devices
- Understand the health and safety issues that arise from individuals' use of ICT and know how they can be minimised

DATA PROTECTION

Some countries have laws to ensure that, when data is stored about individuals, that data is protected. For example, in Singapore, the Personal Data Protection Act ensures that organisations must:

- have an individual's **consent** to collect, use or disclose personal data
- collect, use or disclose personal data in an appropriate manner for the circumstances and must have informed the individual of their purposes
- collect, use or disclose personal data only for purposes that would be considered appropriate to a reasonable person in the given circumstances.

In the UK, there is a law called the Data Protection Act. This law means that organisations who are responsible for using data have to follow rules called data protection principles. These principles mean that they must make sure that the information is:

- used fairly and **lawfully**
- used for limited, **specifically** stated purposes

GENERAL VOCABULARY

consent permission to do something
lawfully keeping to the law
specifically in a detailed or exact way

UNIT 3 — IMPLICATIONS OF DIGITAL TECHNOLOGIES

GENERAL VOCABULARY

adequate large enough in quantity or good enough in quality
European Economic Area (EEA) an area in which goods and services can be traded freely, formed in 1993 by the countries of the European Union (EU) with Norway and Iceland

- used in a way that is **adequate**, relevant and not excessive
- accurate
- kept for no longer than is absolutely necessary
- handled according to people's data protection rights
- kept safe and secure
- not transferred outside the **European Economic Area** without adequate protection.

Under the Data Protection Act, individuals whose data is stored by organisations have the right to:

- access a copy of the information comprised of their personal data
- object to data processing that is likely to cause or is causing damage or distress to the individual
- prevent processing for direct marketing, such as being sent newsletters or emails
- object to decisions that are taken by automated means
- have inaccurate personal data **rectified**, blocked, erased or destroyed in certain circumstances
- claim **compensation** for damages caused by a **breach** of the Act.

GENERAL VOCABULARY

rectified corrected
compensation money paid to someone because they have suffered injury or loss
breach an action that breaks a law, rule or agreement

SKILLS DECISION MAKING
PERSONAL AND SOCIAL RESPONSIBILITY
ETHICS

ACTIVITY

▼ **COMPARING DATA PROTECTION LAW**

Compare the data protection laws from the UK and Singapore. What are the differences?

SKILLS DECISION MAKING
PERSONAL AND SOCIAL RESPONSIBILITY
ETHICS

ACTIVITY

▼ **DATA PROTECTION IN YOUR COUNTRY**

1 Investigate whether your country has laws that protect the data that is stored about individuals.
2 Research a country that does not have data protection laws.

KEY POINT

International agreements are very important to ensure that international organisations can act lawfully.

KEY POINT

Depending on the online services that you use, your data could be stored in countries that have different data protection laws or no data protection laws at all. This means that you would not be able to take action if your rights were abused.

Some countries have international agreements that mean that data can be transferred between countries in the knowledge that they will receive adequate protection.

One example of this is the EU-US Privacy Shield Framework, which aims to ensure that data is protected when it is transferred between the United States of America and countries in the European Union (EU). This is important for American companies like Microsoft®, Amazon®, Twitter and Google™, all of which have large data storage centres in the Republic of Ireland.

SKILLS CRITICAL THINKING
PERSONAL AND SOCIAL RESPONSIBILITY

ACTIVITY

▼ **THE PRIVACY SHIELD FRAMEWORK**

Research how the Privacy Shield Framework protects data transferred between the United States of America and countries in the EU.

COPYRIGHT LEGISLATION

Copyright is a legal power that provides the creator of an original work with the **sole** authority to use and distribute it.

Individual countries have their own laws relating to copyright, and individuals and organisations must obey the laws of the countries in which they operate. Some countries have agreements to stop a publisher stealing work from an author in one country and publishing it in another country. Just like international data protection agreements, international copyright agreements are becoming increasingly important as business becomes more international, partly thanks to the internet.

When a user downloads original work such as software, books, music, images or videos, the work that they download may be protected by copyright. If they live in a country with copyright laws, or a country that is part of an international agreement, then using someone else's work without permission could result in the user facing legal action from the work's copyright owner.

Copyright owners can choose to distribute their works under licences that users must pay for, such as when buying a music track or an app from an online store. Copyright owners can also choose to distribute their works under free licences such as open source or Creative Commons licences, which allow the owner to distribute their work without payment and say how their work can be used.

> **DID YOU KNOW?**
> Creative Commons licences allow owners to distribute their work freely but still protect their rights by specifying how their work can be used, shared and altered by other people.

GENERAL VOCABULARY

legislation a law or set of laws
copyright a legal power that provides the creator of an original work with the sole authority to use and distribute it
sole not shared with anyone else

▲ Figure 9.1 A copyright notice can be used to inform users that work is protected by **legislation**

KEY POINT

In order to protect owners' rights, people must be sure they have the permission to download, use or distribute work.

SKILLS PERSONAL AND SOCIAL RESPONSIBILITY
INTEGRITY
INTERPRETATION
COMMUNICATION
CREATIVITY

ACTIVITY

▼ **CREATIVE COMMONS LICENCES**

1 Research Creative Commons licences. You could do this by doing an internet search using the key terms 'creative commons kiwi video' to find the video, *Creative Commons Kiwi*, which explains how the different licences work.

2 Create a poster that explains the different types of Creative Commons licences that are available.

> **KEY POINT**
> The use of free software licences has made it cheaper for people to access technology, which has helped to narrow the digital divide. This has improved people's access to knowledge, which has helped to narrow the information gap. For more information about the digital divide and the information gap, see pages 125–131.

> **GENERAL VOCABULARY**
> **exemption** having permission to not obey a rule or law
> **parody** an exaggerated imitation for the purpose of humour

> **SUBJECT VOCABULARY**
> **geoblocking** limiting access to internet content based on the user's geographical location (also known as **geolocation rights management**)

When a customer pays for apps, books, music, images or videos, they pay for the right to use them, but this does not usually also include the right to distribute them to others.

Exemption from copyright applies in some situations. In many countries, such as the UK, an example of this is **fair use**. Some examples of fair use are:

- copies, such as copies of books or documents, made by libraries, educational establishments, museums or archives
- recordings of broadcasts for archive purposes
- uses for the benefit of people with a disability
- for non-commercial research or private study
- when used in **parody**.

In order to check that copyright law is not being broken, owners of digital works can protect their work by using copy protection and digital rights management (DRM). These systems are designed to check that the device on which the work is opened is allowed to open it. For example, music files that are downloaded using Apple iTunes®[14] are often protected with DRM.

Geoblocking is often used to prevent online users from accessing digital content. This prevents users in countries with different legal frameworks from accessing copyrighted work.

▲ **Figure 9.2** Organisations can use geoblocking to prevent global access to their work

MONITORING INDIVIDUALS

Digital technologies can be used to monitor individuals. This can have benefits but it can also have significant drawbacks and is considered **controversial**.

> **KEY POINT**
> The use of digital devices and software to monitor individuals is controversial because it affects their right to privacy. It has both benefits and drawbacks for individuals.

> **GENERAL VOCABULARY**
> **controversial** likely to provoke public disagreement

MOVEMENTS

> **SUBJECT VOCABULARY**
> **closed circuit television** (CCTV) a system of cameras placed in public buildings or in the street that are used to help prevent crime

Individuals' movements can be monitored using many methods. Examples include:

- **closed circuit television** (CCTV), which sometimes uses facial recognition software
- automatic number plate recognition (ANPR) cameras used by law enforcement agencies such as the police
- monitoring the use of identification cards, travel cards, passports at borders and bank card transactions

14 ITUNES® IS A TRADEMARK OF APPLE INC., REGISTERED IN THE U.S. AND OTHER COUNTRIES

- identifying devices on networks by their IP or MAC address
- using GPS data shared by apps such as friend finder apps for mobile devices
- GPS trackers that can be attached to items of clothing such as belts.

SKILLS — INTELLECTUAL INTEREST AND CURIOSITY, PERSONAL AND SOCIAL RESPONSINILITY

ACTIVITY

▼ ANTI SURVEILLANCE CLOTHING

Some companies produce clothing that is designed to fool facial recognition systems.

Clothing patterns can contain features that the software interprets as a face. This overloads the system with data, meaning that it is less likely to recognise the actual face of the person wearing the clothing.

1. Investigate how facial recognition software recognises points on a person's face.
2. Do an internet search using the key terms 'Anti surveillance clothing revealed' to watch a video and find other online information about how some clothing is designed to confuse facial recognition technology by overloading it with the very thing it is searching for.
3. Investigate how some CCTV cameras use infra-red light to capture footage in low light or no light areas.
4. Do an internet search using the key terms 'Anti surveillance eyewear infrared' to watch a video and find other online information about how some eyewear is designed to reflect the infra-red light used by CCTV cameras, thereby blocking them from being able to record a face.

DID YOU KNOW?

Some companies produce clothing that is designed to fool facial recognition software. The clothing patterns contain features that the software interprets as a face. This overloads the system with data, meaning that it is less likely to notice the actual face of the person wearing the clothing.

▲ **Figure 9.3** Fashion can be used as camouflage against monitoring systems such as facial recognition software

There are benefits to monitoring individuals' movements, such as being able to:

- find people who are lost, especially young children
- locate nearby friends in order to arrange to meet socially
- identify people on networks

- identify and locate potential criminals at events, such as checking at sporting events for fans who take part in violent behaviour
- keep travellers safe, such as by checking for potential criminals at airports
- verify individuals for financial transactions in order to reduce financial crime.

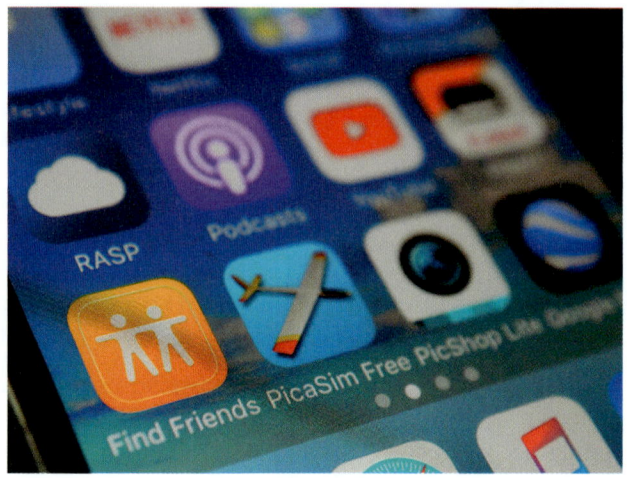

▲ Figure 9.4 Apps provide users with ways of locating their friends and family, though users usually have to give their consent before the app can make their location available to others

However, there are also drawbacks to monitoring individuals' movements, such as:

- compromising people's privacy
- the expense of setting up, monitoring and maintaining systems
- the energy consumption of the systems and the effect on the environment
- making people feel as though they are not trusted.

DID YOU KNOW?
Some parents can use locator devices that clip onto their children's clothing or bags. These devices send an alert to a paired device if their child goes outside a pre-set range.

SKILLS — PERSONAL AND SOCIAL RESPONSIBILITY
REASONING
COMMUNICATION
INTERPERSONAL SKILLS

ACTIVITY

▼ **MONITORING PEOPLE'S LOCATION**

Research the number of children that were reported missing in your country last year. Discuss whether you think it is right for parents to track their children's location. Can you explain your reasons?

COMMUNICATIONS

DID YOU KNOW?
UK mobile phone and internet service providers must keep a record of all customers' phone and online activity for one year.

There are many ways in which individuals' communication can be monitored. For example, parents can use parental control software to monitor their children's online activity and use of applications. Text messages, emails, posts on social networking sites, comments on blogs and web histories are just a few examples of communications that can be monitored and recorded.

In the UK, the Investigatory Powers Act 2016 allows the police and many other agencies to access these kinds of digital communication. This law is controversial and human rights organisations have voiced concerns about the use of these powers.

UNIT 3
IMPLICATIONS OF DIGITAL TECHNOLOGIES
153

▲ Figure 9.5 Some of the most common terms used in the UK's Investigatory Powers Act 2016

> **KEY POINT**
>
> The right to privacy is in conflict with governments' responsibility to protect their citizens.

SAFE AND RESPONSIBLE PRACTICE

Digital technologies offer great opportunities for individuals. However, there are risks associated with their use. For more information about the safe use of digital technologies, see pages 116–119.

SUSTAINABILITY ISSUES

The use of ICT can negatively affect the environment. For example, it can use up natural resources and contributes to long-term harm to the **ecology** of the planet. Table 9.1 shows three ways in which the use of ICT can cause **sustainability** issues and lists some of the ways in which the effects of these issues can be **mitigated**.

▼ Table 9.1 Sustainability issues and mitigating the effects

> **GENERAL VOCABULARY**
>
> **ecology** the biological science that looks at the way in which organisms interact with each other and their environment
> **sustainability** not using up natural resources until they run out; maintaining the balance of nature
> **mitigate** reduce the severity of a problem
> **renewable energy** a source of energy that will not run out when it is used, such as wind power or solar power
> **non-renewable energy** a source of energy that cannot be replaced once it has been used, such as coal or gas
> **energy-efficient** using as little energy as possible
> **hydroelectric** using water power to produce electricity

CAUSE	SUSTAINABILITY ISSUE	MITIGATION
Power requirements of digital devices	The power is produced using **non-renewable energies**, which reduce the planet's natural resources	• Using **renewable energies** • Using more **energy-efficient** devices • Building data centres next to rivers to make use of natural **hydro-electric** power
Power requirements of cooling systems in data centres	Cooling systems use a lot of power, which is produced using non-renewable fuel sources and reduces the planet's natural resources	Building data centres in cold climates to reduce the need to artificially cool the rooms using air conditioners, which use a lot of energy
Use of poisonous substances such as bromine, mercury and chlorine in digital devices	When devices are thrown away, these chemicals leak out and can cause health risks to people's cardiovascular and central nervous systems and to wildlife; they may also cause cancer and lung disease	• Education • Recycling schemes • Laws, such as the EU's Waste Electrical and Electronic Equipment Directive • Using harmless alternative materials for components

DID YOU KNOW?

- The world's biggest data centre uses over 386 million litres of cooling fluid per year.
- Google uses recycled canal water and seawater to cool its data centres in Belgium and Finland.

▲ Figure 9.6 Facebook built this data centre in northern Sweden so that it is cooled by Sweden's cold climate rather than an air conditioning system

SKILLS — INTELLECTUAL INTEREST AND CURIOSITY
PERSONAL AND SOCIAL RESPONSIBILITY

ACTIVITY

▼ **REDUCING THE ENVIRONMENTAL IMPACT**

There are 62 different types of metals that are used in the average smartphone. In 2013, academics at Yale University in the United States of America tried to identify possible replacements for these metals in order to reduce the environmental impact of manufacturing smartphones. They concluded that 12 of these materials could not be replaced by any other substances.

1 Investigate some of the metals used inside smartphones.

2 Do an internet search using the key terms 'Singapore NEA e-waste recycling' to find out about Singapore's guidance on recycling digital devices.

3 Does your country have an e-waste recycling system? What guidance on e-waste recycling is provided by your government?

GENERAL VOCABULARY

implication a possible future effect or result of an action, event or decision

For more information about the sustainability **implications** of digital technologies, see *Unit 1 Digital devices* (page 20).

HEALTH AND SAFETY ISSUES

It is important that you should know about the health and safety risks associated with digital technologies, for both yourself and for others. You also need to know what causes those risks and how to minimise them.

IMPLICATIONS OF DIGITAL TECHNOLOGIES

▼ Table 9.2 Risks to health and safety, their causes and ways of minimising the risk

RISK	CAUSE	HOW TO MINIMISE
Eye dryness and eye fatigue	Looking at a screen for long periods of time can cause dry, sore eyes. Human eyes are sensitive to the short wavelength (blue and blue-green) light emitted by LEDs used in digital devices. Some scientists have said that this can affect our sleep.	• Take breaks and look away from the screen into the distance regularly • Make sure the screen is not too close • Use a large enough screen • Use blue light filters • Use screens that do not flicker • Use suitable lighting and reduce glare of sunlight through windows
Repetitive Strain Injury (RSI), such as Carpal Tunnel Syndrome, which is pain caused by compressing the nerve in the wrist	• Using devices incorrectly • Poor posture (see Figure 9.9)	• Use ergonomic devices • Use ergonomic supports such as wrist pads (see Figure 9.11)
Back and neck ache	Poor posture	• Maintain correct posture when using devices (see Figure 9.8)
Trip hazards	Trailing wires	• Good cable management • Tidy and secure cables in trunking (see Figure 9.12)
Electric shock	• Damaged cables • Liquid on devices	• Use residual current devices (RCDs) on the supply to the electrical circuit • Regular cable inspections • Repair or replace damaged cables • No liquids near devices
Fire	• Overheating • Overloaded plug sockets	• Use cooling devices • Regular maintenance • Install fire extinguishers • Ensure that plug sockets contain fuses that are suitable for the devices that are plugged into them
Injury or death	Failing to notice immediate danger because of distractions caused by a digital device such as a smartphone	Do not use or be distracted by devices when near roads and other hazards

GENERAL VOCABULARY

flicker shine with an unsteady light that goes on and off quickly
glare a bright unpleasant light that hurts the eyes
repetitive strain injury (RSI) pain caused by repeating the same movement many times
posture the way in which you position your body while standing or sitting
ergonomic designed for efficiency and comfort, especially in a working environment
trip hazard an object that a person could trip over
trunking tubes or channels designed to contain cables
residual current device (RCD) a device that interrupts an electrical current to prevent electric shock
overload put too much electricity through an electrical system or piece of equipment
fire extinguisher a metal container with water or chemicals in it, used for stopping small fires
plug socket a point in a wall where you can connect equipment to the supply of electricity
fuse a safety device used in plugs and plug sockets that breaks an electrical current if too much electrical current is supplied

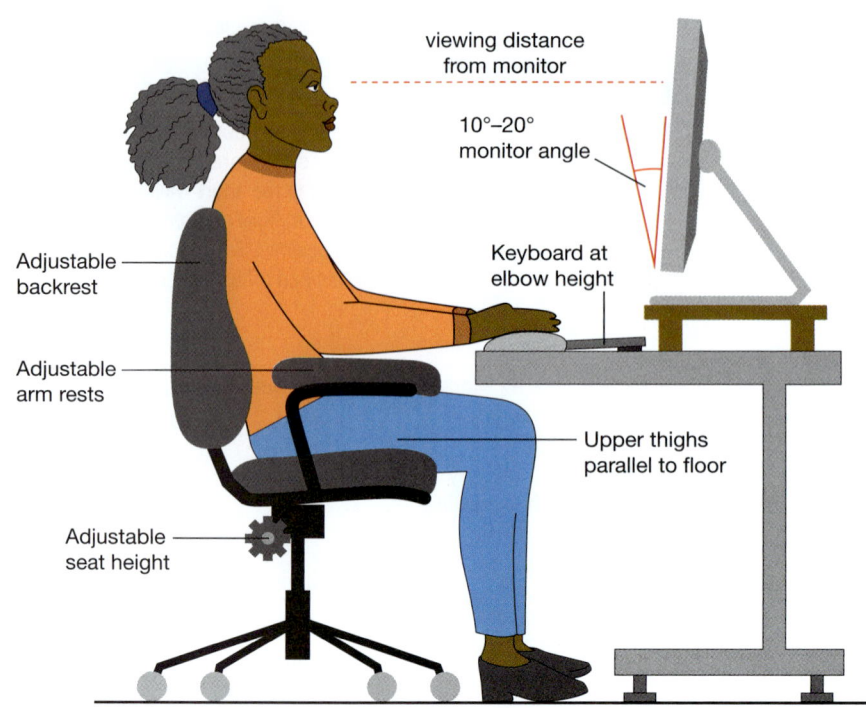

▲ Figure 9.7 Maintaining good posture when sitting at a computer

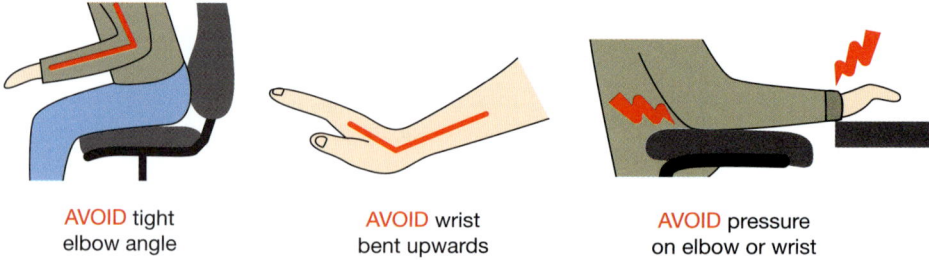

▲ Figure 9.8 Incorrect posture can cause health problems

SKILLS INTELLECTUAL INTEREST AND CURIOSITY
PERSONAL AND SOCIAL RESPONSIBILITY
COMMUNICATION
INTERPERSONAL SKILLS

ACTIVITY

▼ DIGITAL DEVICES AND PERSONAL SAFETY

Do an internet search using the key terms 'ABC News texting while walking' to find an ABC News report, *Texting While Walking Accidents*. Watch the video and then discuss the safety issues related to texting while walking and driving.

SKILLS INTELLECTUAL INTEREST AND CURIOSITY
PERSONAL AND SOCIAL RESPONSIBILITY
INTERPRETATION

ACTIVITY

▼ USING SOCKETS SAFELY

Search 'electrical safety first' and find their guide to avoiding overloading electrical sockets. What do you think of this advice? Is it helpful?

UNIT 3 IMPLICATIONS OF DIGITAL TECHNOLOGIES 157

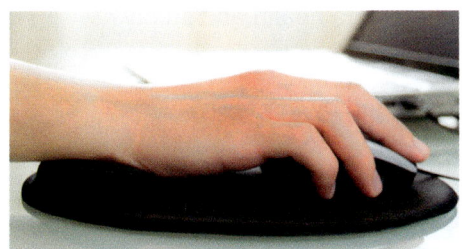

▲ **Figure 9.9** Use of wrist pads can help maintain good posture and reduce the risk to health

▲ **Figure 9.10** Good cable management helps minimise risks to health and safety

As we increase the number of decisions that technology makes for us in our everyday lives, we reduce the control that we have over important decisions that can have an impact on our health and safety. For example, **artificial intelligence** (AI) is now used in self-driving cars and it can make decisions about whether the car should apply the brakes if it is likely to crash into the car ahead, or whether it should swerve to avoid another vehicle. These cars can use sensors to detect whether the car is crossing a lane divider in the road in order to prevent the car drifting into the wrong lane. AI can also read speed limit signs, adjusting the car's speed in order to ensure that the car does not travel faster than the speed limit.

These are all useful tools. However, these AI systems do not have human judgment and cannot apply common sense. Consider the following situations.

- What if a car needs to travel over the speed limit, perhaps to avoid a hazard? Would AI software prevent the car from doing this if it was also supposed to stay under the speed limit?

- What if a car had to swerve to avoid another vehicle, but in doing so veers off the road and into a **pedestrian**? What would the computer decide to do in that situation? Can we know what it decided to do? Can we hold it responsible?

SUBJECT VOCABULARY

artificial intelligence (AI) the ability of a computer program to make decisions that would otherwise be made by humans

DID YOU KNOW?
It is estimated that 94% of car accidents are caused by human error. However, a computer can react much faster than a human.

GENERAL VOCABULARY

pedestrian a person who is walking

KEY POINT
People must be responsible in their use of digital technologies. Digital technologies are not yet capable of human judgement, which means that they are not yet capable of taking ethical or moral responsibility for their actions.

DID YOU KNOW?
The longer that people are not engaged in the driving process because a computer is controlling the vehicle, their reaction times get slower. In some instances, researchers found that people can even fall asleep, leaving the computer to control the vehicle.

SKILLS INTERPRETATION
DECISION MAKING
PERSONAL AND SOCIAL RESPONSIBILITY
INTELLECTUAL INTEREST AND CURIOSITY

ACTIVITY

▼ **USING AUTOPILOT**

Research the use of autopilot in aeroplanes. Do you think humans need to be in control of an aircraft at all times? Do you think the use of autopilot improves the health and safety of passengers and crew?

CHAPTER QUESTIONS

SKILLS PROBLEM SOLVING / ETHICS

1. Which **one** of these is used to reduce the risk to health and safety? (1)
   - A Using a small monitor
   - B Increasing the amount of blue light emitted by a screen
   - C Using an RCD
   - D Working in a room with low-level lighting

SKILLS REASONING / PERSONAL AND SOCIAL RESPONSIBILITY

2. Explain why free software licences have helped to reduce the digital divide. (2)

SKILLS REASONING / PERSONAL AND SOCIAL RESPONSIBILITY

3. Explain why users should be able to give their consent before an app shares their location. (2)

SKILLS INTERPRETATION

4. State **three** types of digital information that can be protected by copyright. (3)

SKILLS INTERPRETATION

5. State **one** method of monitoring an individual's movements and describe how it is used. (2)

SKILLS REASONING

6. Explain why owners of digital information may decide to use copyright. (2)

SKILLS REASONING

7. State **one** benefit to individuals of having their location monitored. (1)

SKILLS REASONING

8. State **one** benefit to individuals of having their communications monitored. (1)

SKILLS REASONING

9. State **one** drawback to individuals of monitoring their location and communications. (1)

SKILLS DECISION MAKING

10. State **three** ways in which organisations should act responsibly to make sure that they protect the data they hold about individuals. (3)

SKILLS REASONING / PERSONAL AND SOCIAL RESPONSIBILITY

11. Explain why the large-scale use of online storage and applications can have a negative effect on the environment. (4)

SKILLS REASONING / INTERPRETATION / PERSONAL AND SOCIAL RESPONSIBILITY

12. Describe **one** way in which individuals can reduce the effect of their use of digital devices on the environment. (3)

10 ONLINE INFORMATION

Living in a connected world means that there is a lot of information available for individuals to find. However, it can be difficult to find good quality information. When you find quality information, it is important that you know how to use it appropriately.

"Getting information off the Internet is like taking a drink from a fire hydrant"
- Mitchell Kapor

LEARNING OBJECTIVES

- Understand that information can be gathered from a wide range of sources
- Be able to select and use appropriate sources of information
- Know how to use search engines effectively
- Be able to evaluate the **fitness for purpose** of available information in terms of accuracy, age, **relevance**, reliability, **bias**
- Understand issues related to copyright: permission to use, acknowledgement of source
- Understand issues related to **plagiarism**: copy and paste, rewriting, **paraphrasing**

GENERAL VOCABULARY

fitness for purpose whether the information is suitable or good enough for the intended use
relevance whether the information relates directly to what you want to know
bias unfairly favouring one point of view, or not considering other points of view
plagiarism using someone else's work and pretending it is yours
paraphrasing expressing what someone else has said in a shorter, clearer or different way
primary source something that you have created yourself
secondary source something that has been created by someone else

INFORMATION SOURCES

Information is available from a wide range of sources. These can either be **primary sources**, which are those that you have created yourself, or **secondary sources**, which are those that have been created by someone else.

▼ Table 10.1 Examples of primary and secondary sources

PRIMARY	SECONDARY
Photographs that you have taken yourself	Newspapers, books and maps
Interviews or questionnaires conducted by you	CDs, DVDs or Blu-rays created by others
Your own blogs, social media posts or emails	Television and radio broadcasts
Your own sound or video recordings	Websites created by other people

SKILLS ADAPTIVE LEARNING

ACTIVITY

▼ **PRIMARY AND SECONDARY SOURCES**

List two more examples of primary sources and two more examples of secondary sources that could be added to Table 10.1

You can decide whether the information that you have found is appropriate for use in a document or digital product by considering whether the information is fit for purpose and for the intended audience. For more information about purpose, see page 163.

If you know the URL of the website you want to access in order to gather information, you can type its name into the address bar of a browser (see Figure 10.2).

HINT

The address bar is not the same as the search field in the web page from a search engine.

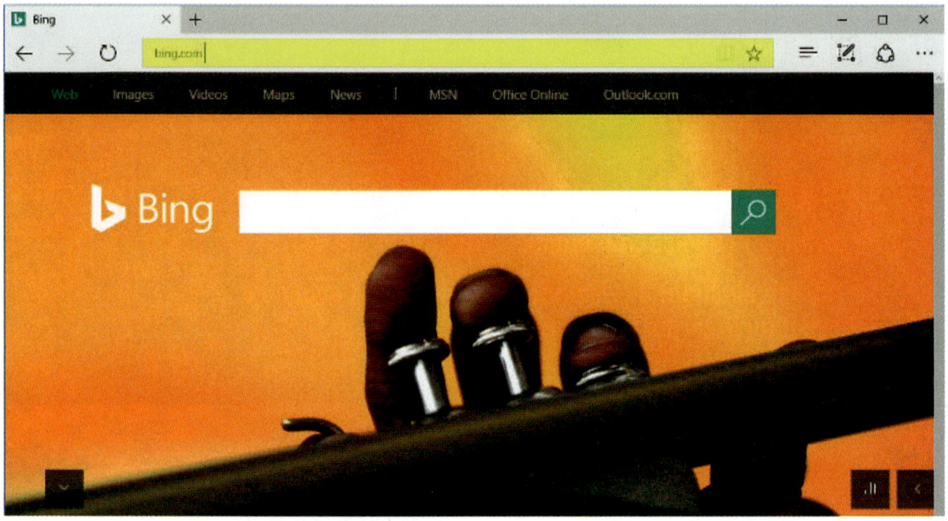

▲ Figure 10.2 The address bar in a browser

SEARCH ENGINES

If you want to find information online and do not know the URLs of any sites that contain that information, you can use a search engine. Search engines compare the words entered by a user with words in a database of web pages. They then show the user the results that are the closest match to their original keywords.

Search engines can be used in browsers, but they are also used by smart personal assistants such as Amazon's Alexa® and Apple's Siri®[14]. These personal assistants allow you to speak your search terms aloud and have results returned through a speaker.

14 SIRI® IS A TRADEMARK OF APPLE INC., REGISTERED IN THE U.S. AND OTHER COUNTRIES

▶ Figure 10.3 Have you used Siri or Alexa?

UNIT 3 — ONLINE INFORMATION

Examples of web-based search engines are:

- Bing
- Creative commons
- Duck duck go
- Google
- Yahoo

For more information about search engines, see *Unit 2 Connectivity* (page 87).

KEYWORDS

SUBJECT VOCABULARY

keywords the words or search terms that a user types into a search engine in order to look for matching information

Keywords are the words or search terms that a user types into a search engine in order to look for matching information. When entering keywords into a search engine, only enter the important words that you think websites will contain. Keep it simple and do not add too many keywords.

SEARCH TYPES

Some search engines allow you to specify the type of information that you are searching for, as shown in Figure 10.4.

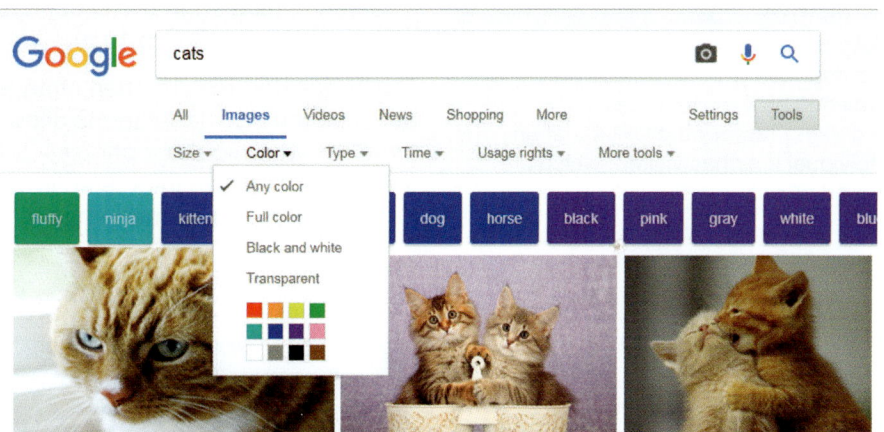

▲ Figure 10.4 Some of the types of information you can find with a search engine

SEARCH TOOLS

Search tools help you to filter the results that the search engine returns, as shown in Figures 10.5 and 10.6.

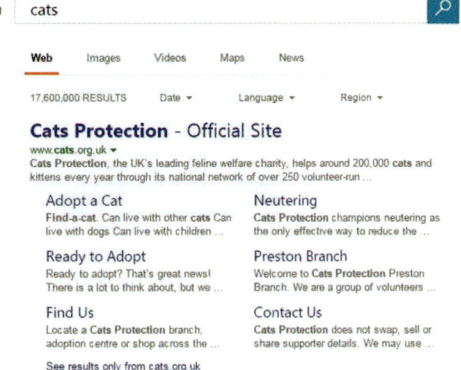

▲ Figure 10.5 Search engines can filter the results by time, date, country and more

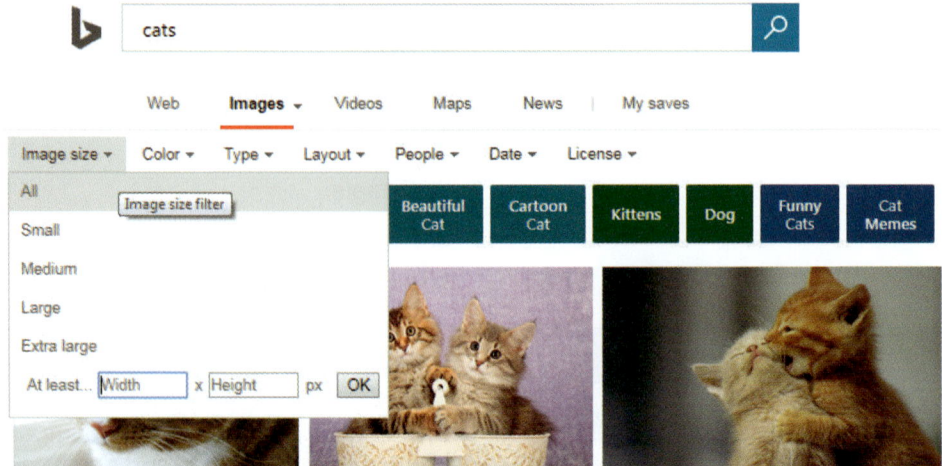

▲ Figure 10.6 When searching for images, search engines can find specific types of images, including those with different types of copyright or **usage rights**

SUBJECT VOCABULARY

usage rights the way in which a piece of information is permitted to be used

SUGGESTED SITES AND AUTOFILL

SUBJECT VOCABULARY

autofill the automatic suggestion of a completed word or phrase that is provided as the user types

browsing history the URLs that an individual user has visited, which are stored in a file

Some search engines give results using **autofill** as soon as you start to type keywords into it (see Figure 10.7). Some browsers also allow you to choose a search engine so that you can type keywords directly into the browser's address bar (see Figure 10.8).

The suggested results often change as you continue to type more text, because the additional terms allow the autofill software to narrow its search for more relevant words or phrases. Similarly, other search engines suggest sites that users might be interested in visiting. These suggested sites can be based on popular searches made by other users or your own **browsing history**.

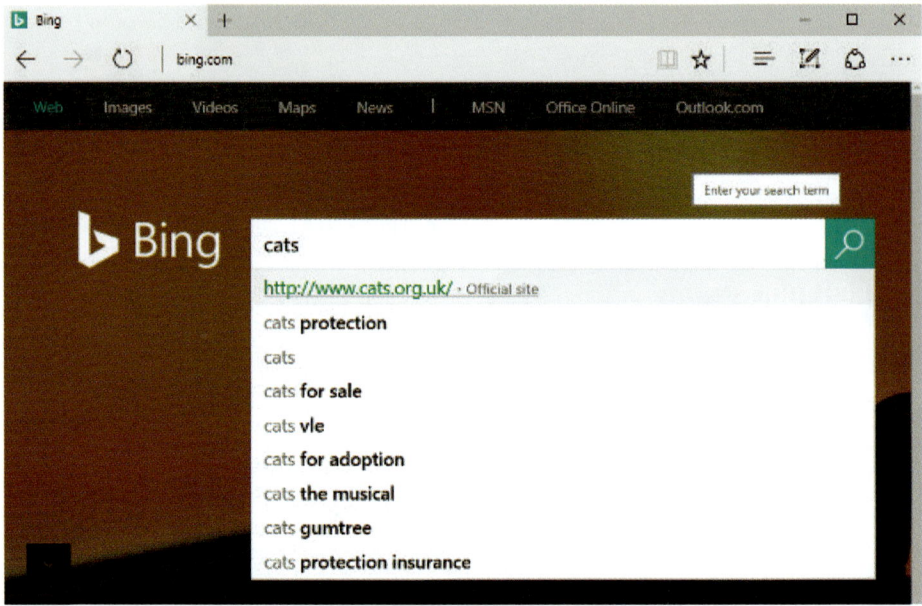

▲ Figure 10.7 Some browsers allow you to select a search engine that will show results when you type into the browser's address bar

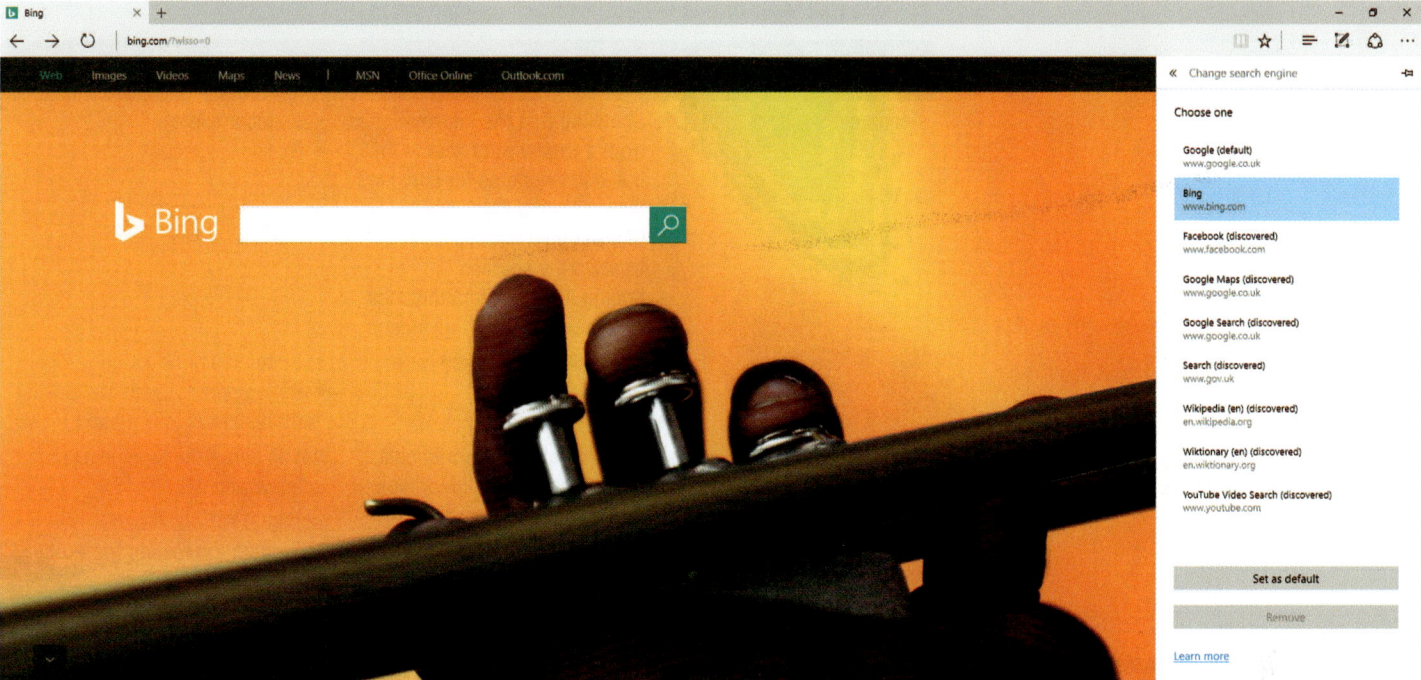

▲ Figure 10.8 You can change the browser's usual search engine in the browser's settings

> **DID YOU KNOW?**
> Some search engines keep users' data and then suggest results based on the user's search history. Others claim to protect users' privacy by not tracking their online behaviour.

SEARCH SYNTAX

SUBJECT VOCABULARY

syntax the rules that describe how words and phrases are used in a language

Syntax is the rules that dictate how words and phrases are used in languages, including computing languages. For example, you can use special characters in searches. This will make the search engine give you more specific results.

AND (+)
Adding + between words will return only results that match **both** words.

NOT (-)
Adding - before a word will return only results that **do not include** that word.

PHRASE MATCHING ("")
Placing speech marks around a group of words will return only results that **include the whole phrase** with the words in that specific order.

FITNESS FOR PURPOSE

When you use information from a primary or secondary source, you need to decide whether it is suitable or good enough for the purpose for which you are planning to use it.

▼ Table 10.2 Methods and reasons for checking information

YOU SHOULD CHECK YOUR INFORMATION'S...	BY...	OTHERWISE IT MIGHT...
Accuracy	• Checking that the information is from a trustworthy source that has good systems for checking facts before publication • Comparing it against other trustworthy sources • Seeing if the information uses evidence to support its claims	• Be incomplete • Be false
Age	Checking the publication date	• Be too old or no longer true • Be too recent if you are looking for historical information
Relevance	Checking that the information's topic matches the topic for which you intend to use it	Not be about the topic you wanted to know about
Reliability	Comparing it against other unrelated sources to see if it matches	Not match the results from other sources of information
Bias	• Checking to see if it provides a range of viewpoints • Considering whether you could use the same information to tell a story from a different perspective • Checking for missing information: are explanations given, or does the information just give the facts? • Checking the use of any statistics and questioning them: who collected the statistics and who funded the research?	• Be too focused on one side of an issue without considering other points of view • Be prejudiced

> **GENERAL VOCABULARY**
> **prejudiced** having an unreasonable dislike of someone or something

COPYRIGHT

If you use information, you should ensure that you have permission to do so. Some information will require you to state the owner or source of the information if you choose to use it. For more information about copyright legislation, see pages 149–150.

> **KEY POINT**
> In some cases, you might not be allowed to use copyrighted work, even if you state the name of the owner or source of the information.

PLAGIARISM

The internet has made information easily available to many people. However, this means that it is becoming more common for people to copy and paste information, sometimes without even checking that it is suitable or true. Sometimes, they may even claim that this information is their own. This is known as plagiarism.

▲ Figure 10.9 Just because something is on the internet doesn't make it true

| UNIT 3 | ONLINE INFORMATION | 165 |

HINT

There are special types of software that can help you to avoid plagiarism. The software will automatically search for phrases and sentences and tell you whether they already exist.

If you use another person's work but fail to state that it is theirs and not yours, you are violating their rights and committing plagiarism. If you do this in your assignments for school, college or university, you will be punished and your marks could be reduced or you could fail the assignment completely.

One way to avoid plagiarism is to rewrite or paraphrase information. When you do this, it shows that you can find information, understand its meaning and then express it in your own words. You should also state where the original information came from. If you found the information online, include the URL, the author's name (if it is available) and the date on which you found the information.

CHAPTER QUESTIONS

SKILLS — PROBLEM SOLVING

1 Which **one** of these is used to match a full phrase in a search? (1)
   A +
   B –
   C @
   D " "

SKILLS — PROBLEM SOLVING

2 State **two** ways in which an image search can be refined. (2)

SKILLS — REASONING

3 State **one** reason why you should check whether information is biased before using it. (1)

SKILLS — INTERPRETATION

4 Describe how a search engine works. (4)

SKILLS — REASONING
PERSONAL AND SOCIAL RESPONSIBILITY

5 Explain why it is important to check whether information is protected by copyright before using it in your own work. (2)

SKILLS — PERSONAL AND SOCIAL RESPONSIBILITY

6 State **one** benefit to students of rewriting information rather than copying it word-for-word. (1)

7 State **three** examples of search syntax. (3)

SKILLS — INTERPRETATION

8 Complete Table 10.3 by stating whether each source is primary or secondary. (8)

▼ **Table 10.3** Identifying primary and secondary sources

SOURCE	PRIMARY OR SECONDARY?
A podcast that you have created	
A video of a discussion that you have with an expert	
Your own copy of a film	
Notes that you take while visiting a museum	
A book that you borrow from someone	
An image that you download from the internet	
Your own recording of a radio broadcast	

ONLINE SERVICES 168   THE CLOUD 176

UNIT 4
ONLINE GOODS AND SERVICES

Assessment Objective 1
Demonstrate knowledge and understanding of Information and Communication Technology (ICT)

Assessment Objective 2
Apply knowledge, understanding and skills to produce ICT based solutions

Assessment Objective 3
Analyse, evaluate, make reasoned judgments and present conclusions

In this unit, you will learn about the types of online services, software and storage, as well as the impact that the availability and use of these has on individuals and organisations. Understanding the ways in which individuals and organisations can access and use online entertainment and commercial services provides new ways of discovering and accessing media and offers new business opportunities.

11 ONLINE SERVICES

Before the development of the internet, people were limited in their ability to access services remotely. Remote access was possible, such as by using the telephone or postal systems for studying, shopping and booking flights. However, making services available online has enabled us to access them anywhere with any connected device. This provides new opportunities, such as up-to-date personalised news and access to learning resources provided by the world's most prestigious universities. We can play synchronised multiplayer games with friends on the other side of the world, and organisations can connect a global workforce to its global customers.

LEARNING OBJECTIVES

- Understand what online services are offered by:
  - shopping sites – basket, checkout, secure payment, product catalogue
  - booking systems for travel, leisure and entertainment
  - banks
  - education and training providers – VLE, online support, online training courses, remote access
  - gaming sites
  - news and other information providers
  - auction sites
  - entertainment providers – on demand, streaming, downloads

- Understand the impact on an individual's lifestyle and behaviour of the availability of goods and services online
- Understand the impact of the internet on the ways that organisations do business
- Understand how transactional data is collected and used: what is collected, cookies, transaction tracking
- Know about targeted marketing and personalisation techniques
- Understand the features and characteristics of online services and local services

TYPES OF SERVICE

Many types of service are available online, such as shopping, banking, education and entertainment services.

SHOPPING SITES

When a user shops online, they use a **product catalogue**. For each product, the catalogue can store:

- an image of the product
- a product description
- the product's price
- **ratings** by customers, shop staff or other people on review sites
- the popularity of the product
- a product code
- the number of items in stock.

GENERAL VOCABULARY

product catalogue a list of products that can be bought
rating a measurement of how good or how popular something or someone is

Products are often grouped into types or categories. These are often displayed in menus with any sub-categories appearing in sub-menus.

KEY POINT

Customers can use the information about products to narrow their results when searching for products.

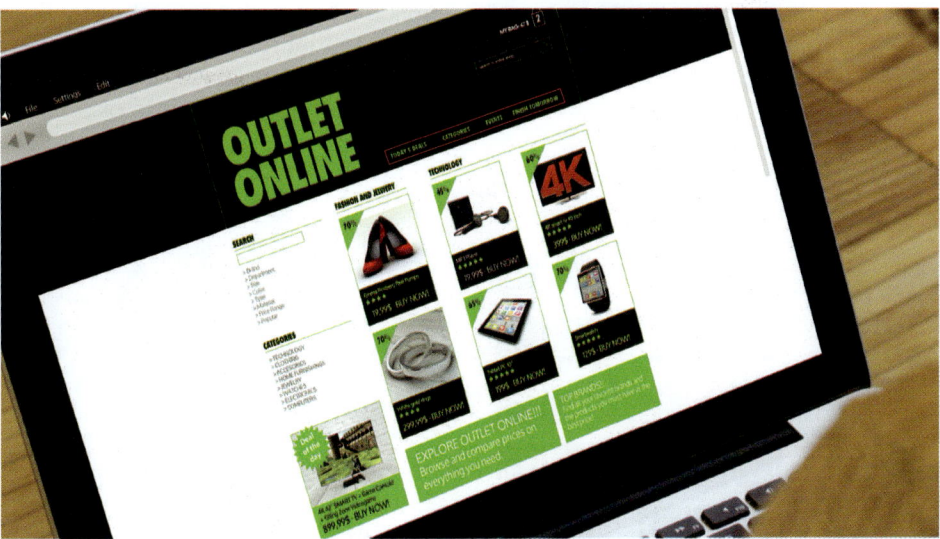

▲ **Figure 11.1** Products are often grouped into categories (shown here, highlighted in red)

When a customer selects a product, they can add it to an online basket or bag (such as 'My Bag' in in Figure 11.1). Baskets keep a record of the items that the customer selects as they shop, so that they do not have to pay for each item separately.

When the customer is ready to pay for everything in the basket, they are directed to the checkout, where they can enter their delivery details and pay for the products in their basket. Sometimes, customers can use **voucher codes** at the checkout in order to receive a discount.

SUBJECT VOCABULARY

voucher code a code representing a specified amount of money that can be used on a shopping website to purchase goods or services

If the customer does not already have an account on that website, they may be asked to create one. Often, customers can shop as a 'guest', so that they do not have to create an account. However, on some websites, this means that they cannot log into the site again later to see their shopping or follow the progress of their order.

Shopping sites often offer secure payment systems that protect customers' payment information when it is transmitted online. For more information about secure websites, see *Unit 3 Operating online* (page 104).

SKILLS EXECUTIVE FUNCTION
INTELLECTUAL INTEREST AND CURIOSITY
SELF-DIRECTION

ACTIVITY

▼ **ONLINE SHOPPING SERVICES**

Visit a shopping site and go through the stages of buying some products to see how the process works. Make sure that you do not complete the checkout procedure unless you actually want to buy those products.

BOOKING SYSTEMS

Train tickets, airline tickets and bus tickets can all be purchased online. Customers can choose their travel times, the number of tickets and the type of tickets that they wish to buy. These tickets can also be added to a basket if the customer is buying tickets for more than one trip. Tickets for leisure and entertainment can also be purchased online in this way.

When customers buy tickets using an online booking system, the tickets are often sent via email, so customers need to register an email address with the service when making purchases. For some types of travel, companies use **e-tickets** that are linked to the customer's passport so that the customer can check in. Some airlines and train companies use QR codes (matrix codes) that can be scanned at airports or on trains.

> **SUBJECT VOCABULARY**
>
> **e-ticket** an electronic version of a paper ticket

▲ Figure 11.2 Travel documents can be loaded onto a smartphone, often using an app

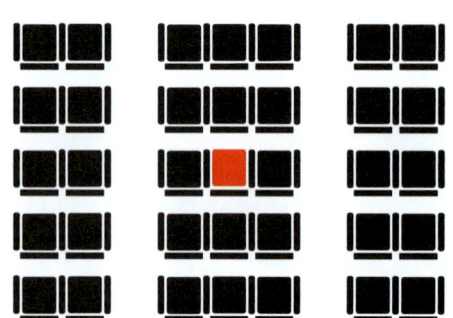

▲ Figure 11.3 Some systems let you choose specific seats

SKILLS INTERPRETATION
COMMUNICATION
INTERPERSONAL SKILLS

ACTIVITY

▼ BOOKING FLIGHTS ONLINE

How does a flight booking system automatically manage the need to only sell tickets to customers if a flight has seats available? Discuss your thoughts with your teacher and the rest of your group.

BANKS

> **GENERAL VOCABULARY**
>
> **balance** the amount of money in a bank account (also known as bank balance or account balance)

> **SUBJECT VOCABULARY**
>
> **balance alert** a service that automatically informs a customer, by text message or email, when the balance of their account reaches a specified amount

Banks offer their customers many online services, including:

- checking **balances**
- setting **balance alerts**
- making payments and transfers
- applying for loans and other financial products
- managing alerts and notifications of payments and balance amounts
- accessing customer service and help systems
- changing personal information.

EDUCATION AND TRAINING PROVIDERS

> **GENERAL VOCABULARY**
>
> **assessment** the process of judging the value or quality of something, such as the quality of a student's work

Online training courses allow learners to access:

- libraries of online journals and reference archives
- online support from teachers and other learners
- learning and **assessment** materials.

This access is provided through virtual learning environments (VLEs). For more information about the function and features of VLEs, see *Unit 3 Operating online* (page 139).

GAMING SITES

Gaming sites are online applications that allow users to play games that are hosted on a remote server. Sometimes these games are multiplayer, so that players control different characters in the game and other players can see their actions in real time. For more information about the function and features of online gaming communities, see *Unit 3 Operating online* (page 138).

NEWS AND OTHER INFORMATION PROVIDERS

News providers give up-to-date access to stories using blogs and notifications that are sent to **subscribers**. Subscribers can choose to receive alerts on stories from a range of categories.

GENERAL VOCABULARY

subscriber someone who signs up for a regular service

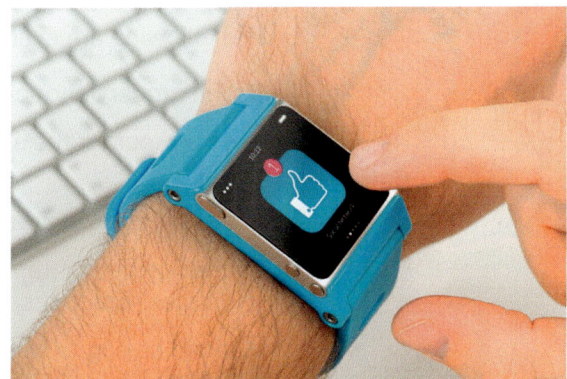

▲ **Figure 11.4** Once a user has subscribed to a service, they can be notified automatically, via an app, of any activity on that service

Other information providers can provide real-time notifications about information such as:

- weather
- sports
- stock markets
- currency values.

AUCTION SITES

GENERAL VOCABULARY

auction a public meeting or website where goods or services are sold to the person who offers the most money for them

Auction sites allow sellers to list items for sale for a certain period of time and allow buyers to offer money for these items. When the auction ends, the buyer who has offered the most money completes a checkout process similar to that used on shopping sites. For more information about shopping sites, see page 168. Most auction sites also allow sellers to list items for sale with a fixed price.

Auction sites provide ratings for buyers. A buyer with a high rating has been rated by sellers for being reliable and paying on time. Sellers can choose to only accept offers from buyers with a high rating. If a buyer does not pay, then the seller can either try to sell the item again or sell it to the buyer who offered the second highest amount of money.

Auction sites also provide ratings for sellers. A seller with a high rating has been rated by buyers for being reliable and sending items promptly. Buyers can choose not to bid on items being sold by unreliable sellers.

If a buyer offers money for an item but someone else offers more money, some auction sites will alert the first buyer via email or app notifications. Some services also alert customers if the auction on an item that they have looked at is going to end soon, so that the buyer does not miss their chance to make an offer for it.

THE IMPACT ON LIFESTYLE AND BEHAVIOUR

The online availability of goods and services has many beneficial impacts on people's lifestyles and behaviour. However, it also has drawbacks.

BENEFITS OF ONLINE GOODS AND SERVICES

Access to online services changes people's lifestyles by giving them more time to do important things such as spending time with family, socialising with friends or working. The American writer Clay Shirky argues that the build-up of free time is a new resource provided to individuals that can be used productively to do the activities that they care about.

The following are examples of the benefits of online goods and services.

Online grocery shopping allows customers to:

- easily reorder the same products that they bought last time, which saves them time
- avoid having to travel to the supermarket
- check whether items are in stock without having to walk around all the different product sections
- avoid having to wait in queues to pay.

Online booking systems for rail travel allow customers to:

- avoid having to go to the station to buy a ticket
- avoid having to queue, saving time
- buy tickets in advance of their journey, which means that they only need to arrive at the station a few minutes before the train leaves
- be notified if there is a delay to their train using live travel information apps.

Online banking allows customers to:

- avoid travelling to the bank to check balances and transfer funds between accounts
- avoid carrying cash, which is safer for the individual.

Online learning services allow users to:

- avoid having to travel to colleges or universities
- avoid having to move closer to colleges or universities, meaning that individuals do not have to move away from their family and friends.

Online information providers allow people to:

- receive weather alerts or traffic advice while they are travelling
- be **rerouted** automatically based on information about traffic conditions ahead.

GENERAL VOCABULARY

reroute to send something such as a vehicle to its original destination using a different route

DRAWBACKS OF ONLINE GOODS AND SERVICES

Some people argue that the use of online services that are constantly available means that, although people spend more time at home with their families, they spend that time using online services such as gaming and social networking sites.

The negative impact of online services on human behaviour is largely unknown. This is partly because online services have not been around long enough to allow people to understand their full impact. However, people should consider the following potential negative impacts of online goods and services.

- The immediate availability of online services could make people less patient and more demanding of others.
- People become more isolated as individuals and detached from their real-world communities, which could make us more detached from the needs of others.
- Some people constantly check their online communications, such as social networking sites, which means that they spend less time connecting with people face-to-face, which reduces their face-to-face communication skills.
- People's use of online services means that there is less need to memorise facts, so there is a negative impact on memory.
- People are becoming accustomed to skim-reading online information, which makes them less likely to pay attention to details.

Table 11.1 sets out the benefits and drawbacks of the online availability of goods and services. For more information about the impact of the internet on individuals, see *Unit 3 Operating online* (pages 110–119).

▼ Table 11.1 The benefits and drawbacks of online services on individuals' lifestyle and behaviour

BENEFITS	DRAWBACKS
More time can be spent with family and friends	More time is spent using online services
Safer lifestyle as there is no need to carry cash, which might put individuals at risk	Individuals can be inconvenienced if no connectivity is available
Individuals are more engaged with creative media like art, photography, videos and drama	Individuals may become less active because they can access services without having to move

THE IMPACT ON THE WAYS THAT ORGANISATIONS DO BUSINESS

The internet has provided new ways for people to work online, such as working from home. For more information about working from home, see *Unit 3 Operating online* (pages 119–121).

The way in which organisations do business has also changed. These changes include:

- improved communication
- access to global markets
- access to a global workforce
- use of big data to understand customer behaviour
- the way in which the organisation secures business information
- increased competition.

For more information about these positive and negative impacts, see *Unit 3 Operating online* (pages 120–121).

SUBJECT VOCABULARY

transactional data data that is sent between digital devices
track collect and analyse data
cookies information that a website leaves on a user's computer so that the website will recognise that user when they use it again
encrypt protect information by putting it into a special code that only some people can read

KEY POINT

Transactional data is not just the data moved during financial transactions, such as moving money from one place to another. It relates to the movement of any data between connected devices.

SUBJECT VOCABULARY

referring website the website previously visited, which linked the user to the website that they are currently visiting
banner advertisement an image, animation or video that displays an advertisement for a product or service in a section of a web page
ad server a web server that stores, delivers and often tracks banner advertisements

TRANSACTIONAL DATA

An online transaction occurs whenever data is sent between devices on the internet. Some of this **transactional data** can be **tracked** online by network devices. This data is stored in **cookies**. It is possible to **encrypt** cookies when they are transferred between devices online.

You have already considered the tracking of data in *Unit 2 Connectivity* (pages 80–83), when you learned about the ways in which devices are identified on a network. Data tracking was also considered in *Unit 3 Operating online* (pages 151–152), when you learned about the ways in which individuals' movements and communications can be monitored.

Examples of data that can be stored as cookies include:

- the time and date of the transaction
- IP addresses
- the **referring website**
- the products or services or the categories of products and services that a user has previously viewed or bought
- items added to the user's online shopping basket
- buttons pressed by the user
- data entered into web forms, such as name, address and credit card information.

Cookies can be manually deleted by the user or set to expire after a specified period of time, as shown in Figure 11.5.

```
HTTP/1.1 200 OK
Content-type: text/html
Set-Cookie: borg=no; Expires=Thu, 05 Apr 2063 00:00:00 GMT
```

▲ **Figure 11.5** The third line of this reply (from a web server to a client's HTTP request) shows that a cookie being sent by this server is set to expire

There are different types of cookies.

- **Session cookies:** These are only stored until a web page is closed in the browser.
- **Persistent cookies:** These are used to record information about the user's use of the internet over time. They can be used to keep a user logged into an online account so they do not have to log in every time they visit a website. These cookies also allow advertisers to track users' use of the internet.
- **Third-party cookies:** These can be used to personalise users' online experience or to send targeted adverts that are more relevant to an individual user. For example, they are used when web pages contain content such as **banner advertisements** for other websites. For more information about banners, see *Unit 6 Software skills* (page 256).

Targeted marketing is advertising that is matched to people based on their attributes or their browsing history. Third-party cookies are used to do this. For example, if a user visits a web page that displays banner advertisements from an **ad server**, the ad server can store a cookie on that user's device. If the user then visits a different web page that uses the same ad server, another cookie will be stored on their device. Because the ad server can request the

UNIT 4   ONLINE SERVICES   175

> **DID YOU KNOW?**
> You can change the settings of your browser to block third-party cookies.

cookies each time the banner loads, the web pages that their banner has been loaded from can also be tracked. The ad server can then select advertisements to display in the banner that match the user's browsing history.

▲ **Figure 11.6** Cookies can be used to track users' online behaviour

CHAPTER QUESTIONS

SKILLS   PROBLEM SOLVING

1 Which **one** of these is **not** provided by banks as an online service? (1)
   A Paying in cheques
   B Transferring money
   C Viewing an account's balance
   D Applying for a loan

SKILLS   PROBLEM SOLVING

2 State **two** ways in which education providers can use online services to help learners. (2)

3 State **three** features of shopping sites. (3)

SKILLS   REASONING

4 Explain why auction sites provide ratings for buyers. (2)

SKILLS   REASONING

5 Explain why banks use HTTPS for their online services. (3)

SKILLS   REASONING

6 Explain the benefit of e-ticketing for airline flights. (2)

SKILLS   INTERPRETATION

7 State **one** drawback of the use of third-party cookies. (1)

SKILLS   PROBLEM SOLVING

8 State **three** examples of data that can be stored in cookies. (3)

SKILLS   INTERPRETATION

9 State the difference between session cookies and persistent cookies. (1)

SKILLS   PROBLEM SOLVING

10 State the way in which news services can use a feature of smartphone apps to keep users up to date. (1)

SKILLS   CRITICAL THINKING
              REASONING
              ADAPTIVE LEARNING
              PRODUCTIVITY
              COMMUNICATION
              PERSONAL AND SOCIAL RESPONSIBILITY

11 Discuss how the use of cookies by organisations impacts on individuals. (8)

12 THE CLOUD

The cloud is the term used to describe the internet when it is used to provide software or space for storing information, rather than relying on local storage.

When you use software stored on your hard drive to work with files, you are using local hardware. You use your computer's resources and this still provides the best performance because there is no network connectivity slowing the transfer of data.

When you use the cloud, you use the internet to access applications and/or files stored on servers housed in data centres. You might use the cloud to use a web application like Twitter or Prezi, or synchronise files stored in a local folder with online data storage.

LEARNING OBJECTIVES

- Understand the impact of cloud-based services: hosted applications, storage
- Understand the features and characteristics of hosted applications software and locally installed software

HOSTED APPLICATIONS SOFTWARE

Web applications (web apps) are stored on online servers. The application runs on an online server and the user interface for the application is displayed in a web browser. Web apps are also known as **hosted applications** because the software is **hosted** on a server. For more information about the client-server model, see *Unit 2 Connectivity* (page 89).

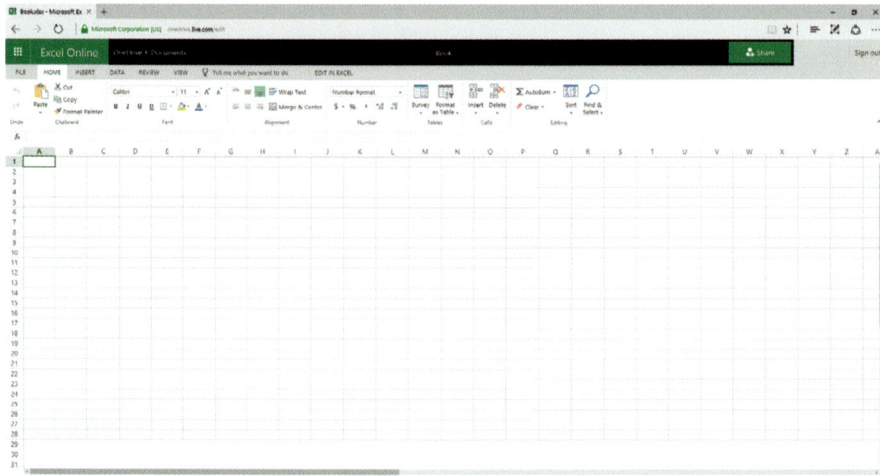

▲ Figure 12.1 A web app runs in a browser

Hosted applications are only available with an internet connection and can be affected by latency and bandwidth, which can create a poor user experience. For example, they can lead to slow **application loading times** or a delay between user input and activity in the browser, which makes the application seem **unresponsive**. For more information about the impact of latency and bandwidth on the user experience, see *Unit 2 Connectivity* (pages 67–68).

GENERAL VOCABULARY

unresponsive not reacting to something or not affected by it

SUBJECT VOCABULARY

application loading time how long it takes an application to load

KEY POINT

Having fewer complex features in hosted software means that less data is required to be processed by the server. This makes the user experience smoother and easier.

To reduce latency and the need for bandwidth, hosted applications usually do not offer as many features as some locally installed software, though they may still have some advanced features. Hosted applications often use online data storage. For more information about online data storage, see page 178.

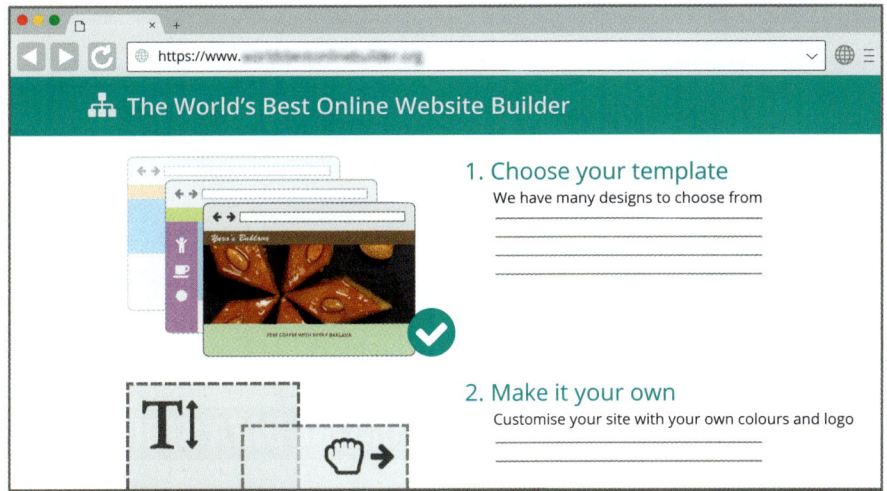

▲ Figure 12.2 There are many online versions of web authoring software that let people without any specialist knowledge create a website

Because hosted software uses the client-server model, it means that multiple clients can use the same application or even the same file at the same time. This gives users the ability to work on a document together. Many hosted applications also have chat features and tracking features that allow users to add and resolve **edits** and comments.

GENERAL VOCABULARY

edit (noun): a change to a document

▼ Table 12.1 The benefits and drawbacks of hosted applications

BENEFITS	DRAWBACKS
Accessible from many types of connected device	Only accessible using an internet connection
Can include the use of online data storage to save files online	User experience can be affected by high latency or low bandwidth
Features that enable collaboration	Not as many features as locally installed software

For more information about collaborative working, see *Unit 3 Operating online* (page 113). For more information about software (including locally installed software), see *Unit 1 Digital devices* (pages 42–57).

SKILLS ADAPTIVE LEARNING INTERPRETATION

ACTIVITY

▼ **HOSTED AND LOCAL SOFTWARE**

For each type of application listed in Table 12.2, give one example of a hosted version and one example of a local version. Two examples of the first type of application (word processing) has been done for you. Then list features that they share and any features that are unique to either hosted or local software.

▼ Table 12.2 Comparing hosted and local applications software

TYPE OF APPLICATION	HOSTED			LOCAL	
	EXAMPLE	UNIQUE FEATURES	SHARED FEATURES	UNIQUE FEATURES	EXAMPLE
WORD PROCESSING	Google Docs™				LibreOffice Writer
IMAGE EDITING					
SOUND EDITING					
PRESENTATION					
EMAIL					
SOCIAL MEDIA					

ONLINE DATA STORAGE

Just like hosted applications, online data storage can be accessed from anywhere from any device with an internet connection. This also has its benefits and drawbacks, as listed in Table 12.3.

▼ Table 12.3 The benefits and drawbacks of online data storage

BENEFITS	DRAWBACKS
• Files are often backed up automatically • The storage is scalable • Sharing data is easier • Many providers offer unlimited storage packages, so less need to buy additional local storage • Enables collaboration • More local storage made available for locally installed apps and local files	• Possible data protection issues if stored on servers in a different country • Dependent on online storage provider for security • File transfer speeds are much slower than local storage • Only accessible using an internet connection • Some software not available as hosted applications so files cannot be opened without being downloaded • Often have to pay for additional storage space if more space is needed

SUBJECT VOCABULARY

scalable something that is able to grow or shrink in order to meet demand, such as at busy times of day

data protection issues problems with maintaining security of data and information

cloud a term used to describe the internet when it is used to provide software or space for storing information, rather than relying on local storage

SKILLS EXECUTIVE FUNCTION
REASONING
INTERPRETATION
PERSONAL AND SOCIAL RESPONSIBILITY

ACTIVITY

▼ CHOOSING ONLINE DATA STORAGE

Create a short presentation (no more than 5 slides) to explain the benefits and drawbacks of online data storage. Try to only use images that are distributed under a free licence.

THE IMPACT OF THE CLOUD

Cloud-based services include hosted applications and online data storage.

Many different hosted applications and online data storage solutions are available. This means that developers of locally installed software are operating

SUBJECT VOCABULARY

netbook a computer that does not have lots of storage or fast processors

▲ Figure 12.3 The development of computers like netbooks and Chromebooks has provided a cheaper way for people to access the internet

in a very competitive marketplace. They have responded by adding more features to their software, and providing their own cloud-based applications and online data storage solutions that can link with their locally installed software.

The development of cloud-based services has made it possible for manufacturers to sell inexpensive devices such as the Google Chromebook™ or **netbooks**. These devices do not need a lot of storage because they can simply access hosted applications and online data storage. This reduction in cost has allowed more people to access technology and has helped to reduce the digital divide. For more information about the digital divide, see *Unit 3 Operating online* (pages 125–128).

Cloud-based services can help organisations, as they can provide organisations with scalable solutions to suit their business needs. They also help organisations to save on the cost of buying, housing and maintaining their own servers.

Cloud-based services can provide individuals with access to a variety of online services including:

- shopping and auction sites
- booking systems for travel, leisure and entertainment
- banking
- VLEs and **massive online open courses** (MOOCs)
- gaming
- news and other information
- entertainment services such as on-demand television and radio.

For more information about the impact of the internet on individuals, organisations and society, see *Unit 3 Operating online* (pages 110–121). For more information about the impact of online services, see pages 168–175.

Cloud-based services can also provide access to online communities, including:

- social networking sites
- online work spaces
- user-generated reference sites such as wikis and forums
- user-generated content sites such as video-sharing sites, blogs and websites
- social bookmarking sites.

For more information about online communities, see *Unit 3 Operating online* (pages 132–145).

CHAPTER QUESTIONS

SKILLS ▶ PROBLEM SOLVING

1 Which **one** of these is used to store hosted applications? (1)
   A Laptop
   B Smartwatch
   C Server
   D Tablet

SKILLS ▶ REASONING

2 State **three** benefits of using online data storage. (3)

SKILLS ▶ PROBLEM SOLVING

3 State **three** online services provided by cloud-based services. (3)

4 State what is meant by the term 'cloud'. (1)

UNIT 5
APPLYING INFORMATION AND COMMUNICATION TECHNOLOGY

Assessment Objective 1

Demonstrate knowledge and understanding of Information and Communication Technology (ICT)

Assessment Objective 2

Apply knowledge, understanding and skills to produce ICT based solutions

Assessment Objective 3

Analyse, evaluate, make reasoned judgments and present conclusions

In this unit, you will learn how to use a range of software effectively to combine information using suitable layouts and styles and apply appropriate editing techniques before reviewing the outcomes against the original requirements. Understanding how to apply ICT will make sure that the digital products you create achieve the desired purpose and are fit for use.

13 APPLYING ICT

When you apply ICT, you need to work effectively and appropriately with a range of digital tools, including application software, to produce ICT solutions in a range of different contexts. You also need to be able to reflect critically on your performance, analysing and evaluating your own and others' use of digital tools.

In *Unit 6 Software skills*, you will gain knowledge of a variety of application software that you will then be able to apply.

LEARNING OBJECTIVES

- Use the following software effectively:
  - word processing
  - database management
  - spreadsheet
  - web authoring
  - presentation (multimedia)
  - graphics
- Select appropriate software applications to meet needs
- Understand the difference between data and information
- Use:
  - text
  - numbers
  - images
  - animation
- Enter, organise, develop, refine and format information, applying editing techniques to meet needs
- Bring together and organise different types of information to achieve a purpose
- Produce information that is fit for purpose and audience, using accepted layouts and house styles
- Use styles appropriately, including serif and sans serif fonts, colour choice
- Work accurately and proofread, using software facilities where appropriate for the task
- Review the outcomes of the use of software applications by comparing the digital product with the original requirements
- Identify strengths and weaknesses in a digital product and suggest possible improvements
- Make modifications to improve the outcomes
- Evaluate the selection, use and effectiveness of ICT tools and facilities used

EFFECTIVE AND APPROPRIATE USE OF SOFTWARE

In *Unit 6 Software skills*, you will learn to use different pieces of software effectively. In order to work effectively, you also need to be able to select appropriate applications to meet the needs of a task. Table 13.1 lists different types of applications and some of the appropriate uses of those applications.

▼ Table 13.1 Application software and the purposes for which they can be used

TYPE OF APPLICATION	TASKS
Word processor	• Writing letters • Writing menus • Producing reports • Writing essays • Writing books
Database management	• Entering, editing and searching data • Producing reports
Graphics	• Creating images • Manipulating and editing images
Web authoring	Creating web pages and websites
Presentation	Creating slides to display multimedia content to accompany a talk
Spreadsheet	• Performing calculations, such as tax or student grades from test percentages • Modelling scenarios • Financial budgeting • Producing graphs and charts to visualise data as information

> **SUBJECT VOCABULARY**
>
> **multimedia** a combination of more than one medium, such as audio and video together

> **SUBJECT VOCABULARY**
>
> **data** raw numbers, text, sounds, images or animations, which are meaningless until they are processed
>
> **information** data that has been processed to be given context and meaning

> **GENERAL VOCABULARY**
>
> **context** the circumstances or background of something, such as information or an event

THE DIFFERENCE BETWEEN DATA AND INFORMATION

Data is raw and unprocessed numbers, text, sounds, images or animations. In this form, data is meaningless.

Information is the term used to describe data after it is processed to be given **context** and meaning.

▼ Table 13.2 Examples of data and information

EXAMPLE OF DATA	CONTEXT	EXAMPLE OF INFORMATION
February	Average temperatures in Kenya	The warmest month in Kenya
59, 79, 81, 90, 93, 99, 111	Students' marks	Grades 5, 6, 7, 8, 8, 9, 9
Deep Thought	Characters in the books of Douglas Adams	Deep Thought is a fictional computer created by the author Douglas Adams
[image]	Photographs taken on cobbled streets	This is a photograph of light reflecting off stone, which you may not have recognised without the context, as at first it looks like water

An animation can be completely meaningless until it is given context. Imagine an animation of a sphere circling another sphere. This could be an animated logo for a company, a representation of the Earth circling the Sun, or any number of other things. Until the context is known, the animation cannot inform people.

Similarly, the sound of a beep could represent a number of things. It could be an app notification, an effect for a game or a sound used in an alarm system. Until the context is known, the sound is just data.

SKILLS ADAPTIVE LEARNING
EXECUTIVE FUNCTION
COMMUNICATION

ACTIVITY

▼ **CONSIDERING CONTEXT**

Consider other examples of animations and sounds that may not have meaning until context is applied to make them into information. Create a table similar to Table 13.2 to contain your examples.

DIFFERENT TYPES OF DATA

Data may come in different forms, such as text or images.

TEXT

SUBJECT VOCABULARY

characters the letters and symbols used to write text

Example of text data: characters.

Possible method to produce meaning from text data: the syntax that is used.

Uses of text data: words, email addresses, product codes, postal codes.

NUMBERS

Examples of numeric data: integers, decimals, currency, percentages.

Possible methods to produce meaning from numeric data: graphs, charts.

Use of numeric data: to perform calculations.

SUBJECT VOCABULARY

alphanumeric containing both letters and numbers

> **KEY POINT**
>
> Text data can contain numbers but numeric data cannot contain text. Text data is therefore sometimes referred to as **alphanumeric** data.

IMAGES

Examples of image data: bitmap graphics, vector graphics. For more information about bitmap and vector graphics, see *Unit 6 Software skills* (page 239).

Possible methods to produce meaning from image data: the surrounding information (such as the rest of the web page or page of text), informative text within the image, **metaphor** and **semiotics**.

Uses of image data: logos, photographs.

GENERAL VOCABULARY

metaphor a figure of speech in which two things that are not literally similar are equated with one another, such as 'the moon was a white balloon in the sky'

semiotics the interpretation of signs and symbols

> **KEY POINT**
>
> Numeric data is data that can be used to perform calculations.

ANIMATION

Examples of animation data: SWF files (commonly known as 'Flash® files') and animated GIF files.

Possible methods to produce meaning from animation data: use of storytelling techniques, surrounding information, informative text within the animation.

Uses of animation data: web banners and other digital adverts.

HINT

GIFs can also be static. Animated GIFs are a special type of GIF that contain frames. For more information about frames, see *Unit 1 Digital Devices* (page 9).

UNIT 5 APPLYING ICT

SOUND

▲ Figure 13.1 An example of sound data shown as image data

Possible method to produce meaning from sound data: processing the sound data through a digital-to-analogue converter on a sound card and attaching a speaker. However, with some sounds, especially sounds that sound similar to one another, additional data such as text, video or images may be required to produce meaning from sound data.

Uses of sound data: music, speech.

ENTER, ORGANISE, DEVELOP, REFINE AND FORMAT INFORMATION, APPLYING EDITING TECHNIQUES TO MEET NEEDS

When you work with application software, you will enter data using input devices such as keyboards, mice and microphones. Selecting the appropriate data, editing it and refining it turns this data into information. In *Unit 6 Software skills*, you will use the editing features of application software to organise the layout of the information, as well as to develop, **refine** and format the information to meet the needs of your chosen design.

Table 13.3 shows examples of the features of different applications used in this process.

GENERAL VOCABULARY

refine make changes to improve something

pagination the process of giving a number to each page of a book, magazine or document

▼ Table 13.3 Methods of turning data into information using different application software

TYPE OF APPLICATION	ENTER	ORGANISE	DEVELOP	REFINE	FORMAT
WORD PROCESSOR	• Text • Images • Graphs • Charts	• Paragraphs • **Pagination** • Bullet points • Tables • Wrapping	• Add image captions • Duplicate text and images	• Spell check • Thesaurus	• Style • Size • Emphasis • Colour • Export or publish
DATABASE MANAGEMENT	• Data into tables	• Sort • Filter	• New fields • Relationships	• Queries • Group • Validation	• Reports • Export or publish
GRAPHICS	• Images • Text	• Layers • Positioning	• Resize • Animation	• Filters	• Export or publish options
WEB AUTHORING	• Text • Images • Buttons • Animation	• Tables • Frames	• Hyperlinks • Navigation	• Menus	• Font enhancements • Alignment
PRESENTATION	• Text • Images • Buttons • Sound Video	• Content on slide • Slide order	• Animations • Transitions	• Notes • Timings	• Master slide • Font
SPREADSHEET	• Numbers • Text	• Sort • Filter • Use of columns and rows	• Functions • Formulae • Graphs • Charts	• Chart features • Absolute referencing	• Cell • Column • Row • Sheet • Print layout

For more examples of how this process can apply to each type of application software, see *Unit 6 Software skills*.

PURPOSE

SUBJECT VOCABULARY

purpose what something (such as a digital product) is required to do

When you use application software to create digital products, you will combine and organise information in order to achieve a **purpose**. When you are developing a digital product, it is important that you ask yourself whether your product fulfils the required purpose. At every stage, ask yourself whether this product meets the needs of the task.

USER

Your users are the people who will use or view the digital product that you produce. For example, if a product is designed for children, it is likely to use a different style than if it is designed for adults. This means that, in addition to checking that the product is fit for purpose, you should also check that it is fit for the intended user.

LAYOUTS

SUBJECT VOCABULARY

layout the way in which text and/or images appear on a page

Different types of digital products use different **layouts**. For example, when creating a presentation, you set text and images out in a certain way. When creating a memo, you set text and images out in a different way and, when creating a poster, text and images will be set out differently again.

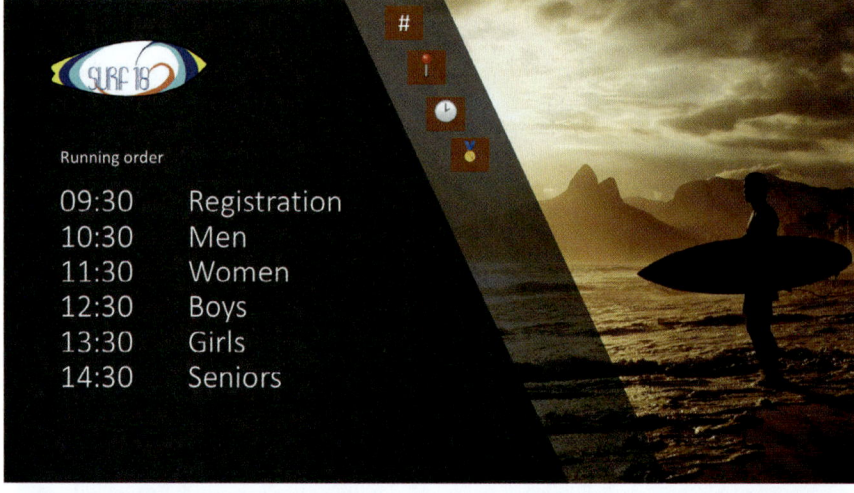

▲ Figure 13.2 The layout of a presentation is different to the layout of a memo

UNIT 5 — APPLYING ICT — 187

▲ **Figure 13.3** Organisations will often have a **house style**, which shows where content should be placed on each copy of a digital product

The following are some of the elements to consider when laying out information.

- **Title and logo position:** Titles and logos are usually placed at the top.
- **Images:** Consider the overall appearance of a document when arranging images. If images appear in a document with text, then the text can be made to flow around or through the images. For more information about laying out images and text, see *Unit 6 Software skills* (pages 223–228).
- **White space:** Good use of white space means not leaving large amounts of empty space between text and images, but also providing enough space to avoid packing the information together too tightly. Figures 13.4 and 13.5 are examples of too much and too little white space.

> **SUBJECT VOCABULARY**
>
> **house style** an organisation's preferred style of writing and layout of content
>
> **white space** the part of a page or digital product that is left blank
>
> **digital assets** content used in a digital product such as digital images

▲ **Figure 13.4** Too much white space can make products look empty and digital assets isolated

▲ **Figure 13.5** Too little white space can make products look too full and confusing

- **Document styles:** Some word-processed documents, such as formal letters, arrange information in specific ways.

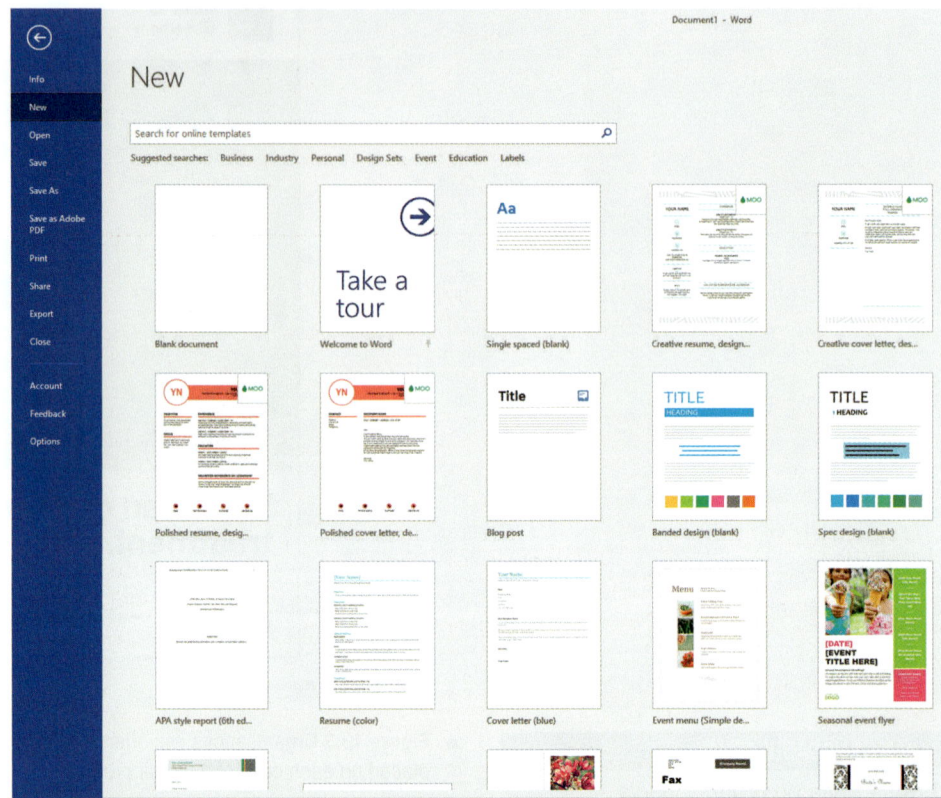

▲ Figure 13.6 Some applications use templates to help you layout your information

HOUSE STYLES

As you have already learned, some organisations have a house style that specifies how their documents and other digital products should be laid out. This makes sure that the organisation's **corporate identity** is maintained, meaning they are immediately recognisable to anyone looking at their digital products.

> **GENERAL VOCABULARY**
>
> **corporate identity** the way an organisation presents itself to the public

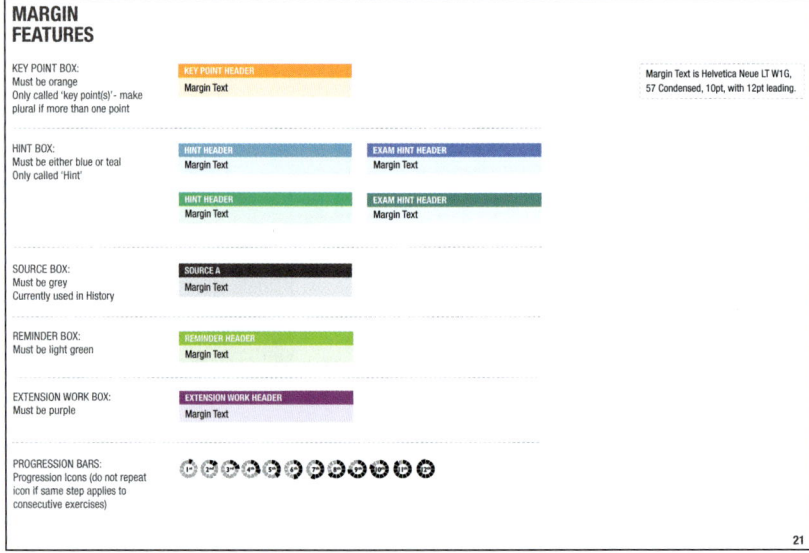

▲ Figure 13.7 An example of a house style document

UNIT 5 — APPLYING ICT

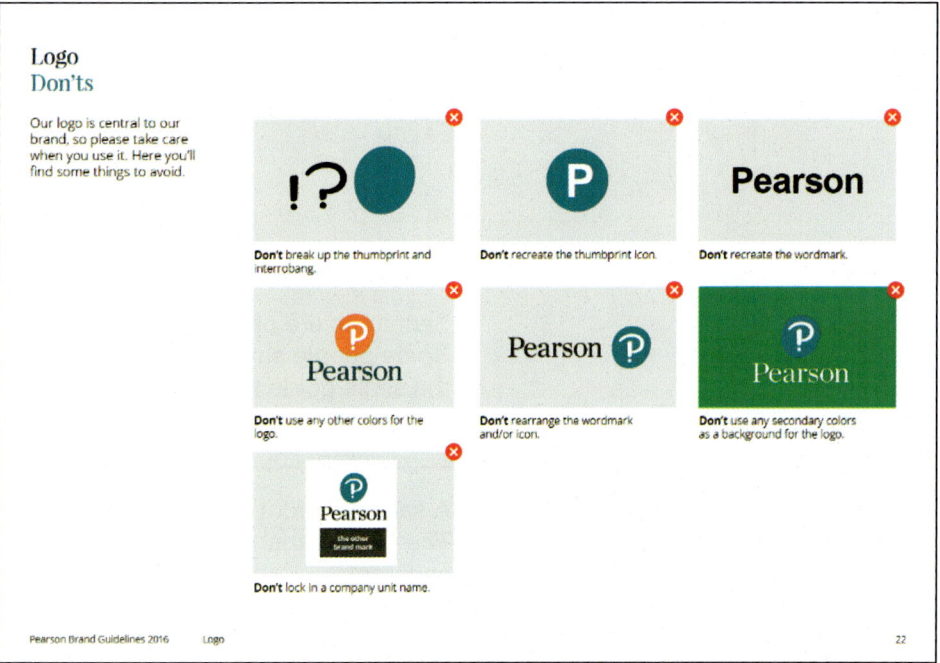

▲ **Figure 13.8** Organisations are often very specific about how people should use their **branding**

House styles usually include guidelines for how designers should treat components such as:

- images
- colours
- logos
- typeface or font style
- white space
- layouts.

GENERAL VOCABULARY

branding the distinctive design that identifies an organisation and its products

SKILLS — INTELLECTUAL INTEREST AND CURIOSITY, REASONING, COMMUNICATION, INTERPERSONAL SKILLS

ACTIVITY

▼ BRANDING

Do an internet search using the keywords 'Twitter brand resources' to find Twitter's brand guidelines. Review the guidelines and discuss them with the rest of your class. Why do you think Twitter has brand guidelines? Is it important for organisations to have such guidelines?

FONT STYLES

There are two main font styles: serif and sans serif.

SERIF

A serif font is a typeface that adds a short, flat line, known as a serif, to the ends of some letters, as shown in Figure 13.9. For example, Times New Roman is a serif font.

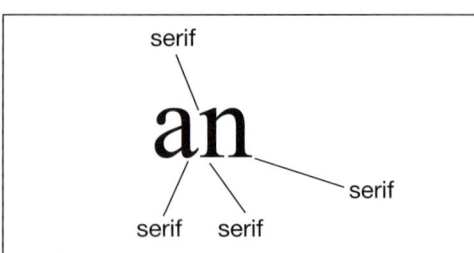

▲ **Figure 13.9** Serifs are used in serif fonts, such as Times New Roman

Serif fonts are often used in printed media, such as books and newspapers. Some people say that serif fonts are easier to read on a printed page because the serifs guide the reader's eye from one letter to the next. However, this point of view has been challenged by others.

SANS SERIF

A sans serif font is a typeface that does not add serifs to the ends of letters. The word 'sans' means 'without' in French. For example, Verdana is a sans serif font.

▲ **Figure 13.10** Verdana is a sans serif font

Sans serif fonts are often used in digital products. This is because they may have to be read on digital devices that use lower resolution screens. A low-resolution screen may not be able to show the detail of serif fonts, which will make the text more difficult to read. However, as screen resolution improves, it is less likely that the use of serif fonts will cause this problem.

> **KEY POINT**
>
> In products that are designed for higher resolution screens and for print, the choice between serif or sans serif font is often made on the basis of **aesthetics**. However, some people consider sans serif fonts to be more accessible, especially for people who have visual impairments or learning difficulties that affect their reading.

> **GENERAL VOCABULARY**
>
> **aesthetics** the study of visual beauty, especially in art

> **HINT**
>
> Don't underestimate the power of using **monochrome** or **greyscale**. Sometimes this simple approach can result in a clean-looking and effective design.

> **SUBJECT VOCABULARY**
>
> **monochrome** using a range of shades of one colour
> **greyscale** using a range of shades of grey

COLOUR CHOICE

You can add colour to digital products by including colourful backgrounds, images, buttons or logos. Alternatively, you can use different-coloured text, such as in paragraphs, links and headings.

▲ **Figure 13.11** Greyscale can be very effective

EMOTION AND MEANING

GENERAL VOCABULARY

convey communicate or express something such as a message or an emotion

Colour can be used to suggest a certain mood or atmosphere. When using colour in digital products, you must consider the purpose and audience of your product. For example, if you are creating a poster for an activity day for children, your colour choice should **convey** different emotions to the emotions conveyed by a poster for a ghost tour for adults. The first poster should convey fun and excitement while the other will need to suggest mystery and fear.

 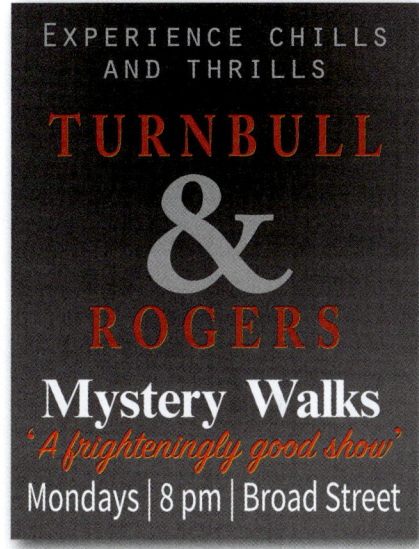

▲ Figure 13.12 These posters use different colours to convey very different moods

HARMONY

GENERAL VOCABULARY

harmonious things that work well together or in harmony
colour wheel a circle that is used to show the relationships between colours by evenly spacing the three primary colours (red, blue and yellow) around it; secondary and tertiary colours, which are produced by combining primary colours, are displayed in between the primary colours
complement to make a good combination with someone or something else
analogous similar to another situation or thing so that a comparison can be made
high contrast very different from each other
theme a particular style

Once you have considered the emotional effect of the colours that you will use, you can create a colour pattern. Some patterns of colour work well together. These can be described as **harmonious** colours.

A **colour wheel**, such as that shown in Figure 13.13 shows that some colours **complement** and contrast with each other. These colours are the colours opposite to one another on the wheel. Other colours are **analogous**, and these colours are next to each other on the wheel.

▲ Figure 13.13 Colours opposite each other on the colour wheel complement each other and can be used to produce bright and lively colour patterns

Not all colours in a product need to be **high contrast**. A pattern of analogous colours works well for objects in a product that need to follow a **theme**, such as the buttons, banners and links in a website.

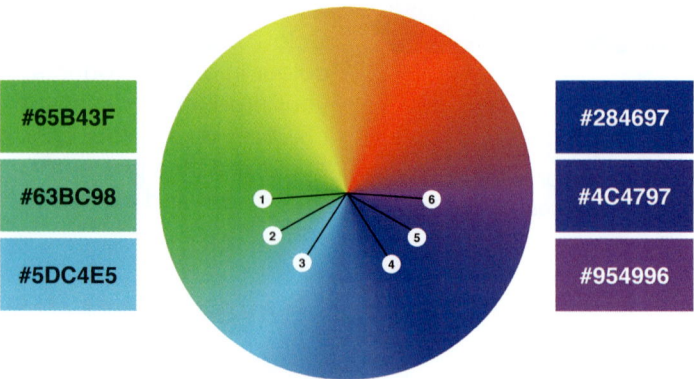

▲ Figure 13.14 Analogous colours are next to each other on the colour wheel

GENERAL VOCABULARY

split-complementary colours a pattern of three colours identified by choosing one colour, identifying its complementary colour and selecting the colours that are analogous to its complement (such as red and two varying shades of green)

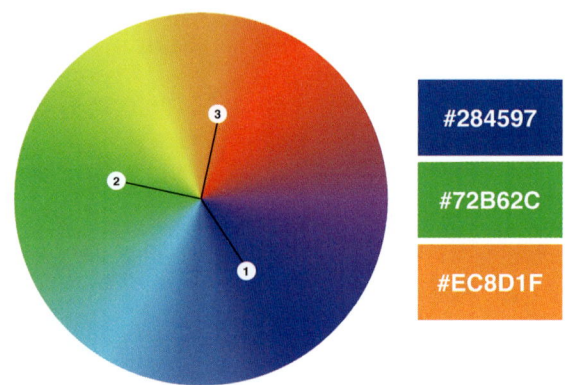

▲ Figure 13.15 **Split-complementary colours** can provide more choice of colours

SKILLS SELF-DIRECTION
INTELLECTUAL INTEREST AND CURIOSITY

ACTIVITY

▼ **CHOOSING COLOUR PATTERNS**

Find some web applications that allow users to create colour schemes, such as Paletton, Galactic Ink Sphere or Coolors. Try out different combinations of colours and see which colours work well together.

CONTRAST

GENERAL VOCABULARY

contrast the degree of difference between the light and dark parts of an image
colour-blind unable to see the difference between all or some colours
distinguish recognise the difference or differences between two things

KEY POINTS

Take care when choosing colours for objects that appear on colourful areas of a layout.

If two or more objects appear together in a product, such as text on a background, then the colours that you choose must be suitable so that the objects can be seen or read clearly. In particular, there must be enough **contrast** between them. For example, using light yellow text on a white background will make the text difficult to see against the background. It may not be visible at all to some people, such as people who are **colour-blind**.

Some colours do not work well together and can cause problems for some people. For example, red and green should not be used together because people with many types of colour blindness cannot **distinguish** between them.

Red and green should never be seen

▲ Figure 13.16 Can you read this text?

ACCESSIBILITY

When you are designing a digital product, you must remember that many people suffer from sight-related conditions that will affect their ability to be able to read the information on your digital products. One example of this is colour-blindness.

You have already learned about the fact that the use of red and green together can cause problems for people who are colour-blind. However, there are many types of colour blindness. Some people will see colours differently to the way in which you intended it, so it is important to check what they will see to ensure that they can see all of the necessary information.

Figure 13.17 shows the effects of one type of colour-blindness. The top row shows the colours that someone without colour-blindness would see. The bottom row shows the same colours, but as they would be seen by someone with a type of colour-blindness called protanopia.

▲ **Figure 13.17** The effects of protanopia

SKILLS INTELLECTUAL INTEREST AND CURIOSITY
PERSONAL AND SOCIAL RESPONSIBILITY

ACTIVITY

▼ ACCESSIBILITY OF DIGITAL PRODUCTS

Other conditions also affect the accessibility of a design, such as partial-sightedness. Find out about partial-sightedness and the accessibility needs of people with this condition.

CHECKING CONTENT

It is important to check that the content in a digital product is correct before it is published.

AUTOMATED CHECKING TOOLS

It is easy to make mistakes when entering data using application software. However, many applications provide automatic tools to help you check your work, such as spelling and grammar checkers. These tools sometimes indicate spelling and grammar errors as you type, such as by underlining them in red, but you can also run these tools manually.

HINT

It is important that you select the correct language for your spell checker. For example, American English and British English use different spellings for some words.

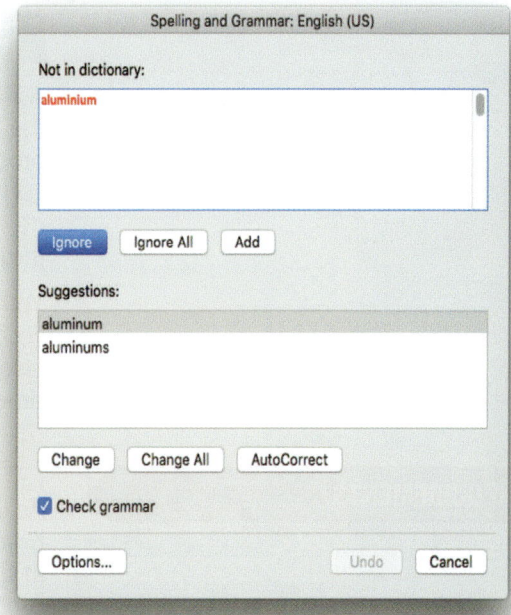

▶ **Figure 13.18** A UK spelling being highlighted as incorrect by a spell checker set to US English

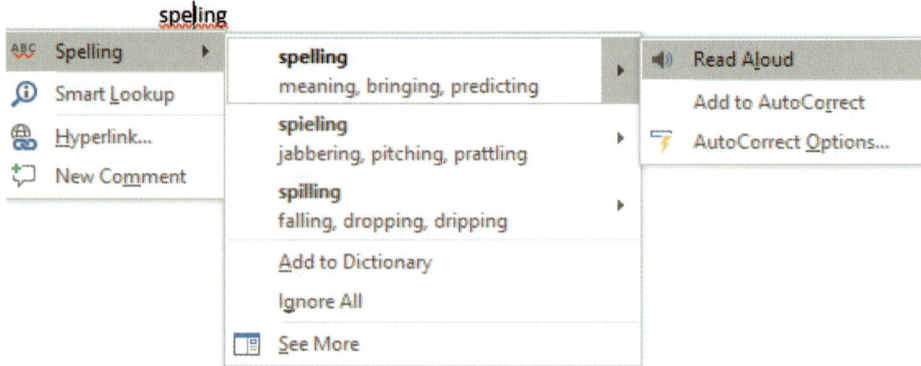

▲ Figure 13.19 A spell checker picking up a spelling error

Some tools will also identify contextual errors. Contextual errors are made when words that are spelled correctly are not used in the correct context. For example, when referring to items that belong to a group of people, the word 'there' is often used when 'their' would be correct.

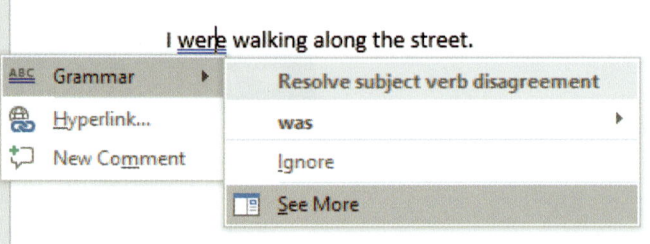

▲ Figure 13.20 A spell checker picking up a grammatical error

PROOFREADING

While automated tools are useful, they will not always find every error. This means that it is important to proofread your own work, particularly as the spell checker may suggest changes with which you disagree.

REVIEWING OUTCOMES

As you create your digital products, you should regularly check that they meet the requirements that you have been asked to meet. You should consider the products' strengths and weaknesses, which will help you to understand how you will update and improve those products. This process is called iterative development and allows you to improve your products by being critical throughout the process of creating them.

You should also review products after you have created them. This will allow you to identify ways in which those products could be further improved and also to consider how you could improve the process by which you created the products if you were asked to create similar products again in the future.

REQUIREMENTS

As you develop a digital product, it is important to compare what you are producing with the requirements of the task. You should do this several times, at different stages of the development process as well as once the final product has been produced.

SKILLS — CONTINUOUS LEARNING, SELF-MONITORING

ACTIVITY

▼ CHECKING A PRODUCT AGAINST REQUIREMENTS

Compare the document in Figure 13.21 against the following requirements.

- SET the orientation to landscape.
- ENTER 'Task A1' and your name, candidate number and centre number in the footer.
- SAVE the word-processed document as TASK A1.

How many of the requirements have been met?

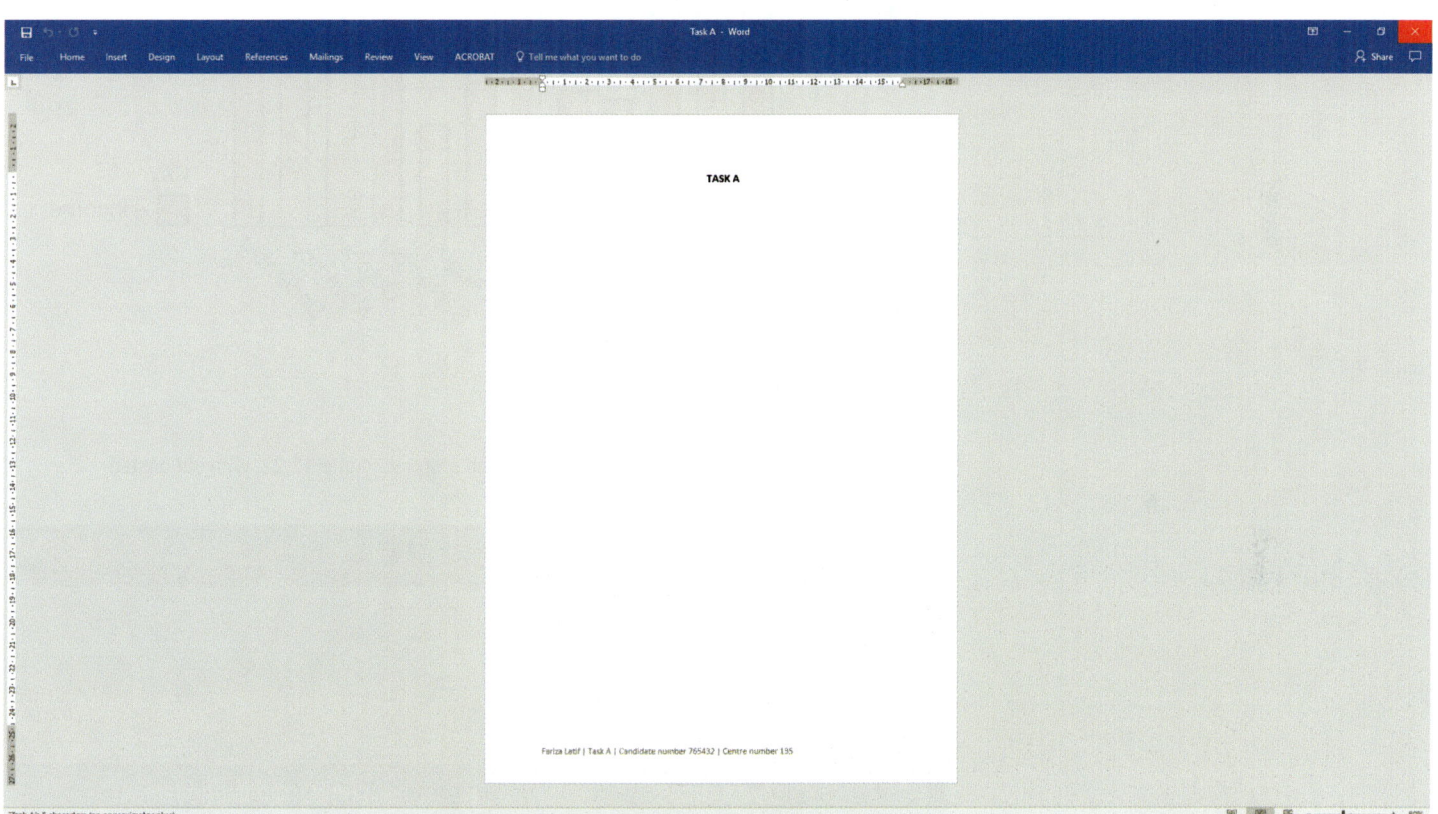

▲ Figure 13.21 A document created to meet the requirements set out in the activity

You can see that the document in Figure 13.21 meets none of the requirements.

- SET the orientation to landscape: The page orientation is set to portrait, not landscape as required. For more information about page orientation, see *Unit 6 Software skills* (page 227).
- ENTER 'Task A1' and your name, candidate number and centre number in the footer: 'Task A' has been entered, rather than 'Task A1' as required.
- SAVE the word-processed document as TASK A1: The document has been saved as 'TASK A', rather than 'TASK A1' as required.

STRENGTHS, WEAKNESSES AND SUGGESTED IMPROVEMENTS

GENERAL VOCABULARY

perspective a point of view or way of thinking about something, especially one that is influenced by the type of person you are or by your experiences

You can identify strengths and weaknesses in your own products. It is also a good idea to ask others to look at your products in order to identify strengths and weaknesses as well. Other people will look at your product from a different **perspective** and will not be as biased as you may be about your own work.

Imagine that you have produced the graph in Figure 13.22. A friend has reviewed the graph for you and has identified the strengths, weaknesses and suggested improvements in Table 13.4.

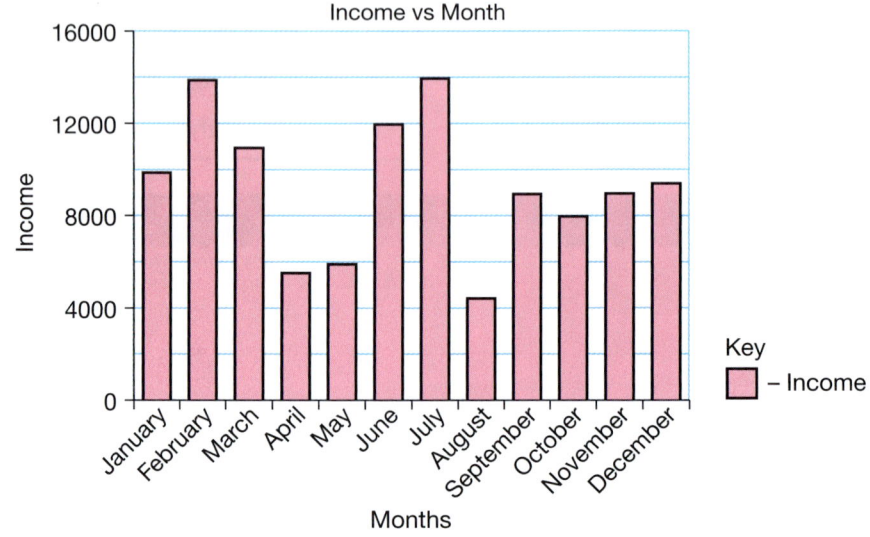

▲ **Figure 13.22** The original graph

▼ **Table 13.4** The strengths and weaknesses of the graph in Figure 13.22, with suggested improvements

STRENGTHS	
Good choice of chart type	
All months are present and clear	
There is a title	
WEAKNESS	**SUGGESTED IMPROVEMENT**
Title is quite small Title does not need to contain 'vs Month', as months are given so it is obviously monthly income	Increase title size Remove 'vs Month'
Legend (key) is unnecessary	Remove legend
It is not clear what currency the income is in	Add currency
The x and y axes do not need labels as it is obvious that these are months and income is given in title	Remove labels from each axis
It is not clear which year this relates to	Add year to title

GENERAL VOCABULARY

legend (also known as a key) the words that explain a picture, graph or map

Once potential improvements have been identified, it is important to make those changes. Figure 13.23 shows the improved version of the graph.

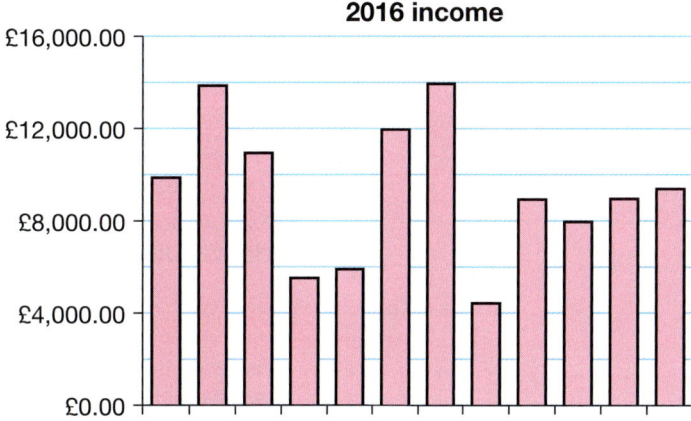

▲ Figure 13.23 The improved version of the graph with all changes made

EVALUATION

The **evaluation** process is very important, as it helps you to reflect on what went well and what you could improve for next time. When you complete an evaluation, you should think back to how you applied your knowledge of ICT. To help you do this, you can ask yourself a number of questions about your selection and use of the application software and the effectiveness of your products.

GENERAL VOCABULARY

evaluation the process of assessing something thoroughly

SELECTING THE APPLICATION SOFTWARE

- Did you select the best application for the job? For example, if you created a web page, did you use a text editor, a word processing tool or a dedicated web authoring application?
- Did you consider using alternative applications? If you did, what criteria did you use to decide which applications to consider?
- Why did you choose the application that you used? If there was a better choice of application, why did you not choose that one?
- What features made your choice of application appropriate? Were any of the application's features **unique** to it?
- How familiar were you with the application that you chose? Did that affect your decision to select it?

GENERAL VOCABULARY

unique the only one of its kind

USING THE APPLICATION SOFTWARE

- Did you make the best use of the application's features?
- Did you apply skills that you learned during the course?
- Were there any additional skills that you applied that you had to learn elsewhere, such as from tutorial videos on the internet?
- Did you learn any new skills through your use of the application? Did you gain confidence in your use of those new skills?
- Did your understanding of the application's features improve? How?
- Did your efficiency in the use of the application's features improve? For example, did you learn to increase the speed at which you gave commands to the application, perhaps by using keyboard shortcuts, or found that you were becoming more efficient because you were more familiar with the application's menus?

EFFECTIVENESS OF YOUR PRODUCTS

- Did your products meet the needs of the client or brief you were given? How do you know?
- Were your products suitable for purpose and their intended audience? How do you know?
- Did you ask other people to check your products and did you make good use of the feedback you received?
- Did you review others' products? Did you provide useful feedback on those products? How did that help you to improve your own skills and understanding?

> **KEY POINTS**
> - Answering these evaluative questions honestly will help you to write a meaningful evaluation.
> - Do not simply focus on your own use of time.
> - Be honest in your discussion about your own work. Saying your work needs improving gives you a chance to explain how and why, which shows that you have a good understanding of the process of producing digital products. Even if your work is very good, it is very likely that it can be improved and that you can make useful additions to it.

CHAPTER QUESTIONS

SKILLS: PROBLEM SOLVING

1 Which **one** of these data types is used to store a photograph? (1)
   - A Image
   - B Number
   - C Text
   - D Sound

SKILLS: REASONING

2 Explain **one** reason why it is important to use white space well when designing a digital product. (2)

SKILLS: INTERPRETATION

3 State **one** type of data and describe how it can be turned into information. (2)

SKILLS: SELF-MONITORING

4 Identify **three** errors in this text. (3)

How was I suposed two know Mr Singh.

SKILLS: REASONING

5 Explain why using a house style can improve finished products when multiple documents are created for one organisation. (2)

6 State what is meant by the term 'serif font'. (1)

SKILLS: DECISION MAKING / INTERPRETATION

7 State **one** drawback of using serif fonts on devices with low-resolution screens. (1)

SKILLS REASONING

8 Using the colour wheel, identify and state the name of the colour that contrasts most with red. **(1)**

SKILLS INTERPRETATION

9 State **one** accessibility need relating to the use of colour in product designs. **(1)**

SKILLS REASONING

10 State why it is important to proofread your work to check for errors. **(1)**

| FILE MANAGEMENT 202 | WORD PROCESSING 208 | GRAPHICS 239 | PRESENTATION 248 |
| WEB AUTHORING 262 | SPREADSHEETS 276 | DATABASE MANAGEMENT 307 | |

UNIT 6
SOFTWARE SKILLS

In this unit, you will learn how to manage files and use the features of a range of application software to allow you to produce effective digital products for a range of scenarios. There are many different applications available for you to use, and each chapter in this unit discusses only a few of the available applications. However, it should not matter which application you choose to use as you will learn about common tools and features.

Assessment Objective 1
Demonstrate knowledge and understanding of Information and Communication Technology (ICT)

Assessment Objective 2
Apply knowledge, understanding and skills to produce ICT based solutions

Assessment Objective 3
Analyse, evaluate, make reasoned judgments and present conclusions

14 FILE MANAGEMENT

Over your lifetime, you will probably create many thousands of digital files. Unless you are organised, these files can easily get lost on your devices. Managing your files carefully will save you time and will help you to find the files that you are working on. It will also help you to locate old files that you can repurpose for a different use.

Naming your files properly will ensure that you always work on the correct version of a file. It is also important to use the correct file types, because this allows you to share your files with other people and guarantees that they will be able to view the finished product.

File security is another important part of file management. This will protect your files and prevent unauthorised users from changing their contents.

LEARNING OBJECTIVES

- Save work regularly and keep information secure
- Use sensible filenames and formats
- Create and manage files and folder structures

SKILLS EXECUTIVE FUNCTION
SELF-DIRECTION
REASONING

HINT
The keyboard shortcut to save a file is Ctrl+S on a Windows computer or Command+S on OS X for Apple Mac®.

SAVING WORK

When you are creating digital products, it is important that you save your work regularly. This is to make sure that you have a copy of your work in case the application crashes or you lose power to your computer. This should include saving your work frequently to secondary storage. For more information about secondary storage, see *Unit 1 Digital devices* (pages 38–41).

ACTIVITY

▼ SAVING A FILE

1. Create a new word processor document and save the document with the filename 'time'.
2. Time how long it takes you to save a file using each of the following methods.
   - Use a keyboard shortcut to save the file to secondary storage.
   - Use the mouse to save the file to secondary storage.
3. Compare the time taken to save the file by each method. Which one took longer?
4. Discuss why you think different methods of saving a file are available.

DID YOU KNOW?
Many applications will save your work to a temporary file. You may be able to use this to recover your work if the application crashes.

SECURING FILES

You can secure your files by adding a password to be able to read or edit the file, as shown in Figure 14.1.

For more information about passwords and encryption, see *Unit 3 Operating online* (page 100) and *Unit 2 Connectivity* (page 90)

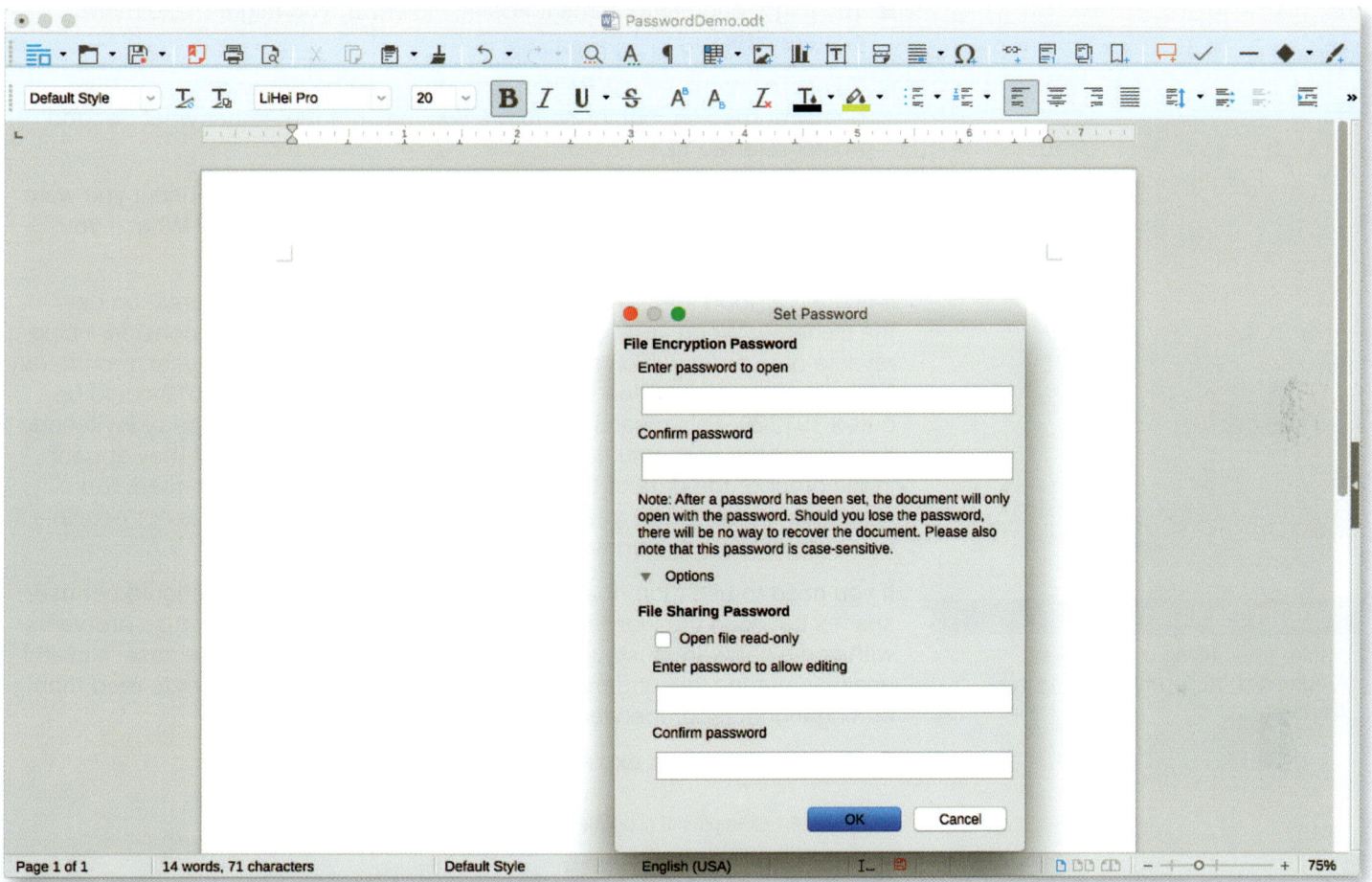

▲ **Figure 14.1** Applications often have **built-in** features that allow you to secure your files

SKILLS ▶ EXECUTIVE FUNCTION

GENERAL VOCABULARY

built-in forming a part of something, from which it cannot be separated

HINT

If you are using Microsoft® Word, you can protect the document with a password using the Protect Document options in the Info section of the File menu.

ACTIVITY

▼ **SECURING A FILE**

1 Create a new word processor document and type a secret message into it.

2 Protect the document with a simple password that you can remember easily.

3 Save the document and close it.

4 Open the document again. What happens?

NAMING FILES

It is important to use sensible filenames. A sensible filename describes the contents of a file so that it can be found easily.

For example, imagine that you are creating a poster for a sports club and have to name your file. The following points are some of the considerations that will help you to decide on a good filename.

- You might choose to name it Poster. However, you might make more posters later.
- You could name it First Poster, to be followed by Second Poster, Third poster and so on, but in the future you may not remember what Second Poster referred to.
- You could name it Sports Club Poster, but what would happen if you were asked to create a different sports club poster in the future? What if you needed to create more than one poster for the same club?

It is often a good idea to add the date of the event or the file creation date in the filename. When you add a date to a filename, you should consider using reverse date order, which means giving the date in the order: year, month, day. For example, an invitation to a party on the 26th December 2019 could be dated 191226. This means that, if you create lots of different party invitations throughout the year, you can sort them by name order so that they appear in the order of the date of the parties. Because the date is reversed, the filenames are sorted by year first, then month, then day. This is not possible if you write dates in the conventional order: day, month, year.

If you need to use more than one word in your filename, you should not use spaces between the words. This is because the spaces can cause problems with some software. Instead, you can use **snake case**. Snake case is useful because putting_an_underscore_between_each_word is easier to read than puttinganunderscorebetweeneachword.

Table 14.1 shows and explains two sensible filenames.

> **SUBJECT VOCABULARY**
>
> **snake case** using underscores (underlines) to separate words in a filename

▼ Table 14.1 Examples of good filenames

PRODUCT	FILENAME	REASON
A poster for the City Sports Club's Summer 2018 Activity Week	CSC_Summer18_ActWeek	• CSC for City Sports Club • Summer18 for the date • ActWeek for the event (Activity Week) • _ used to separate words (snake case)
A presentation to your school about a fundraising day on 16th November 2018	School_Charity_Presentation_181116	• Describes the event • Uses snake case • Gives the date in reverse so that the files will appear in date order when they are sorted by name

VERSIONING

As you make changes to a file, you can name it with a version number. This is known as versioning and it allows you to return to earlier versions of the same document at a later date. For example, the first version of CSC_Summer18_ActWeek from Table 14.1 could be called CSC_Summer18_ActWeek_v1, as shown in Figure 14.2.

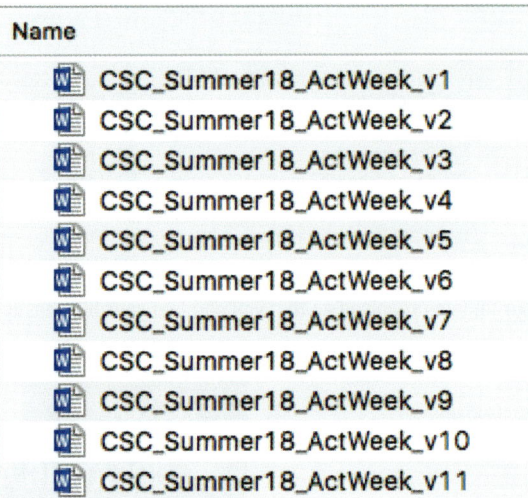

▲ Figure 14.2 An example of versioning

You could also include the date in your versioning by using the format MAJOR.REVISION.BUILDdate.BUILDnumber. For example, 1.2.161226.5 specifies the following information.

- MAJOR: version 1
- REVISION: 2
- **BUILDdate**: 161226 (26th December 2016)
- **BUILDnumber** (from that BUILDdate): 5

The filename is now CSC_Summer18_ActWeek_v1.2.161226.5. However, this filename is very long. To reduce its length, you could organise your files in a folder. If you create a folder to hold all the versions of the CSC Summer 2018 Activity Week files, as shown in Figure 14.3, you don't need to repeat the same text in the filenames.

▲ Figure 14.3 A folder titled CSC_Summer18_ActWeek containing versions of files

SUBJECT VOCABULARY

build date the date on which a file was created

build number the number within a series of versions from the build date

FOLDERS

You can use a folder structure to keep your folders and files organised. For example, in Figure 14.3, none of the files used the word 'poster' in their filename. This means that you may not be able to tell that they were posters. However, because the CSC_Summer18_ActWeek folder contains poster files, you could place it inside a folder called Posters. This ensures that your files remain organised and also lets you know what type of documents are inside the folder. In turn, the Posters folder could be placed inside a folder called Word Processed Documents, as shown in Figure 14.4.

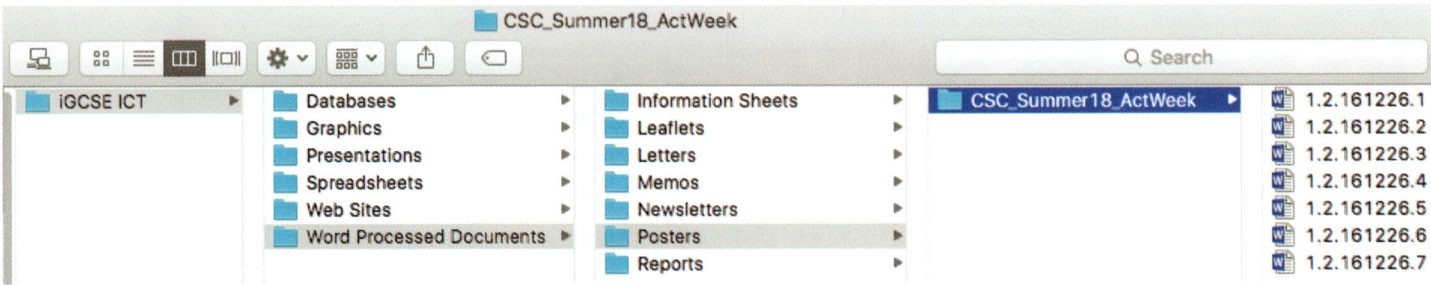

▲ Figure 14.4 Keep your folders organised so that you can find your files easily

SKILLS EXECUTIVE FUNCTION

ACTIVITY

▼ CREATING A FOLDER STRUCTURE

Create folders for your International GCSE ICT work so that you can keep all your files organised.

FILE FORMATS

GENERAL VOCABULARY

compatible two or more things that are able to function properly when they are used together

Software applications can only read files that are saved in **compatible** formats. For example, presentation applications cannot open files saved in a format used by spreadsheet applications. It is good practice to save your files in a format that will be compatible with the software that you will use to edit it.

When saving files, you can choose to save them in different formats. For example, you might choose to save your work in an older format so that it can be read by people who use older versions of the software. Software is often backwards compatible, which means that newer versions of application software can read files created using older versions. However, sometimes you will find that older versions of the software cannot read files created using a newer version.

HINT

Formats are often identified by **file extensions**.

SUBJECT VOCABULARY

file extension the letters at the end of the name of a computer file, which show what type of file it is, such as .doc

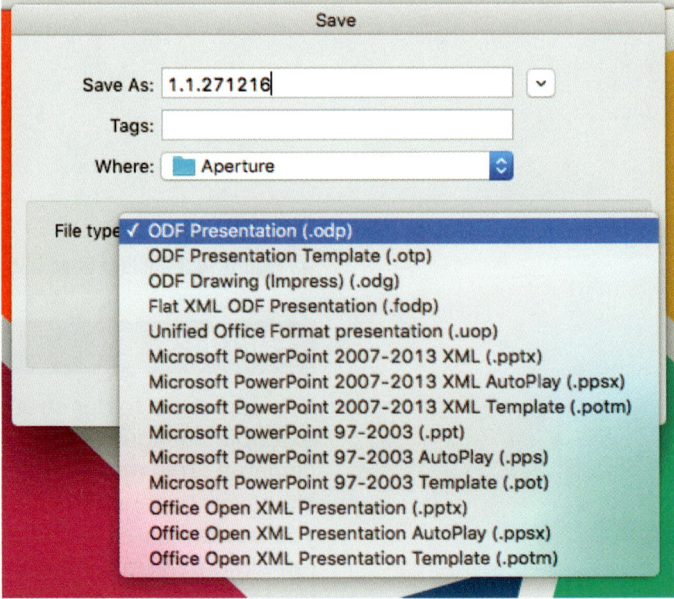

▲ Figure 14.5 Files can be saved in different formats, such as ODF Presentation (.odp) in this example

UNIT 6 — FILE MANAGEMENT

Files that are saved in application file formats are often only able to be viewed and edited by applications that are compatible with that format. See Table 14.2 for examples.

> **DID YOU KNOW?**
> Published file formats can usually be viewed in a web browser, whereas application file formats usually cannot be viewed in a web browser.

When you have finished editing a file, you may wish to publish or export it. Publishing or exporting the contents of the file in a published file format creates a final version of the file. Your audience will be able to view the file, but they will not be able to change it easily using application software.

KEY POINT
You need to use specific application software in order to open any files stored in that application's file format. In comparison, published file formats can be read by a wider range of applications.

SUBJECT VOCABULARY
transparency areas of an image that do not have a colour value, including white, are made see-through; if transparency is unavailable due to the file format, those areas are displayed as white

▼ Table 14.2 Examples of application file formats and their related published file formats

APPLICATION TYPE	APPLICATION	APPLICATION FILE FORMAT	PUBLISHED OR EXPORTED FILE FORMAT
Word processor	Microsoft® Word	.docx	.pdf
Presentation	LibreOffice® Impress	.odp	.ppsx
Graphics	GIMP	.xcf	.jpeg .png
Web authoring	Serif® WebPlus	.wpp	.html

Different published graphics file formats have different properties. For example, to keep the **transparency** of an image, you could choose to export it as a .png file.

CHAPTER QUESTIONS

SKILLS PROBLEM SOLVING

1. Which **one** of these is the most sensible filename for a logo created for a school? **(1)**
   A Logo-1
   B FinalLogo
   C School_Logo_v1.02
   D 102 School

SKILLS REASONING

2. Explain why it is important to save work regularly. **(3)**

SKILLS REASONING

3. State the reason why including versions in filenames is useful when developing a digital product. **(1)**

SKILLS PROBLEM SOLVING

4. State **three** published file formats. **(3)**

SKILLS INTERPRETATION

5. Describe how a user could use the MAJOR.REVISION.BUILDdate.BUILDnumber filename format to help them to find files at a later date. **(3)**

SKILLS PROBLEM SOLVING

6. State **one** method used to secure a file. **(1)**

SKILLS REASONING

7. State the reason why exporting a file is different from saving the file. **(1)**

15 WORD PROCESSING

Word processing software is used to produce documents such as letters, reports, newsletters, posters, leaflets, information sheets or fact sheets and memos. There are many word processing applications available. Some of them, such as LibreOffice® Writer, are free to download. In this chapter, you will learn about tools that are found in different applications such as LibreOffice Writer and Microsoft® Word.

You may be very familiar with one particular word processing application, but they all have common features. It should not matter whether you choose to use an application shown in this book or an application from a different developer. What is most important is that you choose one that allows you to demonstrate your skills, knowledge and understanding of the specification.

LEARNING OBJECTIVES

- Enter or edit text that is appropriate for a given context using accurate spelling, punctuation and grammar
- Enter, edit and format text using: bullets, numbering, sub-numbering, alignment, tabs, line spacing, colour, font size and style, text wrap, text boxes
- Use columns and/or tables: horizontal and vertical text alignment, merge and split cells, gridlines, borders, shading
- Use page layout: headings, sub-headings, lists, templates, header, footer, portrait, landscape, page breaks, page numbering
- Integrate in a single document: charts, tables, images, callouts/autoshapes, text from different files, text boxes, grouping, layering (in front of/behind), values from spreadsheets
- Produce documents in these document types: letter, report, newsletter, poster, leaflet, information sheet (fact sheet), memo
- Use standard conventions: salutation, complimentary close, date, subject, logo
- Use mail merge: mail merge from word processed, spreadsheet and database documents

SUBJECT VOCABULARY

cursor a movable point on a screen that identifies the point that the user's input will affect

ENTER AND EDIT TEXT

When you open a word processing application, it will open a new document or ask you to choose a type of document to open. When you type into the document, characters will appear beside the **cursor**.

The I-beam (sometimes called the I-cursor) is the mouse cursor that you can use to choose the insertion point for text or to highlight text to edit or format.

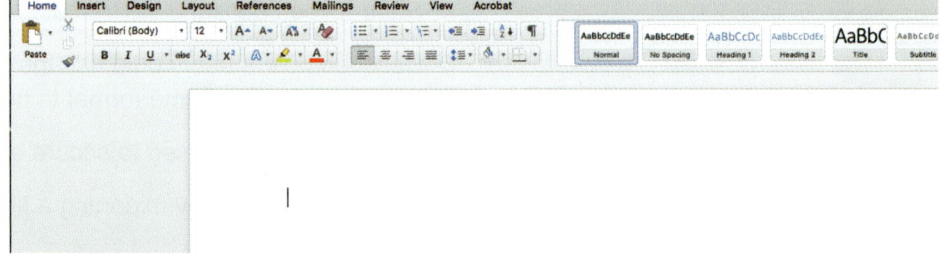

▲ Figure 15.1 The I-beam

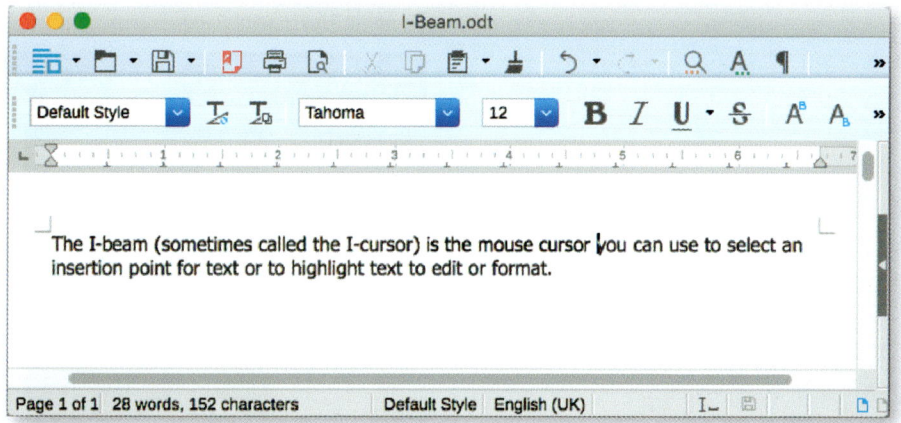

▲ Figure 15.2 In this screenshot from LibreOffice Writer, the insertion point has been positioned between the words 'cursor' and 'you'

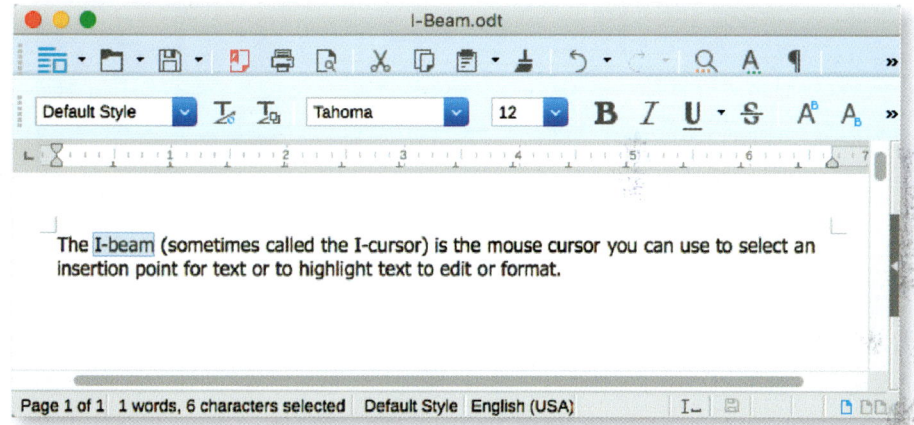

▲ Figure 15.3 In this screenshot from LibreOfficer Writer, the I-beam has been used to highlight the text 'I-beam'

Text is entered using the letter and number keys on the keyboard. However, you can also use other keys on the keyboard when creating a document. Some of those keys are shown in Table 15.1.

▼ Table 15.1 Common keys and their functions

KEY	IMAGE	FUNCTION
Return		Creates a new line and moves the insertion point to that new line
Space		Inserts a space between characters
Caps Lock		Sets the text entry mode to upper case (capital) letters

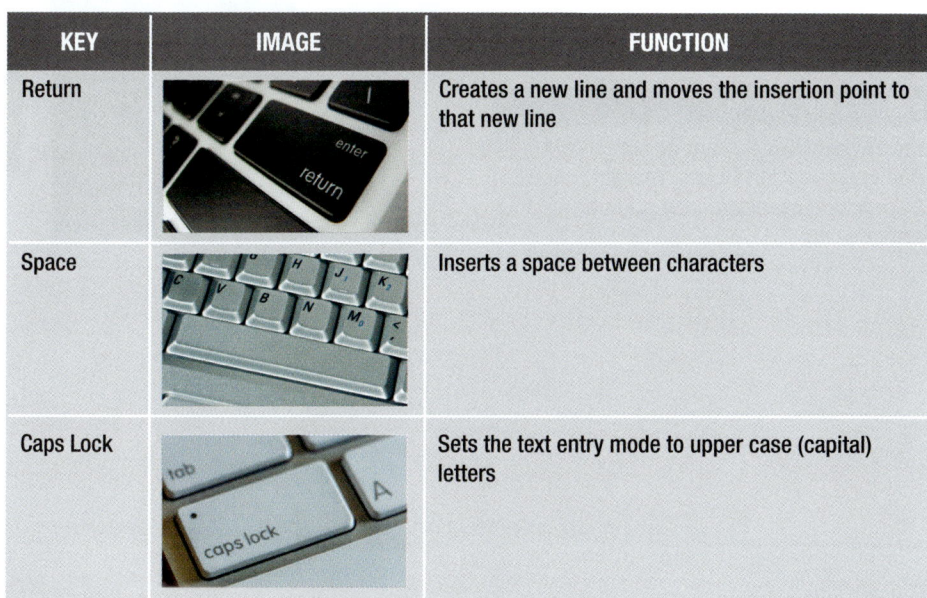

▼ Table 15.1 – *continued*

KEY	IMAGE	FUNCTION
Backspace		Removes the text to the left of (behind) the insertion point, either one character at a time or entire highlighted sections of text.
Delete (Del)	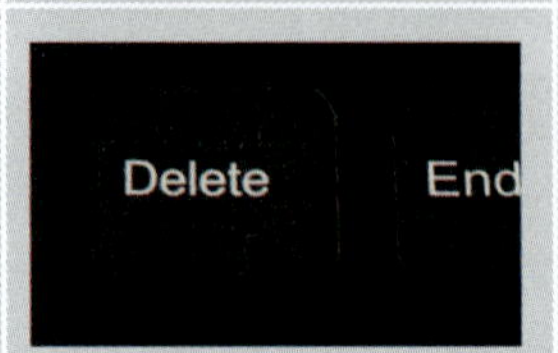	Removes the text to the right of (in front of) the insertion point, either one character at a time or entire highlighted sections of text.
Shift		• Used to access second-function characters or commands. For example, the second-function symbols in Figure 15.4 are <, > and  ?. ▲ **Figure 15.4** First- and second-function symbols on a keyboard • Used to create capital letters by holding down the shift key while pressing a letter.
Insert		Switches between insert mode and overtype mode. Insert mode lets you enter text to the right of the insertion point, moving the existing text along as you type. In overtype mode, the characters to the right of the insertion point are replaced by the text entered.
Tab		Moves the insertion point to the next **indent marker**. In Figure 15.4, each number in the image is aligned with an indent marker. For more information about tabs, see page 216.

SUBJECT VOCABULARY

indent marker a point at which text can be moved in from a margin, used to produce standardised spacing between text

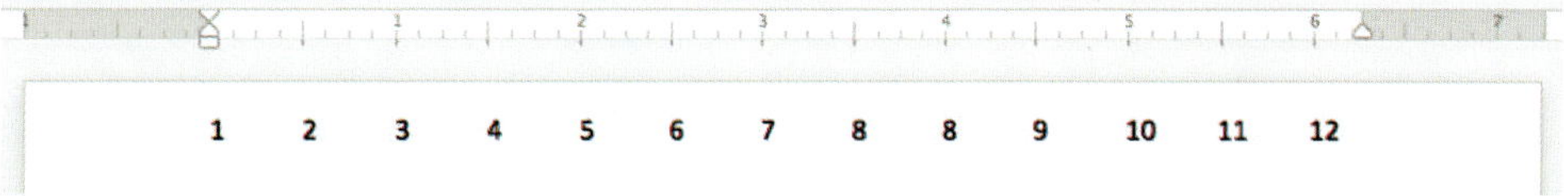

▲ Figure 15.5 Indent markers in Microsoft Word

SKILLS — EXECUTIVE FUNCTION

> **ACTIVITY**
>
> ▼ **USING THE KEYS**
>
> Find and practise using all of the keys listed in Table 15.1

> **HINT**
>
> The Return key is often mistakenly called the Enter key. Most keyboards have separate Return and Enter keys. They can usually be used interchangeably, but some applications use them to carry out separate functions.

SPELLING, PUNCTUATION AND GRAMMAR (SPAG)

To help you check your spelling, punctuation and grammar, you can use automated checking tools to proofread your work as you type.

In Figures 15.6 and 15.7, the automatic checking tools in Microsoft® Word and LibreOffice Writer indicate that 'thi' is misspelled. You can see that both applications indicate the misspelling with red underlining. Both applications also indicate a grammatical error ('a' instead of 'an') with blue underlining.

Neither tool highlights the incorrect use of the word 'muse', which should read 'mouse', because 'muse' is also a word that is spelled correctly. This is one reason why it is important to proofread your work yourself, rather than only relying on checking tools, because automated systems will not pick up all errors.

The I-beam (sometimes called the I-cursor) is thi muse cursor you can use to select a insertion point for text or to highlight text to edit or format.

▲ Figure 15.6 Automatic spell checker running on text in LibreOffice Writer

The I-beam (sometimes called the I-cursor) is thi muse cursor you can use to select a insertion point for text or to highlight text to edit or format.

▲ Figure 15.7 Automatic spell checker running on text in Microsoft Word

You can check your spelling, punctuation and grammar by running a spell check. This is usually selected from the Tools menu. The checking tool will also check for punctuation errors, but you should also check this yourself by proofreading your work.

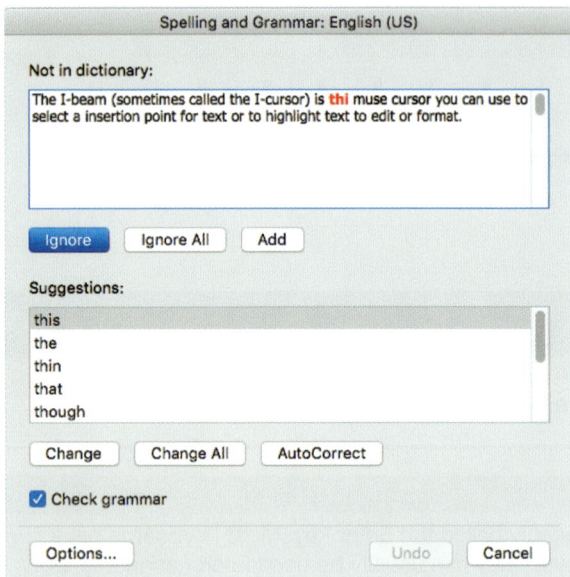
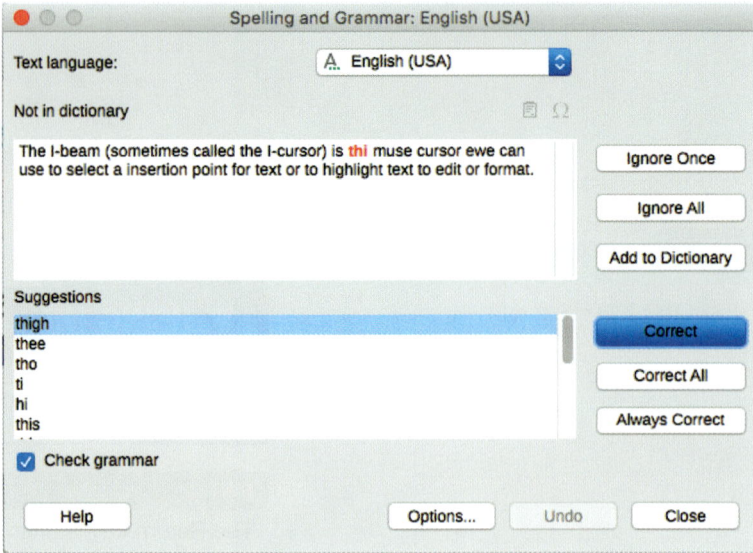

▲ **Figure 15.8** The spell-checking tools in Microsoft Word (left) and LibreOffice Writer (right) suggest different words to replace the incorrectly spelled word 'thi'

FORMATTING

You can use a range of effects to change the appearance of your document. Word processing software usually provides a number of formatting tools, as shown in Figure 15.9.

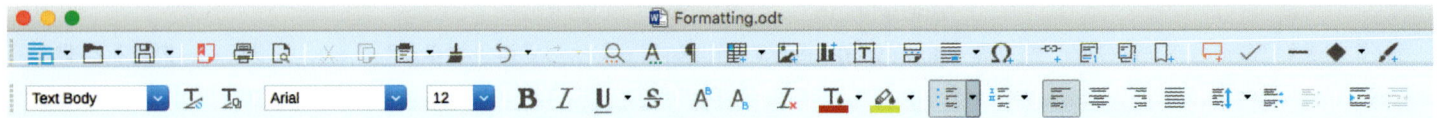

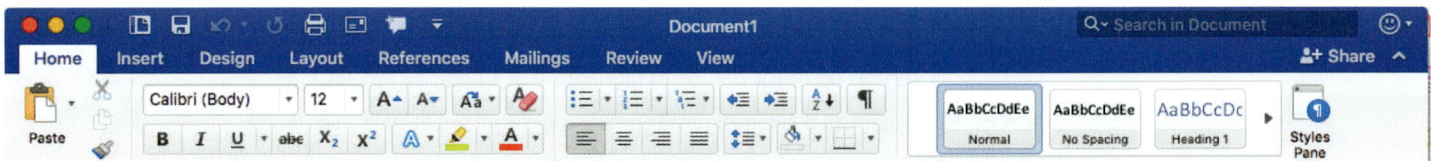

▲ **Figure 15.9** The formatting tools available in LibreOffice Writer (top) and Microsoft Word (bottom)

It is standard to use some formatting techniques for certain documents but not for other documents. Examples of this can be seen in the section on document types on pages 230–236.

PARAGRAPH FORMATTING

Paragraph formatting affects the layout of the document.

BULLET POINTS

To emphasise key points in your document, you can use bullet points. Bullet points are set out as a list, with each point on a separate line, preceded by a symbol. Usually this symbol is a filled-in circle, but you can use many different symbols including squares, arrows and ticks or crosses.

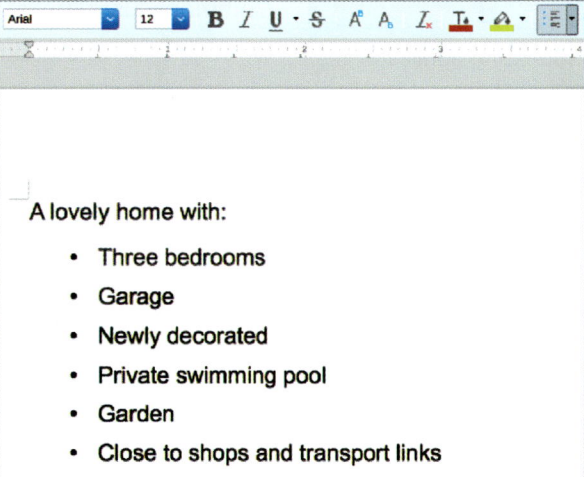

▲ **Figure 15.10** This screenshot from LibreOffice Writer shows that the bullets icon on the right has been selected by the user

For example, aif you were asked to describe the features of a house for sale, you might list those features with bullet points.

A lovely home that has:

- three bedrooms
- garage
- private swimming pool
- garden.

You can also use sub-bullets, which add a secondary bullet list within the main bullet list.

A lovely home that has:

- three bedrooms
  - double with built-in wardrobes
  - double
  - single
- garage
- private swimming pool
- garden.

You can change the bullet symbol by selecting the drop-down menu next to the bullets button, as shown in Figure 15.11.

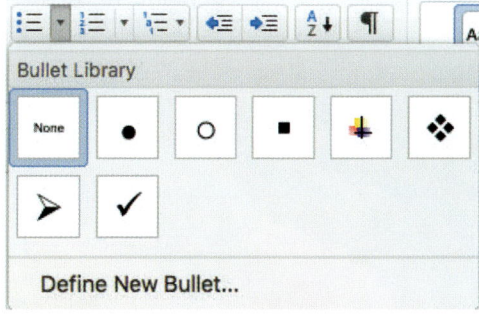

▲ **Figure 15.11** Some different bullet symbols available in Microsoft Word

> **HINT**
> Different word processing applications have different built-in styles.

> **GENERAL VOCABULARY**
> **priority** the thing that is most important or that needs attention before anything else

Commonly used bullet symbols include:

❑ check box, which is good for to-do lists or tick lists

⍰ star

➢ arrow

❖ flower.

NUMBERING

Numbering is used for ordered lists, either when it is important to show a numerical order or to show that some items take **priority** over others. Numbering can use numbers (1, 2, 3, 4), letters (a, b, c, d), and Roman numerals (i, ii, iii, iv).

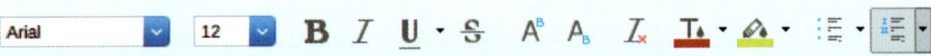

▲ **Figure 15.12** This screenshot from LibreOffice Writer shows that the numbering icon on the right has been selected by the user

For example, if you were asked to write instructions for how to boil an egg, you could use a list using numbers, starting at **1**.

How to boil an egg.

1. Add water to pan
2. Boil water
3. Add egg
4. Boil egg for 4 minutes
5. Remove egg
6. Eat

Alternatively, you could use a list using letters, starting at **a**.

How to boil an egg.

a. Add water to pan
b. Boil water
c. Add egg
d. Boil egg for 4 minutes
e. Remove egg
f. Eat

Sometimes, as with bullets and sub-bullets, you need to show more than one level of point. To do this as part of a numbered list, you could use sub-numbering.

A list of points.

1. First point
2. Second point
   a. First part of second point
   b. Second part of second point
3. Third point
4. Fourth point

UNIT 6 — WORD PROCESSING — 215

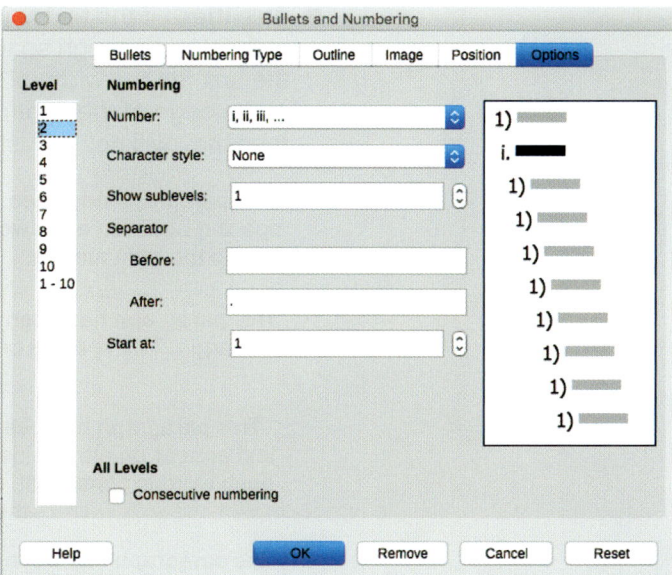

▲ **Figure 15.13** You can choose the style of bullet or number for different levels; in this screenshot from LibreOffice Writer, the style of the second level (selected left) has been set to use Roman numerals (previewed right)

SKILLS ▸ EXECUTIVE FUNCTION

ACTIVITY

▼ MAKING A LIST

Write a list explaining a simple task that you do every day, such as cleaning your teeth or making a cup of tea. Is the order important? Will you use a numbered list or bullets?

ALIGNMENT

SUBJECT VOCABULARY

page margin in a word processing application, the white area of the ruler ends and the grey part begins

Alignment refers to the position in which text appears on the page. For example, text can be aligned so that it starts on the left **page margin** or so that it finishes on the right page margin. This is done using the alignment buttons shown in Figure 15.14.

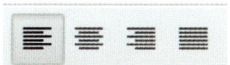  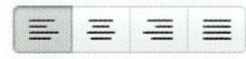

▲ **Figure 15.14** Alignment buttons in three different word processing applications (left to right: Google Docs™, LibreOffice Writer, Microsoft Word)

DID YOU KNOW?

You can use the mouse to alter the size of the page margins.

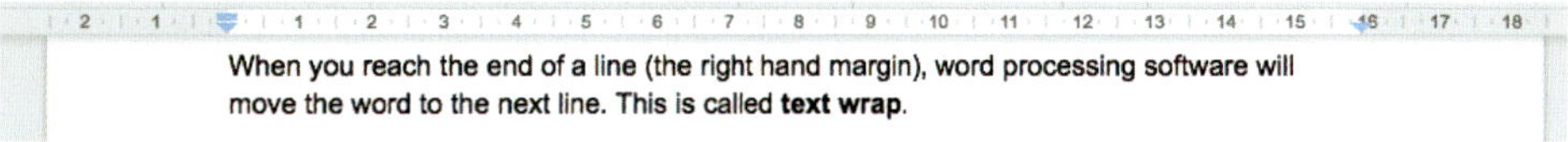

When you reach the end of a line (the right hand margin), word processing software will move the word to the next line. This is called **text wrap**.

▲ **Figure 15.15** The page margins in Google Docs

- **Left-aligned:** If the text is left-aligned, the beginning of each line of text will start at the edge of the left page margin.
- **Right-aligned:** If the text is right-aligned, the end of each line of text will finish at the edge of the right page margin.
- **Centre-aligned:** If the text is centre-aligned, the middle point of each line of text will sit at the middle point of the page between the left and right page margins.

- **Justified:** If the text is justified, it will start at the edge of the left page margin and enough space will be added between words and letters so that the text fits the width of the page, with the last character of each line ending at the edge of the right page margin. If there are only a few words on a line, then they will not be justified.

This paragraph has been **left aligned** so that it starts at the left margin. The spacing between each word is consistent, so some lines do not stretch all the way to the right margin.

This paragraph has been **right aligned** so that the lines of text end at the right margin. The spacing between each word is consistent, so some lines do not begin on the left margin.

This paragraph has been **centre aligned** so that equal parts of each line of text appear on either side of the centre line of the page. The spacing between each word is consistent, so not all the lines of text stretch all the way to either the right or the left page margin.

This paragraph has been **justified** so that it starts at the left page margin and ends at the right page margin. The spacing between words changes so that all the lines of text stretch all the way across the page (except for the final line, which is not long enough to be justified).

▲ Figure 15.16 Examples of text alignment

TABS (INDENTATION)

You can use tabs to move text away from a margin or to produce standardised spacing between text.

```
This
        text
                uses
                        tabs
                                before
                                        each
                                                word,
                                                        not
                                                                spaces
```

▲ Figure 15.17 This text has been spaced using tabs

LINES SPACING

You can change the line spacing of your document if you want to add more space between the lines of text. This can improve the readability of the document and provides space for people to make hand-written notes in between the lines of your text when printed.

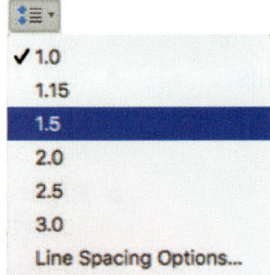

▲ Figure 15.18 The different line spacing options in Microsoft Word

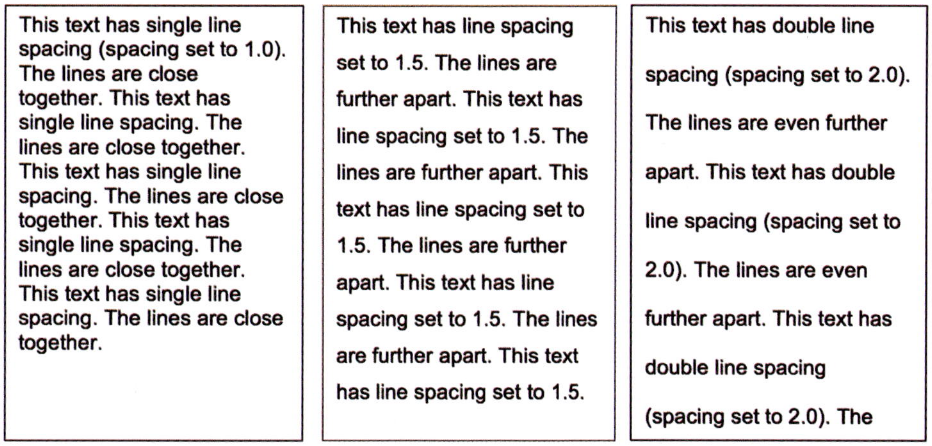

This text has single line spacing (spacing set to 1.0). The lines are close together. This text has single line spacing. The lines are close together. This text has single line spacing. The lines are close together. This text has single line spacing. The lines are close together. This text has single line spacing. The lines are close together.
This text has line spacing set to 1.5. The lines are further apart. This text has line spacing set to 1.5. The lines are further apart. This text has line spacing set to 1.5. The lines are further apart. This text has line spacing set to 1.5. The lines are further apart. This text has line spacing set to 1.5.
This text has double line spacing (spacing set to 2.0). The lines are even further apart. This text has double line spacing (spacing set to 2.0). The lines are even further apart. This text has double line spacing (spacing set to 2.0). The

▲ **Figure 15.19** Examples of different line spacing in LibreOffice Writer

TEXT WRAP

When you reach the right page margin at the end of a line, word processing software will move the last word to the next line if it is too long to fit on the current line. This is called text wrap and is shown in Figure 15.20.

When you reach the end of a line (the right hand margin), word processing software will move the word to the next line. This is called text wrap.

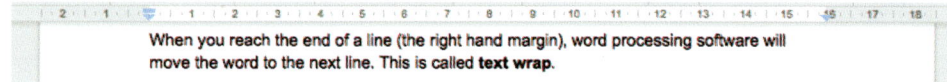

▲ **Figure 15.20** In this screenshot from Google Docs, the word 'move' cannot fit at the end of the line so it has been wrapped to the next line

FONT FORMATTING

Font formatting affects the appearance of the text in your document.

COLOUR

You can change the colour of the text using the tools listed in the Format or Font menu, as shown in Figure 15.21.

A
Automatic
Theme Colors
Standard Colors
More Colors...
Gradient

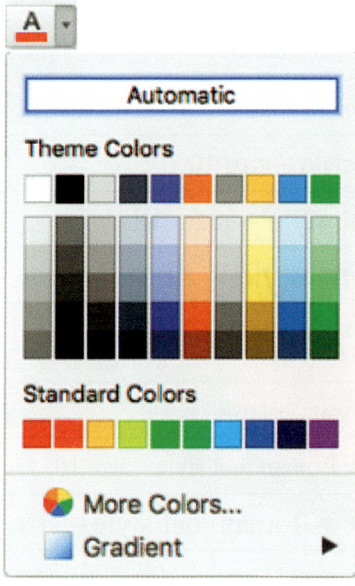

▲ **Figure 15.21** Changing the colour of text in Microsoft Word

FONT SIZE AND STYLE

The text that you enter can be made larger or smaller by altering the font size, as shown in Figure 15.22. Using different font sizes is useful if you are trying to show a visual hierarchy, in order to make some items in a document look more important than others.

> **DID YOU KNOW?**
> Font sizes can be set before or after you start typing.

▲ **Figure 15.22** Font size can be changed using a drop-down menu in LibreOffice Writer

The font can also be changed using a drop-down menu, as shown in Figure 15.23. For example, you could choose to use one font style for the body text and a different font style for headings, but it is often best to limit the number of fonts used in a document.

> **DID YOU KNOW?**
> Font styles can also be set before or after you start typing.

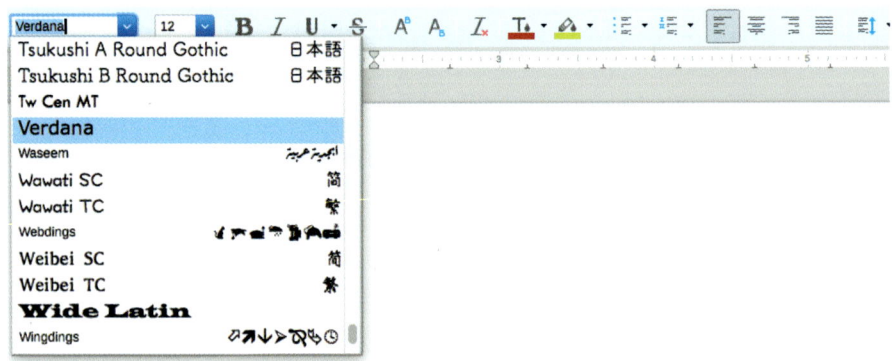

▲ **Figure 15.23** Word processing software such as LibreOffice Writer comes with many built-in font styles and more can be installed if necessary

Tables 15.2 and 15.3 show some examples of different font styles and sizes.

▼ **Table 15.2** Sans serif fonts

Arial font style – size 8	Trebuchet MS font style – size 8
Arial font style – size 10	Trebuchet MS font style – size 10
Arial font style – size 12	Trebuchet MS font style – size 12
Arial font style – size 14	Trebuchet MS – size 14

▼ **Table 15.3** Serif fonts

Times New Roman font style – size 8	Garamond style – size 8
Times New Roman font style – size 10	Garamond font style – size 10
Times New Roman font style – size 12	Garamond font style – size 12
Times New Roman font style – size 14	Garamond font style – size 14

TEXT BOXES

You can use a text box to place text in a precise location on the page. The text box creates a moveable and resizable area of a document that has its own margins, as shown in Figure 15.24.

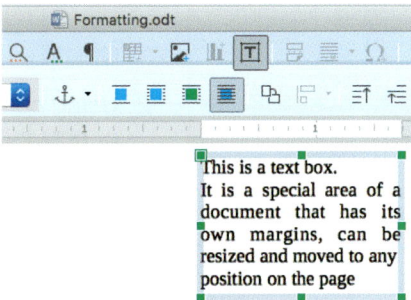

▲ **Figure 15.24** A text box in LibreOffice Writer

COLUMNS

You can choose to have your lines of text laid out in vertical columns, rather than running all the way across the page. This is the sort of layout you generally see in newspapers and newsletters.

When you want text from the first column to move up into a second one, you can use a column break from the Breaks menu.

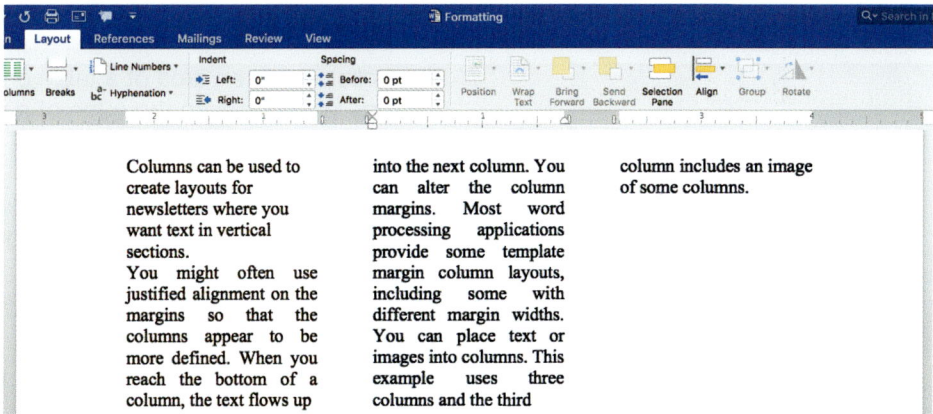

▲ **Figure 15.25** A document laid out using a column layout in Microsoft Word; read the text for more guidance on the use of alignment in columns

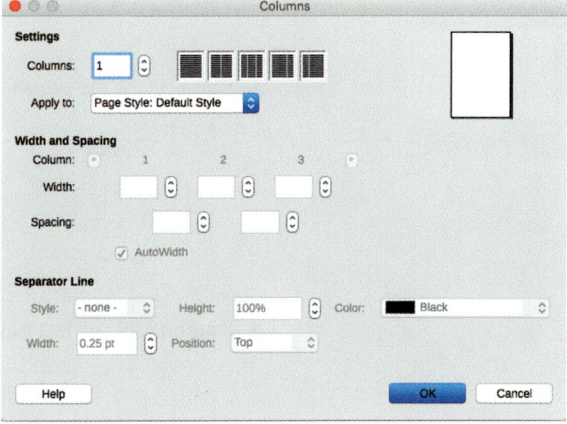

▲ **Figure 15.26** Most word processing applications, such as LibreOffice Writer, provide advanced options for columns

SKILLS: EXECUTIVE FUNCTION, COMMUNICATION

ACTIVITY

▼ USING COLUMNS

1. Create a new document.
2. Using columns, create a newsletter layout for your school or for a club or activity that you enjoy.
3. Discuss the advantages and disadvantages of using columns.

TABLES

Another way to arrange text in a document is by using tables. Tables are useful for displaying comparisons between different pieces of text. Like columns, they keep the text aligned but have more features than columns.

A table is made up of rows and columns of cells. For example, in the table shown in Figure 15.27, the red-shaded area is a **row** of four cells. The area with thick borders is a **column** of three cells.

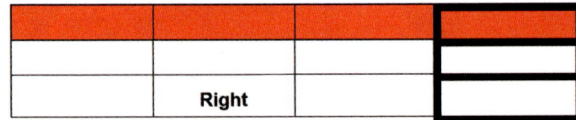

▲ Figure 15.27 A table

Right-clicking on an area of a table enables you to insert or delete rows and columns. You can drag the edge of a row or column to change the height of the row or the width of the column. You can also autofit the table to the page width or to the contents. When you use autofit, the word processing application automatically adjusts the widths and heights of the table's rows and columns in order to fit the page or the table's content.

ALIGNMENT

Just like the body text on a page, the text in cells can be aligned left, right or centre, or it can be justified. Text can be also be aligned to the top, the middle or the bottom of a cell.

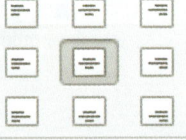

▲ Figure 15.28 The alignment options for text in a table in Microsoft Word

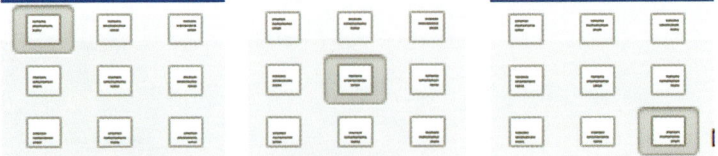

▲ Figure 15.29 Cell text alignment options in Microsoft Word

▲ Figure 15.30 Aligning text in a cell

MERGE

GENERAL VOCABULARY

merge combine two or more things into one thing

You can **merge** different cells together to form one large cell. This is useful for creating headings in tables, as shown in Figure 15.31.

The four cells in the top row of this table have been merged together			
		These two cells have been merged	

▲ **Figure 15.31** Merging cells

SPLIT

GENERAL VOCABULARY

split divide or separate something into different parts or groups

In some word processing applications, you can also **split** cells in a table. Cells can be split vertically and horizontally, as shown in Figure 15.32.

Before splitting

One cell				
	Two	cells		
	Three	cells	here	

After splitting

Split	into two			
	Two cells split into…			
	…one column and two rows			
	Three cells split into…	…two columns and one row		

▲ **Figure 15.32** A table before and after some of its cells have been split

One example of using this feature would be to show groups of information, as in the fitness training plan in Figure 15.33.

Section 1 (Base)	Week 1	2 × 30-minute run
		3 × 10-minute rowing
	Week 2	2 × 40-minute run
		3 × 15-minute rowing
Section 2 (Endurance)	Week 3	3 × 45-minute run
		4 × 10-minute rowing
	Week 4	3 × 50-minute run
		4 × 20-minute rowing
Section 3 (Taper)	Week 5	3 × 25-minute run
		3 × 15-minute rowing
	Week 6	2 × 30-minute run
		2 × 10-minute rowing

▲ **Figure 15.33** A training plan with some cells merged to show the way in which information is grouped

SKILLS: EXECUTIVE FUNCTION

ACTIVITY

▼ **MERGING AND SPLITTING CELLS**

Recreate the training plan shown in Figure 15.33. Do you find it easy to use the merge and split functionality?

GRIDLINES

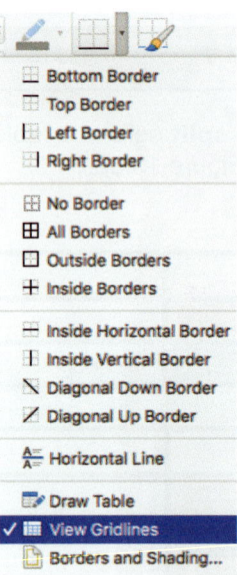

▲ Figure 15.34 Gridlines can be activated from the Borders menu in Microsoft Word

Some word processing applications have a gridlines feature that makes the table layout visible while you are working with it. However, the gridlines are not printed or shown when the final version of a document is exported.

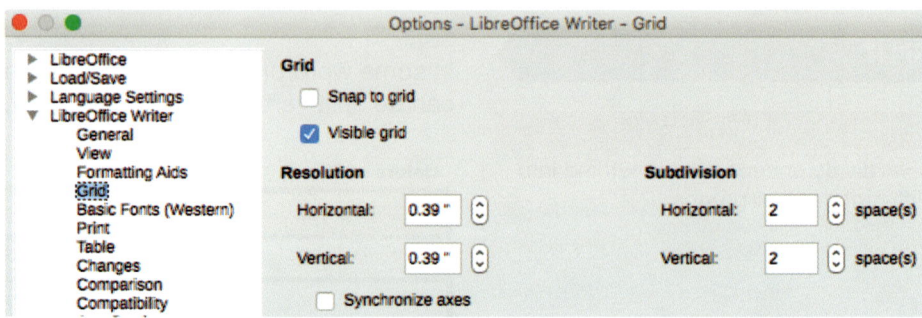

▲ Figure 15.35 In LibreOffice Writer, the grid can be made visible in the Options settings

▲ Figure 15.36 A table in Microsoft Word with and without visible gridlines

With visible gridlines

Cell 1	Cell 2	Cell 3	Cell 4
Cell 5	Cell 6	Cell 7	Cell 8
Cell 9	Cell 10	Cell 11	Cell 12

Without visible gridlines

Cell 1	Cell 2	Cell 3	Cell 4
Cell 5	Cell 6	Cell 7	Cell 8
Cell 9	Cell 10	Cell 11	Cell 12

▲ Figure 15.37 A table in LibreOffice Writer with and without visible gridlines

HINT

In Figure 15.37, the greyed-out gridlines are only visible in LibreOffice Writer. If you printed your document or exported it as a PDF, etc. these gridlines would not be visible. See page 206 for more information about application file and published file formats.

BORDERS

Unlike gridlines, **borders** are visible when the document is printed or published. You can change the thickness and colour of the borders. Some word processing applications allow you to add **patterned** borders or repeated images to create a patterned border.

SUBJECT VOCABULARY

borders lines that surround the cells in a table

GENERAL VOCABULARY

patterned decorated with a pattern

SHADING

▲ **Figure 15.38** The cell shading options in Microsoft Word

You can use shading to apply different colours to different cells. For example, some of the cells in Figure 15.34 are coloured in order to highlight cells that have been merged or split. Similarly, in Figure 15.36, some cells are highlighted to make the table easier to read.

PAGE LAYOUT

The page layout relates to how content is positioned on the page.

HEADINGS AND SUB-HEADINGS

To make the layout of your document consistent, you can use heading and sub-heading styles. These styles can be applied to heading text in order to apply a particular font style, size, formatting and colour to headings throughout a document. Figure 15.39 shows an example of heading styles.

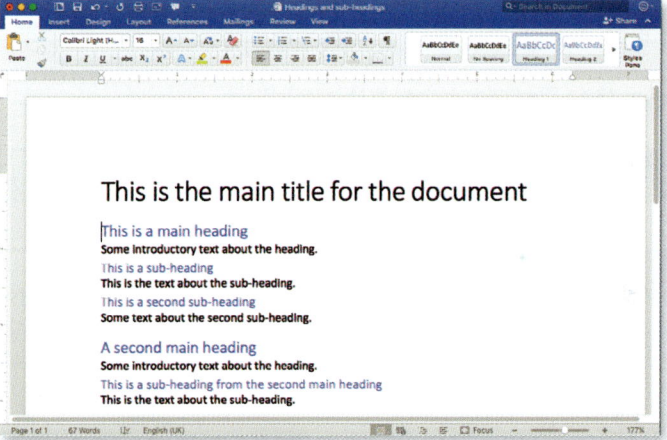

▲ **Figure 15.39** This document in Microsoft Word shows that Heading 1 has been selected for the text, 'This is a main heading'

When styles are applied to headings and sub-headings, they can also be used to create an automatic table of contents.

▲ **Figure 15.40** This table of contents in Microsoft Word is created automatically from the styles applied to the text in Figure 15.39

SKILLS ▶ EXECUTIVE FUNCTION

ACTIVITY

▼ **CREATING A TABLE OF CONTENTS**

1. Recreate the document shown in Figure 15.39 using the heading styles available in your chosen word processing application.
2. Create a table of contents from these headings as shown in Figure 15.40.

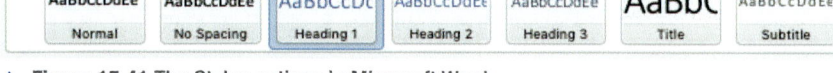

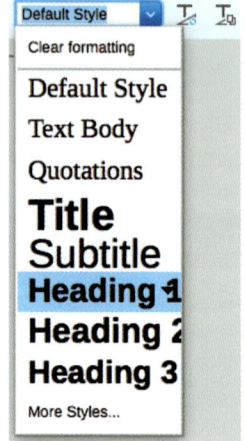

▲ Figure 15.41 The Styles options in Microsoft Word

▲ Figure 15.42 The Styles options in LibreOffice Writer

LISTS

You learned about bullets and numbering on pages 213–215.

TEMPLATES

You can create documents using an existing template. Using a template gives your documents a consistent style. In a business or organisation, this consistency is known as a house style. For more information about house styles, see *Unit 5 Applying Information and Communication Technology* (pages 188–189).

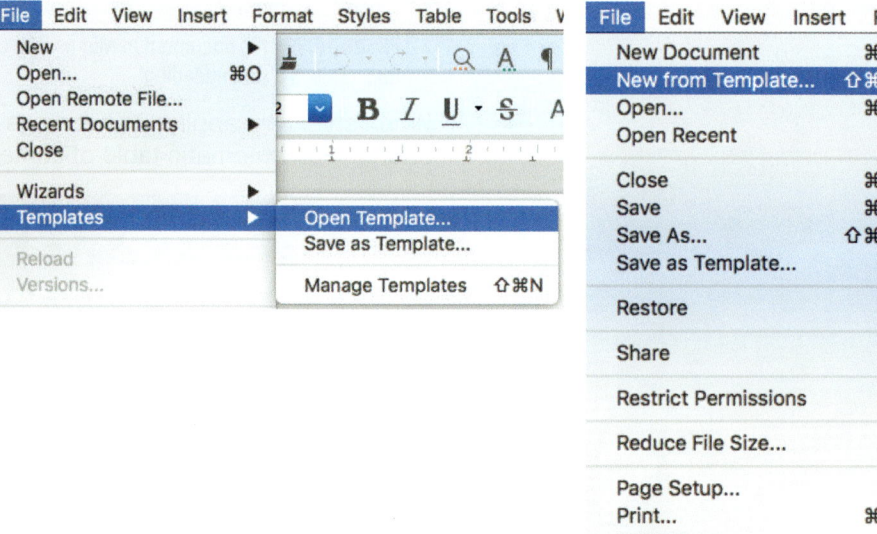

▲ Figure 15.43 You can often access templates by choosing the Templates option from the File menu (left to right: LibreOffice Writer and Microsoft Word)

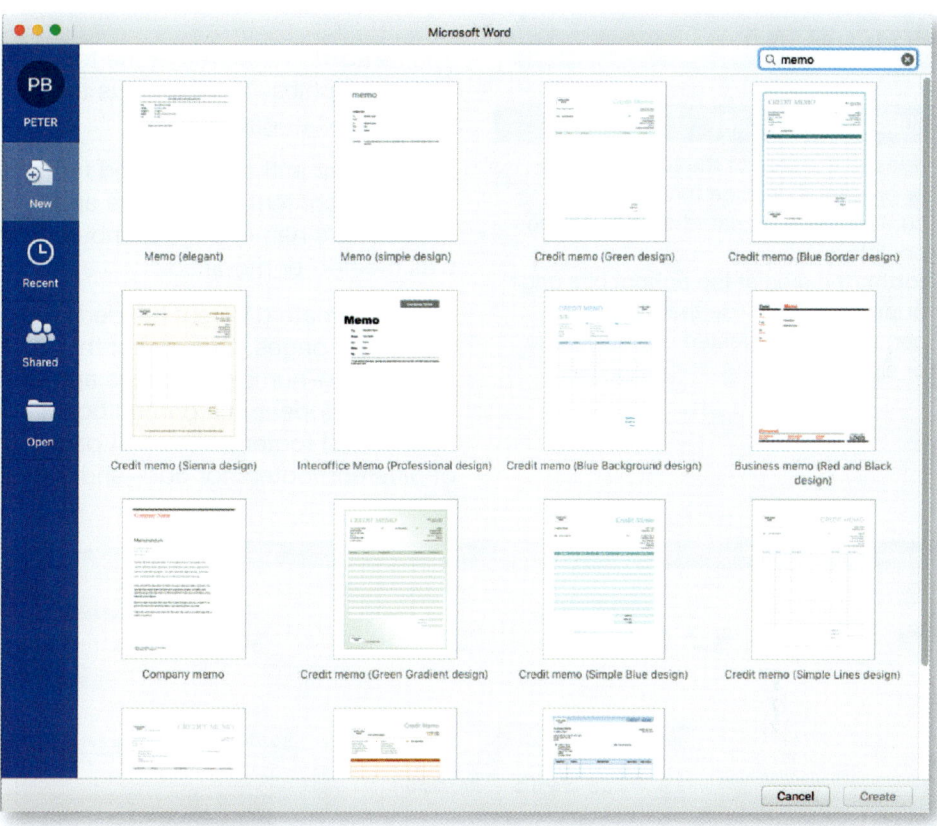

▲ **Figure 15.44** Some applications have a feature that lets you search for online templates

You can also create your own templates by creating a document and saving it as a template from the File menu. The next time that you or someone else uses your template, you or they will be able to save the file as a document based on that template. For example, Figure 15.45 shows a new template that can be used to create chapters for a recipe book. In some applications, once the template file is saved, it will then appear in the list of available templates (see Figure 15.46).

▲ **Figure 15.45** A new template in Microsoft Word for a chapter of a recipe book

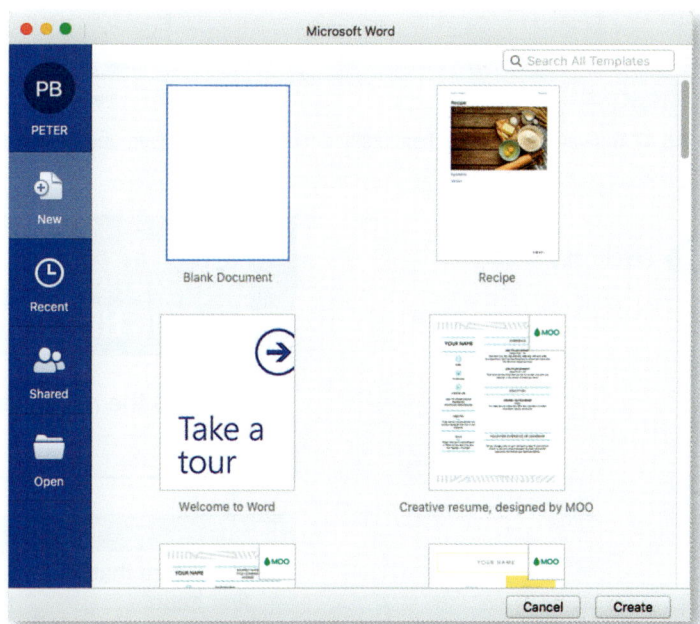

▲ **Figure 15.46** After saving the file as a template, it appears in the New Document window in Microsoft Word

HEADER AND FOOTER

SUBJECT VOCABULARY

header the area at the top of a page or presentation slide that contains content to be repeated on every page or slide

footer the area at the bottom of a page or presentation slide that contains content to be repeated on every page or slide

The **header** is the area at the top of a page in a document. It can contain text or graphics. The **footer** is the area at the bottom of a page that can also contain text or graphics.

The content in the header and footer is usually repeated on every page. Common content for headers and footers includes the title of the document, the author's name, page numbers and the date and time when the document was created or modified.

You can create different headers and footers for odd-numbered and even-numbered pages. One use of this is to place page numbers on the bottom right of odd-numbered pages and bottom left of even-numbered pages, as they may appear in a printed book. You can also choose not to show the header and footer on the first page. Figure 15.47 shows an example of this use of different footers for odd- and even-numbered pages and the first page.

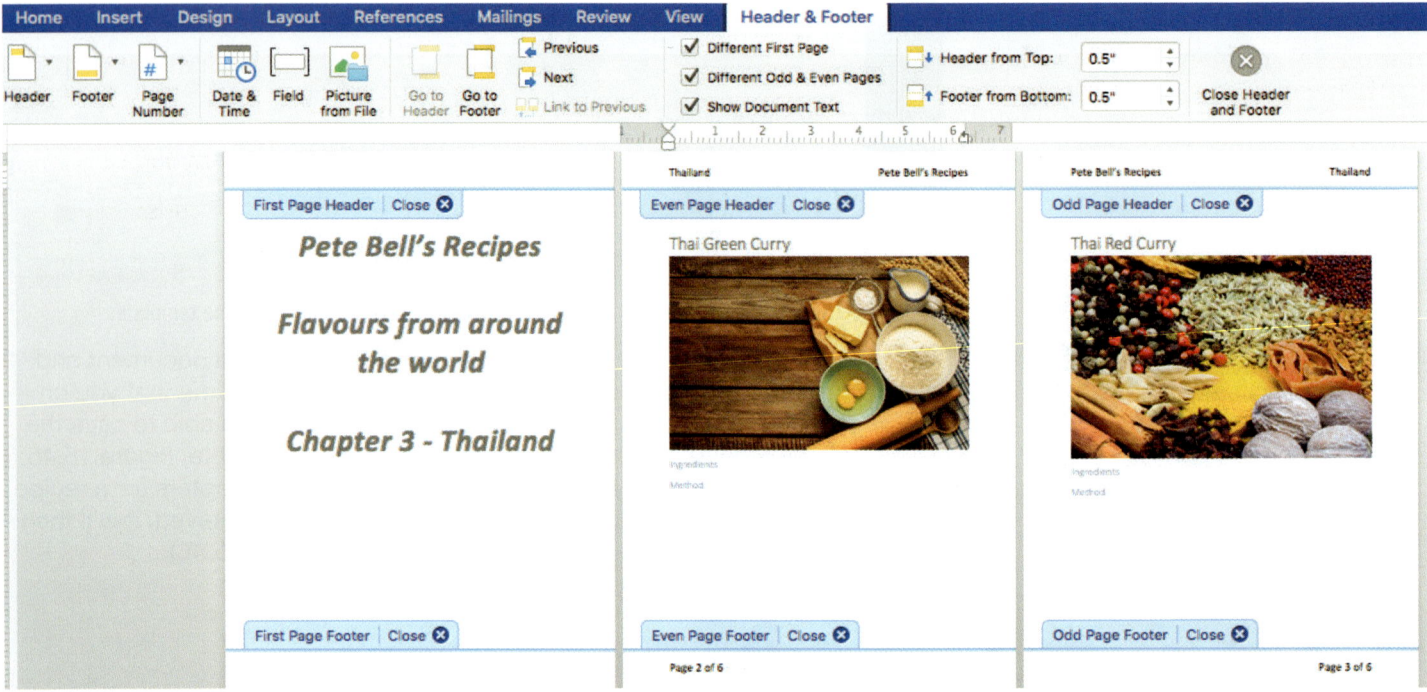

▲ Figure 15.47 You can set different headers and footers for odd, even and first pages of a document

SKILLS EXECUTIVE FUNCTION

ACTIVITY

▼ USING HEADERS AND FOOTERS

Recreate the recipe layout using the headers and footers shown in Figure 15.47.

HINT
- Make sure that you select the option to apply a different header and footer to the first page.
- Select the option to apply different headers and footers to odd- and even-numbered pages, so that they would print correctly if printed in a book format.

UNIT 6   WORD PROCESSING   227

PAGE BREAKS

GENERAL VOCABULARY

page break the point in a word-processed document where one page ends and a new page begins.

HINT

It is a common mistake to repeatedly press the Return key until a new page is created, rather than simply inserting a page break.

If you want to start a new page, such as for a new section or chapter in a document, you can insert a **page break**. This can be done using the mouse to select the Breaks menu or using the keyboard by pressing Ctrl+Enter on a Windows® PC or Command+Enter on an Apple® Mac®.

Inserting a page break ensures that the gap at the bottom of the page on which the page break is inserted will be maintained, no matter what happens to the text on the page. This means that text on the next page will not appear at the bottom of the first page, even if text on the first page is deleted.

However, this is not the case if the Return key is used repeatedly to push text onto the next page. In this case, if you add text at the end of the first page, the text on the next page may be pushed down to accommodate all the line returns. Alternatively, if you delete text from the first page, you may find that the text at the top of the next page comes back onto the first page.

ORIENTATION

The orientation of a document affects the layout of the document. There are two orientations, as shown in Figure 15.48:

- portrait, with the long side of the page vertical like a portrait painting
- landscape, with the long side of the page horizontal, like a landscape painting.

The default page orientation is portrait.

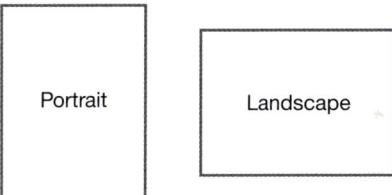

▲ **Figure 15.48** Landscape and portrait orientations

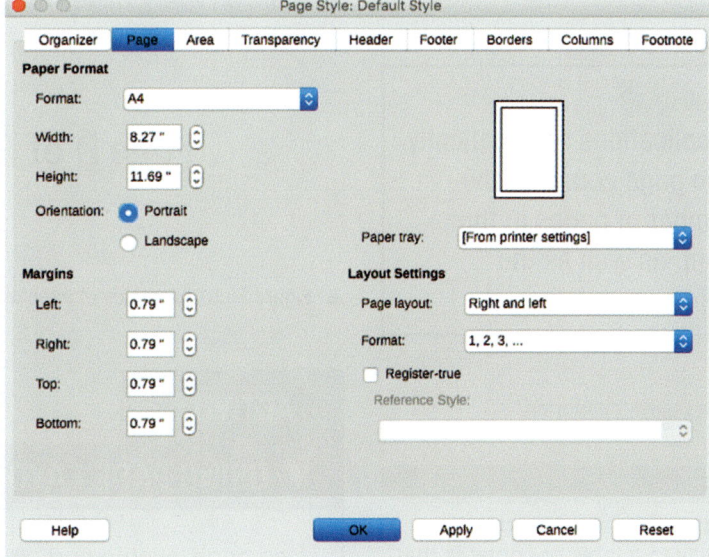

▲ **Figure 15.49** Page Options allows you to change the orientation of the document in LibreOffice Writer

Changing the orientation will change the orientation of every page in the document.

If you want to include a mixture of orientations in your document, as shown in Figure 15.50, you need to use section breaks or manual breaks. Section breaks can work in the same way as page breaks, but they split the document into different sections, each of which can have a different orientation.

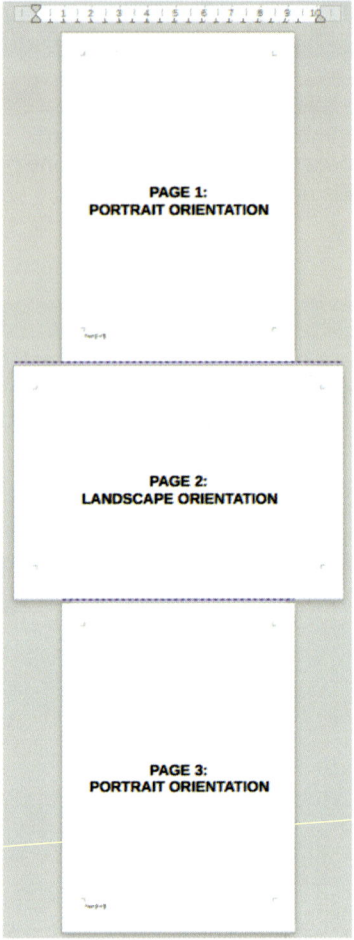

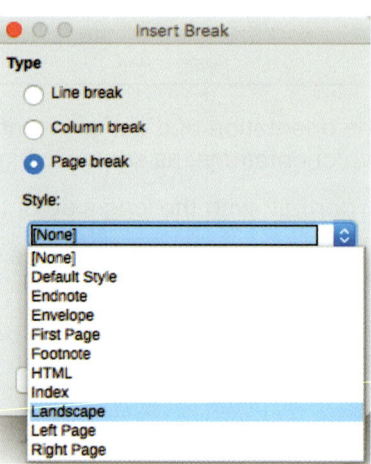

HINT
In Microsoft Word, use section breaks and the orientation setting to achieve the effect shown in Figure 15.50.

▲ **Figure 15.50** In LibreOffice Writer, a landscape page break is used to set the second page to landscape orientation

PAGE NUMBERING

Page numbers can be included in the footer as a repeated element that appears on every page. They can be set to automatically increase as the document gets longer.

DID YOU KNOW?
Some applications automatically show the page count, or the total number of pages in the document, as well as the current page number.

▲ **Figure 15.51** Examples of page numbering in LibreOffice Writer and Microsoft Word

SKILLS ▸ EXECUTIVE FUNCTION

HINT
Page numbers can also be added automatically to a table of contents that you create using heading styles.

ACTIVITY

▼ **USING PAGE LAYOUTS AND PAGE NUMBERING**

Use page layouts and page numbering to recreate the document shown in Figure 15.50.

DOCUMENT ELEMENTS

You can insert different types of elements into a document.

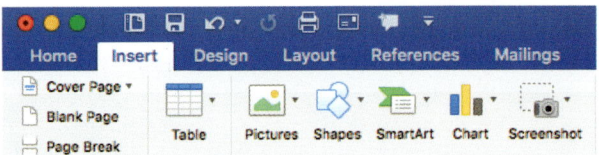

▲ Figure 15.52 Most document elements can be inserted from the Insert tab in Microsoft Word

> **HINT**
> In some applications, images are referred to as pictures.

> **GENERAL VOCABULARY**
> **flow chart** a diagram showing a sequence of actions or events in a process or system
> **callout** a text box or shape designed to attract attention to the text that it contains or the object to which it points

These document elements include:

- charts and values from spreadsheets
- tables (see page 220)
- images, including screenshots
- videos, as shown in Figure 15.53
- shapes, as shown in Figure 15.54, including lines, geometric shapes, arrows, mathematical shapes, **flow chart** symbols, stars and banners and **callouts**
- text from other files, usually by copying it and then pasting it into your document
- text boxes (see page 219).

▲ Figure 15.53 Many types of element, such as video, can be inserted into a document

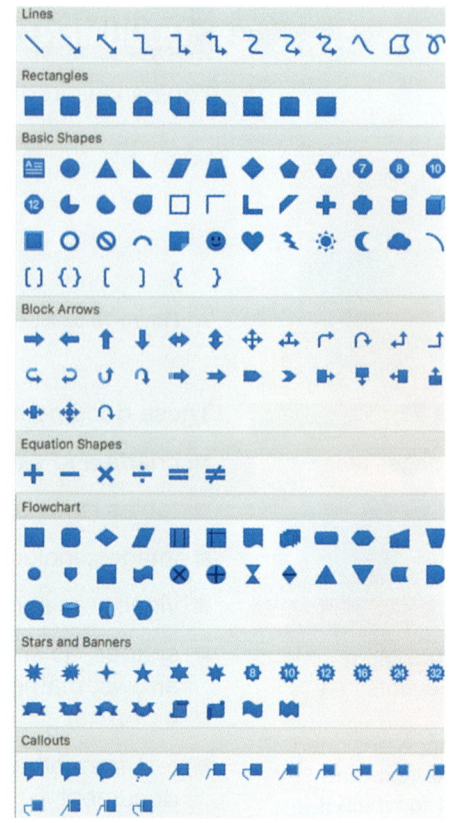

▲ Figure 15.54 Many different types of shape can be inserted into a document

After you have inserted different elements into a document, you can group them or layer them. Grouping elements allows you to edit or move elements together, so that they do not get separated. Layering allows you to position them in front of or behind each other or the main text.

DOCUMENT TYPES

Word processing software can be used to create a number of different types of document, including letters and posters.

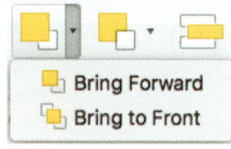

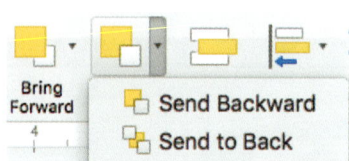

▲ Figure 15.55 Layer options in applications such as Microsoft Word allow you to position different document elements in front of or behind each other

LETTERS

GENERAL VOCABULARY

convention an agreed way of doing something

salutation a phrase used at the beginning of a letter or speech, such as 'Dear Mr Bell'

complimentary close the part of a letter that comes immediately before the sender's signature

When creating letters, it is a **convention** to start the document with a **salutation** and end it with a **complimentary close**. Table 15.4 contains examples of salutations and corresponding complimentary closes.

▼ Table 15.4 Examples of salutations and complimentary closes

SALUTATION	COMPLIMENTARY CLOSE
Dear Mr Bell,	Yours sincerely,
Hi, Mr Bell!	Kind regards,

When creating a letter, it is also conventional to:

- include your own address, the recipient's address and the date of the letter
- put these different elements in standard places on the page, as shown in Figure 15.56
- sign the letter by hand.

Some application software provides templates that will provide a letter layout for you.

▲ **Figure 15.56** An example of a letter layout in Microsoft Word

REPORT

A report is a formal document that is used to bring together and present information about a specific topic. To help present the information as clearly as possible, most reports are split into sections with each section having a heading.

> **HINT**
> Longer reports usually have a table of contents.

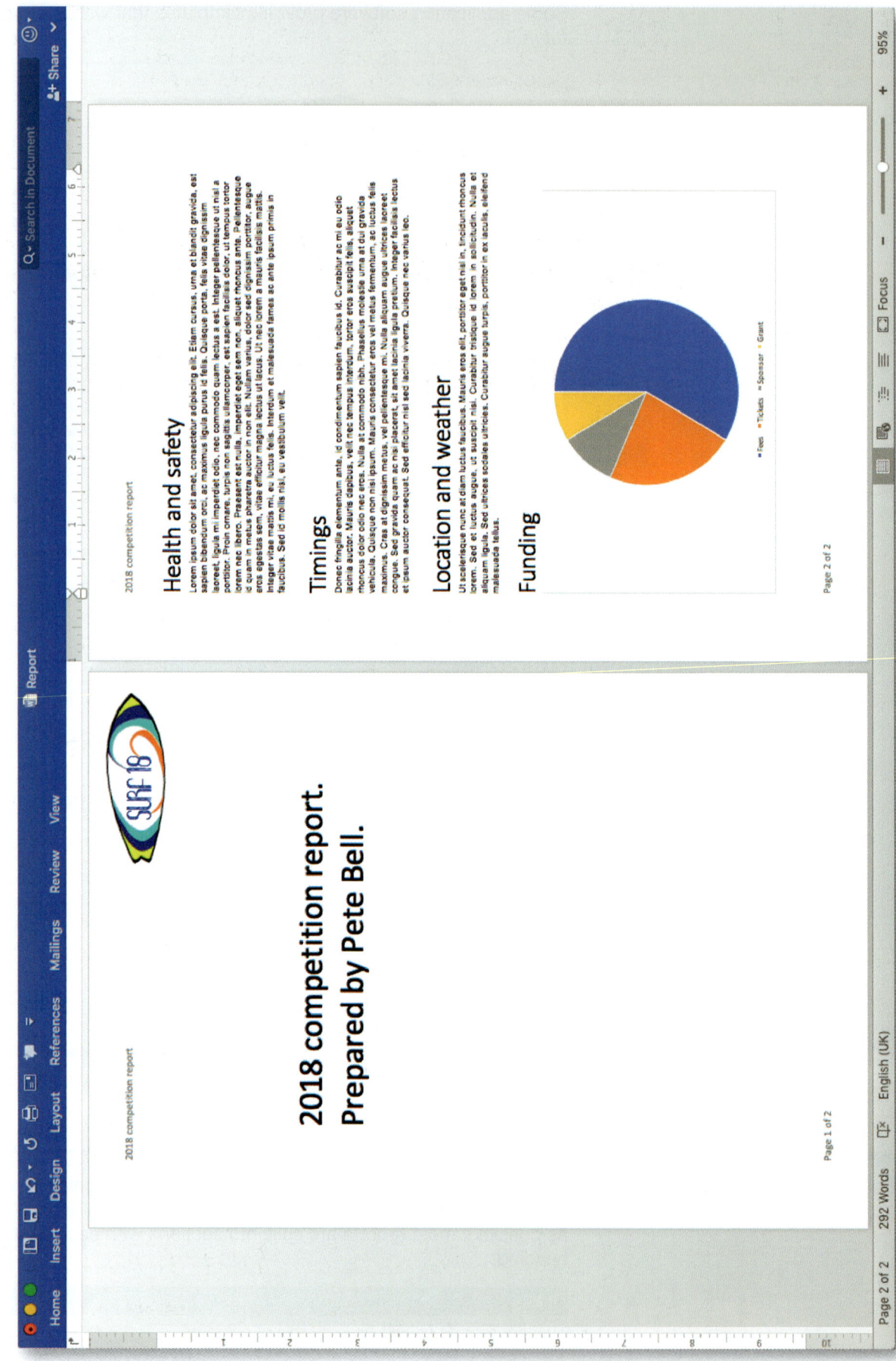

▲ Figure 15.57 An example of a report layout in Microsoft Word

NEWSLETTER

Newsletters are a less formal way of distributing information, such as to members of a club or society. Typically, newsletters use a column layout, as shown in Figure 15.58. For more information about column layouts, see page 219.

▲ Figure 15.58 The layout for the first page of a newsletter in Microsoft Word

POSTER

A poster is used to draw people's attention to something as they walk past it in the street or see it displayed on a notice board. A well-designed poster should not contain too much information, as people are unlikely to spend a lot of time reading it. When you are designing a poster, you should try to stick to just the

> **HINT**
>
> Simplicity is the key to good poster design. Instead of **cluttering** the poster with minor details, you could provide a QR code that links to a website containing all of the less important details. Keep the colours and fonts simple, too.

> **GENERAL VOCABULARY**
>
> **clutter** cover or fill a space with too many things, making it untidy and difficult to use
> **equidistant** at equal distances
> **intersection** the point at which two lines or roads cross each other

most important things that you want people to remember, such as dates and times or locations.

In a poster, one large image is often better than many different images.

You can use design principles such as the rule of thirds when you are designing digital products. The rule of thirds is a design principle that relies upon visualising a product as being divided into nine equal segments, divided by two **equidistant** horizontal lines and two equidistant vertical lines. Key components should be placed along the lines, or on or close to the **intersection** points of these lines.

▲ **Figure 15.59** The sky, background landscape and water/beach in this poster are approximately positioned on the imaginary horizontal lines; the surfer is positioned at an intersection, making it a focal point

> **HINT**
>
> Increase the page size, for example from A4 to A3, before you start creating your poster.

LEAFLET

A leaflet is a document used to distribute information or advertise products or services. Like newsletters, leaflets use columns (see page 219), but in leaflets this layout is used to create a design that can be folded once the document is printed. This produces the effect of separate pages.

▲ **Figure 15.60** This double-sided, folded leaflet in Microsoft Word uses a two-column design; note how the front page is on the right-hand side of the first page and the back page is on the left-hand side of the first page

> **KEY POINT**
>
> It is important to check how your printer prints double-sided documents to ensure that the leaflet prints as you expect it to.

INFORMATION SHEET OR FACT SHEET

Information sheets and fact sheets usually contain more information than you would place on a poster, for example. They are designed to be handed out to people in the street as flyers, given out at meetings or left on information stands for people to pick up.

An information sheet is usually a single, unfolded page, but they can be double-sided. The page size is usually set to **A5** and the page orientation is often set to portrait.

GENERAL VOCABULARY

A5 a standard size of paper (like A4 or A3) that is used in Europe and Japan and measures 148 × 210 mm

▲ Figure 15.61 An example of an information sheet in Microsoft Word

MEMO

Memo is an **abbreviation** of the word memorandum and means a brief note or message. Memos are commonly used within businesses to convey information quickly and clearly. The language and tone used in memos is less formal than the language used in a letter. When you are creating a memo, it is conventional to specify the subject, as shown in Figure 15.62, to make it clear to the **recipient** what the memo refers to.

GENERAL VOCABULARY

abbreviation a shortened version of a word or phrase

recipient someone receiving a letter or document

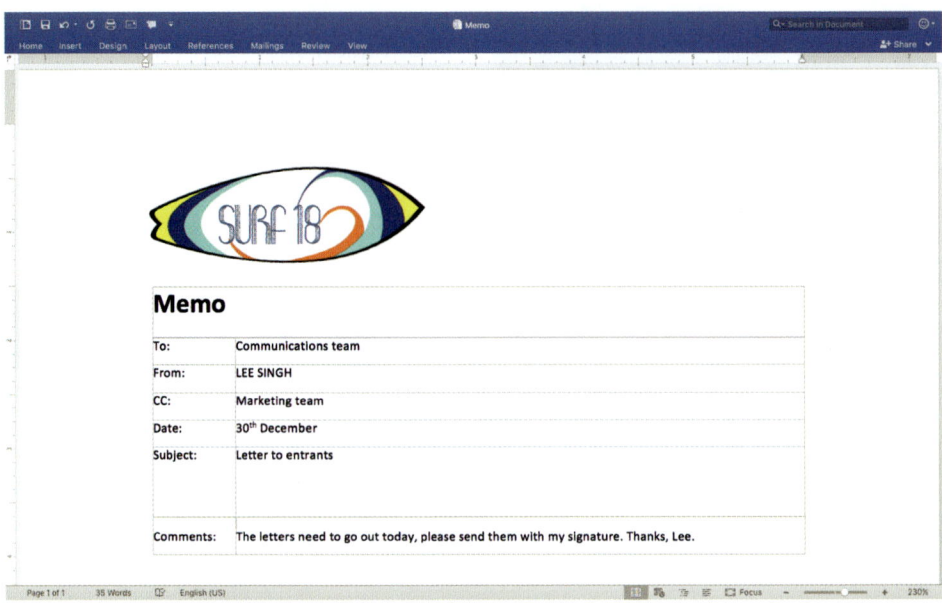

▲ Figure 15.62 An example of a memo in Microsoft Word

MAIL MERGE

Mail merge is used when you want to send the same document to many people but would like to **personalise** part of the document for each individual recipient. For example, you may want to add individual names and addresses to different copies of the same letter or to include personalised information in the text of a document, so that it appears to have been created for each recipient individually.

Mail merge uses two files:

- a data source
- a main document.

For example, if an organisation wants to send a letter to thousands of customers, they would only create one standard letter. This acts as the main document. The personalised information would not be typed into the letter, but stored as records in a data source. After the user chooses where the fields from the records in the data source should appear in the main document, the word processing application automatically puts the individual information from the data source into the main document and then prints or exports the individualised files.

> **DID YOU KNOW?**
> Some applications give you the option to email the document to email addresses if they are included in the data source.

> **HINT**
> A data source file can be created in a:
> - word processing application
> - spreadsheet application (see page 276)
> - database management application (see page 329).

> **GENERAL VOCABULARY**
> **personalise** design or change something so that it is suitable for a particular person

> **HINT**
> You will learn more about mail merging on pages 329–330.

> **KEY POINT**
> The benefit of mail merge is that personal information does not have to be manually entered into the document for each person. This saves many hours of repetitive work.

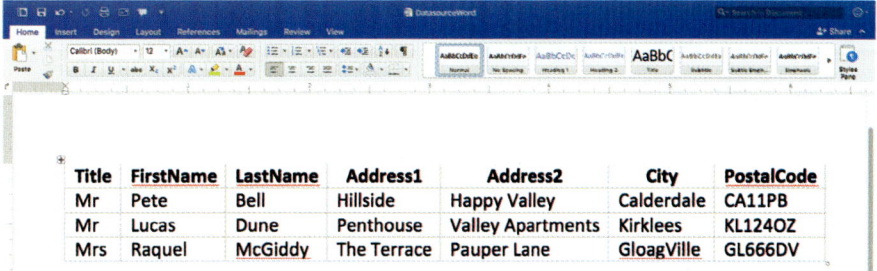

▲ Figure 15.63 A data source created in a word processing application (Microsoft Word)

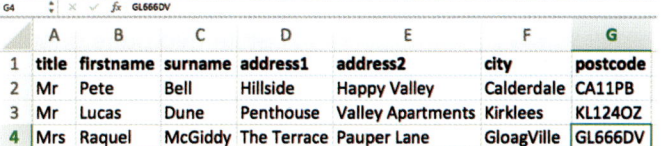

▲ Figure 15.64 A data source created in a spreadsheet application (Microsoft® Excel®)

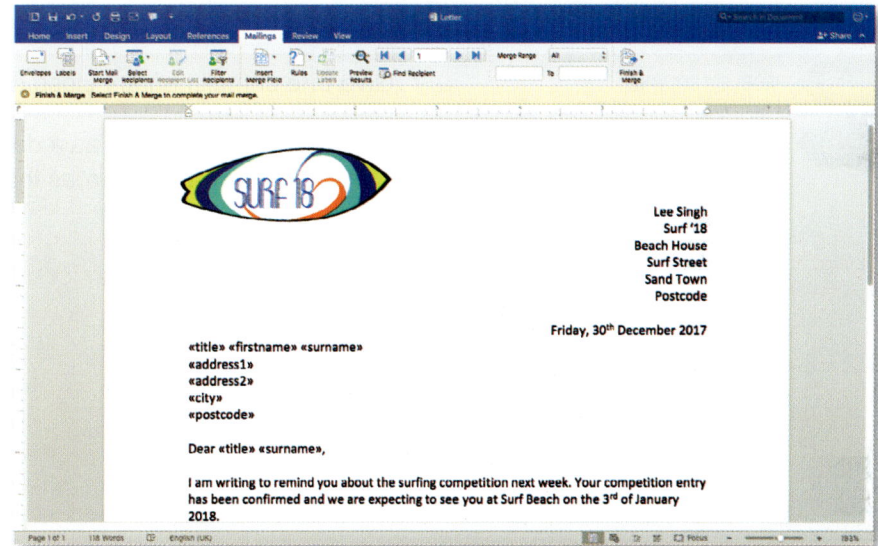

▲ Figure 15.65 The main document with the merge fields added from the data source

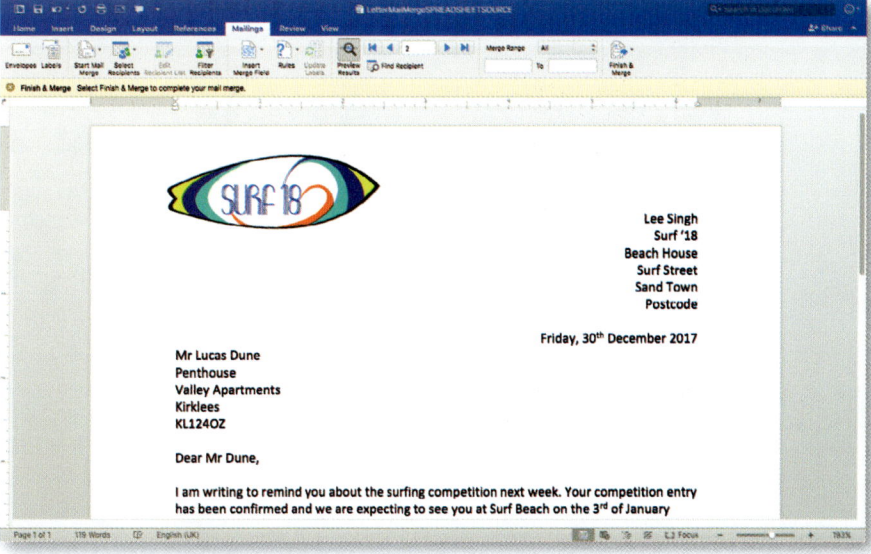

▲ Figure 15.66 The merged document showing the data from second record in the data source shown in Figure 15.64

CHAPTER QUESTIONS

SKILLS — INTERPRETATION

1. Which **one** of these document types is most likely to use columns? (1)
   - A Report
   - B Memo
   - C Letter
   - D Newsletter

SKILLS — REASONING

2. Explain why an automatic spell checker will not pick up all text errors. (2)

SKILLS — PROBLEM SOLVING

3. State **two** page orientations. (2)

SKILLS — INTERPRETATION

4. Identify **three** items that could be placed in a page footer. (3)

SKILLS — INTERPRETATION

5. Describe how mail merge can be applied to a document. (4)

SKILLS — PROBLEM SOLVING

6. Give **one** salutation that can be used in a formal letter. (1)

SKILLS — PROBLEM SOLVING

7. Give **one** complimentary close that can be used in a letter. (1)

SKILLS — PROBLEM SOLVING

8. A database can be used as a data source for a mail merge. State **two** other data sources that can be used for a mail merge. (2)

16 GRAPHICS

Graphics software is used to create and edit images. You may need to create graphics for use in other digital products, such as presentations or web pages. In this chapter, you will learn about tools that are found in different applications such as Microsoft® Paint, Google Drawings and LibreOffice® Draw.

LEARNING OBJECTIVES

- Explain features of image types: bitmap, vector
- Create images: combining basic shapes and text, rectangles (including square), circles (including ovals), lines, triangles, arrows, text boxes
- Edit images: image editing, cropping, adding captions/text, editing/deletion of unwanted aspects

FEATURES OF IMAGE TYPES

Graphic software can produce two types of images:
- bitmap images
- vector graphics.

BITMAP IMAGES

Bitmap images are used for photographs and scanned documents. They are made up of small squares called pixels. Each pixel is a tiny square of one single colour. Images that use more pixels are said to be higher resolution than images that use fewer pixels, meaning that the image is a better-quality image. This is shown in Figure 16.1.

▲ **Figure 16.1** The left side of this image uses fewer pixels than the right side of the image

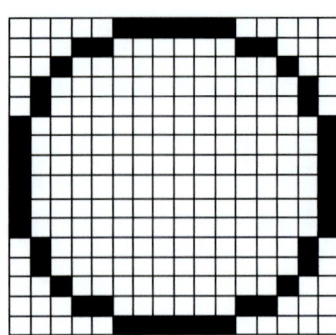

▲ Figure 16.2 Using a 256-pixel grid (right) allows you to represent a circle more accurately than using a 9-pixel grid (left)

Higher resolution images require more storage than lower resolution images because data has to be stored for a larger number of pixels. This means that higher resolution images have larger file sizes than lower resolution images.

If a bitmap graphic is **enlarged**, then each pixel is enlarged. This means that if the image is enlarged too much, individual pixels become visible. This is referred to as pixilation and can be seen in Figure 16.3.

GENERAL VOCABULARY

enlarged made bigger

▲ Figure 16.3 An image will pixelate when enlarged, as the individual pixels are made more obvious

VECTOR GRAPHICS

GENERAL VOCABULARY

co-ordinates a set of numbers that give the exact position of a point on a map or image

stylised drawn, written or performed in an artistic style that does not appear real or natural

Vector graphics do not pixelate when enlarged because they are made up of points or **co-ordinates** and lines. These are recalculated each time the image is redrawn, either by a printer or on a screen. Although vector graphics can look unrealistic or **stylised** when compared with bitmap images, they create much smaller files because data for each pixel does not need to be stored.

Vector graphics can be used to create image styles that are difficult to achieve in a bitmap image. For example, they are often used to create cartoons, technical illustrations and landscapes used in computer games, all of which need to be redrawn at different sizes in some way for the purposes of animation and to give the appearance of depth and movement.

Figure 16.4 shows the key difference between vector graphics and bitmap images. Because a bitmap image is made up of thousands of pixels, it pixelates when the viewer zooms in too far. The vector graphic does not pixelate because it is made of a series of simple mathematical co-ordinates, which means that, when the viewer zooms in, the image is accurately reproduced at a larger size.

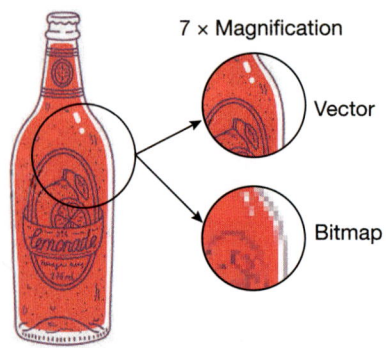

▲ Figure 16.4 The differences between vector graphics and bitmap images

HINT

Basic shapes, such as arrows, can be created by combining other shapes, such as a rectangle and a triangle, or by drawing them using lines.

CREATE IMAGES

When creating images, you must be able to combine basic shapes such as squares, rectangles, circles, ovals, triangles and arrows.

Although you can use specialist graphics applications, many of these shapes are also available in applications that are not obviously associated with graphics, such as Microsoft Word. For more information about the shapes available in word processing applications, see page 229. Often, you can choose from a range of basic shapes or create your own from lines. You also need to be able to incorporate lines and text, including text boxes.

Lines, shapes and text can have their fill colours altered, as shown in Figure 16.5.

▲ **Figure 16.5** The square has been drawn in Google Drawings and the fill colour has been altered from blue to red

The colour and thickness of the outside lines defining the shape can also be altered, as shown in Figure 16.6.

KEY POINT

Lines surround areas that can be filled with colour. The lines themselves can also be given a colour or left uncoloured.

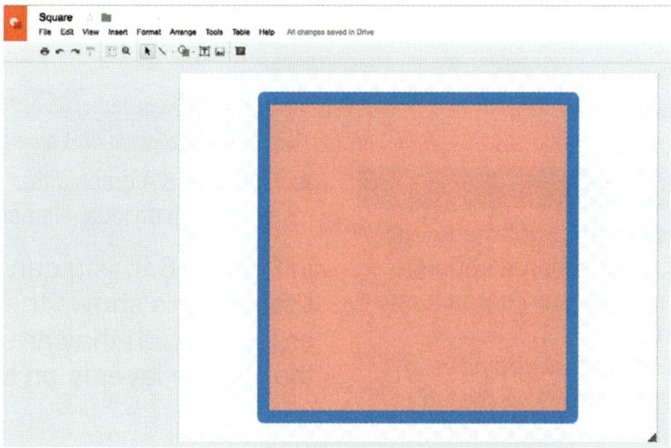

▲ **Figure 16.6** The square's line colour and thickness has been altered

Figure 16.7 shows an example of the way in which basic shapes can be combined to produce an image. The basic shapes used to make the image on the left are shown on the right.

▲ Figure 16.7 An image created in LibreOffice® Draw that uses 12 basic shapes

Figure 16.8 is an example of a graphic produced using curved lines filled with colour.

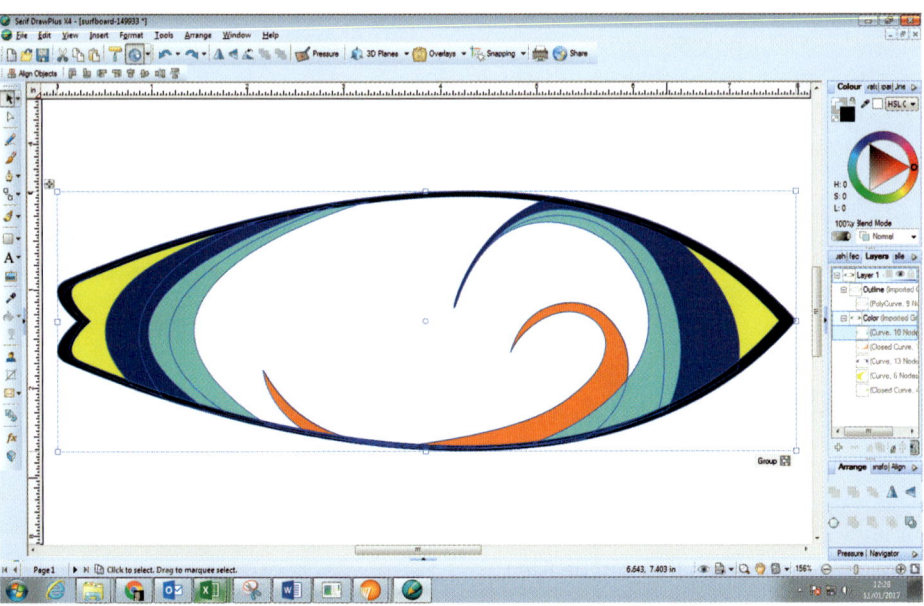

▲ Figure 16.8 A graphic that uses curved lines, some of which are filled with colour; the layers show the individual elements used to create the image

In Figure 16.9, you can see the list of **layers** as displayed in LibreOffice Draw®. This shows the individual elements used to create the image and the order in which they are placed on the **z axis**. In Figure 16.9, you can see that the Outline layer is on top of the Color layer on the z axis.

SUBJECT VOCABULARY

layers individual sections of the image; each layer is positioned on a separate plane of the z axis and can contain one or more elements

z axis the dimension that provides an image's depth and allows elements to appear in front of or behind other elements

UNIT 6 GRAPHICS 243

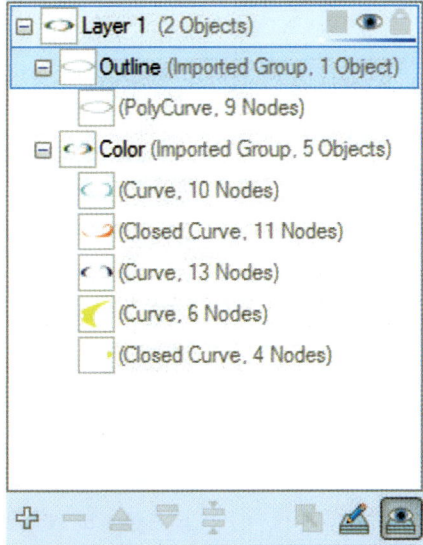

▲ **Figure 16.9** The layers used to create the image in Figure 16.8 (this is a close-up of the feature on the right of the screen in Figure 16.8)

SKILLS EXECUTIVE FUNCTION
ADAPTABILITY
CREATIVITY

ACTIVITY

▼ USING SHAPES AND LINES

1 Using shapes and lines, create your own version of the penguin graphic shown in Figure 16.7.
2 Create a logo for an ice cream company using shapes and lines.

EDIT IMAGES

Image editing tools allow you to change an image in a number of ways.

RESIZE AND ROTATE

GENERAL VOCABULARY

rotate move in a circular motion around a central point

SUBJECT VOCABULARY

resize point a point at which an image can be dragged to be resized
rotate point the pivot point around which an image can be rotated

You can resize or **rotate** an image by clicking the image with your mouse to show its handles. These are the **resize points** and **rotate points** shown in Figure 16.10.

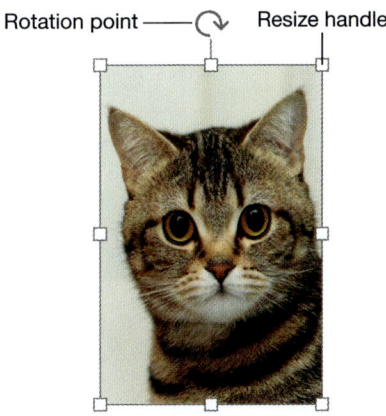

▲ **Figure 16.10** Once an image is selected with the mouse, the eight handles that act as resize points and the rotate point will be visible

UNIT 6 — GRAPHICS

SUBJECT VOCABULARY

dragging moving with the mouse
aspect ratio the ratio of an image's width and height

GENERAL VOCABULARY

distorted twisted out of shape
proportions the relative sizes of different parts of an object or image

Resizing an image by **dragging** the handles in the corners of the image maintains the image's **aspect ratio**. However, resizing the image by dragging the handles on the sides of the image does not maintain its aspect ratio, meaning that the image appears **distorted**.

▲ **Figure 16.11** This image has been resized by dragging from the top or bottom, which means that it has lost its aspect ratio and has become distorted

HINT

Some applications require you to hold down the Shift key while dragging from the corner to maintain the aspect ratio and the **proportions** of the image.

CROPPING

Cropping an image means cutting off and deleting part or parts of it in order to make it a particular size or shape. For example, the image in Figure 16.12 has an original aspect ratio of 4:6. Figure 16.12 shows the image once it has been cropped to 5:7 and 8:10.

▲ **Figure 16.12** Cropping allows images to fit different aspect ratios or to remove unwanted parts of an image

SKILLS EXECUTIVE FUNCTION
COMMUNICATION
REASONING

ACTIVITY

▼ **CROPPING AN IMAGE**

1 Using the internet, find an image of a soccer match and crop the image so that it only shows the player with the soccer ball.
2 Discuss the reasons why using a high-resolution image provides a better result when cropping.

ADDING CAPTIONS AND TEXT

GENERAL VOCABULARY

caption a short title, description or explanation of an image
slogan a short and easy-to-remember phrase, often used in advertising

Text can be added to an image. For example, you might add a **caption** to a photograph or add a **slogan** or strapline to a logo.

EDITING OR DELETING UNWANTED PARTS OF AN IMAGE

If there are areas of a bitmap image that you do not want, you can either erase them or recolour them so that they blend in with surrounding areas of the image. Figure 16.13 shows some of the tools available to do this in Microsoft Paint.

▲ **Figure 16.13** Tools in Microsoft Paint

Most applications have a Colour Picker tool that allows you to select a colour from a nearby area of the image and then use a brush or pencil tool to cover the unwanted area with the selected colour. For example, you can remove the tower in the background of Figure 16.14 by picking the colours around it, as shown in Figure 16.15, and using a brush tool with this colour to paint over the tower, as shown in Figure 16.16. Doing this improves the image, as shown in Figure 16.17 and 16.18.

▲ **Figure 16.14** The tower on top of a building on the right of this image is unwanted

▲ **Figure 16.15** The Colour Picker has been used to select the colour around the tower, which is now ready to be used as Colour 1

▲ **Figure 16.16** The tower has been removed

▲ **Figure 16.17** The same image after the tower has been removed

▲ **Figure 16.18** Before editing and after editing; the edit has improved the image now the tower has been removed from the background

UNIT 6 | GRAPHICS

SKILLS EXECUTIVE FUNCTION

ACTIVITY

▼ **EDITING AN IMAGE**

1 Using the internet, find an image of a landscape or natural scene.
2 Open the image in a bitmap graphics editing application.
3 Find an element of the image that you would like to remove, such as a building or power line, and edit this element from the image.

GENERAL VOCABULARY

breach break a law, rule or agreement

HINT

Be careful that you do not **breach** the image owner's copyright by editing an image that should not be edited. You may not be permitted to alter the image. For more information about copyright, see *Unit 3 Operating online* (page 149).

CHAPTER QUESTIONS

SKILLS PROBLEM SOLVING

1 Which **one** of these needs to be maintained in order to prevent an image from becoming distorted? **(1)**
  A Z axis
  B Aspect ratio
  C Rotation
  D Grouping

SKILLS REASONING

2 Explain why vector graphics do not pixelate when they are enlarged. **(3)**

SKILLS INTERPRETATION

3 Describe how layers can be used to create an image. **(2)**

4 State the name of the small elements that make up a bitmap image. **(1)**

SKILLS REASONING

5 Give **one** drawback of using vector graphics to represent natural objects. **(1)**

SKILLS INTERPRETATION

6 State **two** ways of removing unwanted parts of an image. **(2)**

17 PRESENTATION

Presentations are most often used to support a person delivering information on a topic to an audience. They are a great way of adding context to a speech and engaging your audience. In this chapter, you will learn about tools that are found in different applications such as Microsoft® PowerPoint® and LibreOffice® Impress.

Presentations are made up of a series of slides that are usually displayed on a large screen. Each slide can contain text and image content related to a section of the presentation, and each slide can use effects to draw attention to important information. As a speaker moves between sub-topics, the slides can be advanced so that the audience is presented with content that is relevant to each new sub-topic.

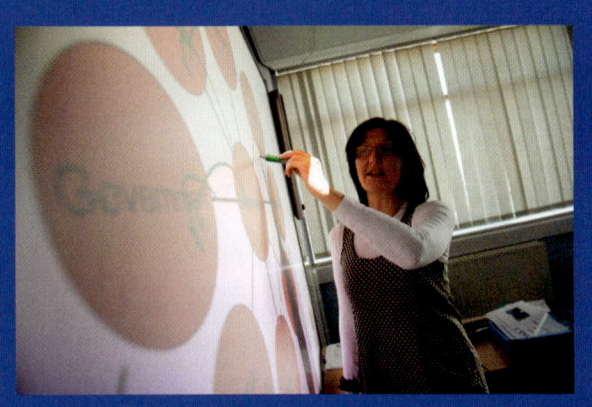

LEARNING OBJECTIVES

- Create a template/master slide: placeholders, footer, slide number, background, font enhancements (bold, italic, underline)
- Create slides: insert text, images, action buttons, hyperlinks; add animation, transition effects
- Print: handouts (two to a page, three to a page), notes pages, full page, headers and footers

GENERAL VOCABULARY

consistent done the same way
layout the way in which elements are arranged and structured
design the choices that are made concerning the style of a product

TEMPLATE AND MASTER SLIDE

To ensure that your presentation has a **consistent layout** and **design**, you can use a template or theme. Figure 17.1 shows some of the templates available in Microsoft PowerPoint.

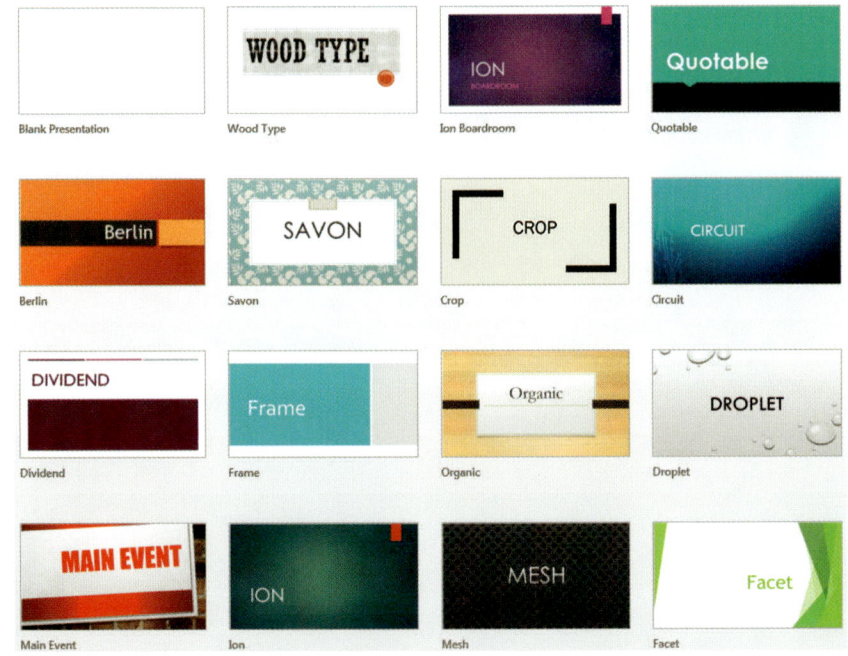

▲ Figure 17.1 Examples of slide design templates or themes in Microsoft PowerPoint

DID YOU KNOW?
Templates are also known as themes or slide decks.

As well as templates that affect the appearance of every slide in the presentation, presentation applications also provide several different slide layouts that you can use within a presentation. For example, when you open a new presentation, the first slide is usually set up using a Title Slide layout, as shown in Figure 17.2.

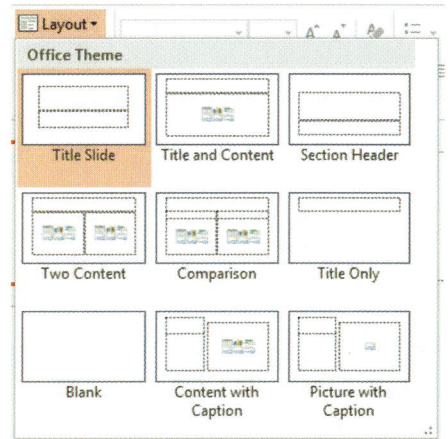

▲ **Figure 17.2** Slide layouts in Microsoft PowerPoint

All templates use the same group of slide layouts, some of which are shown in Figure 17.2, but each template has an individual design that is based on a master slide or **slide master**. The slide master content can only be edited using the Slide Master view, which is accessed in Microsoft PowerPoint by choosing Slide Master from the View tab.

You can produce your own template by editing an existing slide master theme, such as the Blank Presentation theme.

Figure 17.3 shows that this user has selected the slide master from the list on the left (highlighted in orange). Changes made to the design of the slide master will also be made on the individual slide layout masters, which appear underneath the slide master in the list on the left. However, if you want all slides that use a particular layout to share a design feature, then you can edit the design on the slide master for a particular layout, too.

SUBJECT VOCABULARY

slide master (or master slide) in a slide presentation, a template slide that specifies the layout and appearance of content slides

KEY POINT

You are not editing the content on the slides that you will present when you edit the template in Slide Master view.

HINT

Make sure you close the Slide Master view when you want to start adding content to your slides, otherwise every bit of content you add may be added to every slide.

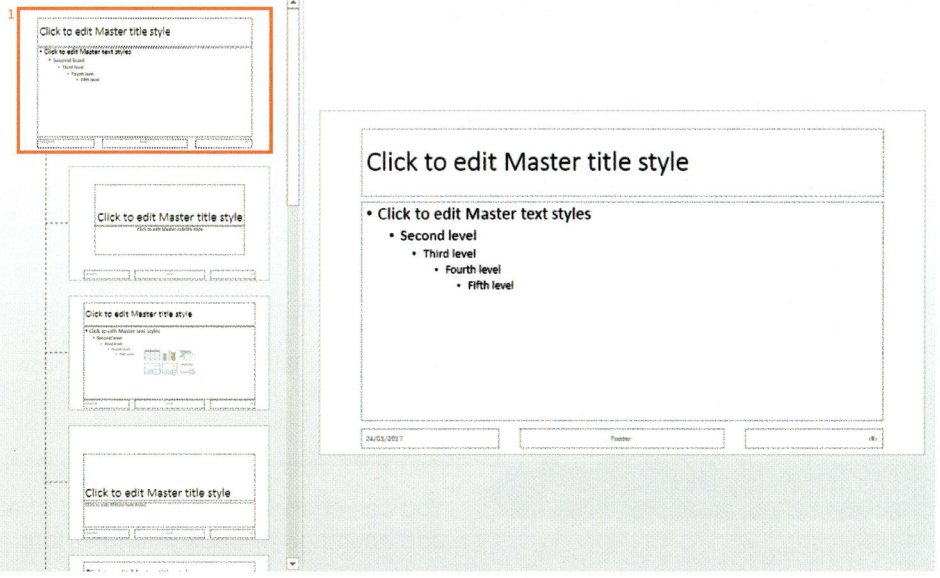

▲ **Figure 17.3** Slide Master view in Microsoft PowerPoint; any changes made to the main slide master will be applied to every slide layout master

PLACEHOLDERS

GENERAL VOCABULARY

placeholder an area in a layout, such as a slide layout, into which content can be placed

The slide master contains **placeholders** for content. These can be made available or unavailable by selecting Master Layout in the Slide Master tab.

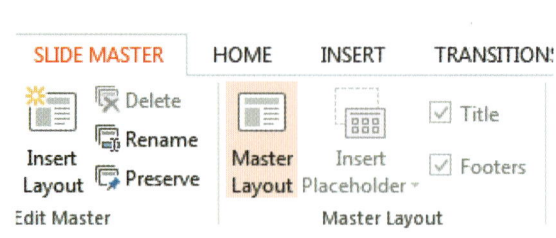 

▲ **Figure 17.4** Selecting Master Layout in Microsoft PowerPoint (left) opens the Placeholders window (right), which lets you choose which placeholders to make available on each slide

SUBJECT VOCABULARY

clip art images, photographs or pictures that you can copy and use in your own computer documents

HINT

Bou can add more placeholders to slide layout masters by selecting the Insert Placeholder option on the Slide Master tab. You can add placeholders for text, pictures, tables, charts, **clip art**, videos and more.

DATE AND TIME, FOOTER AND SLIDE NUMBER

At the bottom of a slide layout, you can format the way in which the date and time, footer and slide number will appear on each slide. They will appear on the slides in your presentation if they are selected from the Header and Footer window after the Master View is closed, as shown in Figure 17.5.

KEY POINT

You can create separate slide masters for each layout. This means that elements can be made to appear differently on slides with different layouts, and ensures that every slide that uses a particular layout will use the same format.

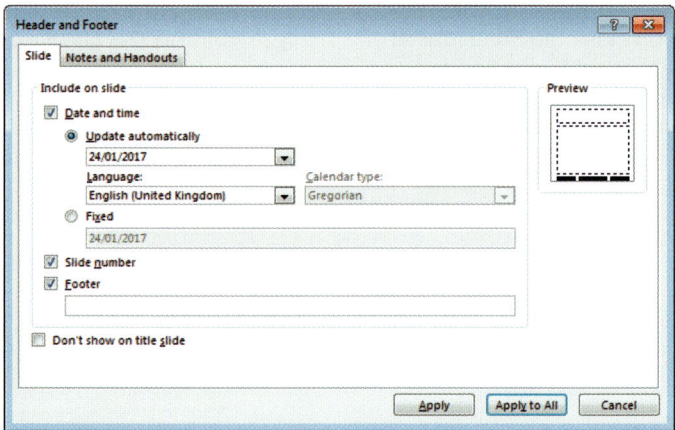

▲ **Figure 17.5** The Header and Footer window is available from the Insert tab in Microsoft PowerPoint

BACKGROUND

You can change the background of all slides using the slide master. You can add an image or background colour.

You should always make sure that your text can still be read if you change the background colour or image (as shown in Figure 17.6). If you are using a light background colour, use dark text, and if you use a dark background colour, use lighter-coloured text. This will ensure that the text stands out against the background.

▲ **Figure 17.6** The text on this slide is not easy to read

If you are using an image as your background, consider increasing the brightness of the image until it becomes very light or washed out (see Figure 17.7). This will ensure that dark coloured text will **stand out** against it, as shown in Figure 17.8. Alternatively, you could apply a slightly transparent background colour to the text placeholders, as shown in Figure 17.9. This makes the text readable but also retains the original colours of the image.

GENERAL VOCABULARY

stand out easily seen or noticed

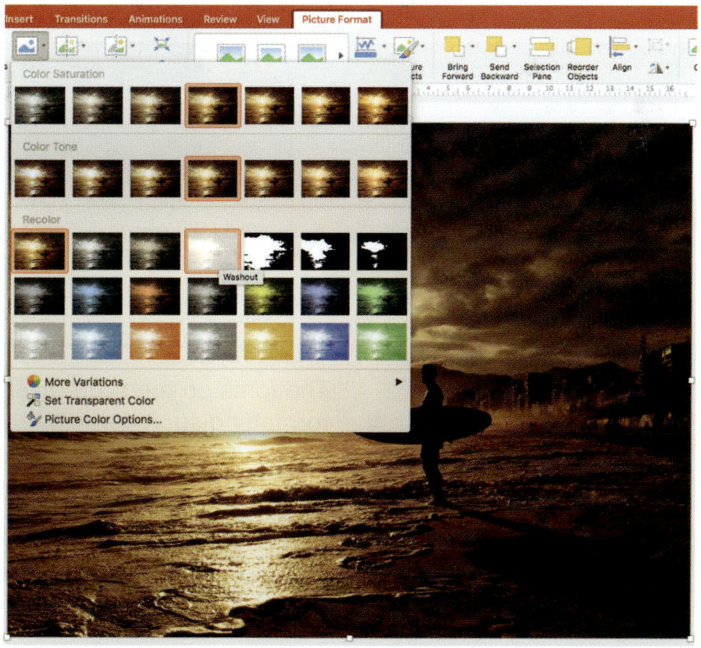

▲ **Figure 17.7** Applying a washout effect in Microsoft PowerPoint

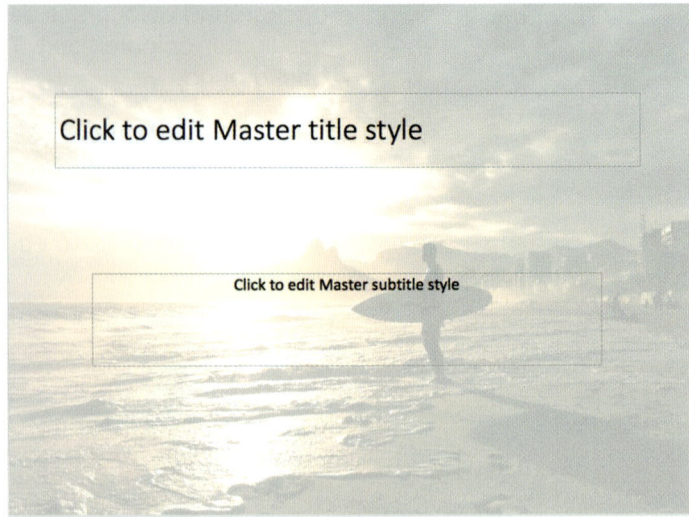

▲ **Figure 17.8** Once the washout effect has been applied, the text is easy to read

▲ **Figure 17.9** Applying a slightly transparent background colour to text placeholders makes it easy to read the text on the slide without affecting the colours in the image

FONT ENHANCEMENT

GENERAL VOCABULARY
enhance add emphasis

SKILLS ▸ EXECUTIVE FUNCTION

The fonts on the slide master or slide layout masters can be **enhanced** using formatting such as bold, italic or underlining.

ACTIVITY

▼ **CREATING A TEMPLATE**

Recreate the template shown in Figure 17.9. If you are using Microsoft PowerPoint, follow the instructions below.

1. Create a new presentation using a Blank Presentation template.
2. From the View menu, choose Slide Master.
3. Hide the Footers (from the Master Layout group on the Slide Master tab).

4 Add an image of your choice to the slide master, so that it appears as the background on all slide layouts.

5 Change the background colour of the content placeholders on the first four slide layout masters. For each placeholder:
   - right-click the placeholder and select Format Shape
   - set a Solid fill, using a colour that matches a prominent colour in the image
   - change the transparency to 50%.

6 Close Slide Master view.

7 Save your file.

SLIDES

Once you have set up your template and slide master, you can begin to add content to your individual slides.

TEXT AND IMAGES

HINT

You can also create new text boxes on a slide. However, if you do this too much, the use of text boxes will make the presentation's layout less consistent.

You can add text and images into the content placeholders on your slides. If you add a lot of text to a placeholder, the text will automatically resize so that it fits the placeholder.

Try to limit the amount of text that you use on each slide. Presentations are not meant to repeat everything that the speaker says, but should give a few key points as a visual guide or reminder for the audience. If the audience is too busy reading lots of text on the slide, they may not be listening to what the speaker is saying.

Sometimes, images can be much more powerful than words. You can even use images or charts to summarise the point or points that you are making on each slide without using any text at all. For example, compare Figures 17.10 and 17.11. Both slides give the same information, but Figure 17.11 requires the audience to do less reading.

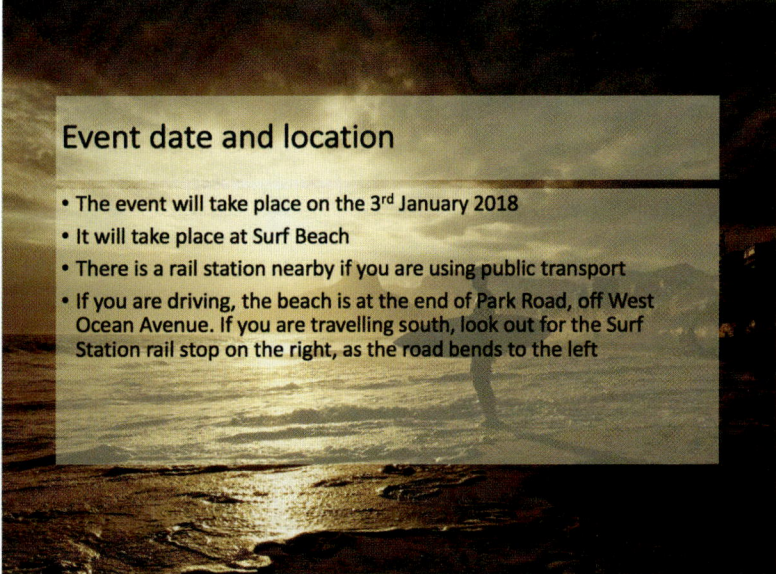

▲ Figure 17.10 This slide provides lots of information in bullet points

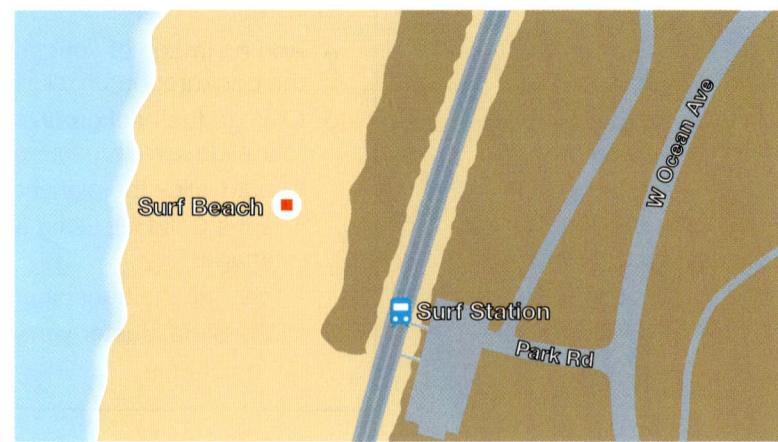

▲ **Figure 17.11** This slide provides the same information given in the slide in Figure 17.10, but it requires almost no reading

> **KEY POINT**
> Do not put notes on your slides. Slides are not meant to be used as speaker notes. For more information about speaker notes, see page 259.

ACTION BUTTONS

Presentation applications can be used to create interactive navigation using action buttons. Figure 17.12 shows some examples.

Action buttons have several uses. For example, if a teacher wanted to use a large touch screen, such as an interactive whiteboard, to show a presentation on a topic to a class, they might not want to walk to the keyboard to advance the slide each time. Instead, they could use action buttons that would allow them to advance the slides by pressing on the interactive whiteboard's screen.

▲ **Figure 17.12** Action buttons in Microsoft PowerPoint come with **ready-made** actions, but you can alter their actions

> **GENERAL VOCABULARY**
> **ready-made** already prepared or made and ready to be used immediately

The action buttons feature is only available in Microsoft PowerPoint and can be accessed from the Shapes menu on the Insert tab.

▲ **Figure 17.13** The Shapes menu in Microsoft PowerPoint

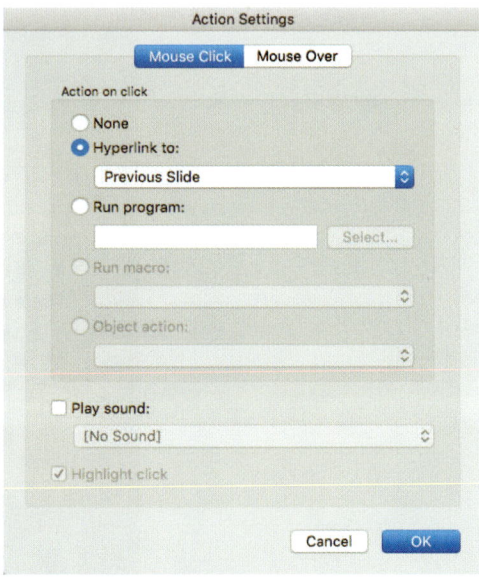

▲ **Figure 17.14** Action settings for action buttons appear when you insert an action button into a Microsoft PowerPoint presentation

Action buttons are also used in kiosk displays, such as the one shown in Figure 17.15. Kiosks allow users to control navigation using a touch screen interface.

If you are using buttons to allow users to **navigate** through your presentation, you might want to deselect the On Mouse Click setting from the Transitions tab.

If you do not **deselect** this setting, users who control the presentation with a touch screen will find that pressing any area of the screen will cause the presentation to advance to the next slide. This may cause problems as users will expect that only the buttons control slide navigation.

▲ Figure 17.15 A touch screen kiosk display

SUBJECT VOCABULARY

navigate move around a piece of application software or a system, such as from one slide to the next

deselect remove something from a list of choices on a computer

HINT

There are two ways of disabling the On Mouse Click setting in Microsoft PowerPoint.
1. Go to the Transitions tab and deselect On Mouse Click.
2. Set the presentation to run in kiosk mode by going to the Slide Show tab, selecting Set Up Slide Show and selecting the option, Browsed at a kiosk, as shown in Figure 17.16.

 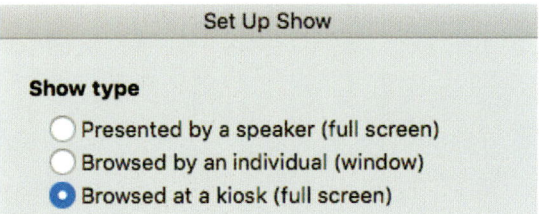

▲ Figure 17.16 You can set your Microsoft PowerPoint presentation to run in kiosk mode

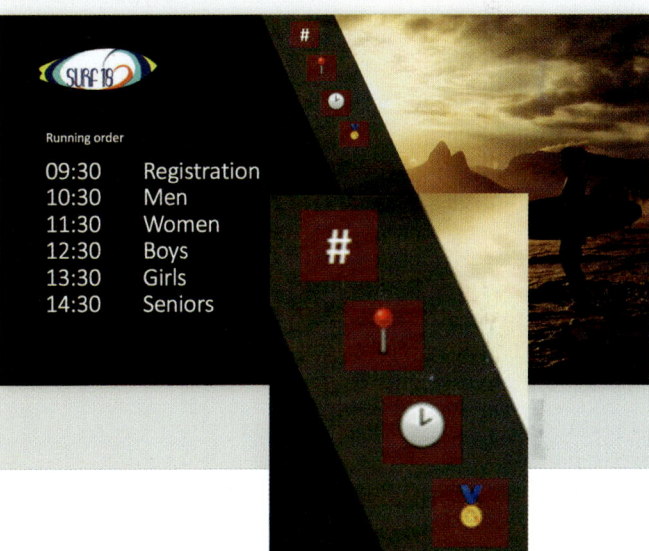

▲ Figure 17.17 This Microsoft PowerPoint presentation uses four **custom** action buttons to lead to different individual slides

GENERAL VOCABULARY

custom specially made for a specific purpose or altered from an original form to serve a specific purpose

SKILLS ▶ EXECUTIVE FUNCTION

ACTIVITY

▼ USING ACTION BUTTONS

1. Open the file 'Surf18.pptx'.
2. Right-click on the buttons and choose Action Settings to see their settings.
3. View the presentation by pressing F5 on the keyboard or selecting the Play From Start button on the Slide Show tab. Try using the buttons. Notice how the buttons are the only way to navigate through the slide show. If you click on an area of the slide, rather than on the buttons, nothing will happen.
4. Press the Escape (Esc) key on the keyboard to end the show.

> **SUBJECT VOCABULARY**
>
> **macro** a function that runs a set of instructions to perform a task

Although this feature is only found in Microsoft PowerPoint, other applications also allow you to create buttons. For example, you can create buttons in LibreOffice Impress by using the Form Control menu, selecting the Push Button feature and setting a **macro** for that button. You can then make the macro control what should happen when the button is pressed.

▲ Figure 17.18 Creating a Push Button in LibreOffice Impress

HYPERLINKS

During a presentation, you may want to open content from outside the presentation slides, such as a web page or a spreadsheet in a folder on your computer. You can insert a hyperlink to do this, as shown in Figure 17.19.

Hyperlinks can open:

- local files
- online content
- slides in the current presentation or custom shows
- email addresses (used to compose a new email in the user's default email application with the address field already filled in).

Hyperlinks can be added onto images or text, which is then clicked to access the hyperlink.

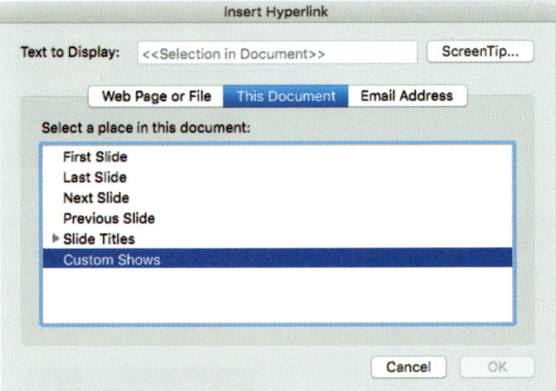

▲ Figure 17.19 Hyperlinks can be inserted to allow users to navigate to content inside or outside the presentation slides

ANIMATIONS

Animations are visual effects that add emphasis and movement. They are used to draw attention to important information, and they can be added to slide content such as text, pictures, shapes, tables, SmartArt graphics and other objects. Figure 17.20 shows some examples of animation effects in Microsoft PowerPoint.

▲ Figure 17.20 Examples of animation effects in Microsoft PowerPoint

UNIT 6 PRESENTATION

SUBJECT VOCABULARY

transitions (in a slide presentation) the effects that occur when a user moves from one slide to the next

▲ **Figure 17.21** The Animation Pane button in the Animations tab in Microsoft PowerPoint

SKILLS ▶ EXECUTIVE FUNCTION

SUBJECT VOCABULARY

entrance effect an animation effect that occurs when an object is brought onto a slide during a presentation
exit effect an animation effect that occurs when an object leaves a slide during a presentation

HINT

Animations are not the same as transitions.
- **Transitions** are applied to slides.
- Animations are applied to content on slides.

You can control the order in which the animations on a slide occur using the Animation Pane, which is accessed through the Animations tab as shown in Figure 17.21. You can set animations to happen on a mouse click, or automatically. Objects' animations can be timed to run at the same time as or after other objects' animations.

ACTIVITY

▼ APPLYING ANIMATIONS

1. Open the file 'Surf18.pptx'. This is a presentation that is designed to be used at a sporting event on a touch screen kiosk.
2. Apply **entrance effects** to the map objects on the second slide to make the objects enter automatically, one after the other. Make sure that the First Aid box and the red cross symbol enter at the same time, and do not apply animation to the slide title, the buttons, the image, or the logo.
3. Apply a Fade **exit effect** to the red cross symbol.
4. Apply a Fade entrance effect to the red cross symbol. This will help to draw the user's attention to it.
5. Animate the text on the Results slide (the final slide). Choose an effect which is appropriate for sports results.
6. View the presentation.
7. Save the presentation to a suitable folder.

TRANSITIONS

GENERAL VOCABULARY

preview see something before choosing it or publishing it
duration the length of time that something continues

Slide transitions are the effects that occur when a user moves from one slide to the next.

You can choose from a range of ready-made transition effects, as shown in Figure 17.22. Clicking one of the available effects allows you to **preview** the effect. You can set the **duration** for each transition and can define whether the transition should occur On Mouse Click. You can also set the transition to occur after a set period of time using the After functionality.

The chosen transition and its settings are applied to the active or selected slide. You can also apply the same transition to all slides using the Apply To All functionality. Applying the same transition to all slides can improve the consistency of your presentation.

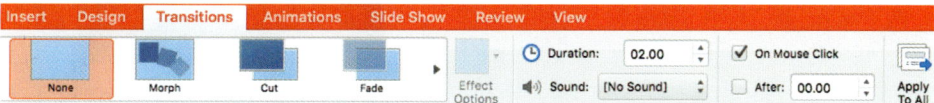

▲ **Figure 17.22** Different transition effects can be found on the Transitions tab in Microsoft PowerPoint

HINT

Do not use too many animations or transitions because they lose their impact when they are overused.

PRINT

If you need to print your presentation, there are several different print layouts available. Your choice will depend on the purpose of printing your presentation.

HANDOUTS

Handouts are given to your audience so that they have a copy of the information that you are presenting. This can help your audience to follow your presentation more easily and allow them to take notes on the slides.

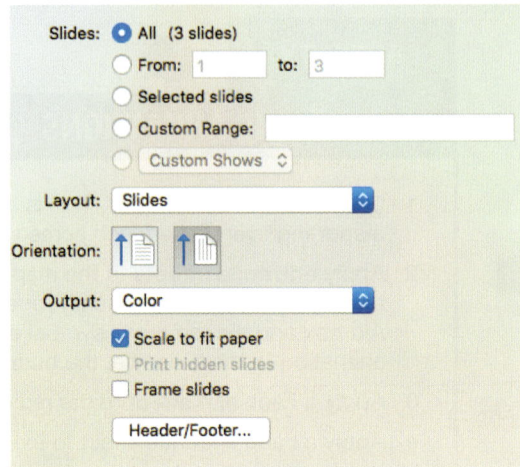

▲ **Figure 17.23** The Print options available in Microsoft PowerPoint

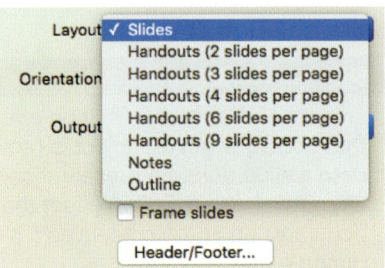

▲ **Figure 17.24** Selecting the Layout or Print Layout menu shows a variety of print layout options

The most common handout layouts are Handouts (2 slides per page) and Handouts (3 slides per page). These layouts are shown in Figure 17.25.

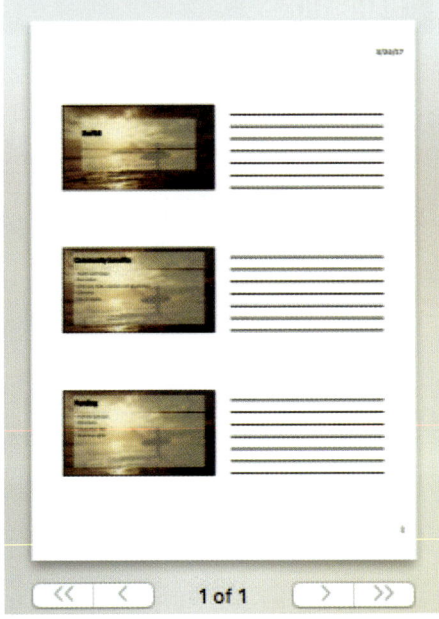

▲ **Figure 17.25** The Handouts (3 slides per page) print layout includes writing lines to the right of each slide, which are useful if you expect your audience to take notes

NOTES PAGES

When giving a presentation, you or the person speaking may need to refer to notes. Presentation applications provide a Speaker Notes section with each slide where you can add notes for the presenter, as shown in Figure 17.26. You can use this to add a complete script for the presenter to follow, or a few points that need to be explained.

▲ **Figure 17.26** Speaker notes for each slide can be added underneath the slides in Microsoft PowerPoint

If you want the notes to be visible when you print the presentation, you can select the Notes or Notes Pages print layout, as shown in Figure 17.27. Having printed speaker notes allows presenters the freedom to move around with their notes, perhaps controlling the slideshow remotely.

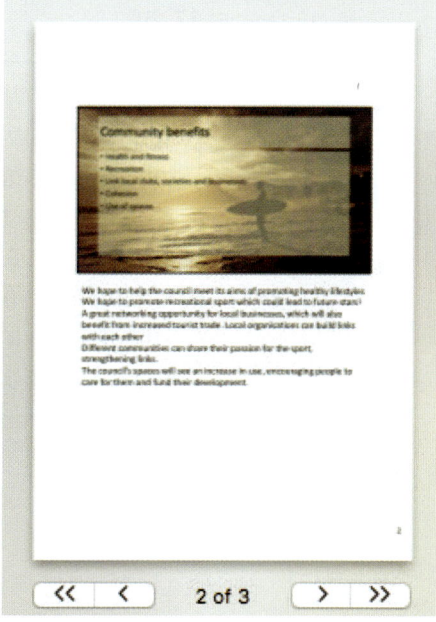

▲ **Figure 17.27** Choosing the Notes layout option prints the notes underneath an image of the slide

> **KEY POINT**
> You may not be the one to present your presentation. Your notes should be detailed enough for any presenter to use.

You can also use the Notes field to add speaker notes about hyperlinks that need to be clicked or important information about timings that the presenter should know.

FULL PAGE

Choosing the Slides or Full Page Slides print layout gives the result shown in Figure 17.28. This print layout is useful if you want to create posters from the slides, which you can display.

▲ **Figure 17.28** Choosing the Slides print layout allows you to print one slide per page

HEADERS AND FOOTERS

When printing your presentation, you can choose to print information in the header and footer, such as the time and date, slide numbers and a standard footer. You can do this by selecting Header/Footer or Edit Header & Footer in the Print settings and selecting the appropriate fields, as shown in Figure 17.29.

> **DID YOU KNOW?**
> You can show your presentation in Presenter View from the Slide Show tab. This feature is shown in Figure 17.30 and:
> - shows the notes for the current slide on the screen
> - gives you a preview of the next slide
> - can help you to keep track of slide timings.
>
> This feature means that you do not have to print notes pages, so it saves paper and is better for the environment.

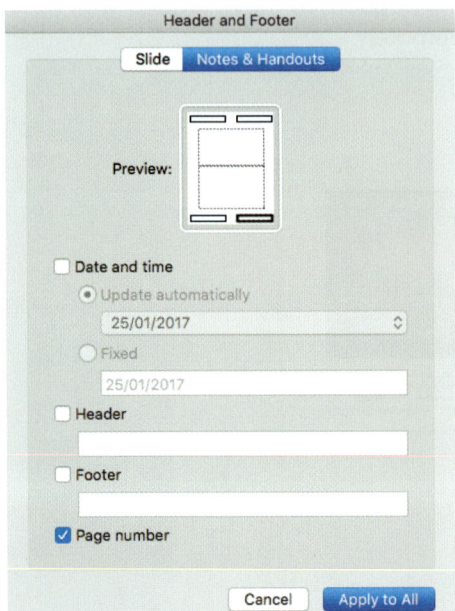

▲ **Figure 17.29** Header and footer options for the Notes & Handouts layout in Microsoft PowerPoint

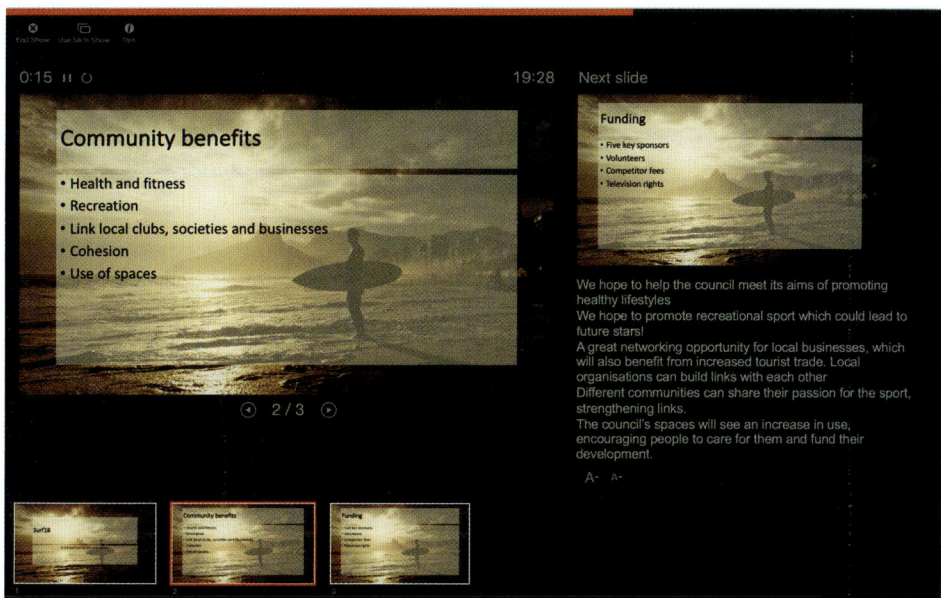

▲ **Figure 17.30** Presenter View in Microsoft PowerPoint

CHAPTER QUESTIONS

SKILLS INTERPRETATION

1. Which **one** of these would make a presentation most readable? (1)
   A Low contrast between background and text
   B Dark background and dark text
   C Light background and light text
   D High contrast between background and text

SKILLS REASONING

2. State the reason why using a slide master gives a consistent layout. (1)

SKILLS REASONING

3. State **one** reason why it is not appropriate to place lots of text on a slide. (1)

SKILLS PROBLEM SOLVING

4. List **three** font enhancements that can be applied to text. (3)

SKILLS INTERPRETATION

5. Describe how transitions can be used in a presentation. (2)

SKILLS INTERPRETATION

6. Give **one** way of reducing the amount of text on a slide while providing the same amount of information. (1)

SKILLS REASONING

7. Explain why action buttons would be useful for presentations shown in kiosk mode. (2)

SKILLS INTERPRETATION

8. Give **two** destinations that hyperlinks can link to from within a presentation. (2)

SKILLS PROBLEM SOLVING

9. List **three** print layouts available for presentations. (3)

SKILLS INTERPRETATION

10. Describe **two** ways in which Presenter View can support a speaker during a presentation. (4)

18 WEB AUTHORING

Web pages are documents containing Hypertext Markup Language (HTML), which is the language of the World Wide Web. HTML code is read by web browser software, which carries out the instructions provided by the HTML code and displays the resulting output as a web page.

Browsers display web page content and also content that is linked from a page.

To create web pages, you can either write HTML in a text editor or use a specialist application such as Adobe® Dreamweaver®. Specialist applications allow you to place content on a page without having to know the syntax (computer language) of HTML. The application will often allow you to edit the HTML that it produces automatically. You can also use some word processing and presentation applications to create web pages, although their functionality is limited.

In this chapter, you will learn about the tools available in applications such as Adobe Dreamweaver, KompoZer and Amaya. You will also see how a plain-text editor and specialist programming text editor can be used to create web pages.

LEARNING OBJECTIVES

- Use a template: tables/frames, standard page features, banners, menu/navigation
- Insert text, images, buttons, animation
- Format a web page: headings, subheadings, body text, alignment
- Use HTML code: insert hyperlinks, insert images, font enhancements

HINT
A website can contain one or more web pages.

SKILLS EXECUTIVE FUNCTION

SUBJECT VOCABULARY
WYSIWYG ('What You See Is What You Get') when something is presented on screen exactly as it will look when the finished product is output or published

TEMPLATE

Creating a template ensures that all of your web pages will have a consistent appearance and layout. Once you have created a template, you can add content and edit each page individually.

ACTIVITY

▼ CREATING A NEW PAGE

1. Create a new page.
2. View the HTML code or use the split view to see the HTML side by side beside the design.

Creating web pages by placing elements on a page rather than writing HTML is an example of what is known as **WYSIWIG** editing. This makes creating web pages much easier and has enabled more people to contribute to the World Wide Web. This in turn has had a significant impact on individuals, organisations and society. For more information about the impact of the internet, see *Unit 3 Operating online* (pages 109–131).

UNIT 6 — WEB AUTHORING

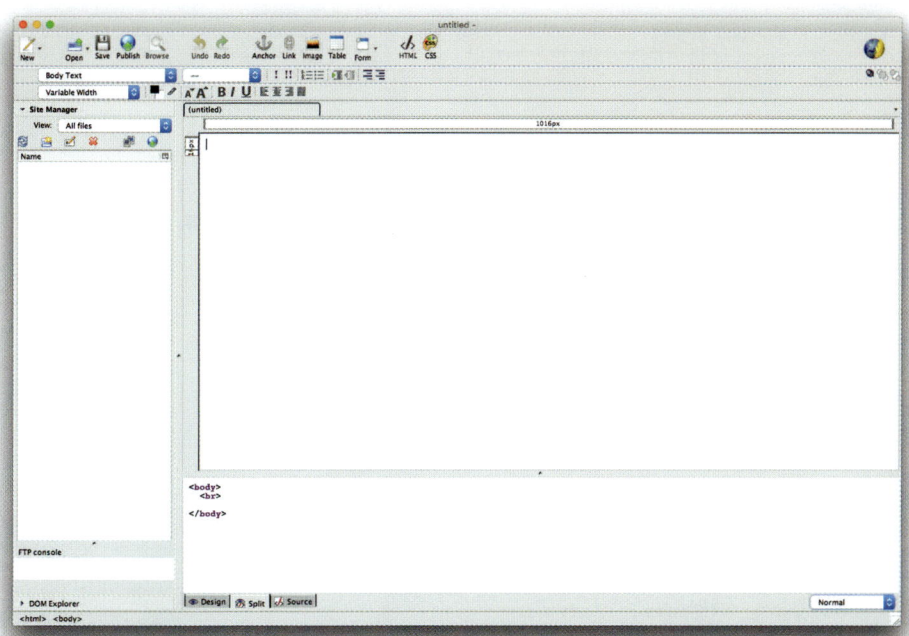

▲ **Figure 18.1** KompoZer can work as a WYSIWYG web authoring application and creates the HTML in the background as the user edits the content

TABLES AND FRAMES

GENERAL VOCABULARY

merging combining or joining together several things in order to form one single thing

grid a pattern of straight vertical and horizontal lines that cross each other, creating cells

SKILLS EXECUTIVE FUNCTION ADAPTABILITY

GENERAL VOCABULARY

guideline a line used as a visual guide

SUBJECT VOCABULARY

cell padding the space *inside* cells in a table that determines how close to the edge of the cell the content will be placed

cell spacing the space *between* cells

Tables can be used to create a layout template, which specifies how content should be placed on a page. When the page is resized, the table will stretch to fit the page. This means that the page will keep its layout even when viewed on devices with different sized screens.

Merging cells in a table allows you to create more complex layouts than using a simple **grid**.

ACTIVITY

▼ CREATING A TABLE

1. Insert a 5 x 5 table into the new page that you created in the previous activity (page 262). For more information about tables, see pages 220–223.

2. Set the table width to 100% so that it will stretch to fit any window size or screen size.

3. Format the table so that its borders will not be displayed by a web browser by setting the border thickness to 0. You will still see **guidelines** in the application to help you place content in cells.

4. Set all **cell padding** and **cell spacing** to 0.

5. Check to make sure your settings match those in Figures 18.2a and 18.2b, then select OK.

6. Merge\join the cells on the top row.

7. Save the file as 'index.html'.

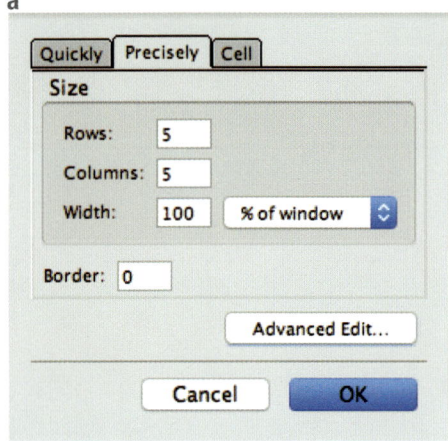

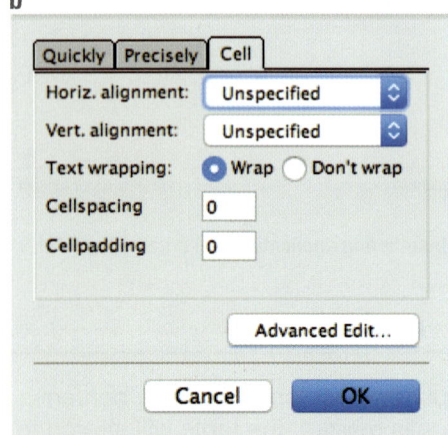

▲ **Figure 18.2** Settings to use when inserting a table into a web page for the Activity

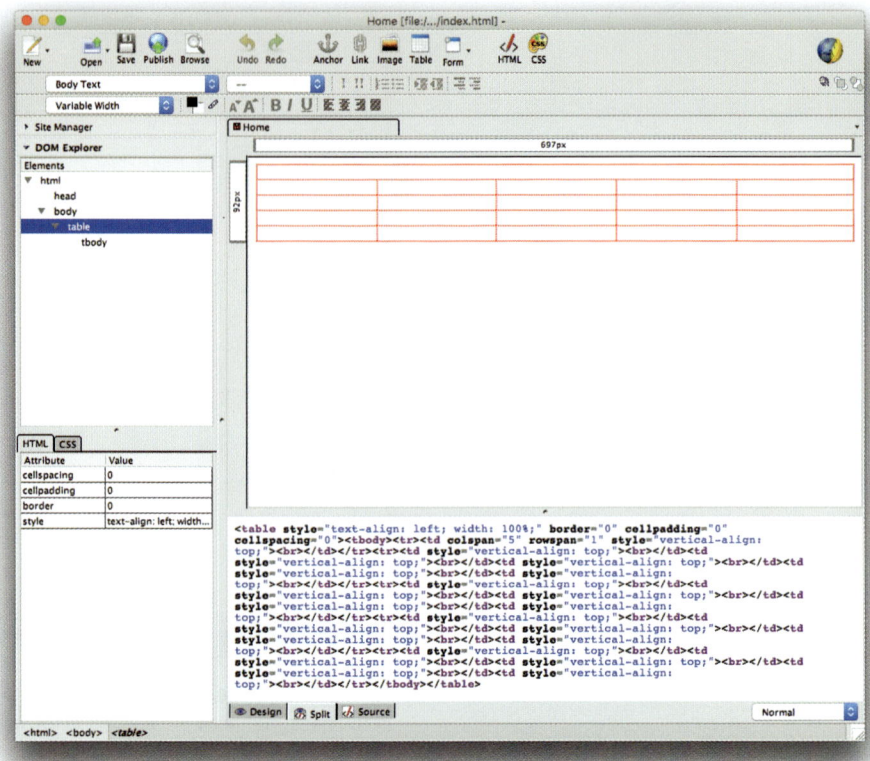

▲ **Figure 18.3** Guidelines showing the outline of the table are displayed in the web authoring application, but the border settings in Figure 18.2a will not allow them to be displayed by the browser

Frames are areas of a page that can be defined to display other web pages. They are not supported in the latest version of HTML, which at the time of writing is HTML5.

STANDARD PAGE FEATURES

There are certain features that appear on most web pages, such as hyperlinks and menus.

HYPERLINKS

A hyperlink is a link that can be clicked in order to go to another location, often a web page hosted on a web server connected to the internet. You can insert hyperlinks that allow users to move to a position on a page in the current document, open documents from the current website or open documents from other online locations. This collection of linked content is known as the World Wide Web.

You can also create links that open the user's email application ready to send a pre-formatted email to a specified address.

ACTIVITY

▼ INSERTING A HYPERLINK

1 In the bottom left cell of your table, type the word 'Search'.
2 Highlight the word, then insert a hyperlink by typing 'http://www.google.com' into the Link Location field, as shown in Figure 18.4.
3 Save the file.

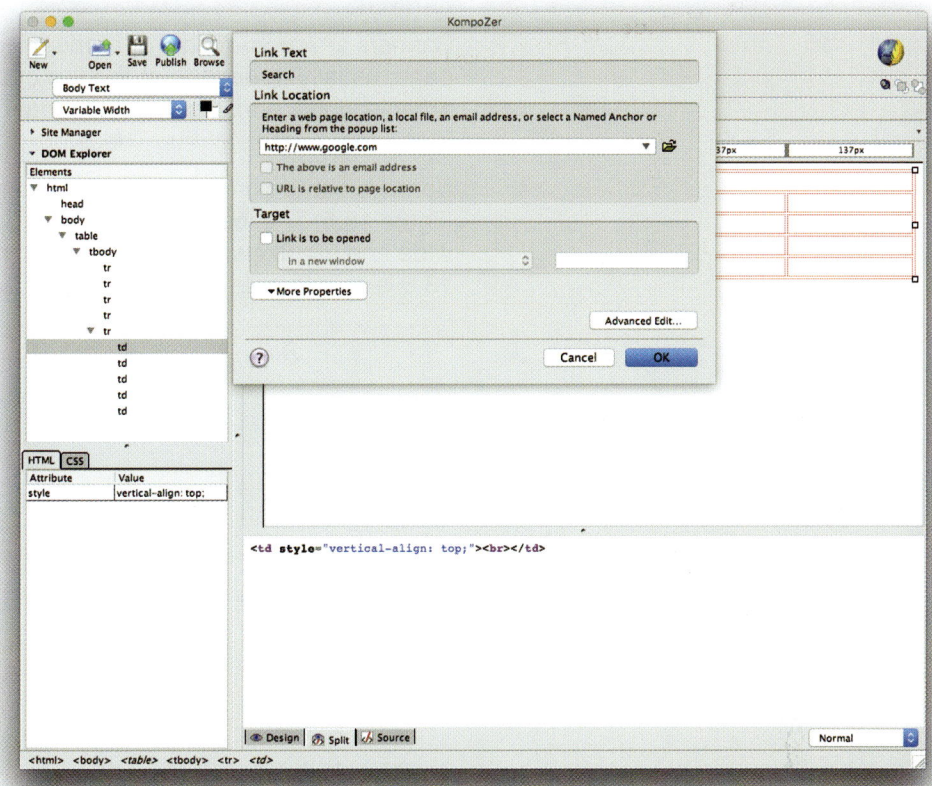

▲ Figure 18.4 Hyperlinks are underlined and coloured blue by default, though you can change this if the page design requires

ACTIVITY

▼ VIEWING THE HTML

View the HTML that has been generated by the application so far.

BACKGROUND COLOURS

The background colour is the colour displayed as the background of a web page. You can also set an image as the background for a web page. If you do use an image, make sure that the colour of the text on the page contrasts well with the colour of the image.

SKILLS EXECUTIVE FUNCTION ADAPTABILITY

SUBJECT VOCABULARY

Hex colour value 6 hexadecimal characters which represent the amount of red, green and blue in the colour

HINT

Try to match the colours on your page so that there is consistency across the different elements you use.

ACTIVITY

▼ SETTING THE BACKGROUND COLOUR

1 Format the page colour (in KompoZer, use 'Page Colors and Background' from the Format menu).
2 Use the **Hex colour value** #FCD957
3 Save the file.

For more information about colour choice and its impact on accessibility, see *Unit 5 Applying Information and Communication Technology* (pages 190–193).

BANNERS

Banners are promotional or marketing images that can be added to a web page, usually appearing at the top of the page. The image will often use the organisation's house style, but some banners advertise goods and services from other organisations. These are known as third-party banners.

Banners can be created using different standard dimensions as shown in Figure 18.5. The leaderboard banner is a standard-sized banner (728 pixels wide and 90 pixels high) that can be placed at the top of a web page. Figure 18.6 is an example of a leaderboard banner.

▲ Figure 18.5 Banners can be made in a variety of dimensions

▲ Figure 18.6 A leaderboard banner

SKILLS ► EXECUTIVE FUNCTION ADAPTABILITY

HINT
See pages 271–272 for more information about alignment.

ACTIVITY

▼ INSERTING A BANNER

1 Centre-align the merged cells at the top.
2 Insert the file 'banner.jpeg' into the top row of merged cells in the table. It should look like Figure 18.7. The banner background matches the background colour of your web page.
3 Save the file.

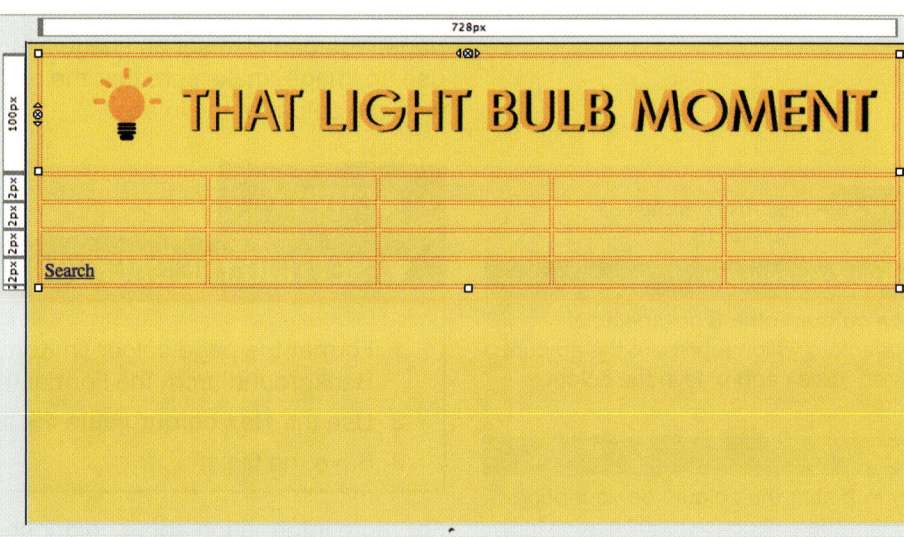

▲ Figure 18.7 Banner placed at the top of the page

GENERAL VOCABULARY
animation moving images

SKILLS
EXECUTIVE FUNCTION
ADAPTABILITY

HINT
See page 218 for more information about font styles.

KEY POINT
The links that you have just created to the Contact and News pages are known as relative links. This is because these pages will exist in the same (related) folder as the page on which the links appear.

GENERAL VOCABULARY
duplicate copy something exactly

MENU OR NAVIGATION

Menus allow the user to navigate or move around a website. Menus are collections of hyperlinks that are inserted into text, images, buttons or **animation**.

ACTIVITY

▼ **CREATING A MENU**

Follow the steps to create a menu using text placed in the cells of your table.

1. Centre-align the three middle cells underneath the banner.
2. Add the text 'Home' to the first cell, 'Contact' to the second cell and 'News' to the third cell.
3. Format all the text in the page, including the 'Search' text that you added earlier, so that it uses a sans serif font, such as Verdana.

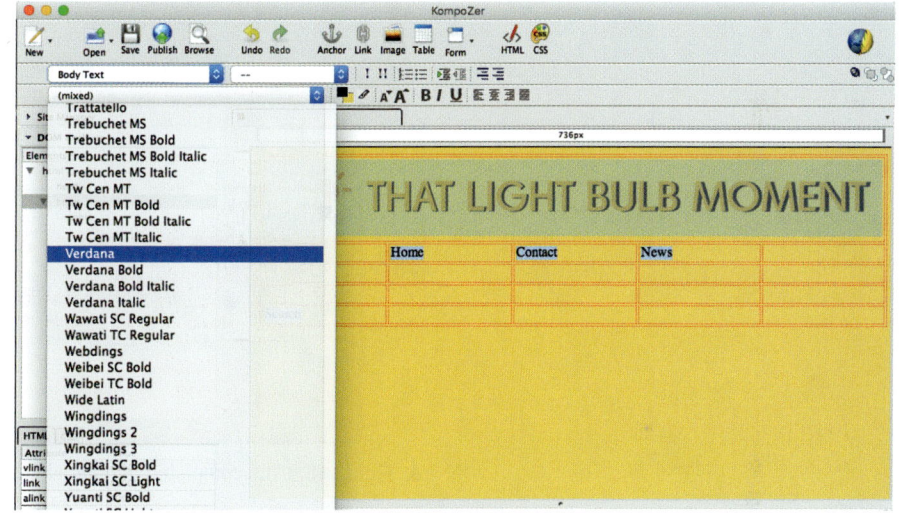

▲ Figure 18.8 Selecting a different font

4. Select the text 'Home' and use the Link field to insert a hyperlink to the document 'index.html'.
5. Repeat step 4 for 'Contact', inserting a hyperlink to 'contact.html', which you will create later.
6. Repeat step 4 for 'News', inserting a hyperlink to 'news.html', which you will also create later.
7. Save the file.

You now have a template page that you can **duplicate** before adding page-specific content.

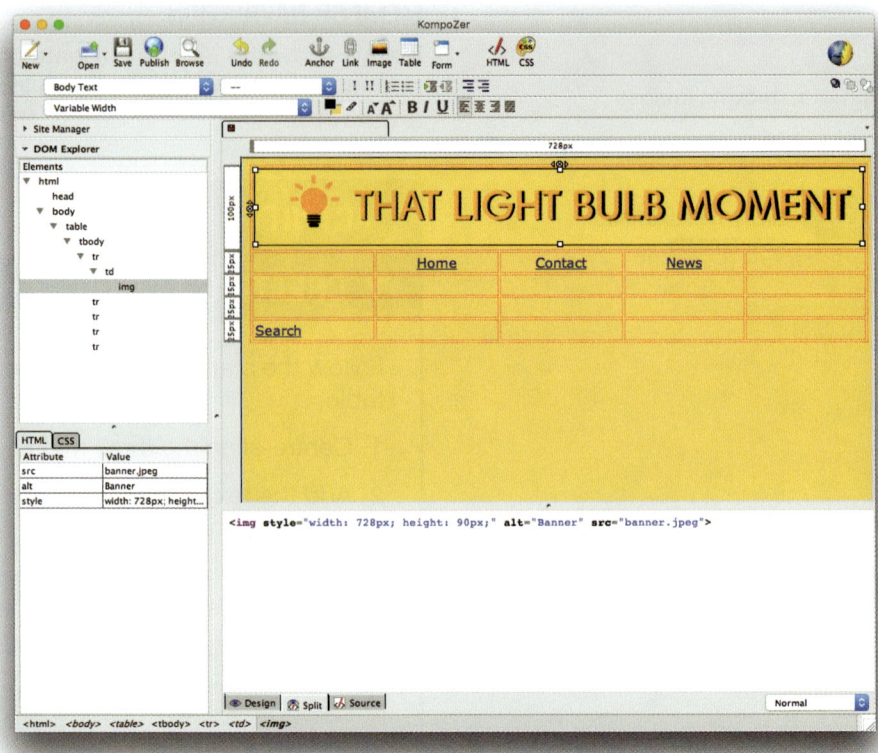

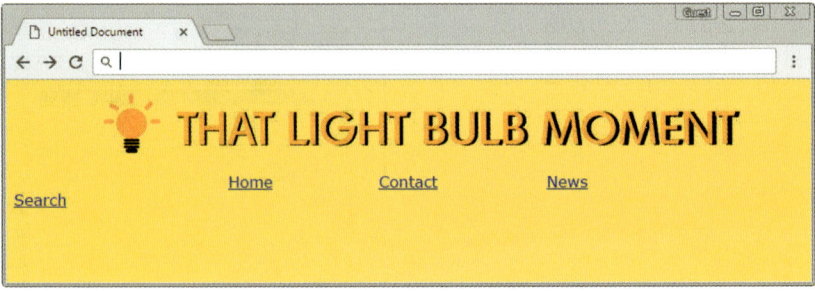

▲ Figure 18.9 The completed template in KompoZer and displayed in a browser

PAGE NAME (FILE NAME)

When you set up the template for your web page you named it 'index.html'. This is because this name causes web browsers to load this page first by default, making it the first page that visitors to your website will see. In other words, 'index.html' will act as your website's **home page**.

> **SUBJECT VOCABULARY**
>
> **home page** the introductory or main page of a website

EXECUTIVE FUNCTION
ADAPTABILITY

ACTIVITY

▼ CREATING OTHER PAGES

Make two copies of the file 'index.html' and rename them 'contact.html' and 'news.html'.

> **KEY POINT**
>
> The page 'index.html' will function as your website's home page, so you do not need to create a separate file named 'home.html'.

CONTENT

The content of a web page can include text, images, buttons and animation.

TEXT

SUBJECT VOCABULARY

voice recognition a system in which a computer takes input from a human voice

Text can be entered using either the keyboard or **voice recognition** software, just as when using other applications.

You can format text using styles and alignment tools, which you will learn more about later in this chapter (page 271).

IMAGES

HINT

You should store images in the same folder as your web pages. This means that you do not have to worry about referencing other folders, especially if you move or rename the image folder.

SUBJECT VOCABULARY

alt text alternative text that is displayed if an image cannot be loaded

GENERAL VOCABULARY

visual impairment a condition that means that someone is unable to see normally

You can insert images such as banners and photographs into your web pages. When you do this, the web page creates a link to the location of the image. If you move the image to a different folder, the link may break and the image will not appear until you re-establish the link.

You can either insert images using the Insert menu or by dragging and dropping the images into the document using the mouse.

ALT TEXT

Alt text is alternative text that is displayed if an image cannot be loaded. When you add an image to a web page, you can specify the alt text that will be associated with the image, which can be displayed if the image cannot. For more information about alt text, see page 273.

KEY POINT

Alt text is used for accessibility reasons. For example, it is read aloud by the screen readers used by some people with **visual impairment**.

BUTTONS

You can add hyperlinks to images to make them act like buttons. Users can click on the image to move around the page or to open other pages or documents, just as they can by clicking on hyperlinked text.

ANIMATION

You can include animation files such as .swf files or animated .gif files in your web pages. These can be used to draw the user's attention to important content.

▲ **Figure 18.10** Animated content is created by sequencing a series of images together

SKILLS EXECUTIVE FUNCTION ADAPTABILITY

ACTIVITY

▼ **ADDING ANIMATION**

1. Open the file 'news.html'.
2. Add the animation file 'bulb.gif' into the cell beneath the text 'Home', as shown in Figure 18.11.

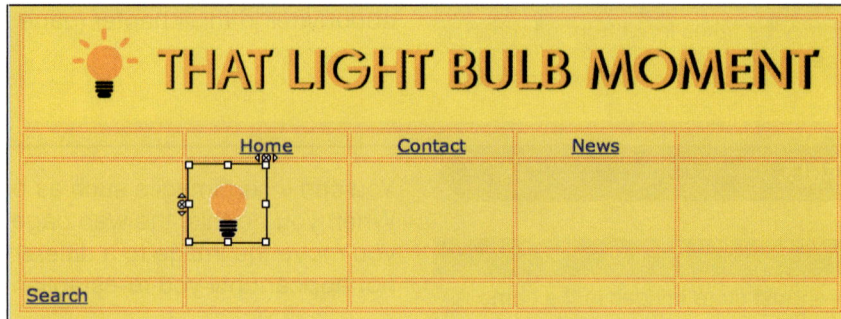

▲ Figure 18.11 Adding an animation file

3. Left-align the animation.
4. Save the file.
5. View the file in a browser to see the animation working.

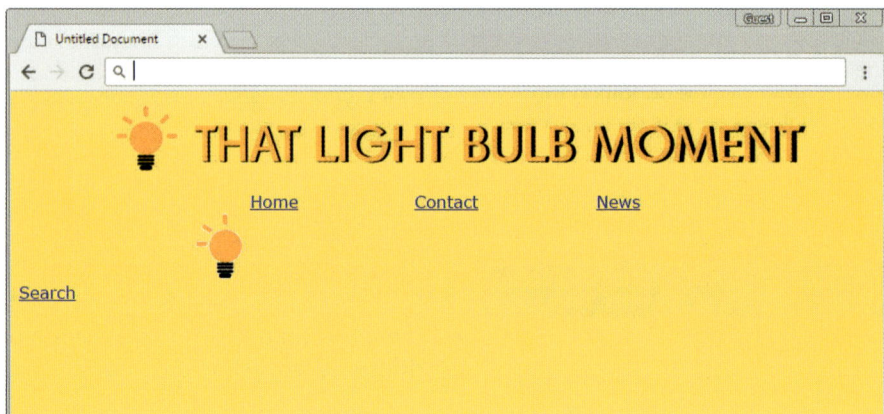

▲ Figure 18.12 The animation in the page

FORMAT

The content of a web page is formatted using styles and alignment.

STYLES

You can apply styles to headings, subheadings and **body text** in order to make their appearance consistent within the web page and across every web page in the website. For more information about styles, see page 218.

GENERAL VOCABULARY

body text the text in the main part or body of the document

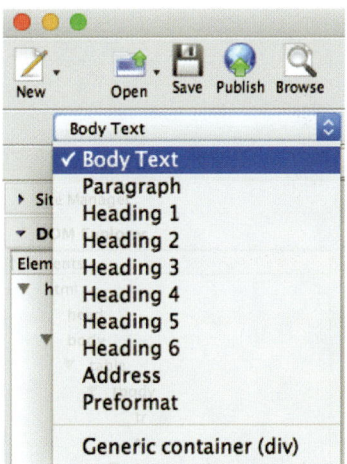

▲ Figure 18.13 There are several levels of heading available

ALIGNMENT

You can align content left, right or centre. For more information about alignment, see pages 215 and 220.

HTML

You have already learned about some ways of using HTML, but there are other ways of using HTML you might use.

You can write HTML in a simple text editor, as shown in Figure 18.14.

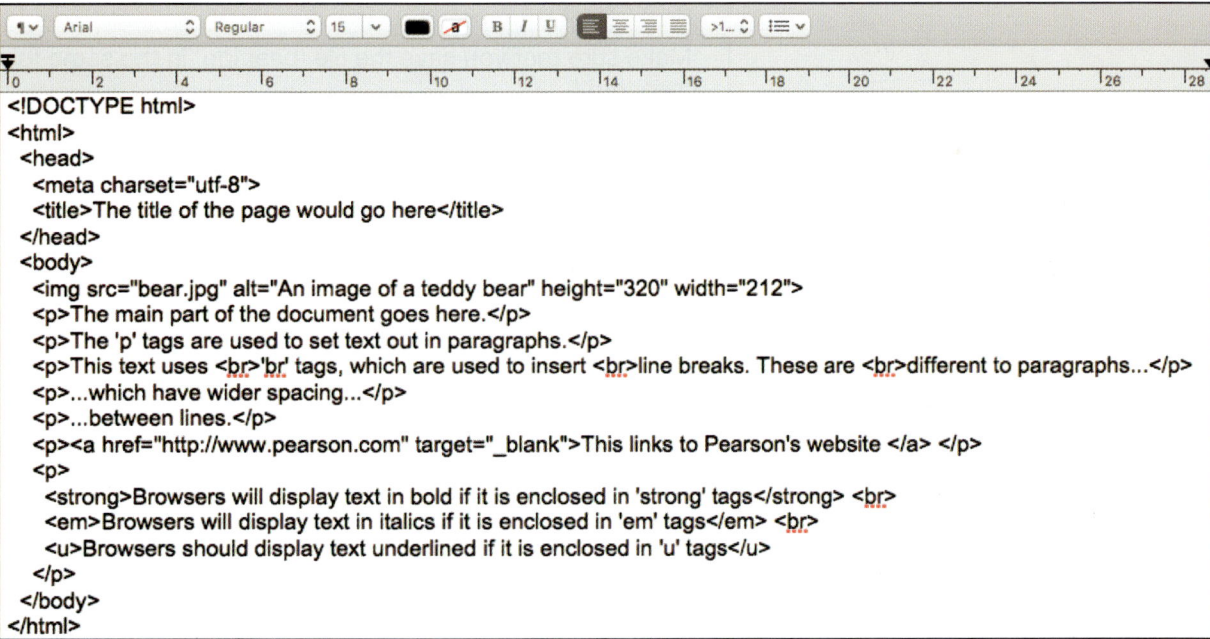

▲ Figure 18.14 HTML being edited in a simple text editor

SUBJECT VOCABULARY

markup the tags surrounding elements of text that indicate the purpose of the text and instruct the browser how to handle (display) them

HINT

Some **markup** uses tags enclosed in `<>` and `</>` pairs. The `/` character in the second tag is used to let the browser know that the tag has ended. Others, like `<img>`, do not need to be ended.

```
index.html
1   <!DOCTYPE html>
2   <html>
3     <head>
4       <meta charset="utf-8">
5       <title>The title of the page would go here</title>
6     </head>
7     <body>
8       <img src="bear.jpg" alt="An image of a teddy bear" height="212" width="320">
9       <p>The main part of the document goes here.</p>
10      <p>The 'p' tags are used to set text out in paragraphs.</p>
11      <p>This text uses <br>'br' tags, which are used to insert <br>line breaks. These are <br>different to paragraphs...</p>
12      <p>...which have wider spacing...</p>
13      <p>...between lines.</p>
14      <p><a href="http://www.pearson.com" target="_blank">This links to Pearson's website </a> </p>
15      <p>
16        <strong>Browsers will display text in bold if it is enclosed in 'strong' tags</strong> <br>
17        <em>Browsers will display text in italics if it is enclosed in 'em' tags</em> <br>
18        <u>Browsers should display text as underlined if it is enclosed in 'u' tags</u>
19      </p>
20    </body>
21  </html>
```

▲ **Figure 18.15** HTML being edited in Atom, an open source programming text editor that **colour codes** the markup to help the developer see the structure of the document

GENERAL VOCABULARY

colour code mark with, or write in, different colours to represent different categories of information

SKILLS ▶ EXECUTIVE FUNCTION

ACTIVITY

▼ **VIEWING THE OUTPUT OF CODE**

Open the file 'bear.html' and view the output for this code in a web browser.

Make sure that you save the file 'bear.jpg' in the same folder as the file 'bear.html'.

INSERT HYPERLINKS

GENERAL VOCABULARY

anchor fasten something firmly so that it cannot move

SUBJECT VOCABULARY

attribute something that provides additional information about an HTML element

required attribute an attribute that must be present for the element to work as intended

element an individual component of a web page (for example, `<a>` ... `</a>` is a hyperlink element)

Figure 18.16 shows the hyperlink used on line 14 in Figure 18.15.

```
<a href="http://www.pearson.com">This links to Pearson's website</a>
```

▲ **Figure 18.16** A hyperlink

This markup provides the following information.

The `<a>` element has one **required attribute**: `href`.

- The `<a>` tag is used to **anchor** the hyperlink to some text, an image or another **element** on the page.
- The attribute href is used to tell the browser that the next thing it reads (after the "=" will be the hyperlink (which must be surrounded by quotation marks).
- The text that the browser should display then follows the opening anchor tag.
- The `</a>` tag closes the anchor.

By default, a linked document will be displayed in the current browser window. This means that the browser will replace the current page with the linked one. However, you can specify where the linked document should be opened by using a `target` attribute, as shown in Figure 18.17.

```
<a href="http://www.pearson.com" target="_blank">This links to Pearson's website </a>
```
▲ Figure 18.17 Using a target attribute

The example in Figure 18.17 uses the target attribute _blank. Table 18.1 shows the other target attributes that can be set for a hyperlink.

▼ Table 18.1 Target attributes used for hyperlinks

TARGET ATTRIBUTE	DESCRIPTION
_blank	Opens in a new window or tab
_self	Opens in the same frame as the frame in which it was clicked (default)
_parent	Opens in the parent frame
_top	Opens in the full body of the window

INSERT IMAGES

An image is used on line 8 in Figure 18.15.

```
<img src="bear.jpg" alt="An image of a teddy bear">
```
▲ Figure 18.18 An image

The `<img>` tag has two required attributes: src and alt.

- The `src` attribute specifies where the image is.
- `alt` is the attribute used to tell the browser what alternative text should be used.

Images are not **embedded** in web pages: they are referenced from web pages. This means that the HTML references the source (`src`) or the image and the browser fetches the image from the source and displays it.

Images can either be referenced from an online location or a local file. In this example, the browser will expect to find the file 'bear.jpg' in the same folder as the file 'bear.html' because the source does not specify a different folder or location. If the browser does not find the image in the specified location, it will display a **placeholder**.

GENERAL VOCABULARY

embed make something, such as a graphic, part of something else, such as a web page

placeholder an empty shape that represents the size and location of a missing image

KEY POINT

Images are not embedded in web pages. Instead, they are referenced from web pages.

ANALYSIS
PROBLEM SOLVING

ACTIVITY

▼ USING ALT TEXT

1 Using Figure 18.15, identify the alt text for the file 'bear.jpg'.
2 Open the file 'index.html' while the file 'bear.jpg' is not in the same folder. Note how the alt text is still displayed.

By default, an image will be displayed at its original size. However, you can specify the size of the image by using the height and width attributes, as shown in Figure 18.19.

```
<img src="bear.jpg" alt="An image of a teddy bear" height="212" width="320">
```
▲ Figure 18.19 Using height and width attributes

PAGE TITLE

The page title is displayed in the tab at the top of the browser window.

```
<title></title>
```

▲ **Figure 18.20** The title tags are read by the browser, which then displays the text between them on the tab

SKILLS — EXECUTIVE FUNCTION

ACTIVITY

▼ USING TITLE TAGS

Switch to HTML view and enter text as the page title between `<title>` and `</title>` as indicated in Figure 18.20.

FONT ENHANCEMENTS

Font enhancements are used to draw attention to important text.

BOLD

The text on line 16 in Figure 18.15 has been styled as **bold** using the tags `<strong> </strong>`.

```
<strong>Browsers will display text in bold if it is enclosed in 'strong' tags</strong>
```

▲ **Figure 18.21** Styling text using 'strong' tags

ITALIC

The text on line 17 in Figure 18.15 has been styled as *italic* using the tags `<em> </em>`.

```
<em>Browsers will display text in italics if it is enclosed in 'em' tags</em>
```

▲ **Figure 18.22** Styling text using 'em' tags

HINT

`<em>` means emphasis.

UNDERLINE

The text on line 18 in Figure 18.15 has been styled as underlined using the tags `<u> </u>`.

```
<u>Browsers should display text as underlined if it is enclosed in 'u' tags</u>
```

▲ **Figure 18.23** Styling text using 'u' tags

It is no longer good practice to use the `<u>` tag to format text as underlined.

There are two reasons for this:

- Underlines are used by browsers to indicate hyperlinks and so underlining other text may confuse users
- In the latest version of HTML (HTML5), `<u>` tags are used to visually highlight text that is stylistically different (e.g. misspelled words or Chinese proper nouns).

However, the alternative way of styling text as underlined (using CSS) is beyond the reach of this qualification. If you do use `<u>` tags, browsers should still support them and be backwards compatible.

UNIT 6 — WEB AUTHORING

SKILLS: ADAPTABILITY, COLLABORATION, RESPONSIBILITY, COMMUNICATION

ACTIVITY

▼ ADDING CONTENT TO WEB PAGES

1. Using the skills that you have learned in this chapter, add appropriate content to the three web pages that you have created: 'index.html', 'news.html' and 'contact.html'.
2. Ask a friend to give you feedback on the pages.
3. Use the feedback you have received to improve your pages.

CHAPTER QUESTIONS

SKILLS: PROBLEM SOLVING

1. Which **one** of these is the HTML element used for a hyperlink? (1)
   - A `<a>`
   - B `<h>`
   - C `<l>`
   - D `<w>`

SKILLS: REASONING

2. Explain why image files should not be moved from their original location once they have been added to a web page. (4)

SKILLS: PROBLEM SOLVING

3. State the use of a table in a web page. (1)

SKILLS: PROBLEM SOLVING

4. State the use of animation in a web page. (1)

SKILLS: PROBLEM SOLVING

5. Which **one** of these is the first file that a browser will display? (1)
   - A index.html
   - B html.html
   - C first.html
   - D homepage.html

SKILLS: DECISION MAKING

6. State **three** types of content that can be added to a web page. (3)

19 SPREADSHEETS

Spreadsheets are used for a number of different purposes, such as performing loan or tax calculations and helping teachers calculate student grades from test percentages. They are used to store numeric data values and perform mathematical calculations on the stored data values. They can also display numeric data values using charts and graphs, which often make it easier for people to understand the data as information and analyse it to find patterns or trends. In this chapter, you will learn about the tools available in applications such as Microsoft® Excel® and LibreOffice® Calc.

LEARNING OBJECTIVES

- Know data types, number, text
- Format a worksheet: currency, percentage, decimal places, date, time, text wrap, row height, column width, gridlines, merge/split cells, cell borders, cell shading, hiding rows and columns
- Use formulae: arithmetic operators (plus, minus, multiply, divide), percentage, single operators, multiple operators, absolute and relative cell referencing, named cells/ranges. Replicate effectively.
- Use functions: SUM, AVERAGE, IF, VLOOKUP/LOOKUP, MAXIMUM, MINIMUM, COUNT (COUNTA, COUNTIF), LENGTH, PRODUCT
- Use other features: multiple worksheets, sorting, filtering
- Add graphs and charts: pie chart, line chart, bar/column chart, scattergram
- Select an appropriate graph/chart and format it effectively adding title, axis labels, legends, axis, scale, trend line as appropriate
- Print selected columns/rows from a worksheet formula view or data view in landscape or portrait format, adding headers and footers, row and column headers

GENERAL VOCABULARY

intersect meet or cross over each other

SUBJECT VOCABULARY

cell reference the name of a cell in a spreadsheet, created by combining a cell's column letter and its row number

COLUMNS, ROWS AND CELLS

Spreadsheets are also known as workbooks. Each workbook is made up of one or more worksheets. Worksheets contain columns and rows, which create cells where they **intersect**.

Each cell is identified by its column and its row. Columns are named using the letters of the alphabet and rows are numbered. For example, the first cell in a spreadsheet is referred to as A1 because it is in Column A and Row 1, as shown in Figure 19.1. The cell's name is known as its **cell reference**.

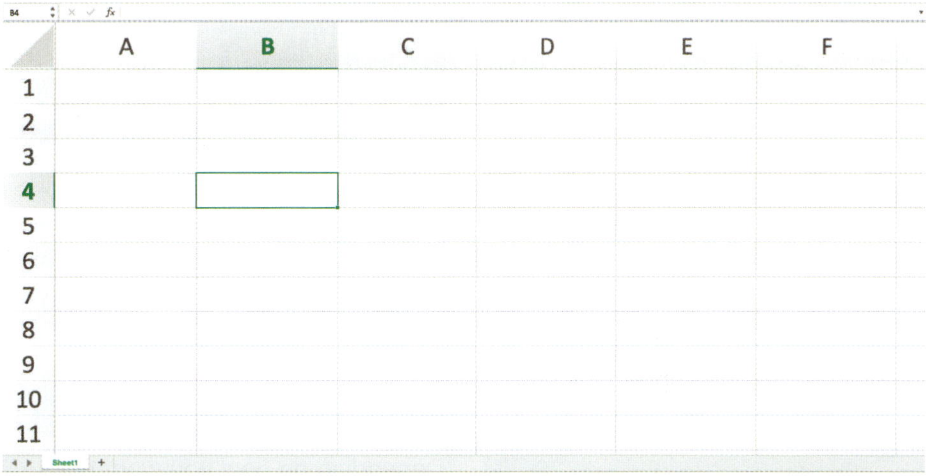

▲ Figure 19.1 A blank spreadsheet in Microsoft Excel

HINT

The column and row headings also highlight the position of the active cell.

SUBJECT VOCABULARY

active cell the selected cell in a worksheet
range a group of adjacent cells in a worksheet

The worksheet in Figure 19.1 is named Sheet1. You can see Columns A to F and Rows 1 to 11.

The **active cell** in a worksheet is the cell that has been selected by a user. In Figure 19.1, Cell B4 is the active cell and is highlighted by a green box. The Name Box in the top left shows B4, because this is the cell reference of the active cell. The Formula Bar does not contain anything because there is no data entered in B4.

RANGES

A cell **range** reference is used to refer to a range of cells. In Figure 19.2, the selected range is B4:D7. A range is made up of the first cell in the range (the one at the top left), followed by a colon (:) and then by the final cell in the range (the one at the bottom right).

	A	B	C	D
1		Mobile phone costs		
2				
3		Talk2U	X-Mob	Set4Calls
4	Handset	£299.00	£399.00	£349.00
5	Calls (per minute)	£0.10	£0.10	£0.10
6	Texts	£0.05	£0.30	£0.01
7	Data (per MB)	£0.99	£0.80	£1.00

▲ Figure 19.2 The cell range B4:D7 has been selected

DATA TYPES

Spreadsheet cells can contain data stored as number data or text data. For more information about different data types, see *Unit 5 Applying Information and Communication Technology* (pages 184–185).

In spreadsheets, number data is defined as data on which you can perform calculations. This means that you would store certain numbers, such as telephone numbers, as text, because you will never need to add together two telephone numbers. Often, telephone numbers also start with a 0, which the spreadsheet would omit if the data was stored as numeric data.

SKILLS — EXECUTIVE FUNCTION
INTELLECTUAL INTEREST AND CURIOSITY
ADAPTABILITY

GENERAL VOCABULARY
fictitious not true or not real

ACTIVITY

▼ STORING DATA AS NUMBER AND TEXT

1. Enter the **fictitious** telephone number 07700900123 into a cell of a spreadsheet. What happens to the initial 0?
2. Change the format of a different cell from number to text. Enter the telephone number into this cell. What happens to the initial 0 now?

FORMATTING

HINT
A quick way of formatting a value as text is to include a leading single quote or apostrophe (') before the value.

Depending on how you want to use the data in your worksheet, you may need to format the cells to match the type of data that you want the cells to contain. You have already learned about one example of this in the previous activity (page 277).

NUMBER FORMATTING

Cells can be formatted to display numeric data values in different ways. Table 19.1 shows some of the most commonly used cell formats.

▼ Table 19.1 Common cell formats used in worksheets

FORMAT	EXAMPLE	NOTES
Currency	£25	Used to display money values. Gives the option for negative numbers to be displayed automatically in different ways, as shown in Figure 19.3. Negative numbers: −£1,234.10 £1,234.10 (£1,234.10) (£1,234.10) ▲ Figure 19.3 Different ways of displaying negative numbers in Microsoft Excel
Percentage	25%	Used to display percentage values as **proportions** of 1. For example, if you want a cell to contain 20%, you need to enter the value 0.2. Entering the value 20 as a percentage will show 2000%.
Number	0.25	The number of **decimal places** used can be selected quickly using the Increase Decimal and Decrease Decimal tools shown in Figure 19.4. These allow you to display numbers to different levels of accuracy. ▲ Figure 19.4 The Increase and Decrease Decimal tools in Microsoft Excel
Date	01/01/2019	Used to display dates using the day, month and year. Short Date and Long Date formats are available, as shown in Figure 19.5. Short Date 24/06/2019 Long Date Monday, 24 June 2019 ▲ Figure 19.5 Examples of different date formats in Microsoft Excel

▼ Table 19.1 – *Continued*

Time	09:00:00	Used to display the time using hours, minutes and seconds. Different formats are available using the Custom format options, as shown in Figure 19.6. 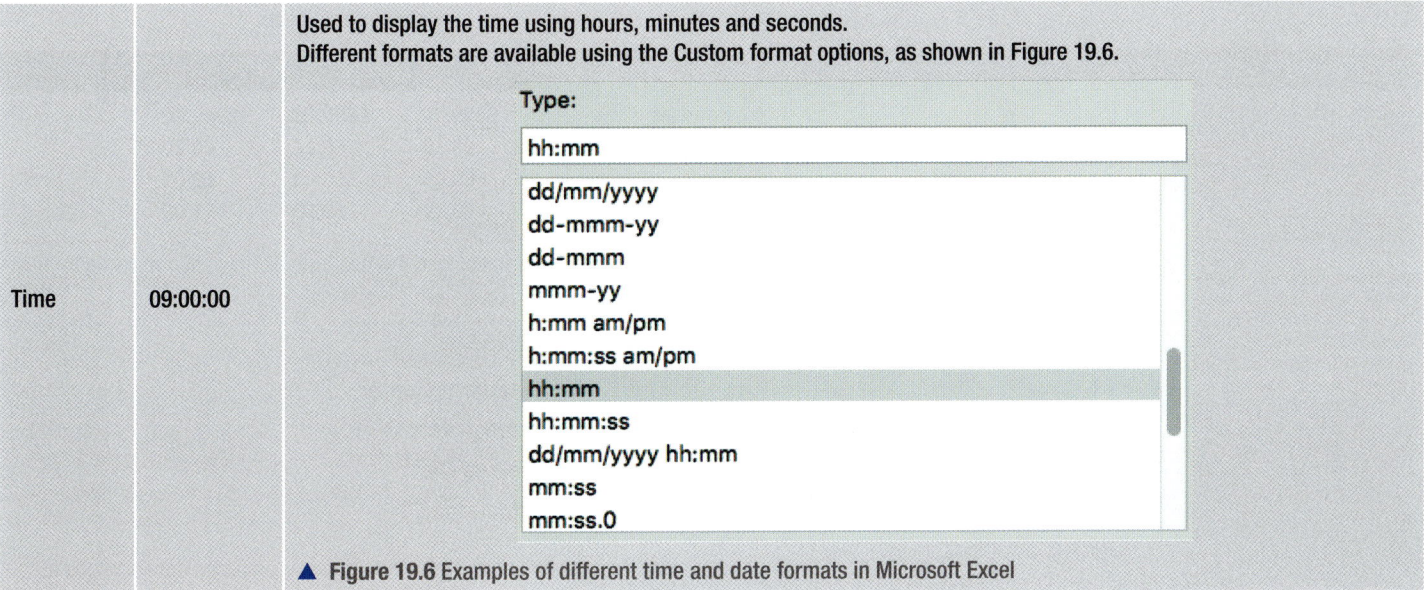

▲ **Figure 19.6** Examples of different time and date formats in Microsoft Excel

GENERAL VOCABULARY

proportion part of a number or an amount of something considered in relation to the whole of it

decimal places the number of places to the right of the decimal point in a number

DID YOU KNOW?

You can also use the accounting format to display currency values.

HINT

The Format Cells window provides more options than can be found in the **toolbar**.

SUBJECT VOCABULARY

toolbar a row of buttons or options at the top of a window that allow you to perform common actions within an application

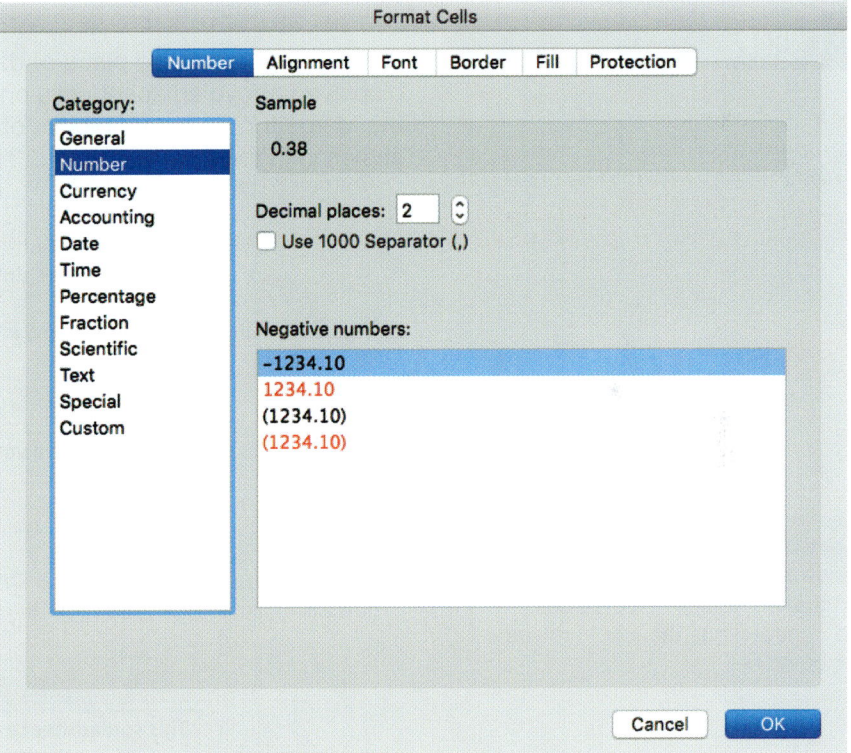

▲ **Figure 19.7** The Format Cells window can be accessed from the Format menu in most spreadsheet applications such as Microsoft Excel

MERGE AND SPLIT CELLS

You can merge and split cells in a worksheet, just as you can with cells in a table created using a word processing application (see page 220). Merge is used when you want text to spread across several cells, as shown in Figure 19.8. Most spreadsheet applications do not have a specific Split command, but let you unmerge cells that have been previously merged, as shown in Figure 19.9.

	A	B	C	D
1		Mobile phone costs		
2				
3		Talk2U	X-Mob	Set4Calls
4	Handset	£299.00	£399.00	£349.00
5	Calls (per minute)	£0.10	£0.10	£0.10
6	Texts	£0.05	£0.03	£0.01
7	Data (per MB)	£0.99	£0.80	£1.00

▲ **Figure 19.8** In this worksheet, Cells B1:D1 have been merged and the new cell reference for these cells is B1

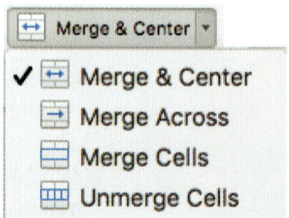

▲ **Figure 19.9** Most spreadsheet applications have various merge and unmerge options, such as these options in Microsoft Excel

TEXT WRAP

When you enter a long piece of data, such as text, into a cell, the text will be displayed above adjacent cells on the same row. You can use Text Wrap and the Merge tool to create blocks of text within a worksheet. This process is shown in Figures 19.10–19.13.

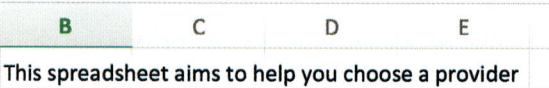

▲ **Figure 19.10** Initially, the text entered in the cell in Column B spreads across four columns

B	C	D	E
heet aims to help you choo			

▲ **Figure 19.11** Applying **Merge and Centre** to three rows of cells in Columns B and C combines these cells, but the start and end of the text are not visible

B	C	D	E
This spreadsheet aims to help you choose a provider			

▲ **Figure 19.12** Applying Text Wrap makes the text appear all together in the same block of cells

B	C	D	E
This spreadsheet aims to help you choose a provider			

▲ **Figure 19.13** The text can then be aligned as you choose (in this case, left-aligned)

SUBJECT VOCABULARY

Merge and Centre a spreadsheet tool that combines selected cells and centre-aligns the text in the new combined cell

ROW HEIGHT AND COLUMN WIDTH

The height of the rows and the width of the columns in your worksheet affect how easy it is to read the information in the worksheet. For example, in Figure 19.14, the contents of Cells A5 and A7 are not fully visible because the column is too narrow to display all the text.

You can change the width of a column by clicking between the column names, as circled in Figure 19.14.

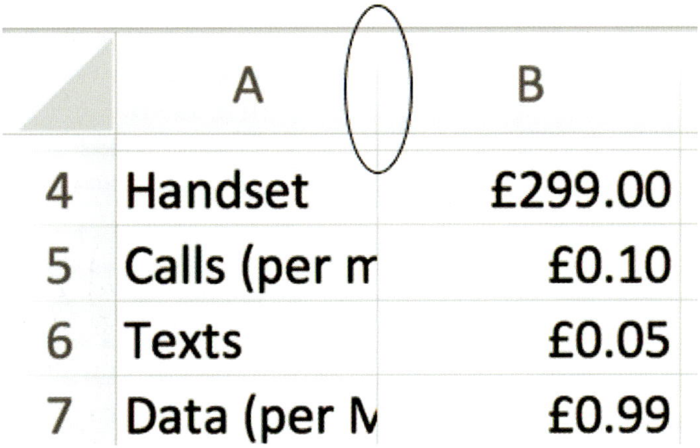

	A	B
4	Handset	£299.00
5	Calls (per m	£0.10
6	Texts	£0.05
7	Data (per M	£0.99

▲ **Figure 19.14** Using your mouse between columns allows you to change the width of the column to the left of your mouse

When you move your mouse to the correct point between columns and rows, the pointer will change to the symbols shown in Figure 19.15.

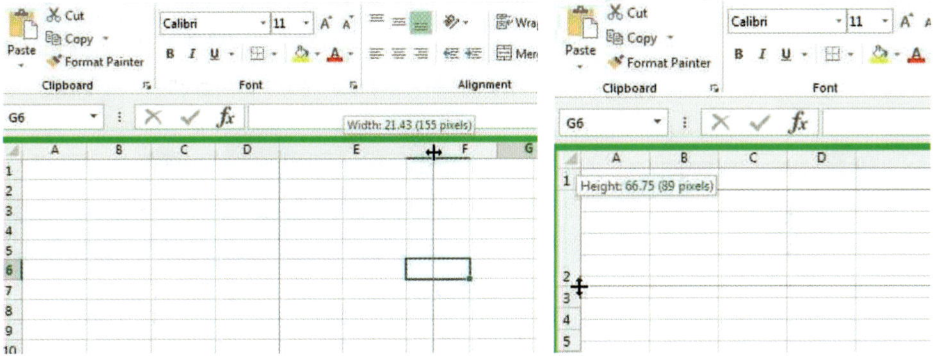

> **HINT**
> If the width of a cell is not wide enough to display numeric data, the application will display placeholder characters instead, such as ########.

▲ **Figure 19.15** The pointer changes shape when you hover your mouse between columns (left) and rows (right)

CELL BORDERS AND SHADING

Borders and shading or colours can be used to emphasise certain cells in a worksheet. They can also be used to make the data easier to read, as shown in Figure 19.16.

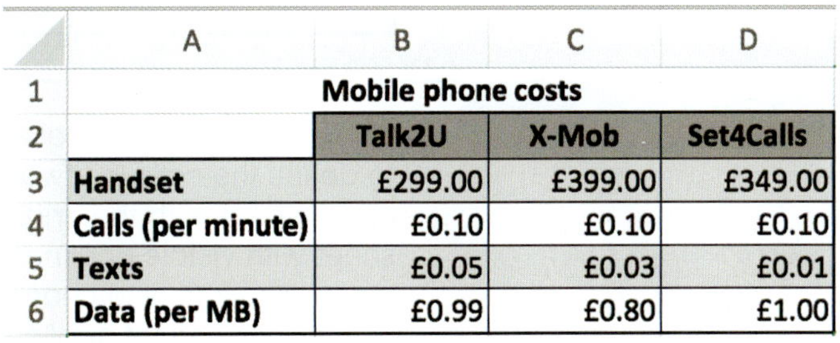

	A	B	C	D
1		**Mobile phone costs**		
2		**Talk2U**	**X-Mob**	**Set4Calls**
3	**Handset**	£299.00	£399.00	£349.00
4	**Calls (per minute)**	£0.10	£0.10	£0.10
5	**Texts**	£0.05	£0.03	£0.01
6	**Data (per MB)**	£0.99	£0.80	£1.00

▲ **Figure 19.16** Borders and shading can be used to make the data in a worksheet easier to read

Most spreadsheet applications offer a lot of different options for borders and shading, as shown in Figure 19.17.

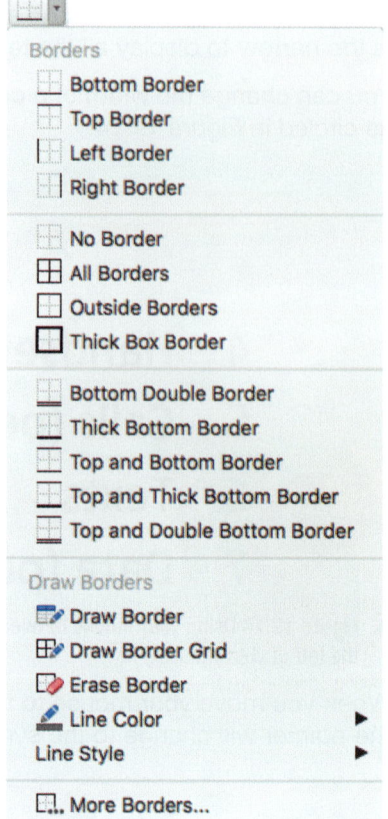

▲ **Figure 19.17** The border and fill options available in Microsoft Excel

SKILLS ▶ EXECUTIVE FUNCTION

ACTIVITY

▼ **FORMATTING A WORKSHEET**

1. Open the file 'format.xlsx'.
2. Set the width of Columns A:I to 20 pixels.
3. Set the height of Rows 1:8 to 20 pixels.
4. Merge Cells C2:D2, F2:G2 and D4:F4.
5. Shade the newly merged cells with a grey colour.
6. Shade Cells B5, H5, C6 and G6 with the same colour.
7. Shade cell range A1:I1 with the same colour.
8. Shade cell range A8:I8 with the same colour.
9. Compare your result with the file 'format_solution.xlsx'. They should look the same.

GRIDLINES

Gridlines are the vertical and horizontal lines that spreadsheet applications use to define the cells in a worksheet. When you print a spreadsheet, it does not usually print with the gridlines visible. However, you can choose to print the sheet with visible gridlines by using an option often found in the Page Layout menu. You can also choose not to display the gridlines when viewing the sheet in the spreadsheet application by changing the option in the View menu, as shown in Figure 19.18.

UNIT 6
SPREADSHEETS

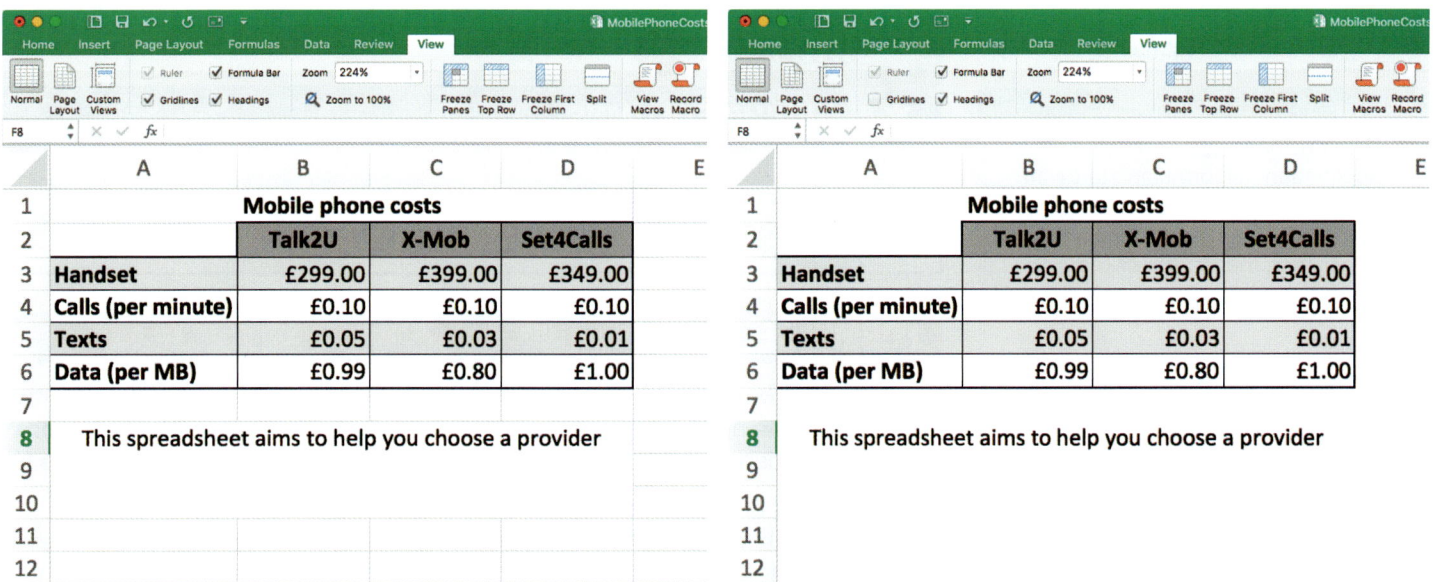

▲ **Figure 19.18** The same worksheet, with and without Gridlines selected in the View menu in Microsoft Excel

> **HINT**
>
> You can change the view of a spreadsheet so that you can see it in Page Layout mode. This shows you how it will look when it is printed.

HIDING ROWS AND COLUMNS

If you do not want or need to show certain rows or columns, you can right-click on them and choose Hide from the options displayed, as shown in Figure 19.19. The data that the hidden rows or columns contain will still form part of any calculations, but they will not be visible on the screen or when printed, as shown in Figure 19.20. If necessary, you can use the Unhide option to make them visible again.

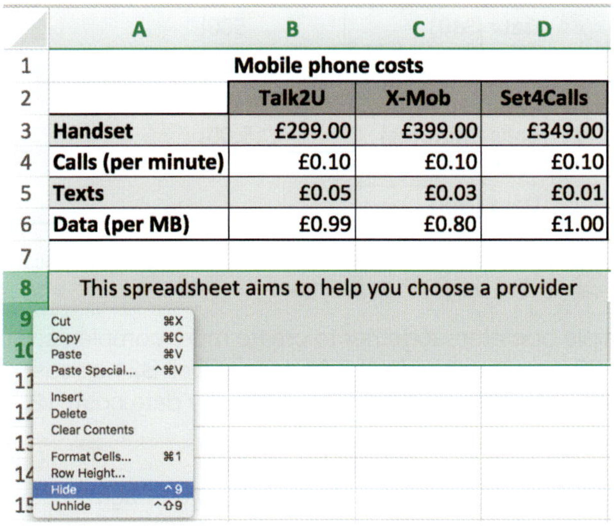

▲ **Figure 19.19** Hiding Rows 8 to 10 in Microsoft Excel

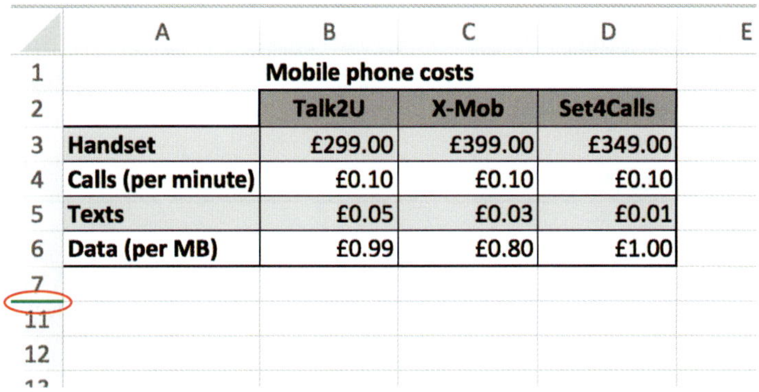

▲ **Figure 19.20** The hidden Rows 8:10 are no longer visible and their location is indicated with a green bar between the row numbers 7 and 11 on the left-hand side of the window

| SKILLS | EXECUTIVE FUNCTION |

HINT

- When using a spreadsheet application, all formulae start with an = sign.
- The character used for multiply is * rather than the letter x or the symbol ×.

SUBJECT VOCABULARY

formula (plural **formulae**) a mathematical operation or calculation
operator a symbol that represents a mathematical action
single operator formula a formula that uses only one operator

ACTIVITY

▼ UNHIDING COLUMNS

1 Open the file 'life.xlsx'.
2 Unhide the hidden column to reveal the content of the column.

FORMULAE

Formulae allow you to carry out arithmetic operations on numeric data stored in cells, such as numbers, currency or percentages. The arithmetic **operators** used in spreadsheet formulae are add (+), subtract (-), multiply (*) and divide (/).

An example of an arithmetic operation is shown in Figure 19.21. In order to find the typical cost of calls for a month with the mobile network Talk2U, the multiplication formula **=B4*B12** has been used to multiply the cost of calls per minute (the number in Cell B4) by the number of minutes typically used each month (the number in Cell B12). When the formula is entered in Cell B17, the product is £15.00, as can be seen in the second image. The formula uses one operator (*), so it is known as a **single operator formula**.

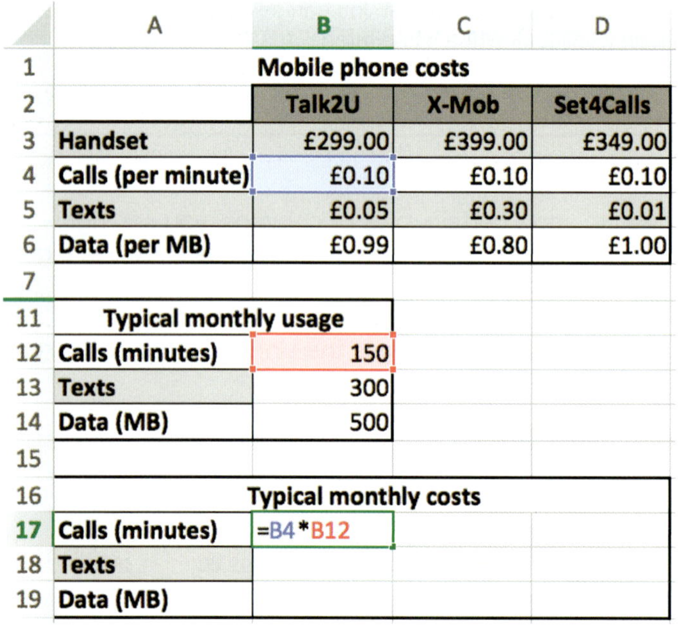

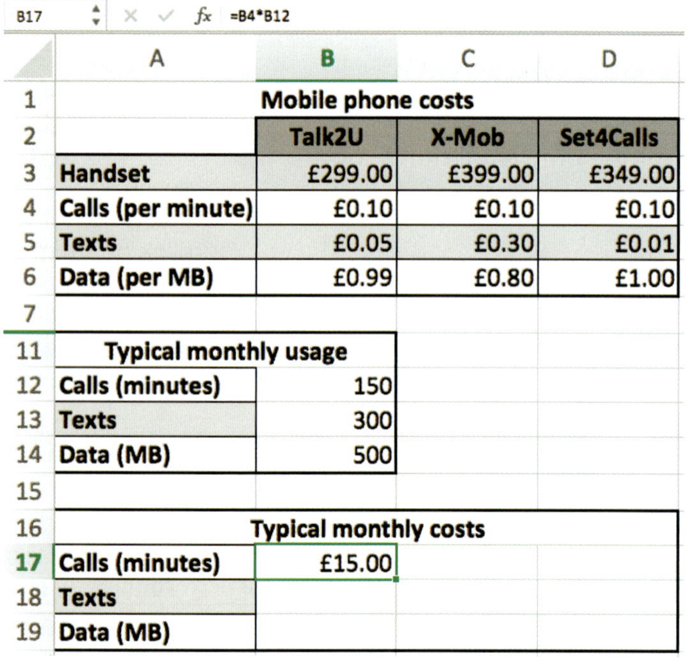

▲ Figure 19.21 A formula is used to multiply values in Cells B4 and B12 to give the typical monthly cost of calls given a typical monthly usage of 150 minutes

You can combine multiple operators together to create more complex calculations, as shown in Figure 19.22. In this example, the formula in Cell B21 is: cost of handset + (monthly call cost + monthly text cost + monthly data cost)*12.

KEY POINT

Using formulae means that you do not have to do the work all over again if the values in the cells change. For example, if new values are entered for cost of calls per minute or for typical monthly call usage, the formula in Cell B17 will automatically recalculate the typical monthly cost for calls with Talk2U.

	A	B	C	D
1		Mobile phone costs		
2		Talk2U	X-Mob	Set4Calls
3	Handset	£299.00	£399.00	£349.00
4	Calls (per minute)	£0.10	£0.10	£0.10
5	Texts	£0.05	£0.30	£0.01
6	Data (per MB)	£0.99	£0.80	£1.00
7				
11		Typical monthly usage		
12	Calls (minutes)	150		
13	Texts	300		
14	Data (MB)	500		
15				
16		Typical monthly costs		
17	Calls (minutes)	£15.00	£15.00	£15.00
18	Texts	£15.00	£90.00	£3.00
19	Data (MB)	£495.00	£400.00	£500.00
20				
21	Yearly cost	=B3+(B17+B18+B19)*12		

▲ **Figure 19.22** Multiple operators have been used in the formula in Cell B21 to perform a more complex calculation

GENERAL VOCABULARY

index (plural **indices**) an exponent or other superscript or subscript number appended to a quantity; for example, in '2^4' the index is 4. In the numbers '2^3' and '6^5', the indices are 3 and 5

HINT

If you use multiple operators in a formula, the calculations are done in the order of operations: Brackets, **Indices**, Division, Multiplication, Addition, Subtraction (BIDMAS). This means that calculations inside brackets will be done first, followed by those involving indices, then division, multiplication and addition, with subtraction calculations being done last.

REPLICATING CELLS

GENERAL VOCABULARY

replicate copy or reproduce something

You can cut, copy and paste formulae between cells in a workbook. However, it is also possible to **replicate** a formula across multiple cells that are above, below or to the left or right of the active cell by using the Fill handle shown in Figure 19.23.

16		Typical monthly costs
17	Calls (minutes)	£15.00
18	Texts	
19	Data (MB)	

▲ **Figure 19.23** The Fill handle is displayed at the bottom right of the active cell in Microsoft Excel

RELATIVE CELL REFERENCING

GENERAL VOCABULARY

product in mathematics, the number you get by multiplying two or more numbers together

times table a list, used especially by children in school, that shows the results when each number between 1 and 12 is multiplied by each number between 1 and 12

By default, formulae use relative cell referencing. This means that, if you copy a formula in one cell to another cell, the copied formula will keep the structure of the original but will change its cell references, so that it refers to cells that are in the same relative positions to the new cell as the cells to the original cell. For example, in Figure 19.24, the formula in Cell E2 can be replicated down to give the **products** of the 3 **times table**. Because the formula uses relative cell references and it will be copied into the same column, the row numbers will change relative to those in E2.

The formula in E2 is =A2*C2

When it is replicated down:

- the formula in E3 will be =A3*C3
- the formula in E4 will be =A4*C4
- the formula in E5 will be =A5*C5
- the formula in E6 will be =A6*C6
- ... and so on.

Figure 19.25 shows a multiplication table that allows the user to enter the number to multiply into Cell D2. Look carefully at the formula displayed in the formula bar, then complete the following activity.

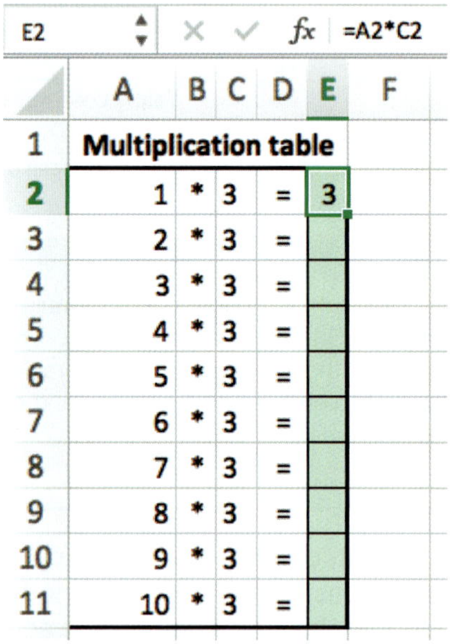

▲ **Figure 19.24** Preparing to replicate a formula in 'multiplicationTable1.xlsx'

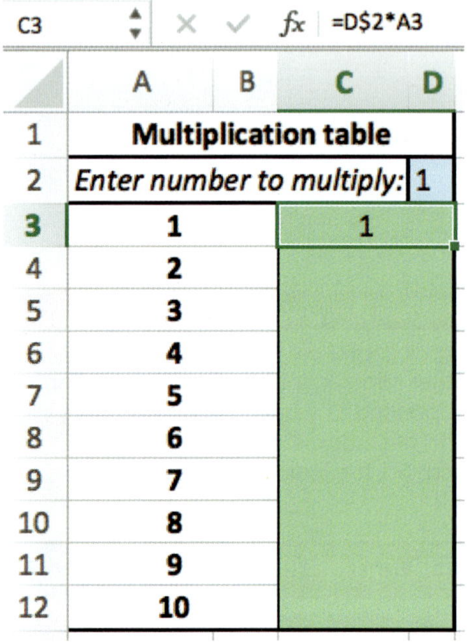

▲ **Figure 19.25** A multiplication table created in Microsoft Excel

SKILLS EXECUTIVE FUNCTION
        TEAMWORK
        RESPONSIBILITY

ACTIVITY

▼ REPLICATING FORMULAE

1 Look at Figure 19.25. With a partner, discuss what the result would be if the formula in Cell C3 was replicated to cell range C4:C12.
2 Open the file 'multiplicationTable1.xlsx'.
3 Replicate the formula in Cell E2 to cell range E3:E11.

ABSOLUTE CELL REFERENCING

GENERAL VOCABULARY

fix attach something firmly to something else so that it stays there permanently

Absolute references are used when you do not want the cell references in a formula to change when the formula is copied from one cell to another. Using absolute referencing **fixes** the references in a formula to particular columns or rows.

SUBJECT VOCABULARY

absolute reference in a spreadsheet, used to fix a cell reference in a formula so that it does not change when it is copied from one cell to another

SKILLS REASONING
COMMUNICATION
EXECUTIVE FUNCTION

An absolute reference is created by adding a $ in front of either the row or column part of the cell reference, or in front of both parts of the cell reference. For example, the active cells in Figures 19.24 and 19.25 contain a multiplication formula. In Figure 19.25, the formula in Cell C3 uses absolute referencing to fix the reference to the row for Cell D2. When the formula is replicated down, each replication of the formula will continue to refer to Cell D2.

ACTIVITY

▼ USING ABSOLUTE REFERENCES

1. The formula in Cell C3 of Figure 19.25 uses D$2 rather than $D$2. Discuss why it was unnecessary to absolutely reference the column (D) in the formula.
2. Open the file 'mobiles1.xlsx'. Cell B17 uses relative referencing. Change it to use absolute referencing and then complete the typical monthly costs section (cell range B17:D19).
3. Check the results of the previous task against the file 'mobiles2.xlsx'.
4. Open the file 'multiplicationTable2.xlsx' and replicate the formula in Cell C3 to cell range C4:C12. Try changing the value in Cell D2.

NAMED CELLS AND CELL RANGES

You can give a descriptive name to a cell or range of cells by selecting the cell or cells and typing a one-word name in the Name Box. This name will now appear in the Name Box whenever a user clicks on that cell or range of cells, as shown in Figure 19.26 and 19.27. Names provide additional information to users of the spreadsheet when they are using cells or cell ranges in formulae or functions.

boundaries	fx	0				
	A	B	C	D	E	F	G
1	Name	Mark	Percentage	Grade			
2	Haseeb	12	34%				
3	Yung Bo	34	97%				Boundaries
4	Waseem	27	77%			0	Fail
5	Ariz	29	83%			40	Pass
6	Ashima	32	91%			60	Merit
7	Zohra	7	20%			80	Distinction
8							
9			Total marks available:	35			

▲ Figure 19.26 The cell range F4:G7 has been named boundaries

total		fx	35			
	A	B	C	D	E	F	G
1	Name	Mark	Percentage	Grade			
2	Haseeb	12	34%				
3	Yung Bo	34	97%			Boundaries	
4	Waseem	27	77%			0	Fail
5	Ariz	29	83%			40	Pass
6	Ashima	32	91%			60	Merit
7	Zohra	7	20%			80	Distinction
8							
9			Total marks available:	35			
10							

▲ Figure 19.27 Cell D9 has been named total

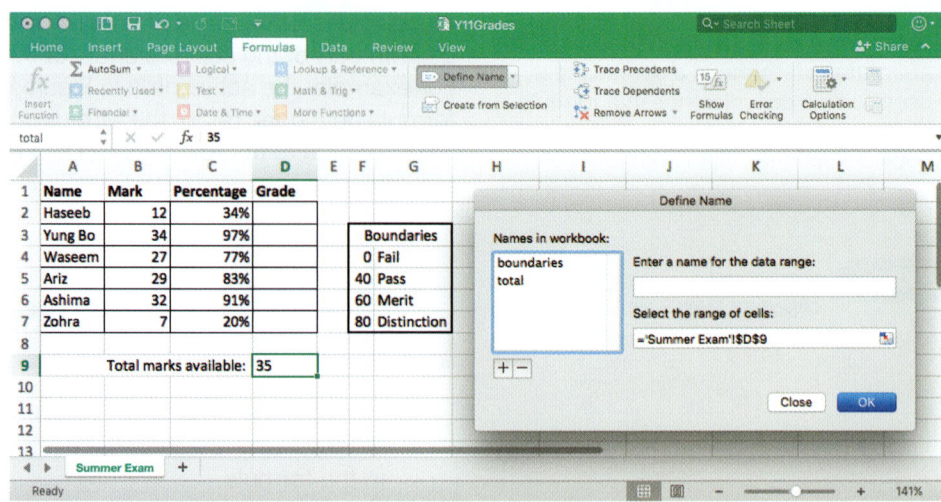

▲ Figure 19.28 Some spreadsheet applications, such as Microsoft Excel, provide other ways to name cells or cell ranges

SUBJECT VOCABULARY

function in mathematics, an expression that represents a complex calculation or process

DID YOU KNOW?

Most spreadsheet applications include approximately 500 functions. If you cannot find a function that suits your needs, you can even create your own, although you are not expected to be able to do that for this qualification.

FUNCTIONS

A **function** is an expression that represents a complex calculation or process. Functions can be used with data for a variety of purposes, such as:

- mathematical
- statistical
- financial
- logical
- text manipulation
- date and time.

MATHEMATICAL AND STATISTICAL FUNCTIONS

Functions can be used to carry out mathematical and statistical operations. Table 19.2 shows the use and examples of specific functions used for these purposes, some of which are shown in use in Figure 19.29.

▼ Table 19.2 Mathematical and statistical functions

FUNCTION	TYPE	USE	IN FIGURE 19.29	EXAMPLE
SUM	Mathematical	Calculates the **total** of a range of values	Cell F5	=SUM(C5:E5)
PRODUCT	Mathematical	**Multiplies** a range of values	Not used	Not used (see Hint)
AVERAGE	Statistical	Calculates the **mean** of a range of values	Cell G5	=AVERAGE(C5:E5)
MINIMUM	Statistical	Returns the **smallest** value in a range	Cell H5	=MIN(C5:E5)
MAXIMUM	Statistical	Returns the **largest** value in a range	Cell I5	=MAX(C5:E5)

GENERAL VOCABULARY

mean in statistics, the mathematical average of a range of values

▼ Table 19.2 Continued...

FUNCTION	TYPE	USE	IN FIGURE 19.29	EXAMPLE
COUNT	Statistical	Counts how many cells contain **numbers**	Cell J5	
COUNTA	Statistical	Counts how many cells are **not empty**	Not used	Not used
COUNTIF	Statistical	Counts how many cells meet some criteria	Cell H12	=COUNTIF(K$4:K$9,G12)

Count cells... ...if they are... ...in range K4:K9...
...the same as the value in Cell G12

GENERAL VOCABULARY

arguments in a spreadsheet, the values or cell references placed inside the brackets of a function that are used by the function when it is carried out

SKILLS
COMMUNICATION
COLLABORATION
RESPONSIBILITY

KEY POINT

Functions will often only include relevant cells in calculations, which can help to prevent errors occurring. For example, the total marks for Ariz (Row 7) is calculated using a SUM function. Ariz did not take Test 2, so he has only taken two tests. The SUM function in Cell F7 only adds together the two numbers in Cells C7 and E7, and ignores the text 'ABS' in Cell D7. However, if the formula in Cell F4 had been replicated down rather than using the SUM function, an error would have been displayed because text cannot be calculated.

HINT

The PRODUCT function multiplies the values from the cells given in its **arguments**. This means that '=PRODUCT(A1,A2)' will do the same as '=A1*A2'. However, the PRODUCT function is useful when you need to multiply multiple cells. For example, the formula '=PRODUCT(B1:B3, C1:C3)' is the same as '=B1*B2*B3*C1*C2*C3'.

ACTIVITY

▼ USING A PRODUCT FUNCTION

Discuss with a partner the benefit of using the following PRODUCT function rather than an equivalent formula: =PRODUCT(A1:A40,D3:D400).

Figure 19.29 shows student marks calculated from three test scores.

Row 4 shows the formulae that could be used to calculate Haseeb's total marks and average marks. You will notice that this row does not show the minimum or maximum marks for the tests that have been taken, the value for tests taken or the student's grade. This is because there is no formula that can do those calculations, so a function would have to be used instead.

Row 5 shows the functions that have been used to calculate the figures for Yung Bo. You will notice that functions have been used for all the calculations, including the total marks and average marks. The same functions have been used to calculate the figures for the students in Rows 6:9.

	A	B	C	D	E	F	G	H	I	J	K
1											
2							Marks				
3		Name	Test 1	Test 2	Test 3	Total	Average	Minimum	Maximum	Tests Taken	Grade
4		Haseeb	12	40	37	=C4+D4+E4	=F4/3				
5		Yung Bo	34	34	39	=SUM(C5:E5)	=AVERAGE(C5:E5)	=MIN(C5:E5)	=MAX(C5:E5)	=COUNT(C5:E5)	=LOOKUP(G5,F12:F15,G12:G15)
6		Waseem	27	29	23	79	26	23	29	3	=VLOOKUP(G6,boundaries,2)
7		Ariz	30	ABS	40	70	35	30	40	2	Merit
8		Ashima	32	29	31	92	31	29	32	3	Merit
9		Zohra	7	13	11	31	10	7	13	3	Fail
10											
11							Boundaries		Total grades		
12							0	Fail	=COUNTIF(K$4:K$9,G12)		
13							20	Pass	0		
14							30	Merit	2		
15							40	Distinction	0		

▲ Figure 19.29 Student marks calculated from three test scores

LOOKUP FUNCTIONS

The LOOKUP and VLOOKUP functions can be used to find a value in an **array** that match a given value. Table 19.3 lists the uses and examples of these functions, which are shown in use in Figure 19.29.

▼ Table 19.3 LOOKUP functions

FUNCTION	USE	IN FIGURE 19.29	EXAMPLE
LOOKUP	Finds a value in a row or column range and then moves to another row or column range to return an associated value	K5	=LOOKUP(G5,F12:F15,G12:G15)
VLOOKUP	Looks in the first column of an array and, when the given value is located in the column, moves across the row to return the value of a cell	K6:K9	=VLOOKUP(G6,boundaries,2)

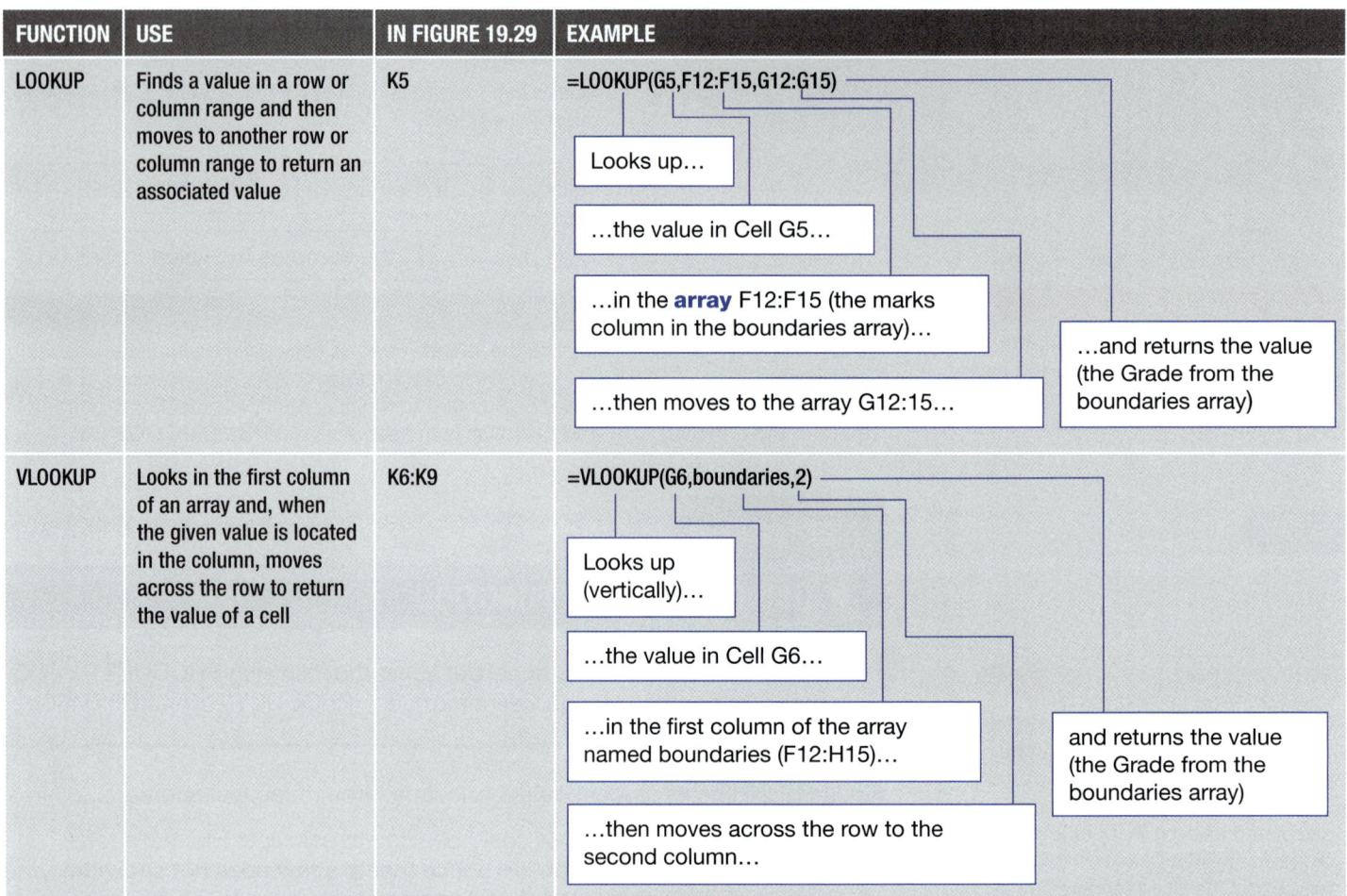

SUBJECT VOCABULARY
array a series of items

HINT
In the VLOOKUP function shown in Table 19.3, boundaries has been set as a named range (as shown in Figure 19.26).

> **DID YOU KNOW?**
> The values in the first column of an array used in a LOOKUP or VLOOKUP function must be in ascending order for these functions to work.

LOGICAL FUNCTIONS

GENERAL VOCABULARY
evaluate return the result of a mathematical expression

Logical functions return values after a test has been carried out, which uses logical conditions that **evaluate** the outcome of the test as either True or False. The most commonly used logical function is IF, which is explained in Table 19.4 and shown being used in Figure 19.30.

SPREADSHEETS

▼ Table 19.4 Logical function IF

FUNCTION	USE	IN FIGURE 19.30	EXAMPLE
IF	Performs a logical test of a condition and returns one thing if the result of the test is TRUE. Can be set to return a different thing if the result of the test is FALSE.	K6	=IF(J6=3,VLOOKUP(G6,boundaries,2),"Incomplete")

Test if...
...do the VLOOKUP (See above)...
...the value in the Cell J6 is equal to 3 (meaning that the student has done all three tests)...
...and if it is...
...and if it is not...
...print the text 'Incomplete'.

Figure 19.30 shows the Grades spreadsheet in which the IF function from Table 19.4 is used in Cell K6.

	A	B	C	D	E	F	G	H	I	J	K
1											
2							Marks				
3		Name	Test 1	Test 2	Test 3	Total	Average	Minimum	Maximum	Tests Taken	Grade
4		Haseeb	12	40	37	=C4+D4+E4	=F4/3				
5		Yung Bo	34	34	39	=SUM(C5:E5)	=AVERAGE(C5:E5)	=MIN(C5:E5)	=MAX(C5:E5)	=COUNT(C5:E5)	=LOOKUP(G5,F12:F15,G12:G15)
6		Waseem	27	29	23	79	26	23	29	3	=IF(J6=3,VLOOKUP(G6,boundaries,2),"Incomplete")
7		Ariz	30	ABS	40	70	35	30	40	2	Merit
8		Ashima	32	29	31	92	31	29	32	3	Merit
9		Zohra	7	13	11	31	10	7	13	3	Fail
10											
11							Boundaries		Total grades		
12						0	Fail		=COUNTIF(K$4:K$9,G12)		
13						20	Pass		0		
14						30	Merit		2		
15						40	Distinction		0		

▲ Figure 19.30 The grades spreadsheet using an IF function in Cell K6

CONDITIONS

In a logical test, conditional operators are used to evaluate the outcome when applied to two numbers. If the condition is met, the outcome is True. If the condition is not met, the outcome is False. Table 19.5 lists some examples.

> **HINT**
>
> When you are working with functions, some spreadsheet applications will provide help to show you how to construct the function, as shown in Figure 19.31.

▼ Table 19.5 Conditional operators

CONDITIONAL OPERATOR	MEANING	EXAMPLE OF USE	RESULT OF EXAMPLE USE
=	Equal to	2 = 2	True
>	More than	2 > 2	False
<	Less than	2 < 2	False
>=	More than or equal to	2 >= 2	True
<=	Less than or equal to	2 <= 2	True

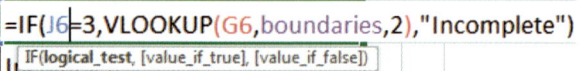

▲ Figure 19.31 Help is shown underneath the function as it is being edited in Microsoft Excel

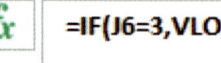

▲ Figure 19.32 The *fx* button provides detailed help on functions in spreadsheet applications such as Microsoft Excel

> **DID YOU KNOW?**
> Most spreadsheet applications provide more detailed information and support, which can be found by clicking the *fx* button next to the formula bar, as shown in Figure 19.32.

Figure 19.33 shows the Function Arguments window, displaying the arguments for the IF function used in Cell K6 of Figure 19.30.

- The Logical_test uses the conditional operator '=' to check IF the value 3 is equal to the value in Cell J6.

- The Value_if_true section of the function is triggered because the value in Cell J6 is 3, which means that the result is TRUE.
  - The Value_if_true section contains a VLOOKUP function, which takes the value from Cell G6 and looks it up in Column 1 of the boundaries array.
  - The value in Cell G6 is 26. When the value 26 is found in Column 1 of the boundaries array, the corresponding value in Column 2 of the same row is returned.
  - The corresponding value in Column 2 of the boundaries array is Pass and is displayed in Cell K6.

- Therefore the final result of this function is Pass (shown as Formula result = Pass at the bottom left of the window in Figure 19.33).

- The Value_if_false section would have been triggered if the result of the Logical_test had been FALSE because the value in Cell J6 had been something other than 3. In this case, the final result of the function would have been the text 'Incomplete'.

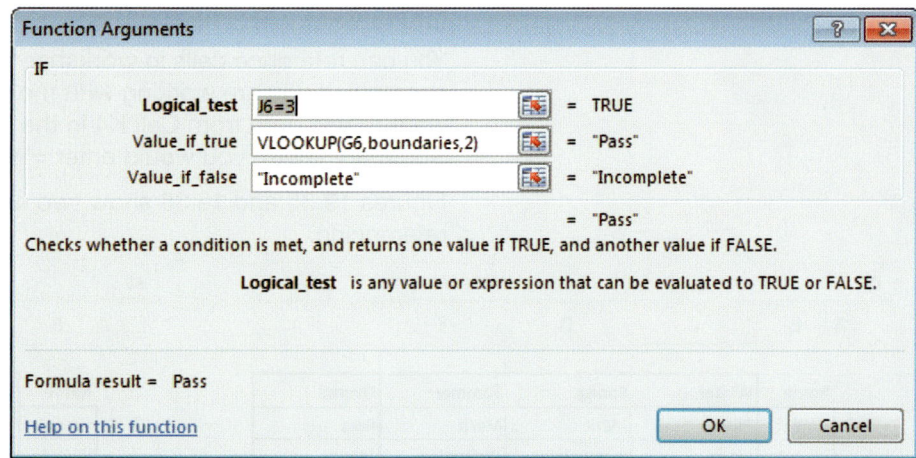

▲ **Figure 19.33** The Function Arguments window in Microsoft Excel

> **DID YOU KNOW?**
> You can nest functions within other functions. Cell K6 in Figure 19.30 and Cell F3 in Figure 19.36 are examples of nested functions.

TEXT FUNCTIONS

Sometimes it is necessary to check the number of letters in a piece of text. This is used in situations when validation is required, such as when filling in an application form. The most commonly used logical function is LENGTH, which is explained in Table 19.6.

▼ **Table 19.6** Text function LENGTH

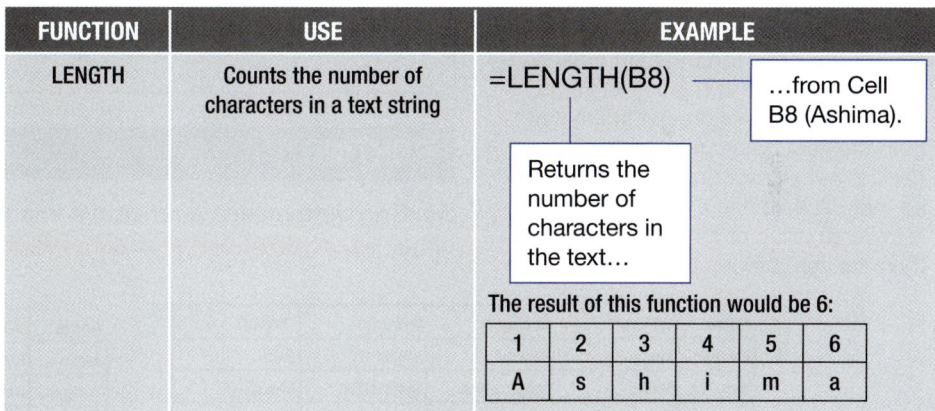

MULTIPLE WORKSHEETS

If you have lots of data about separate but related topics, you might want to use more than one worksheet within a workbook, as shown in Figure 19.34. Using multiple worksheets also helps to make the spreadsheet easier to read.

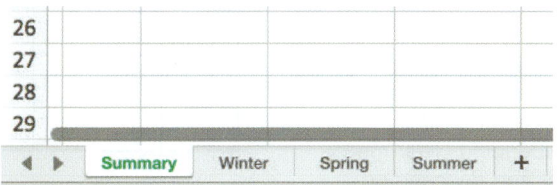

▲ **Figure 19.34** A workbook can contain more than one worksheet

CROSS-SHEET REFERENCING

You can reference cells in worksheets other than the active worksheet. For example, if you are working with the workbook shown in Figure 19.34 and want to use data from Cell K4 in the Winter sheet in a calculation in the Summary sheet, you would enter **=Winter!K4** into a cell in the Summary sheet.

Figures 19.35 and 19.36 show two examples of the use of cross-sheet referencing.

C3		fx	=Winter!K4		
A	B	C	D	E	F
1					
2	Name	Winter	Spring	Summer	Overall
3	Haseeb	Pass	Merit	Merit	Pass
4	Yung Bo	Merit	Incomplete	Distinction	Merit
5	Waseem	Pass	Merit	Distinction	Merit
6	Ariz	Incomplete	Pass	Merit	Pass
7	Ashima	Merit	Distinction	Distinction	Distinction
8	Zohra	Fail	Distinction	Distinction	Merit

▲ **Figure 19.35** Cell C3 in the Summary sheet contains a reference to Cell K4 in the Winter sheet

F3		fx	=VLOOKUP(AVERAGE(Winter!G4,S		
A	B	C	D	E	F
1					
2	Name	Winter	Spring	Summer	Overall
3	Haseeb	Pass	Merit	Merit	Pass
4	Yung Bo	Merit	Incomplete	Distinction	Merit
5	Waseem	Pass	Merit	Distinction	Merit
6	Ariz	Incomplete	Pass	Merit	Pass
7	Ashima	Merit	Distinction	Distinction	Distinction
8	Zohra	Fail	Distinction	Distinction	Merit

▲ **Figure 19.36** Cell F3 contains a nested function that uses multiple cross-sheet references

SKILLS — EXECUTIVE FUNCTION

SUBJECT VOCABULARY

sort in a spreadsheet, arrange data in a particular order

GENERAL VOCABULARY

ascending order arranged in order so that each item in a group of items is higher in value or greater in amount than the item before it in the list

descending order arranged in order so that each item in a group of items is lower in value or smaller in amount than the item before it

ACTIVITY

▼ **UNDERSTANDING CROSS-SHEET REFERENCING**

Open the file 'Grade3.xlsx' to see how cross-sheet referencing has been used in the Summary sheet to summarise students' test results from tests that they sat in winter, spring and summer.

SORTING

Sorting data means arranging it in a particular order. You can sort data in either **ascending order** or **descending order**.

Name	Winter	Spring	Summer	Overall
Haseeb	Pass	Merit	Merit	Pass
Yung Bo	Merit	Incomplete	Distinction	Merit
Waseem	Pass	Merit	Distinction	Merit
Ariz	Incomplete	Pass	Merit	Pass
Ashima	Merit	Distinction	Distinction	Distinction
Zohra	Fail	Distinction	Distinction	Merit

Name	Winter	Spring	Summer	Overall
Ashima	Merit	Distinction	Distinction	Distinction
Yung Bo	Merit	Incomplete	Distinction	Merit
Waseem	Pass	Merit	Distinction	Merit
Zohra	Fail	Distinction	Distinction	Merit
Haseeb	Pass	Merit	Merit	Pass
Ariz	Incomplete	Pass	Merit	Pass

Name	Winter	Spring	Summer	Overall
Haseeb	Pass	Merit	Merit	Pass
Ariz	Incomplete	Pass	Merit	Pass
Yung Bo	Merit	Incomplete	Distinction	Merit
Waseem	Pass	Merit	Distinction	Merit
Zohra	Fail	Distinction	Distinction	Merit
Ashima	Merit	Distinction	Distinction	Distinction

HINT

Because the data in the Overall column is text, ascending order means alphabetical order and descending order means reverse alphabetical order.

▲ **Figure 19.37** Examples of unsorted data (top left), data sorted in ascending order by the Overall column (top right) and data sorted in descending order by the Overall column (bottom)

The data in Figure 19.37 is sorted by the Overall column. You can also sort data by more than one column, as shown in Figure 19.38.

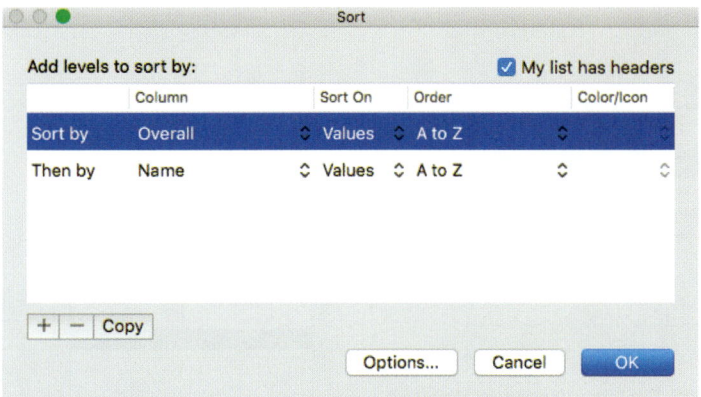

▲ Figure 19.38 Sorting data by more than one column in Microsoft Excel

Name	Winter	Spring	Summer	Overall
Ashima	Merit	Distinction	Distinction	Distinction
Waseem	Pass	Merit	Distinction	Merit
Yung Bo	Merit	Incomplete	Distinction	Merit
Zohra	Fail	Distinction	Distinction	Merit
Ariz	Incomplete	Pass	Merit	Pass
Haseeb	Pass	Merit	Merit	Pass

▲ Figure 19.39 Data sorted using the options set in Figure 19.38

HINT

The students who received an overall Merit are sorted alphabetically by name: Waseem, then Yung Bo and then Zohra. The students who received an overall Pass are also sorted alphabetically by name: Ariz and then Haseeb.

SKILLS EXECUTIVE FUNCTION

ACTIVITY

▼ SORTING DATA

1. Compare the sorted data in Figure 19.39 with the sorted data in Figure 19.37.
2. Open the file 'AusData.csv'.
3. Sort the data by state and then by last_name.

FILTERING

Filtering a worksheet means that data will only be displayed if it meets specified criteria. For example, the data in the Summary worksheet shown in Figure 19.39 can be filtered to show only those students who have received an overall Pass.

▲ Figure 19.40 The Filter icon in Microsoft Excel

To filter data in a worksheet, select a cell within an array of data, then press the Filter icon (shown in Figure 19.40) from the Data tab. This displays filter arrows for the selected data, as shown in Figure 19.41.

Name	Winter	Spring	Summer	Overall
Ashima	Merit	Distinction	Distinction	Distinction
Waseem	Pass	Merit	Distinction	Merit
Yung Bo	Merit	Incomplete	Distinction	Merit
Zohra	Fail	Distinction	Distinction	Merit
Ariz	Incomplete	Pass	Merit	Pass
Haseeb	Pass	Merit	Merit	Pass

▲ Figure 19.41 Selecting the Filter icon displays filter arrows

▲ **Figure 19.42** The Filter window in Microsoft Excel

> **GENERAL VOCABULARY**
>
> **checkbox** a small square space on a document or computer screen into which you can put a mark to select something

Clicking on one of the filter arrows brings up the Filter window, as shown in Figure 19.42. This lets you set the criteria by which the data should be filtered.

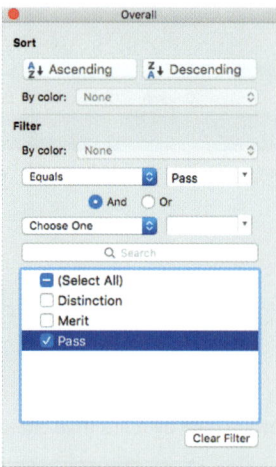

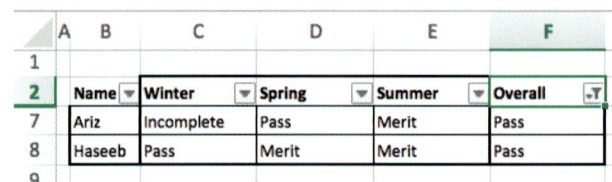

▲ **Figure 19.43** Only selecting the Pass **checkbox** in the filter window means that only Rows 7 and 8 are shown, and the other rows are hidden

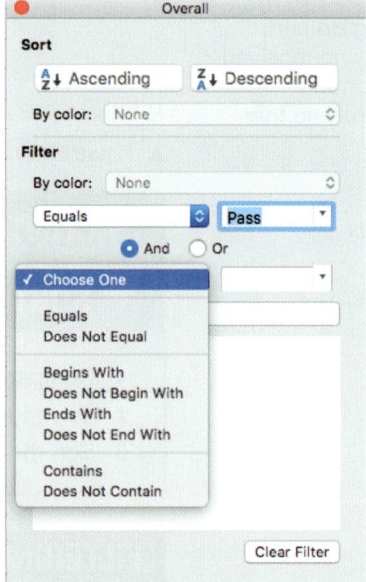

▲ **Figure 19.44** The highlighted menu shows the different ways in which you can filter data in Microsoft Excel

> **HINT**
>
> If the data is numerical, you will be presented with different options, as shown in Figure 19.45.

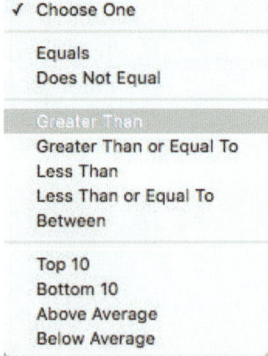

▲ **Figure 19.45** The filter options for numerical data in Microsoft Excel

UNIT 6 SPREADSHEETS 297

SKILLS EXECUTIVE FUNCTION

GENERAL VOCABULARY

rep a sales representative
binder a removable cover for holding loose sheets of paper, magazines and similar items

ACTIVITY

▼ FILTERING DATA

Open the file 'RepData.xlsx' and apply the following filters.
- **Reps** who are from the East region.
- Reps who sold either a **binder** or a pen.
- Reps who sold 30 or more units.

GRAPHS AND CHARTS

Data can be represented visually using graphs and charts. This makes the data easier to analyse and interpret.

For example, look at the table in Figure 19.46, which lists data about annual sea temperatures. It is not easy to interpret this data or see any trends in the data.

The line graph in Figure 19.46 represents the same temperature data in a visual format. The line graph makes the data much easier to interpret and allows the user to see the trend, which is that the temperature fell over the 30-year period 1880–1910.

Year	Annual anomaly (°F)
1880	-0.4700088
1881	-0.3568788
1882	-0.3726612
1883	-0.448443
1884	-0.5897538
1885	-0.6636546
1886	-0.6439392
1887	-0.7616232
1888	-0.5166342
1889	-0.4717926
1890	-0.8875836
1891	-0.6603264
1892	-0.8173098
1893	-0.8148276
1894	-0.84978
1895	-0.6772536
1896	-0.4412844
1897	-0.4894326
1898	-0.78255
1899	-0.578736
1900	-0.4833054
1901	-0.6831072
1902	-0.7883226
1903	-0.9732618
1904	-1.123038
1905	-0.8347986
1906	-0.795843
1907	-0.917685
1908	-1.160703
1909	-1.189773
1910	-1.112769

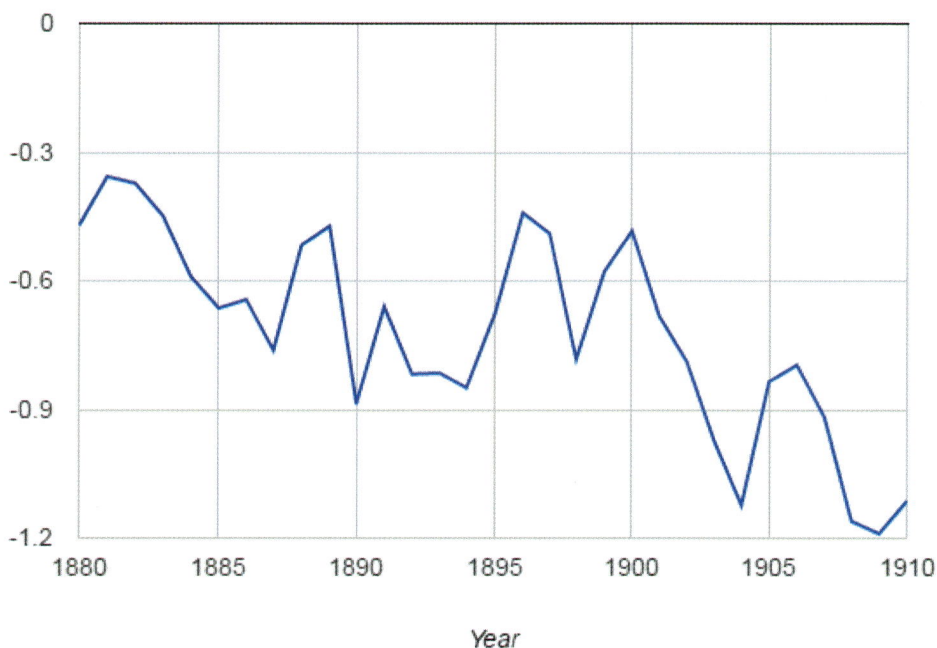

▲ Figure 19.46 The same data represented as a table and as a line graph

CREATE A CHART

You can create a chart by:

- selecting the data you want the chart to represent
- choosing an appropriate chart type from the Charts section of the Insert tab, shown in Figure 19.47.

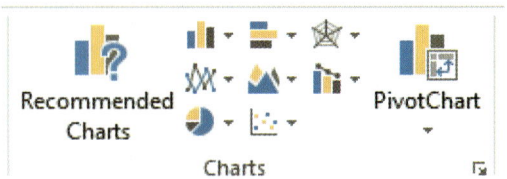

▲ Figure 19.47 Different spreadsheet applications, such as Google Sheets™, provide different types of chart

TYPE OF CHART

The type of chart that you use will depend on the type of data that you want to represent.

PIE CHART

Pie charts are used to represent data as their proportion of a whole. For example, if you wanted to present the proportion of gold medals won by each continent from the data in Figure 19.48, you might choose to create a pie chart. Figure 19.49 is the pie chart created from cell range C1:D21.

	A	B	C	D	E	F	G
1	Rank	NOC	Continent	Gold	Silver	Bronze	Total
2	1	United States (USA)	North America	46	37	38	121
3	2	Great Britain (GBR)	Europe	27	23	17	67
4	3	China (CHN)	Asia	26	18	26	70
5	4	Russia (RUS)	Europe	19	17	19	55
6	5	Germany (GER)	Europe	17	10	15	42
7	6	Japan (JPN)	Asia	12	8	21	41
8	7	France (FRA)	Europe	10	18	14	42
9	8	South Korea (KOR)	Asia	9	3	9	21
10	9	Italy (ITA)	Europe	8	12	8	28
11	10	Australia (AUS)	Oceania	8	11	10	29
12	11	Netherlands (NED)	Europe	8	7	4	19
13	12	Hungary (HUN)	Europe	8	3	4	15
14	13	Brazil (BRA)	South America	7	6	6	19
15	14	Spain (ESP)	Europe	7	4	6	17
16	15	Kenya (KEN)	Africa	6	6	1	13
17	16	Jamaica (JAM)	North America	6	3	2	11
18	17	Croatia (CRO)	Europe	5	3	2	10
19	18	Cuba (CUB)	North America	5	2	4	11
20	19	New Zealand (NZL)	Oceania	4	9	5	18
21	20	Canada (CAN)	North America	4	3	15	22

▲ Figure 19.48 Data about the number of medals won by different teams at the 2016 Rio Olympic Games

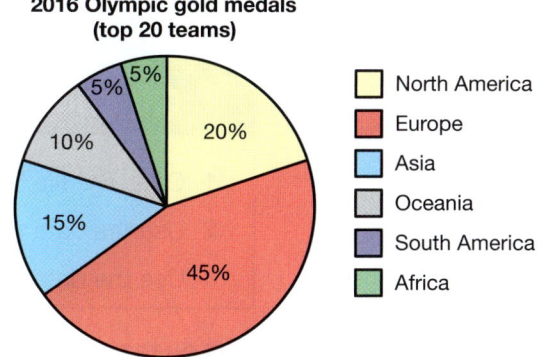

▲ **Figure 19.49** A pie chart showing the proportion of gold medals won by each continent at the 2016 Rio Olympic Games, based on the top 20 teams' results (Figure 19.48)

BAR CHART OR COLUMN CHART

Bar charts and column charts are used to compare values between different categories or groups using horizontal bars (bar chart) or vertical bars (column chart). The categories are placed on the **x-axis** and the values are placed on the **y-axis**.

> **HINT**
>
> A bar chart is often used when one set of data relates to time or if the text used on the category axis is very long.

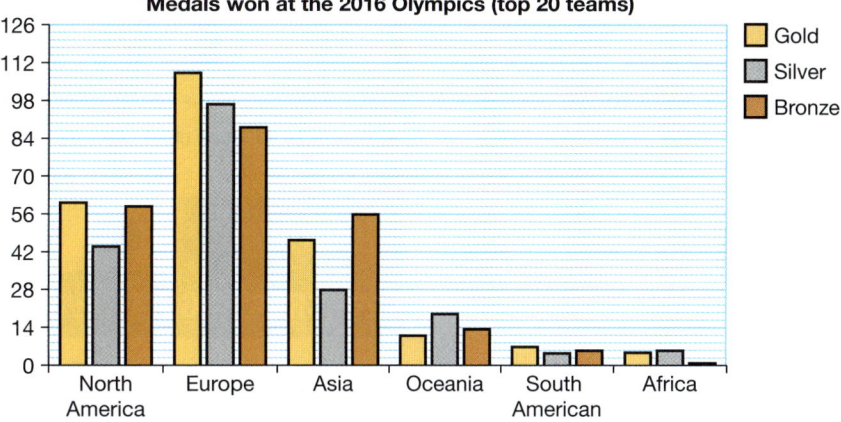

▲ **Figure 19.50** A column chart created from the data from cell range C1:G21 in Figure 19.48

> **GENERAL VOCABULARY**
>
> **x-axis** the horizontal **axis** in a chart or graph
> **y-axis** the vertical axis in a chart or graph
> **axis** a fixed reference line in a chart or graph

> **HINT**
>
> In Figure 19.50, the *x*-axis and *y*-axis are not labelled. This is because the category labels are obviously the names of continents and the title makes it clear what the value labels represent.

> **DID YOU KNOW?**
>
> You should never rely on colour as the only method of conveying information. This is because some people, such as people with colour blindness, may not be able to see the differences between colours. For more information about accessibility, see *Unit 5 Applying Information and Communication Technology* (page 193)

SKILLS EXECUTIVE FUNCTION

ACTIVITY

▼ CREATING PIE CHARTS AND COLUMN CHARTS

1 Open the file 'medals.xlsx'.
2 Use the data to recreate the pie chart shown in Figure 19.49.
3 Use the data to recreate the column chart shown in Figure 19.50.

LINE CHART

Line charts are often used to show how data values change over time. This makes trends easier to see, as shown in Figure 19.51.

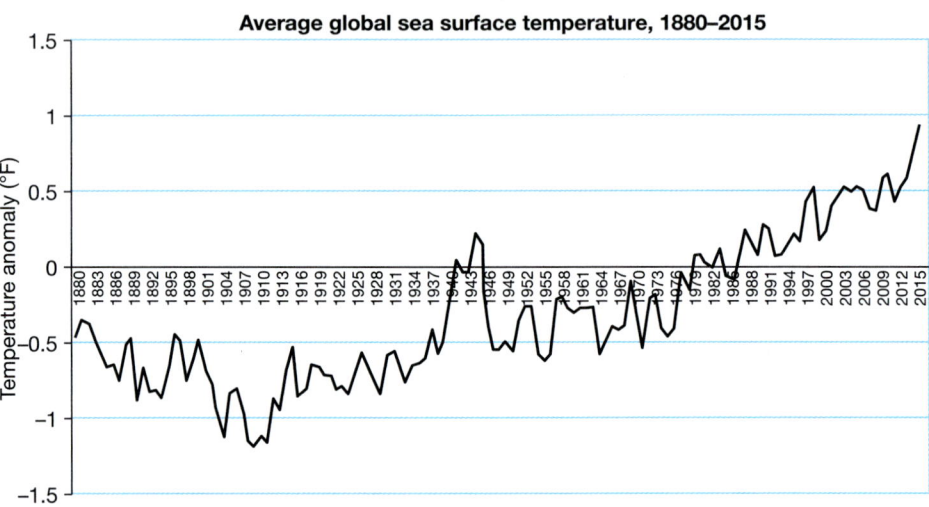

▲ Figure 19.51 A line chart showing global sea surface temperatures

HINT

IfIt is unusual to find an axis in the middle of a chart, but it is appropriate to include the *x*-axis in the middle of Figure 19.51 in order to show clearly the full range of negative and positive numbers in the data set. It is more usual to find the *x*-axis at the base of the chart.

SKILLS EXECUTIVE FUNCTION

ACTIVITY

▼ CREATING A LINE CHART

1 Open the file 'sea.xlsx'.
2 Use the data to recreate the line chart shown in Figure 19.51.

SCATTERGRAM

Scattergrams are used to show relationships between two sets of data values. The *x*-axis is used for one set of values and the *y*-axis is used for the other set of values.

For example, the salary data in Table 19.7 contains data about individuals' age, salary and height.

▼ Table 19.7 Data about individuals' age, salary and height

AGE	SALARY ($)	HEIGHT (CM)
18	18000	162
18	19000	182
19	17000	189

19	13000	174
20	26000	189
20	23000	166
21	25000	165
22	25000	171
23	30000	179
23	32000	168
25	36000	185
27	40000	171
27	50000	180
28	40000	181
28	48000	161
28	49000	179
31	53000	183
33	58000	162
34	100000	183
34	66000	163
34	80000	166
35	93000	188
35	82000	182
39	121000	163
40	88000	188
40	87000	161

GENERAL VOCABULARY

correlation in statistics, the interrelation of two facts, especially when one may be the cause of the other

Figures 19.52 and 19.53 are scattergrams created using the data in Table 19.7. They show that there is a **correlation** between age and salary (that is, older people earn more than younger people) but that there is no significant correlation between height and salary.

▲ Figure 19.52 A scattergram showing that salary increases with an individual's age

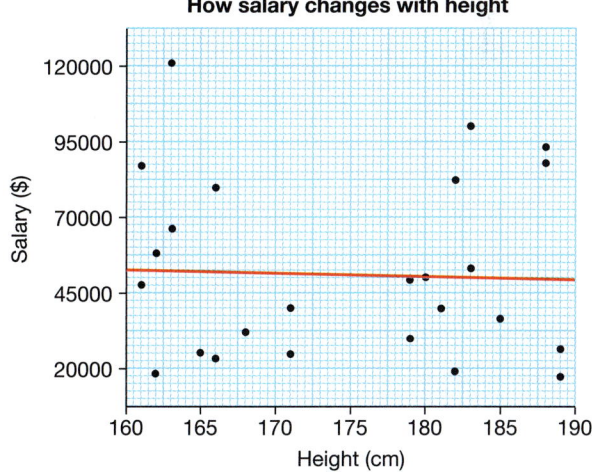

▲ Figure 19.53 A scattergram showing that salary does not change significantly with an individual's height

KEY POINT

The trend lines in Figure 19.52 and 19.53 are used to show the level of correlation between data values. These trends are easy to see from looking at the scattergrams, but they are not easy to see from looking only at Table 19.7.

SKILLS EXECUTIVE FUNCTION

ACTIVITY

▼ CREATING SCATTERGRAMS

1. Open the file 'salary.xlsx'.
2. Use the data to recreate the scattergrams shown in Figures 19.52 and 19.53.

FORMATTING CHARTS

Formatting a chart provides additional information to make the chart more readable and easier to interpret. Table 19.8 shows the different formatting options, their uses and some examples.

▼ Table 19.8 Options for formatting a chart

OPTION	USE	EXAMPLE
Title	Text that explains what the chart represents	In Figure 19.53, the title is 'How salary changes with height'
Axis labels	Text to state what the data on that axis represents	In Figure 19.53, the axis labels are 'Salary ($)' and 'Height (cm)' (these labels include the units of measurement used to measure the data)
Legends	A key to show what colours represent in a chart	In Figure 19.50, the medal colours on the right-hand side of the chart
Axis	The horizontal (x-axis) and vertical (y-axis) lines showing the data categories and data values • In column charts, line charts and scattergrams, the x-axis is used as the category axis and the y-axis is used as the value axis • In bar charts, the x-axis is used as the value axis and the y-axis is used as the category axis	In Figure 19.53, the x-axis values range from 160 cm to 190 cm and the y-axis values range from $10000 to $110000
Scale	The interval between values on an axis	In Figure 19.52, the x-axis values are scaled to show every five years, with each minimum scale value line representing 1 year
Trend line	A line of best fit that shows the general direction in which a group of data values seem to be heading	In Figure 19.52, the straight red line indicating the correlation between age and salary

DID YOU KNOW?

Many spreadsheet applications can now use vector images as illustrations to represent geographic data. For example, Figure 19.54 uses a map to show the number of gold medals won by the top 20 teams at the Rio 2016 Olympics.

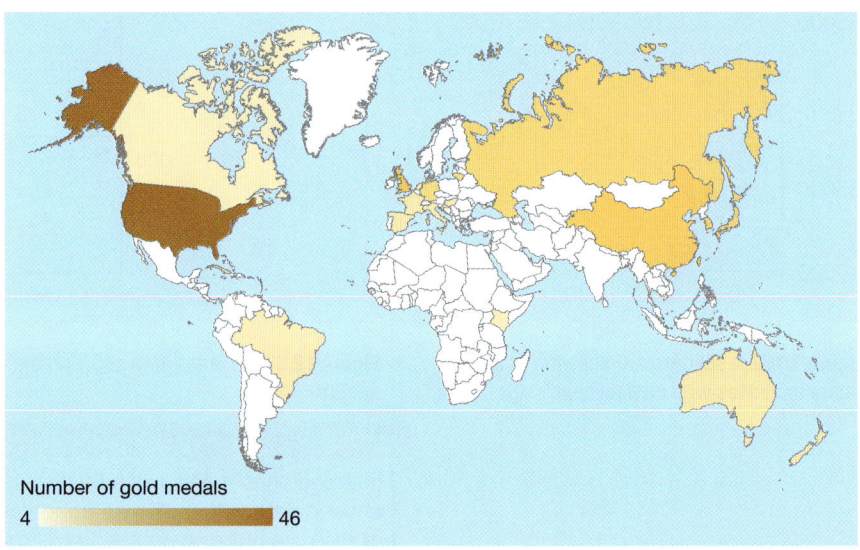

▲ Figure 19.54 The number of gold medals won by the top 20 teams at the Rio 2016 Olympics

PRINTING

DATA VIEW AND FORMULA VIEW

There are two different ways to view a worksheet:

- data view is the default view and it shows the results of formulae contained by the worksheet
- formula view has to be set manually and it shows the formulae used in the worksheet, rather than their results.

To enable formula view, select Show Formulas from the Formulas tab in Microsoft Excel or select Formulas in the View options in LibreOffice® Calc.

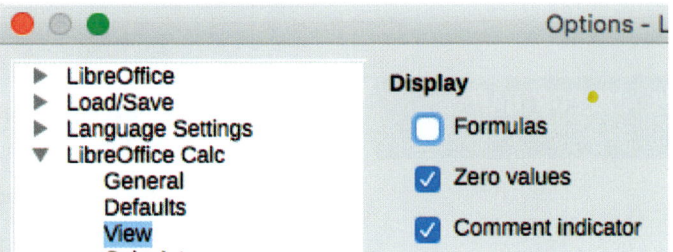

▲ Figure 19.55 The View options in LibreOffice Calc

SKILLS EXECUTIVE FUNCTION

ACTIVITY

▼ USING FORMULA VIEW

1. Open the file 'formulaView.ods'.
2. Show the formulae in cell range B1:B5.

SET A PRINT RANGE

SUBJECT VOCABULARY

dialogue box a box that appears on your computer screen when the program needs to ask the user a question before it can continue to do something; the user clicks on one part of the box to give their answer

You can set a temporary print area or print range by selecting the desired rows, columns or cell range in the spreadsheet and then selecting Print from the File menu. When the Print **dialogue box** appears, choose Print Selection or Selected cells, as shown in Figure 19.56 and 19.57.

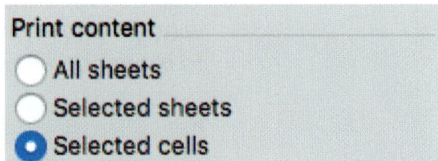

▲ Figure 19.56 Print Selected cells in LibreOffice Calc

▲ Figure 19.57 Print Selection in Microsoft Excel

Alternatively, you can set a permanent print area if you need to print the data frequently.

SKILLS > EXECUTIVE FUNCTION

ACTIVITY

▼ **SETTING A PERMANENT PRINT RANGE**

1. Open the file 'print.ods'.
2. Set the print range by:
   - in LibreOffice Calc, choosing Format > Print Ranges > Add
   - in Microsoft Excel, choosing File > Print Area > Set Print Area.
3. Use Print Preview to check that only the PRINT ME text will print. (You do not actually need to print this.)

LANDSCAPE AND PORTRAIT FORMAT

Spreadsheets are set to print in portrait format by default. The option to set the spreadsheet to landscape format is found by:

- in LibreOffice Calc, choosing Format > Page
- in Microsoft Excel, choosing Page Layout > Orientation.

For more information about landscape and portrait orientation, see page 227.

HEADERS AND FOOTERS

Headers and footers are repeated on every page when a spreadsheet is printed. Often, they include the title of the spreadsheet, the name of the author and the page numbers.

You can access header and footer options:

- in Microsoft Excel, from the Page Layout tab or by clicking the Header & Footer button on the Insert tab
- In LibreOffice Calc, from the Insert menu.

ROW AND COLUMN HEADERS

If your worksheet contains many rows, it will print across multiple pages. However, the column headers will only appear on the first page.

You can repeat a worksheet's column headers on every page by selecting Print Titles on the Page Layout tab in Microsoft Excel. This opens the Page Setup window shown in Figure 19.58. You can then choose which rows or columns to repeat on all printed pages.

> **HINT**
>
> Do not confuse row and column **headings** (1, 2, 3, 4, etc. and A, B, C, D, etc.) with row and column **headers**.

Figure 19.58 shows records from a table of data that contains 500 records. The row headers in cell range A1:F1 are shaded blue. Row 1 ($1:$1) has been selected in the field 'Rows to repeat at top'.

UNIT 6 — SPREADSHEETS — 305

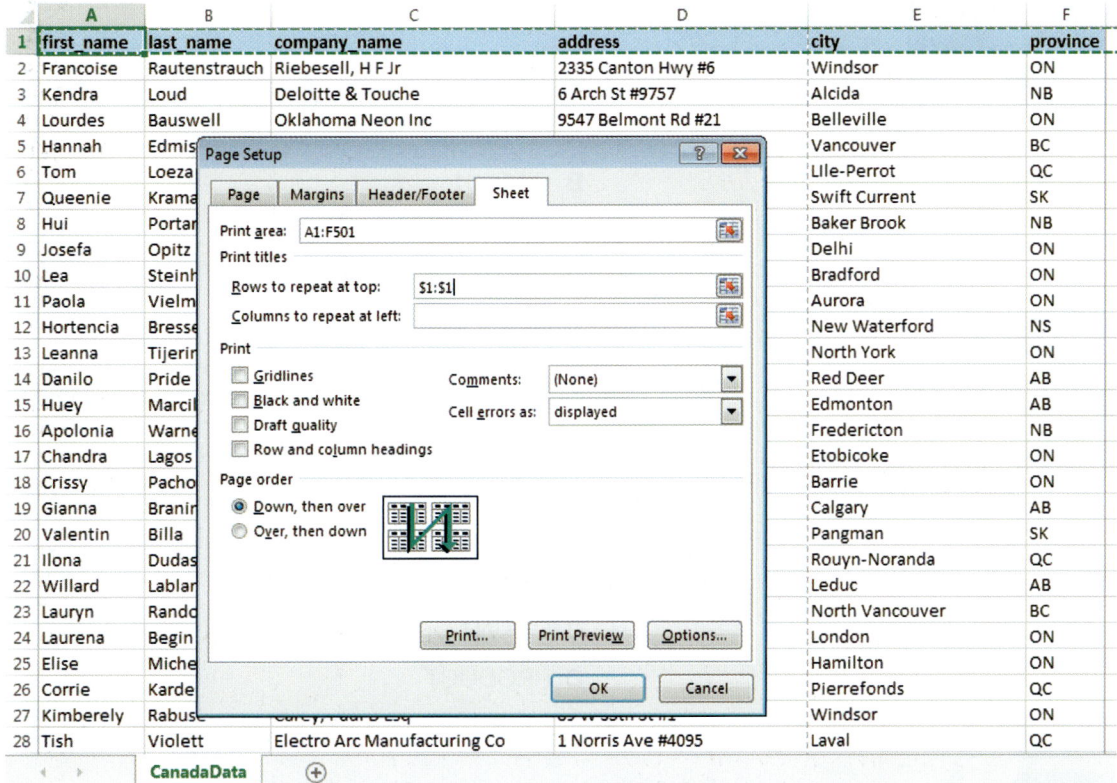

▲ Figure 19.58 The Page Setup window in Microsoft Excel

 SKILLS — EXECUTIVE FUNCTION

ACTIVITY

▼ REPEATING HEADERS

1. Open the file 'Canada.xlsx'.

2. View the file in print preview and preview the different pages to see that the column headers do not repeat on each page.

3. Close print preview.

4. Set the file up so that the column headers repeat on each page.

5. View the file in print preview and preview the pages to check that the headers for the table now repeat on each page.

CHAPTER QUESTIONS

SKILLS — PROBLEM SOLVING

1. Which **one** of these is a cell range reference? (1)
   - **A** G1J1
   - **B** G1 to J1
   - **C** G1 → J1
   - **D** G1:J1

SKILLS — REASONING

2. Explain why named ranges are useful in a spreadsheet. (2)

SKILLS — REASONING

3. Explain why absolute referencing is used in spreadsheets. (4)

SKILLS — PROBLEM SOLVING

4. Which **one** of these functions would you use to calculate the addition of a range of cells? (1)
   - **A** SUM
   - **B** COUNTIF
   - **C** COUNT
   - **D** PRODUCT

SKILLS — PROBLEM SOLVING

5. List **three** types of chart that you could use to represent data. (3)

SKILLS — INTERPRETATION

6. Describe how a VLOOKUP works. (4)

SKILLS — PROBLEM SOLVING

7. State the most appropriate chart type to show the correlation between two sets of data values. (1)

SKILLS — PROBLEM SOLVING

8. State the most appropriate chart type to represent values as a proportion of a whole. (1)

SKILLS — PROBLEM SOLVING

9. State the most appropriate chart type to compare values between different categories or groups. (1)

SKILLS — INTERPRETATION

10. Describe how a trend line can be used with a series of data to make predictions. (2)

SKILLS — INTERPRETATION / REASONING

11. State the advantage of using formulae in a spreadsheet to perform a calculation, rather than working out the answer and manually entering the result. (1)

SKILLS — PROBLEM SOLVING

12. Which **one** of these would evaluate to TRUE? (1)
    - **A** 9 > 11
    - **B** 9 = (5+4)
    - **C** 9 < 5
    - **D** 9 >= 10

UNIT 6   DATABASE MANAGEMENT   307

20 DATABASE MANAGEMENT

Databases allow users to store, organise and search data, as well as outputting it in either a printed or electronic format.

Databases have many uses, such as storing school or college students' academic records, cataloguing and managing stock in shops, organising a collection of books, films or music. Databases are used in banking, police and crime information systems and vehicle registration systems. Many organisations also use databases when sending out letters and emails to customers.

In this chapter, you will learn about Microsoft® Access®, but you could also use LibreOffice® Base or any other database application.

LEARNING OBJECTIVES

- Identify data types: alphanumeric/text, numeric/number, date, currency, logical/Boolean
- Explain the structure of a given database, including: record, field, table, primary key/field, foreign key/field, relationships between tables
- Explain the need for validation and identify validation checks such as range check, presence check, type check, length check
- Sort using a single field, multiple fields, ascending/descending order
- Input information to given tables or forms applying format consistently
- Use search/query using single criterion, multiple criteria, search within results, relational operators, logical operators
- Produce outputs: reports, mail merge documents, specified fields, design view (table structure, searches/queries, forms, relationships), data view (table, search/query results, forms)

GENERAL VOCABULARY

Boolean a Boolean system is based on things that can be either true or false, but not both; it links statements with operators, which are words such as AND, OR, and NOT
monetary relating to money

DID YOU KNOW?

The term Boolean comes from the name of the nineteenth-century mathematician, George Boole.

DATA TYPES

When data is stored in a database, it must be stored as a specific type of data. This makes sure that appropriate operations can be carried out on the data at a later date.

▼ Table 20.1 Common data types that can be stored in a database

DATA TYPE	DESCRIPTION	EXAMPLE OF DATA
Alphanumeric or text	Stores letter, number and special characters such as punctuation	Telephone number: 613-555-0182
Date	Stores dates using day, month and year, and can be presented in different formats	Date of birth: 26/12/2013
Logical or **Boolean**	Store one of two values, such as True or False and Yes or No	'Is 30 greater than 40?': False
Currency	Stores **monetary** values	Cost of ticket for children: $5.99
Numeric or number	Stores numeric values such as distance	Height in centimetres: 178

SKILLS: INTERPRETATION

ACTIVITY

▼ DATA TYPES

Match each example of data in Table 20.2 to the correct data type.

▼ Table 20.2 Matching data types

EXAMPLE OF DATA	DATA TYPE
Magic wand	Numeric or number
17/11/2019	Alphanumeric or text
$40.00	Date
9780435188931	Logical or Boolean
True	Currency

DATABASE STRUCTURE

A database consists of one or more tables. A database with only one table is called a flat file database. A database with more than one table is known as a relational database.

TABLES

A table consists of:

- **records** (as rows) that contain data about **entities**, such as people, films, objects or locations
- **fields** (as columns) that are used to store **attributes** about each entity, such as gender, date of birth or height.

This is shown in Table 20.3.

▼ Table 20.3 A table containing data about books

ISBN	TITLE	AUTHOR	PUBLISHER	YEAR PUBLISHED
0394831039	Danny, The Champion of the World	Roald Dahl	Knopf Books for Young Readers	1975
0307292045	The Hitchhiker's Guide to the Galaxy	Douglas Adams	Harmony Books	1979
0575041714	Mort	Terry Pratchett	Gollancz	1987

CREATE A DATABASE

A **theme park** is creating a database.

- The theme park database stores data about visitors in a table called 'Visitors'.
- The theme park has five **rides**. Data about the rides are stored in a table called 'Rides'.
- Data about tickets are stored in a table called 'Tickets'.
- When visitors pay for a ride, they are given a ticket.
- Tickets can be bought at ticket stalls in the theme park.

SUBJECT VOCABULARY

entity in a database, something that exists as a single and complete unit
attribute in a database, a characteristic, feature, or quality of an entity

GENERAL VOCABULARY

ISBN (International Standard Book Number) a unique number that is given to every book that is published

DID YOU KNOW?
ISBNs are used to uniquely identify books. The ISBN of this book is 9780435188931.

GENERAL VOCABULARY

theme park a themed amusement park containing attractions such as rollercoaster rides
ride a large machine that people ride for fun at a fair or theme park

UNIT 6 DATABASE MANAGEMENT

▲ Figure 20.1 Have you bought tickets at a theme park ticket stall like this?

> **HINT**
> Choose a name for your database that describes the data that it will store.

When you create a new database, you must give it a name. It is then saved immediately to a folder that you can specify.

When the new database opens, you will see a table ready for you to enter data, as shown in Figure 20.2. This view is called Datasheet View.

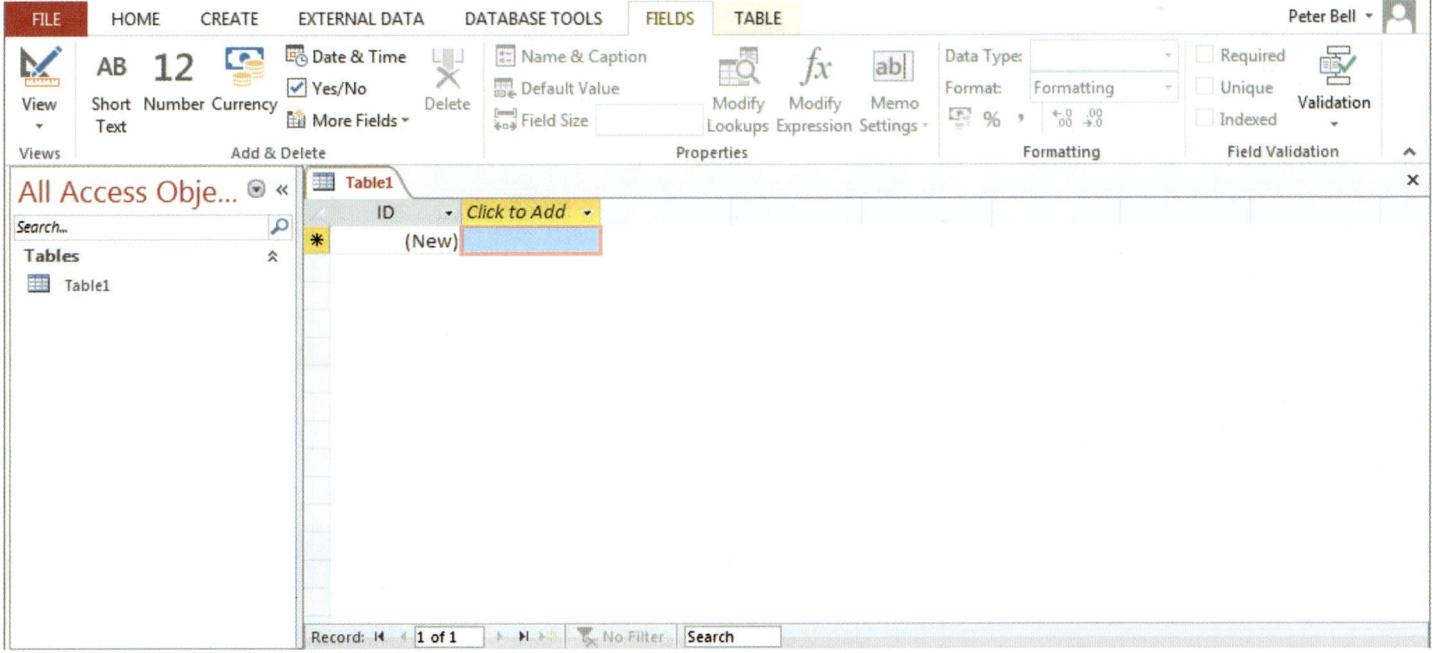

▲ Figure 20.2 When you create a new database, you will see a new table in Datasheet View

▲ **Figure 20.3** The Design View button in Microsoft Access

The next task is to set up the table to store data about visitors. Before you enter data into the table, you should set up the table's fields and data types in Design View, using the button shown in Figure 20.3.

When you name the tables within your database, ensure that you use names that describe the type of data you will store in the table.

ACTIVITY

▼ CREATING A NEW DATABASE

1. Create a new database named 'ThemePark' and store it in an appropriate folder.
2. Open the table in Design View by clicking the button shown in Figure 20.3.
3. Name the table 'Visitors' and save the table.

In Design View, you can enter field names, set the data types stored in each field and add a description to each field, as shown in Figure 20.4. The description should be good enough to help you or someone else understand your fields if it is necessary to edit your design at a later date.

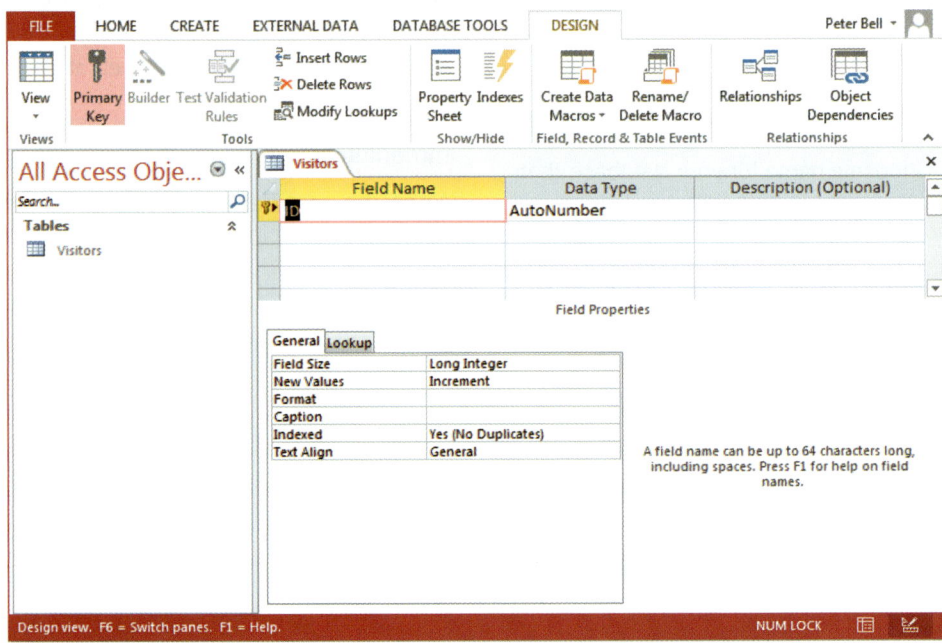

▲ **Figure 20.4** Viewing a table in Design View

ACTIVITY

▼ COMPLETING FIELDS

1. Use the data in Table 20.4 to complete the field name, data type and a description for each field in your Visitors table.
2. Save the table.

UNIT 6 — DATABASE MANAGEMENT

▼ Table 20.4 Field names and data types

FIELD NAME	DATA TYPE
VisitorID	AutoNumber
FirstName	Short Text
Surname	Short Text
DateOfBirth	Date/Time
Gender	Short Text

SUBJECT VOCABULARY

primary key field in a database, the field that holds the primary key, which is a unique attribute stored for each entity

HINT

Often, the primary key is named 'ID' by default, as shown in Figure 20.4.

The first field that you set up (in Table 20.4, the VisitorID) is used as the **primary key field**. Primary key fields hold values that will be unique for each record or entity in the table. For example, In Table 20.3 on page 308, the primary key field is ISBN.

You can choose AutoNumber for the Data Type for the primary key field, as suggested in Table 20.4. This ensures that each record will be given a new primary key value. The primary key value starts at 1 and will go up by 1 each time a new record is added. The primary key is set automatically as the first field when you create a new table.

HINT

The data type for the VisitorID field would be alphanumeric or text (if it was not also the primary key field), as visitor IDs do not need to be calculated and can start with a 0 (which numeric data cannot).

Figure 20.5 shows the completed table design for the Visitors table.

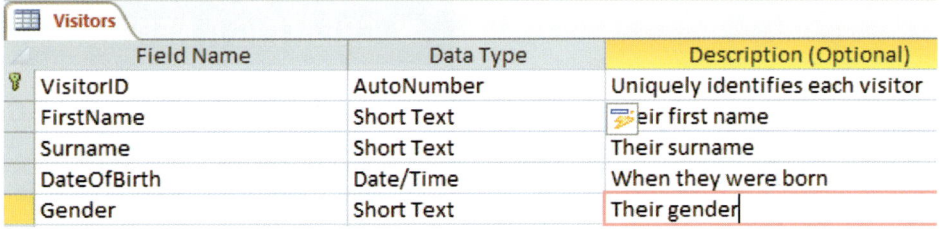

▲ Figure 20.5 A completed table design for the Visitors table in your database

HINT

- You can return to Datasheet View by clicking the View button at the top left of the window.
- If you do not save your file first, you will be prompted to save the file when you change views.

In Datasheet View, the field names appear at the top of each column, as shown in Figure 20.6.

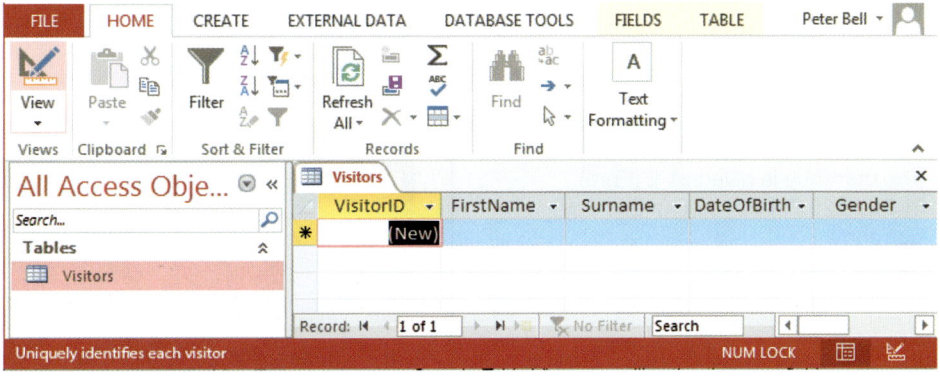

HINT

Any description text that you have entered for the active field appears in the bottom left of the window.

▲ Figure 20.6 A table that has been set up and is ready for data entry

UNIT 6 — DATABASE MANAGEMENT

SKILLS: EXECUTIVE FUNCTION

KEY POINT
You do not need to type the values for VisitorID field because it uses AutoNumber. When you enter data into the FirstName field, the value in the AutoNumber field will be generated automatically.

ACTIVITY

▼ ENTERING RECORDS

Use the information in Table 20.5 to enter 10 records into the Visitors table of your database, saving your table once you have finished.

▼ Table 20.5 Information needed to enter records into the Visitors table

VisitorID	FirstName	Surname	DateOfBirth	Gender
1	Holley	Worland	16/07/1983	F
2	Maryann	Tates	01/04/1999	F
3	Jon	Hannah	23/02/2000	M
4	Hailey	Kopet	11/04/2008	F
5	Farrah	Malboeuf	10/12/1984	F
6	Candra	Deritis	17/01/1998	F
7	Reuben	Hegland	26/12/2010	M
8	Rowan	Thomas	10/08/1977	M
9	Lee	Taylor	06/09/1972	M
10	Luicien	Schmoyer	31/10/1993	M

SKILLS: EXECUTIVE FUNCTION

ACTIVITY

▼ CREATING A NEW TABLE

1. Using the Table option on the Create tab, create a new table in your database and name it 'Rides'.
2. Use Table 20.6 to set up the fields in Design View.
3. Use Table 20.7 to add records in Datasheet View.

▼ Table 20.6 Field names and data types for the Rides table

FIELD NAME	DATA TYPE
RideID	AutoNumber
RideName	Short text
RideFee	Currency

▼ Table 20.7 Records for the Rides table

RideID	RideName	RideFee
1	Looper	€5.00
2	SpinX	€4.00
3	Shuttle	€6.00
4	Slide	€1.00
5	Insanity	€8.00

HINT
The currency is given as € (Euro) in Table 20.7, but you can use any currency.

CREATING RELATIONSHIPS BETWEEN TABLES

In the activities so far, you have created two separate tables: one for visitors and one for rides. When a visitor (record or entity) pays for a ride (record or entity), a ticket (record or entity) is created. This creates a relationship between these tables, as shown in Figure 20.7.

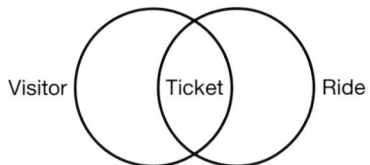

▲ Figure 20.7 Relationships are formed between linked tables

Figure 20.8 shows some other examples of tables that can form relational databases.

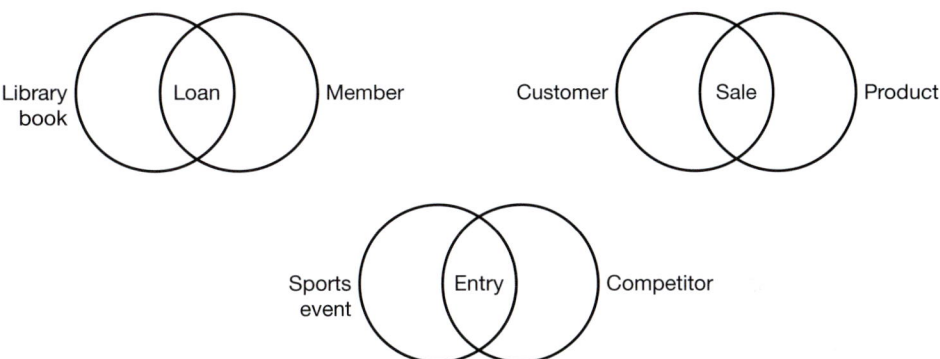

▲ Figure 20.8 Other examples of relationships that can be made between tables for libraries, retailers and sports events organisers

The theme park's database will also contain a third table called 'Tickets'. This table will have four fields:

1 TicketID (the primary key field in this table)
2 RideID (a **foreign key**)
3 VisitorID (a foreign key)
4 RideDate (the date on which the ticket for the ride is valid).

You can view the relationships between tables by selecting Relationships from the Database Tools tab in Microsoft Access.

SUBJECT VOCABULARY

foreign key in a database, a primary key from one table that is used in another table

KEY POINT

A table can only have one primary key. It must be unique. Tables can contain more than one foreign key.

SKILLS EXECUTIVE FUNCTION

KEY POINT

Setting the default value to =Now() makes sense, as it is likely that the user will be entering data about a sale at the time of the sale.

ACTIVITY

▼ CREATING RELATIONSHIPS BETWEEN TABLES

1 Open the file 'ThemePark.accdb'.
2 Open the Tickets table in Design View.
3 Set the Data Type to Number for both VisitorID and RideID.
4 Set the Data Type to Date/Time for RideDate.
5 Set the Format property for RideDate to Short Date.
6 Set the Default Value property for RideDate to =Now(). (This sets the attribute for this field to the current day's date.)
7 Save the Tickets table.

> **HINT**
> Task 8 is important. Tables must be closed before you can change their relationships with other tables.

> **HINT**
> Double-click each table to add them.

> **SUBJECT VOCABULARY**
> **referential integrity** the state of a database when any foreign key field in a table refers to a primary key in a related table

> **HINT**
> When you enforce referential integrity, the database will only allow data to be entered if the related record exists.

> **HINT**
> Because referential integrity is being enforced, an error message appears when you complete Task 20, as shown in Figure 20.10. This is because there is no RideID 7 in the Rides table.

8 Close the Tickets table.
9 Open the Relationships View from the Database Tools tab.
10 Show all three tables by adding them **once**.
11 Close the Show Table window.
12 Drag the RideID field from the Rides table onto the RideID field in the Tickets table.
13 The Edit Relationships window will appear. Check that the Enforce **Referential Integrity** box is selected, as shown in Figure 20.9.

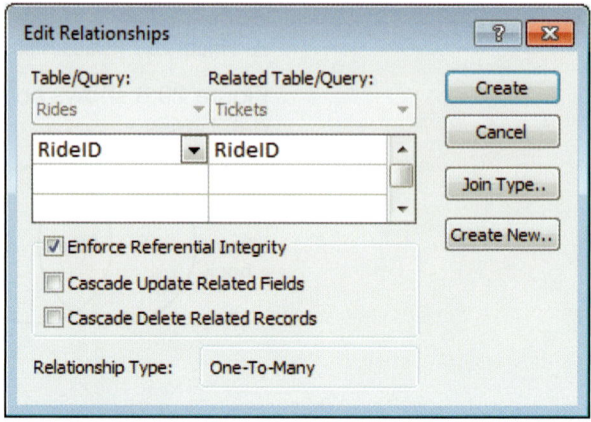

▲ Figure 20.9 Enforcing referential integrity when creating relationships between tables

14 Click the Create button in the Edit Relationships window.
15 Drag the VisitorID field from the Visitors table onto the VisitorID field in the Tickets table.
16 The Edit Relationships window will appear. Check that the Enforce Referential Integrity box is selected.
17 Click the Create button in the Edit Relationships window.
18 Save the Relationships design window.
19 Close the Relationships design window.
20 Open the Tickets table and enter 9 in the VisitorID field and 7 in the RideID field.

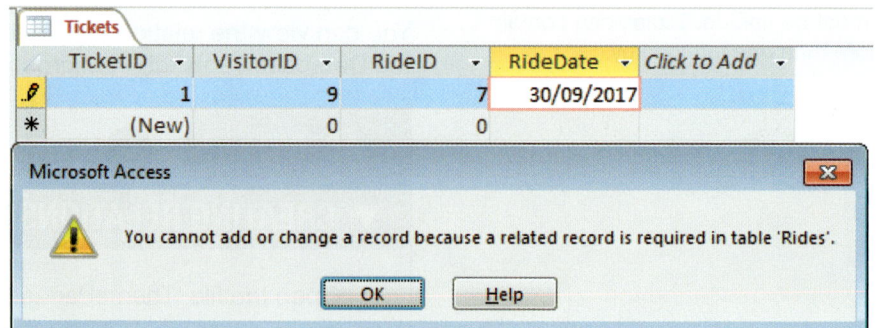

▲ Figure 20.10 Enforcing referential integrity prevents users from entering invalid data

21 Click OK on the error message to close it.
22 Change the RideID to 5 and press the Enter key. This entry should be accepted.
23 Enter four more records into the Tickets table.
24 Save the table.

Enforcing referential integrity is important when creating relationships between tables. This is because it allows you to make sure that only existing data from the Visitors table and the Rides table can be entered into the VisitorID and RideID fields of the Tickets table. This helps reduce data entry errors, because users are less likely to make mistakes by entering invalid data.

Once relationships have been created between tables, data from one table can be looked up using criteria from another. For example, in the theme park database, you could find out the gender of all visitors who bought tickets for the Looper ride to see whether it is more popular with women or with men. This is shown in Figure 20.11.

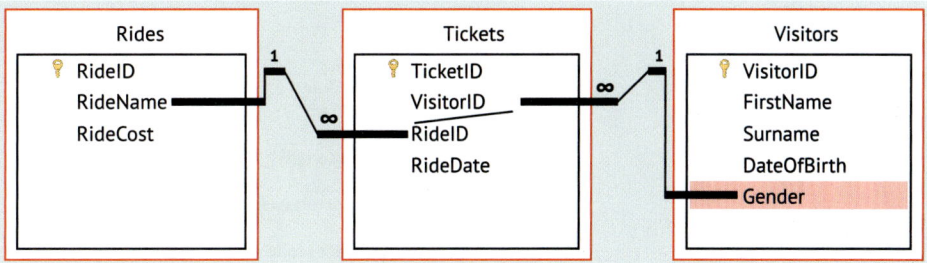

▲ Figure 20.11 The relationships between tables allow related data to be looked up

You will learn more about this when you consider queries later in this chapter.

VALIDATION

SUBJECT VOCABULARY

validation the process of checking if something is acceptable when compared to given criteria

Validation helps to reduce data entry errors. It is used to check that data entered in a field is acceptable when compared to criteria set in the database design. Enforcing referential integrity is one type of validation.

Validation does not check that the data is accurate or correct. It just checks that the data meets criteria and can be accepted by the field. If the data passes a validation check, then it will be stored in the field. If it does not pass the validation check, it will be rejected and an error message will be displayed.

HINT

It is good practice to customise the general error message so that it explains to the user why the data was rejected and why the validation rules were not met. Good error messages help users to understand what they need to do in order to enter valid data.

TYPES OF VALIDATION CHECK

There are four different types of validation check:
- presence
- type
- length
- range.

Table 20.8 lists the purpose and examples of each of these checks.

▼ Table 20.8 The purpose and examples of different types of validation check

TYPE OF CHECK	PURPOSE	EXAMPLE OF DATA	EXAMPLE OF CHECK
Presence	Tests if any data has been entered by checking that the field is not blank	Surname (text)	Has data been entered into the surname field?
Type	Tests if the data entered matches the field's data type	Quantity (number)	Is the entered data numeric?
Length	Tests if the correct number of characters has been entered	Password	Have more than 7 characters been entered?
Range	Tests if data is between two specific values	DateOfBirth (Date)	Is the date between 01/01/1990 and 31/12/2017?

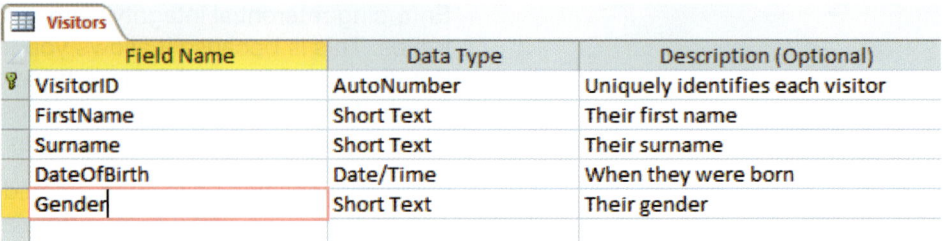

▲ Figure 20.12 Validation rules can be set in the Field Properties in Microsoft Access

SKILLS ▸ EXECUTIVE FUNCTION

ACTIVITY

▼ **SETTING VALIDATION RULES**

1. Open the file 'ThemePark2.accdb'.
2. Open the Visitor table in Design View.
3. Set a validation rule for the Gender field to check that the field only accepts **'M'** or **'F'** (range check and length check) by setting Validation Rule to **'M' Or 'F'**, as shown in Figure 20.13.

General	Lookup
Field Size	255
Format	@
Input Mask	
Caption	
Default Value	
Validation Rule	'M' Or 'F'
Validation Text	Please enter M or F
Required	Yes
Allow Zero Length	Yes
Indexed	No
Unicode Compression	No
IME Mode	No Control
IME Sentence Mode	None
Text Align	General

▲ Figure 20.13 Completed validation rules for the Gender field in the Visitors table

4. Save the table.
5. Switch to Datasheet View.
6. Type 'Male' in the Gender field for VisitorID 3 (Jon).

HINT

- Include the single quotes (' ') around the M and F to denote that they are text values.
- Check that there is data in the field (presence check) by setting Required to Yes.
- Add validation text that will provide help for users if they do not enter valid data.

7 Press Enter to store the data in the Gender field. The error message will display your validation text, as shown in Figure 20.14.

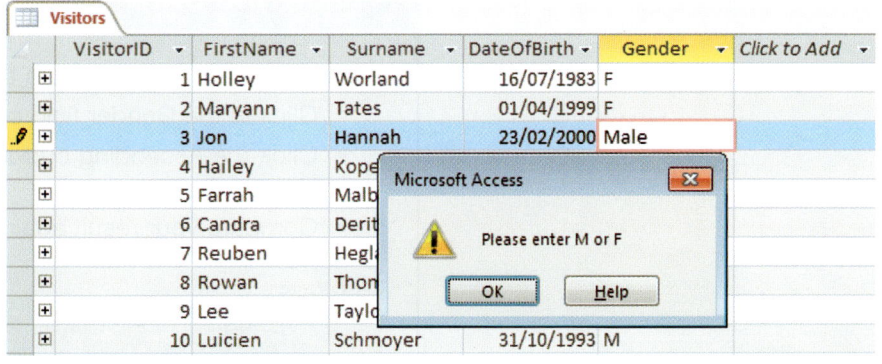

▲ Figure 20.14 A customised validation message helps the user understand what they need to do to enter valid data

8 Press the OK button.

9 Replace text 'Male' with 'F'. The data will be accepted even though Jon is male. This shows that validation checks do not check whether data is accurate, only whether it is acceptable.

10 Replace text 'F' with 'M' for VisitorID 3 (Jon). The data should be accepted.

11 Save the table.

SORTING DATA

You can sort data in either ascending order or descending order. Table 20.9 shows some examples.

▼ Table 20.9 Ascending and descending order

	UNSORTED DATA	ASCENDING ORDER	DESCENDING ORDER
Text	C,B,D,A,E	A,B,C,D,E	E,D,C,B,A
Numeric	4,3,2,5,1	1,2,3,4,5	5,4,3,2,1

Data can either be sorted by the data in a single field or in multiple fields, such as ascending by Surname then descending by DateOfBirth. You can sort data using the tools shown in Figure 20.15.

▲ Figure 20.15 The Sort & Filter tools available in Microsoft Access

For more information about ascending and descending order, see page 294.

SKILLS ▶ EXECUTIVE FUNCTION

ACTIVITY

▼ **SORTING DATA**

1. Sort the data in the Visitors table by Gender in ascending order.
   - Click in the Gender field of any record.
   - Click the Ascending button in the Sort & Filter group on the Home tab.
   - Compare your result against Figure 20.16.

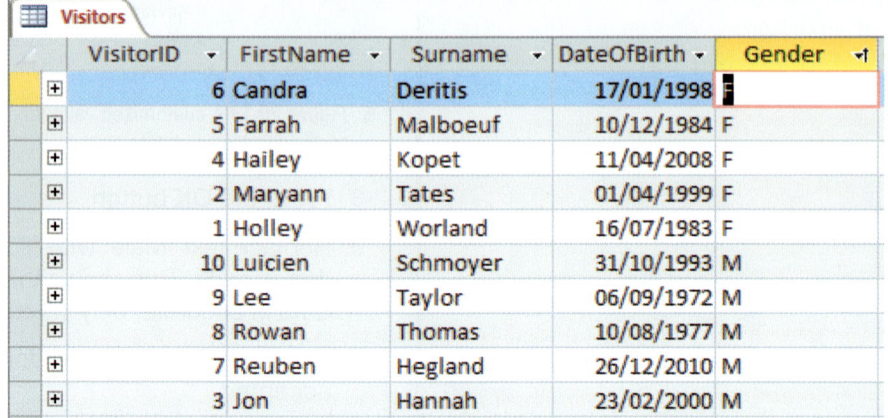

▲ Figure 20.16 The Visitors table has been sorted by Gender in ascending order

2. Sort the data by Gender (in descending order) **then** by DateOfBirth (in descending order).
   - Click in the Gender field of any record.
   - Click the Advanced button in the Sort & Filter group on the Home tab.
   - Select Advanced Filter/Sort.
   - Double click on DateOfBirth.
   - Set both sort options to Descending, as shown in Figure 20.17.

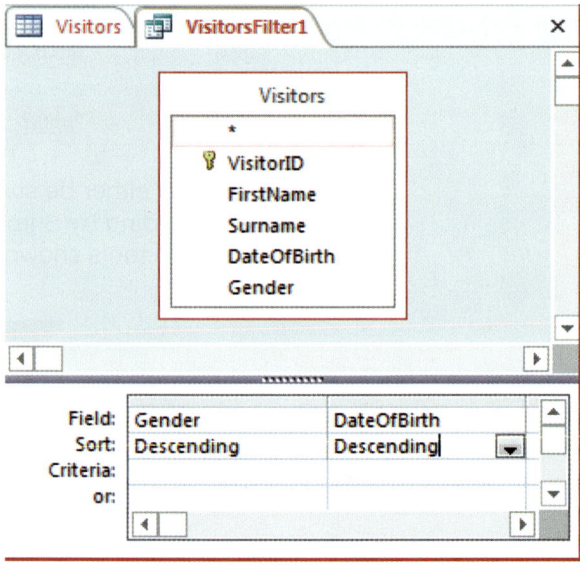

▲ Figure 20.17 The completed Sort options

- Click the Toggle Filter icon (Figure 20.18) in the Sort & Filter group on the Home tab.

▲ Figure 20.18 The Toggle Filter icon in Microsoft Access

- Compare your result against Figure 20.19.

VisitorID	FirstName	Surname	DateOfBirth	Gender
7	Reuben	Hegland	26/12/2010	M
3	Jon	Hannah	23/02/2000	M
10	Luicien	Schmoyer	31/10/1993	M
8	Rowan	Thomas	10/08/1977	M
9	Lee	Taylor	06/09/1972	M
4	Hailey	Kopet	11/04/2008	F
2	Maryann	Tates	01/04/1999	F
6	Candra	Deritis	17/01/1998	F
5	Farrah	Malboeuf	10/12/1984	F
1	Holley	Worland	16/07/1983	F

▲ Figure 20.19 Visitor data sorted by Gender then by DateOfBirth

INPUTTING INFORMATION CONSISTENTLY

You have already input some data into your tables.

When you enter data into a table or a form, you must make sure that you use the same format throughout. For example, if data in a Date field is formatted as DD/MM/YYYY (day, then month, then year), you should always enter it in that format. Do not change the format to MM/DD/YYYY (month, then day, then year) or change the '/' to ':' (DD:MM:YYYY).

Similarly, if names start with a title, such as Mrs, you should make sure that the titles are consistent: do not use 'Mrs.' or 'MRS'.

QUERIES

SUBJECT VOCABULARY

query a request for data results
dynaset a dynamic set of data used to store the results of a query

Queries are used to search for, retrieve and combine data from one or more tables and perform calculations on that data. Queries that retrieve or calculate data from a table are called select queries.

The results of a query are stored in a **dynaset**, which is a **DYNA**mic sub**SET** of data. The data in the dynaset are dynamically linked to the table(s) from which they are selected. **Dynamically linked** means that any change made to the data in the dynaset is also applied to the data in the table from which it was originally selected.

The results of a query are determined by the criteria you enter. You can query records in one or more tables and use one **criterion** or multiple criteria to define the search.

GENERAL VOCABULARY

criterion (plural **criteria**) a standard, rule or piece of information on the basis of which something is decided

SKILLS ▸ EXECUTIVE FUNCTION

ACTIVITY

▼ CREATING A QUERY BASED ON A SINGLE CRITERION

1. Open the file 'ThemePark2.accdb'. This database has had some records added to the Tickets table.
2. Create a new query using Query Design (Figure 20.20) from the Create tab.

▲ **Figure 20.20** The Query Design button in Microsoft Access

3. From the Show Table window, add all three tables by double-clicking them once.
4. Close the Show Table window.
5. Add the fields as shown in Figure 20.21 (four fields from the Visitors table, two from the Rides table and one from the Tickets table).
6. Type **"Thomas"** into the Criteria for the Surname field. This creates a single-criterion query, as shown in Figure 20.21.

> **HINT**
> If you do not enter the quotation marks (" ") around the word, some database management applications will add them for you.

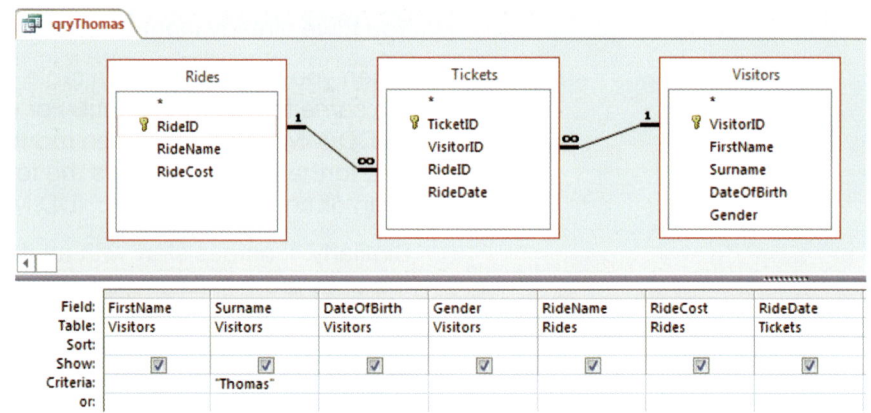

▲ **Figure 20.21** A single-criterion query

7. Save the query as qryThomas.
8. View the query as a dynaset in Datasheet View.
9. Compare your result against Figure 20.22.

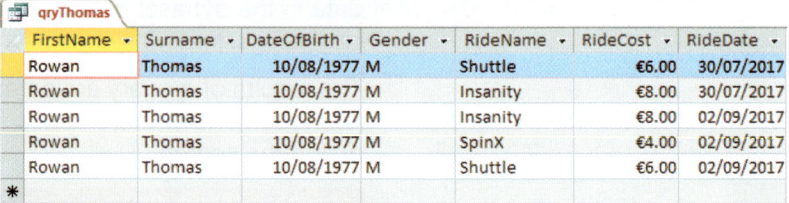

▲ **Figure 20.22** qryThomas in Datasheet View, displaying data from linked tables that matches the criteria

SKILLS > EXECUTIVE FUNCTION

ACTIVITY

▼ CREATING A QUERY BASED ON MULTIPLE CRITERIA (AN 'AND' QUERY)

1 View qryThomas in Design View.

2 Type **"Shuttle"** into the Criteria for the RideName field. This means that the query now contains more than one criterion.

3 Save the query.

4 View the query in Datasheet View.

5 Compare your result against Figure 20.23. Only two records should appear.

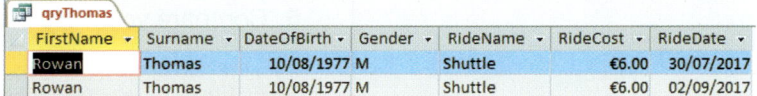

▲ Figure 20.23 The two records that should be displayed when you view qryThomas in Datasheet View

LOGICAL OPERATORS

You can enter logical operators in criteria, as explained in Table 20.10. Logical operators evaluate to either TRUE or FALSE.

▼ Table 20.10 The different logical operators that can be entered in criteria

LOGICAL OPERATOR	WHAT IS TESTED	RESULTS	EXAMPLE
AND	Two or more criteria **must** match	Only results that match (are TRUE for) **all** criteria are shown	Finding records based on multiple criteria across one or more fields
OR	**Either** criteria match	Results that match (are TRUE for) **any** of the criteria are shown	Finding records based on multiple criteria in the same column (see *Activity: Using the logical operator OR*)
NOT	Two or more criteria must **not** match	Only results that **do not** match (are FALSE for) **all** criteria are shown	Exempting (not including) records that match criteria (see *Activity: Using the logical operator NOT*)

SKILLS > EXECUTIVE FUNCTION

ACTIVITY

▼ USING THE LOGICAL OPERATOR 'OR'

1 Create a new query in Design View.

2 Type **"Hannah"** into the Criteria row for the Surname field, as shown in Figure 20.24.

3 Type **"Thomas"** into the Or row for the Surname field, as shown in Figure 20.24.

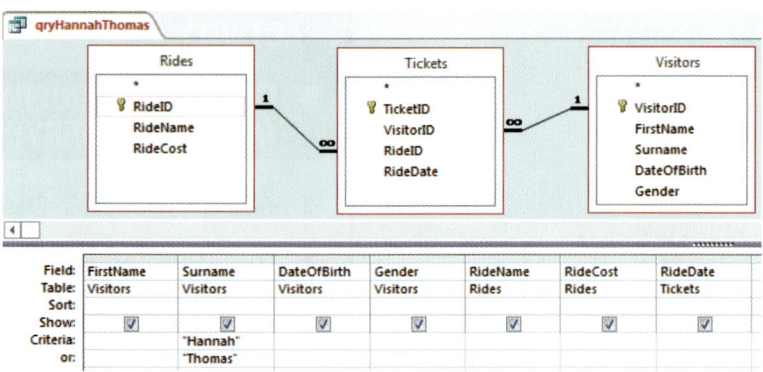

▲ Figure 20.24 Creating a query using OR

4 Save the query as qryHannahThomas.
5 View the query in Datasheet View.
6 Compare your result against Figure 20.25.

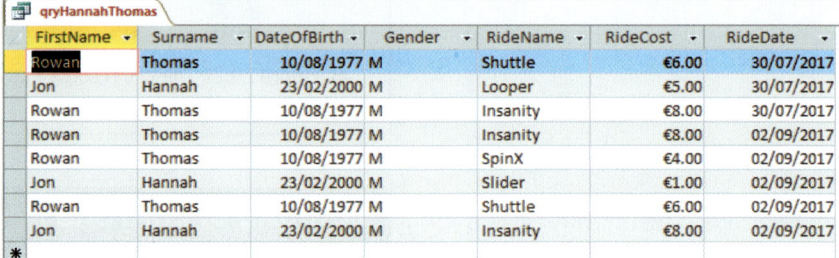

▲ Figure 20.25 The OR query in Datasheet View

7 Return to Design View.
8 Add **"Kopet"** underneath **"Thomas"**.
9 Save the query.
10 View the query in Datasheet View. The query should now return records that match any of the three criteria for Surname.

SKILLS ▶ EXECUTIVE FUNCTION

ACTIVITY

▼ USING THE LOGICAL OPERATOR 'NOT'

1 Using the same query, enter Not "Shuttle" into the Criteria for the RideName field on the row for **"Thomas"**, as shown in Figure 20.26.)

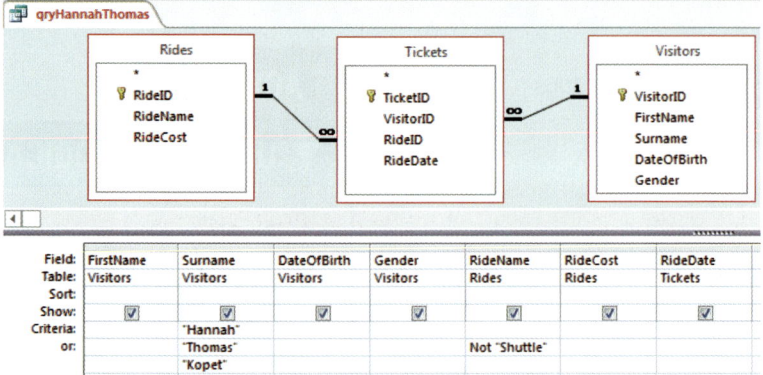

▲ Figure 20.26 Adding a NOT operator to qryHannahThomas

UNIT 6

DATABASE MANAGEMENT

2 Save the query.

3 View the query in Datasheet View.

4 Compare your result against Figure 20.27.

▲ **Figure 20.27** Ticket records for all three visitors are displayed except for tickets for the Shuttle that were bought by visitor Thomas

> **HINT**
> You can sort the data returned from a query using the same method shown earlier in this chapter.

RELATIONAL OPERATORS

You can enter relational operators in criteria, as explained in Table 20.11. Like logical operators, relational operators also evaluate to either TRUE or FALSE.

▼ **Table 20.11** The different relational operators that can be entered in criteria

RELATIONAL OPERATOR	NAME	USE	EXAMPLES THAT WOULD RETURN TRUE
>	Greater than	Checks if the first value is greater than the second value	14>12
<	Less than	Checks if the first value is less than the second value	2<9
>=	Greater than or equal to	Checks if the first value is greater than or the same as the second value	• 2>=1 • 2>=2
<=	Less than or equal to	Checks if the first value is less than or the same as the second value	• 1<=2 • 1<=1
=	Equal to	Checks if the first value is the same as the second value	1=1
<>	Not equal to	Checks if the first value is not the same as the second value	1<>2

> **HINT**
> Entering **< > "Shuttle"** will achieve the same result as querying the logical operator **Not "Shuttle"**, which was used in Figure 20.26.

You can combine logical and relational operators, which is useful when you need to set criteria to find records within a particular date range. For example, you might want to find tickets bought by visitor Thomas in September.

SKILLS ▸ EXECUTIVE FUNCTION

ACTIVITY

▼ **COMBINING LOGICAL AND RELATIONAL OPERATORS**

1 Create a new query in Design View.

2 Enter **"Thomas"** into the Criteria row for the Surname field.

3 Enter **>#01/09/2017# And <#1/10/2017#** into the Criteria for the RideDate field on the same row as **"Thomas"**, as shown in Figure 20.28. This selects only those tickets that have a RideDate of after 00:00 on 1 September 2017 and before 00:00 on 1 October 2017, which means that it will select tickets from September 2017.

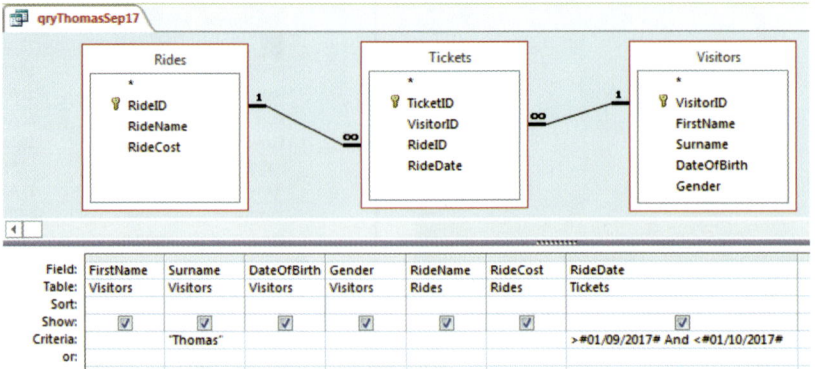

▲ Figure 20.28 This query will select only the rides taken in September by visitors with the surname Thomas

4 Save the query as qryThomasSep17.
5 View the query in Datasheet View.
6 Compare your result against Figure 20.29.

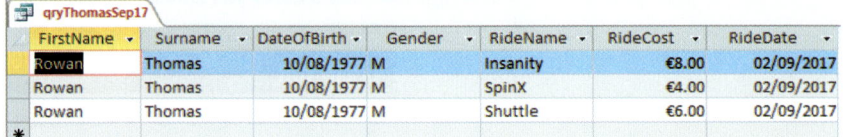

▲ Figure 20.29 The results of a query designed to show tickets bought by visitor Thomas in September

OUTPUTTING DATA FROM A DATABASE

Once data has been input and processed, it can be output in a range of formats. Your choice of format will be decided by the needs of the target audience. Outputs make the data easier for the audience to read and understand.

REPORTS

You can display selected data from a database in a report, which can be viewed on screen or printed. In Microsoft Access, you can create a report based on a query using the Report Wizard from the Reports group on the Create tab, as shown in Figure 20.30.

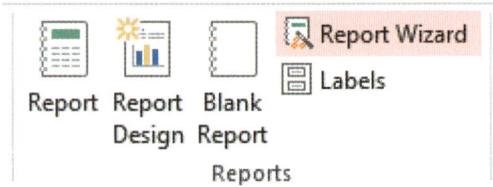

▲ Figure 20.30 The Report Wizard in Microsoft Access

For example, you might want to create a report that shows details of people who bought tickets for different theme park rides in September 2017.

UNIT 6 | DATABASE MANAGEMENT | 325

SKILLS › EXECUTIVE FUNCTION

ACTIVITY

▼ CREATING A REPORT

1. Open the file 'ThemePark3.accdb'.
2. From the Create tab, select Report Wizard from the Reports group.
3. Choose the qryTicketsSep17 query.
4. Add the fields shown in Figure 20.31.

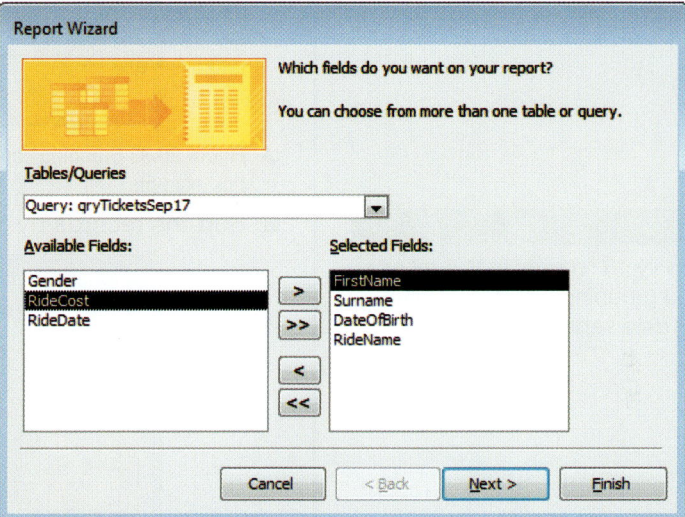

▲ **Figure 20.31** Only add fields that you need to see; some fields are not relevant to this report so they have been left out

5. Click Next.
6. Choose by Rides and then click Next, as shown in Figure 20.32.

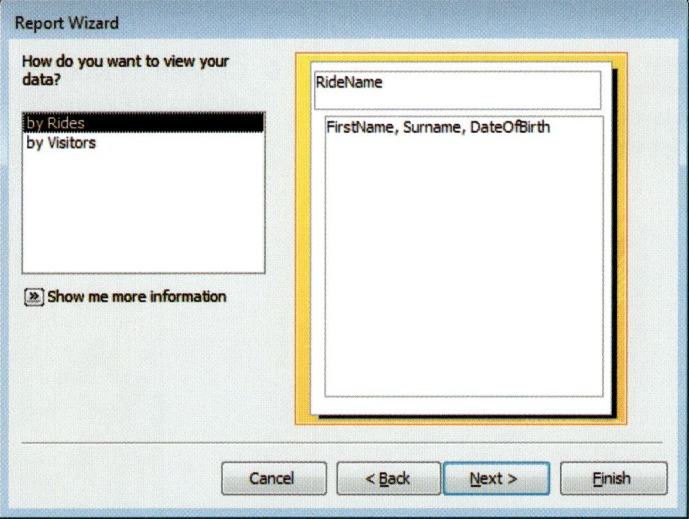

▲ **Figure 20.32** The report will show details by Rides

7. Do not add grouping, as there is not enough data to require it to be grouped. Click Next, as shown in Figure 20.33.

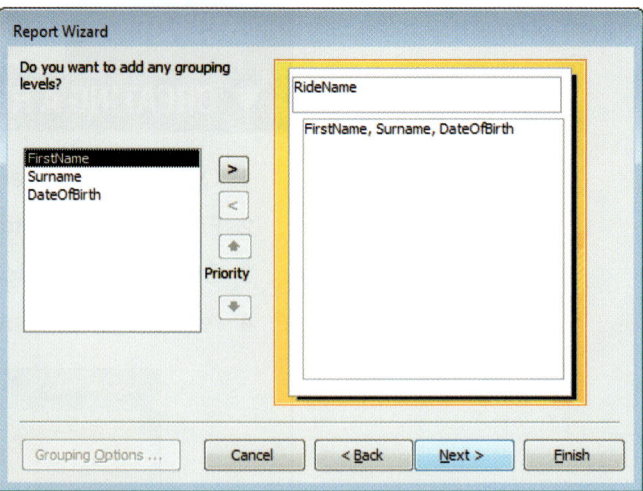

▲ **Figure 20.33** Grouping can help organise the report into headings, but is not necessary in this example

8 Sort the records by Surname, as shown in Figure 20.34.

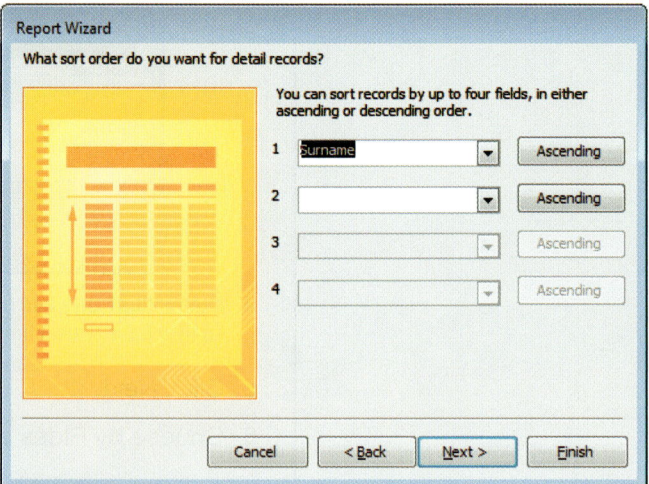

▲ **Figure 20.34** Sorting records

9 Choose a layout option. For this activity, leave it as **Stepped**, as shown in Figure 20.35.

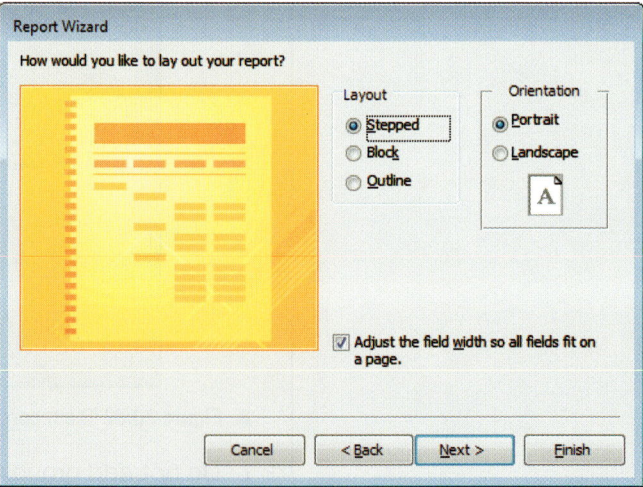

▲ **Figure 20.35** Choosing a layout for your report

HINT

There are only 13 records in this report. Sorting and grouping are more useful with larger data sets.

GENERAL VOCABULARY

stepped a layout format that stages details under each group heading

10. Give the report a meaningful title, such as 'Tickets sold in September'. Do not give it a name like 'Rides', as shown in Figure 20.36, because this does not contain enough detail.

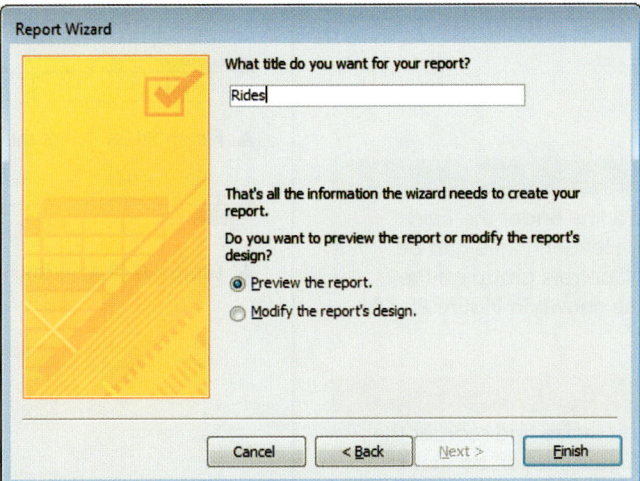

▲ Figure 20.36 'Rides' is not a meaningful title

11. Leave the option set to Preview the report and click Finish to preview the report, as shown in Figure 20.37.

▲ Figure 20.37 Previewing your report allows you to identify any problems, such as the DateOfBirth field not displaying correctly

12. Close Print Preview using the Close Preview button (Figure 20.38).

▲ Figure 20.38 The Close Preview button in Microsoft Access

13. Rename the field names in the Page Header section in order to add spaces between the words, then resize and reorder the field names. You may want to change the formatting of the field names so that they stand out, as shown in Figures 20.39 and 20.40.

▲ **Figure 20.39** Before the field names have been formatted, renamed, resized and reordered

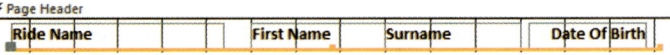

▲ **Figure 20.40** After the field names have been formatted, renamed, resized and reordered

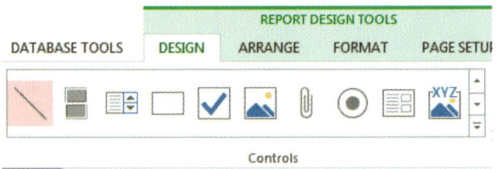

▲ **Figure 20.41** The Controls group on the Design tab

> **HINT**
> You can add a line under the field names in the Header. Lines can be found in the Controls group on the Design tab, as shown in Figure 20.41.

> **KEY POINT**
> Make sure you resize and reorder the fields in the Detail section so that they line up with the field names.

14. Choose Print Preview from the View tab, as shown in Figure 20.42. You will now be able to preview the finished report, as shown in Figure 20.43.

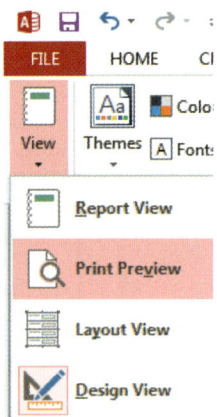

▲ **Figure 20.42** Selecting Print Preview

▲ **Figure 20.43** The finished report, ready to print or email

DATABASE MANAGEMENT

MAIL MERGE DOCUMENTS

Many organisations use databases to produce letters for current and potential customers. A database can be used as a source of data for a mail merge.

For more information about mail merge, see pages 236–237.

SKILLS — EXECUTIVE FUNCTION

ACTIVITY

▼ CREATING A MERGED DOCUMENT

1. Open the file 'MailMergeLetter.docx'.
2. Select the Mailings tab.
3. Choose Use an Existing List from the Select Recipients menu, as shown in Figure 20.44.

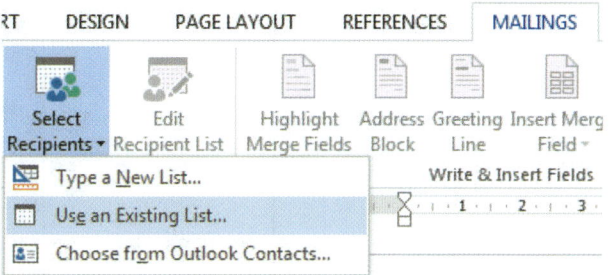

▲ Figure 20.44 Using an existing list to carry out a mail merge

4. Select the database 'MailMerge.accdb' and click Open.
5. Place your cursor after the word 'Dear' and before the comma.
6. From the Insert Merge Field menu, choose first_name and then last_name, ensuring that there is a space between them.
7. Create an address above the 'Dear' text using the same process.
8. Check your result against Figure 20.45.

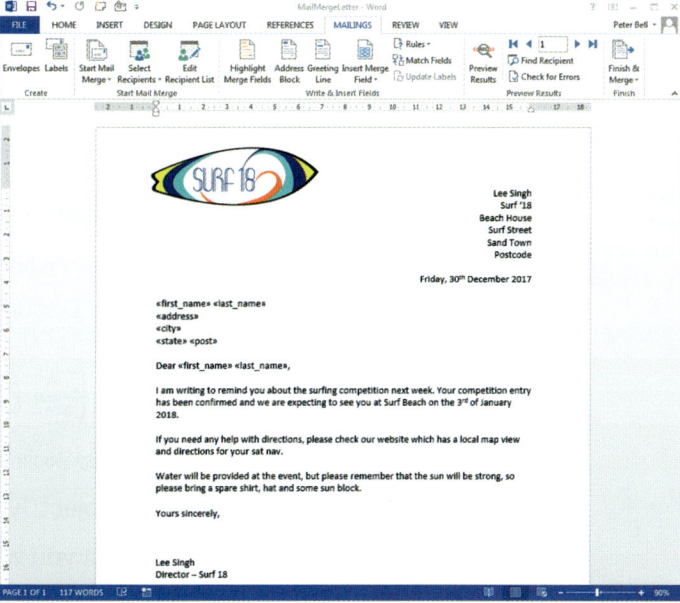

▲ Figure 20.45 The merge is set up

9 Choose Preview Results and then read through the merged records using the arrows shown in Figure 20.46.

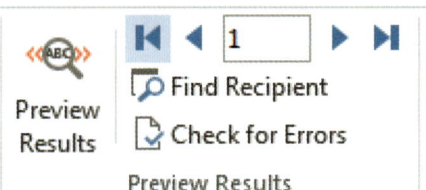

▲ Figure 20.46 Previewing the results of the mail merge using Preview Results

10 When you have checked the results, choose Finish & Merge and select the output you want. If you are using Merge to Printer to print a copy of the merged letter for each record in the database, choose a small range of records to test, as shown in Figure 20.47 on page 330. The database you are using (MailMerge.accdb) has 500 records, so be careful not to print them all.

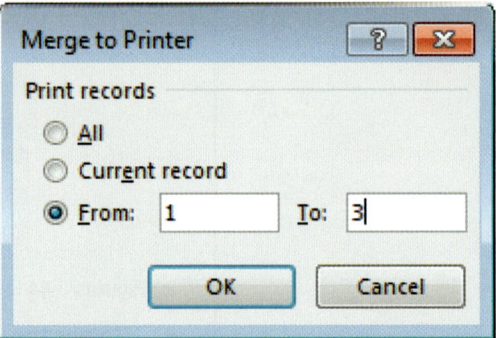

▲ Figure 20.47 Merging to printer

SPECIFIED FIELDS

As well as selecting which fields you want to show in a Report or Mail Merge, you can select which fields you want to show in the Datasheet View of a query. This is done by using the Show checkbox.

DESIGN VIEW

You cannot print from Design View. Instead, you could screenshot your work and paste it into a word processing application. However, you can export the **design characteristics** of a **database object** using the following steps.

- Make sure you have saved all your open objects.
- Select Database Documenter (Figure 20.48) on the Database Tools tab.

🗐 Database Documenter

▲ Figure 20.48 Database Documenter in Microsoft Access

- Select the All Object Types tab.
- Select the object you want to print, as shown in Figure 20.49.

> **SUBJECT VOCABULARY**
>
> **design characteristics** properties of a database object
>
> **database object** an object in a database, such as a table, query or report

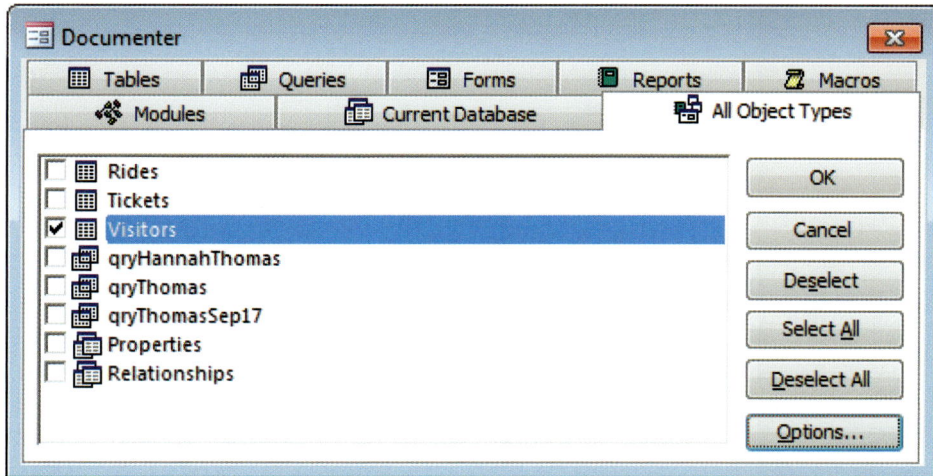

▲ Figure 20.49 Selecting a database object (the Visitors table) in the Database Documenter tool

- In Options, check:
  - the Include for Table area and remove all three ticks from the boxes, as shown in Figure 20.50
  - the Include for Fields area and choose Names, Data Types, Sizes
  - the Include for Indexes area and click Nothing.

- Select OK and, when you are asked if you want to close the table, choose Yes.

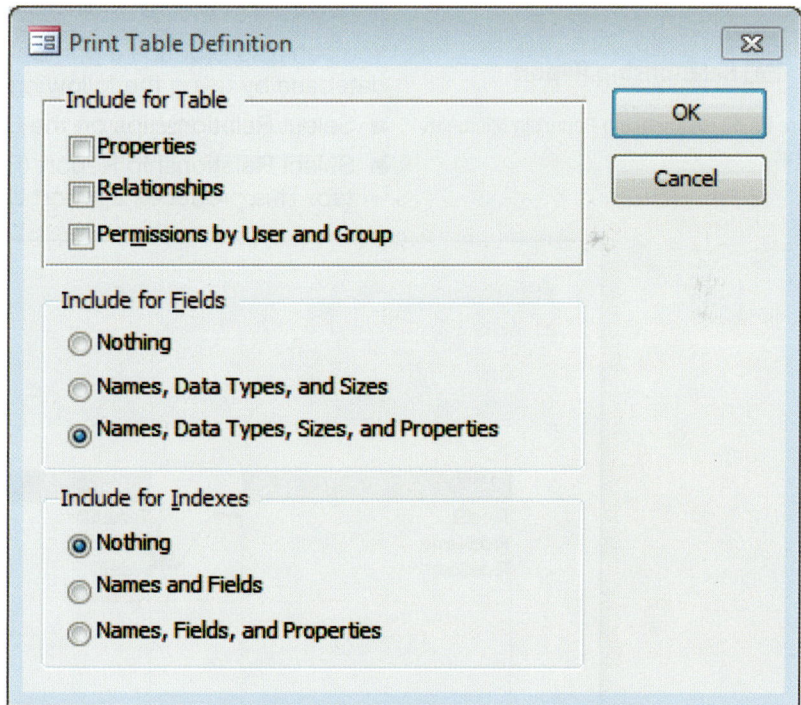

▲ Figure 20.50 Choosing what to include in the printed design documentation

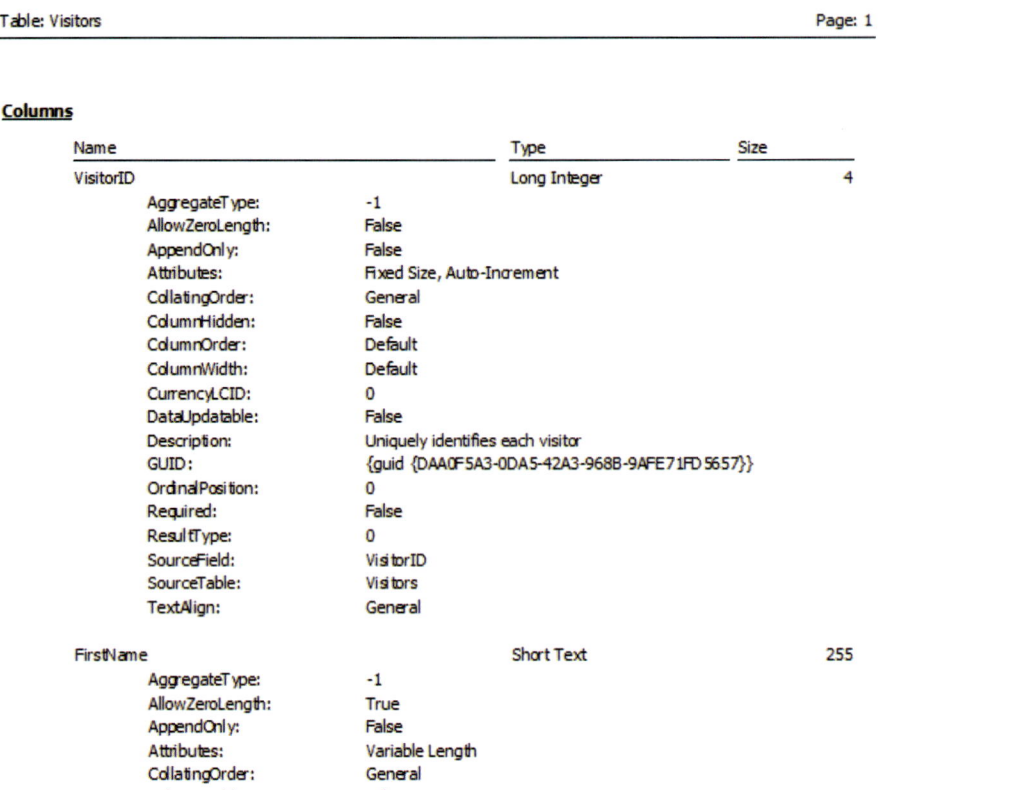

▲ Figure 20.51 The design documentation, ready to be printed

▲ Figure 20.52 Relationship Report in Microsoft Access

You can also produce a printable report that shows the relationships in your database by using the following steps.

- Select Relationships on the Database Tools tab.
- Select Relationship Report (Figure 20.52) in the Tools group on the Design tab. This produces a report like the one in Figure 20.53.

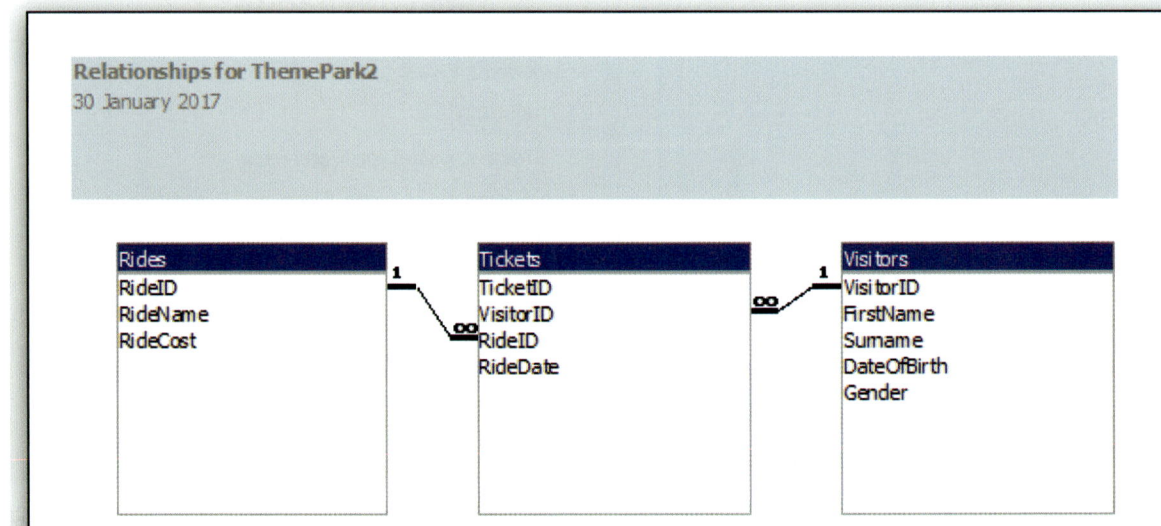

▲ Figure 20.53 A Relationship Report

DATA OR DATASHEET VIEW

Objects in Data or Datasheet View can be printed using Print options in the File menu, as shown in Figure 20.54.

UNIT 6 — DATABASE MANAGEMENT

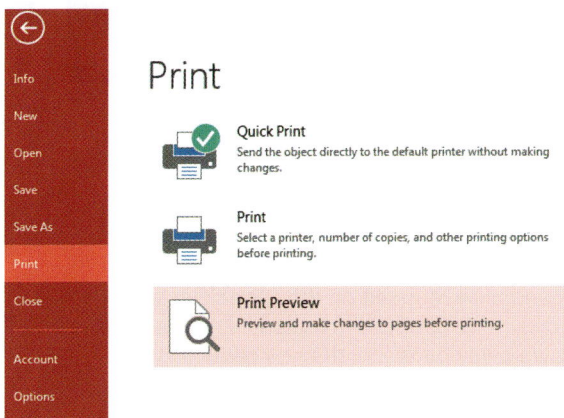

▲ Figure 20.54 The Print options in the File menu in Microsoft Access

HINT

Use Print Preview before printing in order to test that the printed output will be as expected.

CHAPTER QUESTIONS

SKILLS PROBLEM SOLVING

1. Which **one** of these is the most appropriate data type to store data about student grades? (1)
   - A Numeric
   - B Alphanumeric/text
   - C Logical/Boolean
   - D Currency

SKILLS REASONING

2. State the reason why a primary key is used in a database. (1)

SKILLS REASONING

3. State **two** reasons why validation is used in a database. (2)

SKILLS PROBLEM SOLVING

4. List **three** attributes that could be stored about a book entity in a library database. (3)

SKILLS PROBLEM SOLVING

5. Identify **three** validation checks that can be carried out on data. (3)

SKILLS INTERPRETATION

6. Explain why referential integrity is used in databases. (4)

SKILLS PROBLEM SOLVING

7. State the type of validation check that would be used to select all records between specified dates. (1)

SKILLS PROBLEM SOLVING

8. Give the outcome of sorting this data in ascending order: 1,6,4,3,7. (1)

SKILLS PROBLEM SOLVING

9. Give the result of evaluating this relational expression: 14>16. (1)

SKILLS PROBLEM SOLVING

10. A database contains data about boys and girls. Which **one** of these logical operations would return results about only girls? (1)
    - A Boy AND Girl
    - B Boy OR Girl
    - C NOT Boy
    - D NOT Girl

ANSWERS

CHAPTER 1

1. Barcodes save time (1).
   OR
   Barcodes ensure that fewer errors are made when entering product ID numbers (1).
2. These devices are designed to be portable (1).
3. The charge cannot be reduced on the capacitive layer (1) because wool is not a conductive material (1). (The charge is usually drawn away by touch, thereby **reducing** the charge held in the capacitive layer.)
4. Any **three** from: a burglar alarm (1); a web server (1); an engine management system (1); a home heating system (1); many other examples.
5. Laser printers are faster (1) and produce each copy more cheaply (1) than inkjet printers.
6. Any **two** from: architecture (1); product design (1); cartography (1); engineering (1).
7. To reduce the impact (1) on the environment (1) when the finished models are discarded (1).
8. Several answers. For example: An accelerometer (1), used to detect 'tilt' in a game (1), and a light sensor (1), used to alter the brightness of a screen to match the environmental light conditions (1).
9. Several answers. For example: Sensors are used in cars for many reasons. Some examples include detecting whether doors are open, whether seatbelts are secured, whether passengers are in their seats and whether it is dark outside. This type of feedback on the environment can be useful to the driver, so that they know what is around the car. For example, the car could use distance sensors to help drivers to park or avoid collisions. Similarly, cars could use light sensors under the car to help drivers know if they are moving out of a lane on a road and the car's computer could trigger an alarm to alter the driver's course.
   The use of sensors can take some of the need to think away from the driver, allowing them to concentrate on the driving. Sensors can also produce reactions that are quicker than a human's, therefore increasing road safety. However, sensors (and the computers to which they are linked) are not good at making ethical decisions and so, if they sensed a person in the road ahead, they may not be able to decide whether to steer off the road and maybe crash into a wall (potentially injuring the driver) or crash into the person crossing the road, potentially injuring the pedestrian.
   In summary, sensors can be very useful, but humans will always need to take responsibility for their actions and should not become complacent when in charge of a vehicle.
10. Console games use detailed graphics (1), which use a lot of data and therefore data storage (1).
    OR:
    Optical media is required because download sizes would be too big (1) and Blu-ray media has the greatest capacity of all optical formats (1).

CHAPTER 2

1. A piece of software you can use to carry out specific tasks that are not related to the operating system (1).
2. Any **three** from: backup (1); anti-virus (1); defragmentation (1); compression (1); disk management (1).
3. The operating system allows the user to control and manage (1) the computer's hardware (1).
4. So that backup processes can be completed when the system is not in use (1) to avoid file conflicts (1).
5. Compression utilities can free up storage space (1) by reducing the amount of data (1) needed to store a file.
6. By allowing the user to create slides that contain content (1) that support (1) their talk.
7. Several answers. For example: Control software could be used in manufacturing factories (1) to control robots on a production line (1).
8. Several answers. For example: Building companies must adhere to scheduled timelines because multiple resources such as materials and personnel such as electricians need to be coordinated in sequential phases which are dependent upon each other. This ensures that the project hits targets, and forecasts for completion can be provided, with progression monitored so that stakeholders (such as homeowners) can be updated with the progress of the project.
9. Any **three** from: web browser (1); social media (1); SMS (1); email (1); MMS (1); instant messaging (1).
10. Any **two** from: fixing security vulnerabilities or bugs (1); increasing compatibility with newer operating systems (1); improving performance and efficiency (1); introducing new features (1); improving usability (1).

CHAPTER 3

1. Read Only Memory (1).
2. Random Access Memory (1).
3. Increasing the amount of RAM means that more programs can be open at the same time (1) without needing to use virtual memory from storage (1), which has slower access times than RAM (1).
4. Virtual memory is an area of secondary storage (1) used to store data when the computer system does not have enough space in RAM (1).
5. Any three from: volatile (1); instructions can be swapped in and out or temporarily stored (1); used for temporary storage (1); upgradable (1).
6. Flash memory does not have any moving parts (1), so it has low power consumption (1). It also means that it is less susceptible to data loss (1) if the device is knocked or shaken (1).
7. **A** The number of times per second that a processor can carry out instructions (1).

CHAPTER 4

1. **a** Infra-red signals cannot travel as far as Bluetooth signals (1) and the console is sometimes not in range (1).

ANSWERS

OR

Infra-red requires line of sight (1) and the controller is often pointed away from the console when in use (1).

b Loss of connection would give the user a bad experience (1).

2 ▶ Parts of a video file are downloaded to a buffer (1), which is then topped up (1) as the video plays (1).

3 ▶ The user does not have to wait (1) for the full file to be downloaded (1) before it can be played (1).

4 ▶ Several answers. For example: USB (1), Ethernet (1) and HDMI (1).

5 ▶ **B** WAN (1).

6 ▶ People play games with others from all round the world (1) and they want to avoid lag (1) caused by latency (1).

CHAPTER 5

1 ▶ **B** Gateway (1).

2 ▶ Public key encryption does not use the same key (1) to encrypt and decrypt the data (1).

3 ▶ Firewall (1).

4 ▶ IP address (1) and MAC address (1).

5 ▶ IPv4 did not provide enough unique addresses (1) to service the number of devices being connected to the internet (1).

6 ▶ Any **two** from: working from home (1); avoiding geolocation rights management (1); making secure payments (1).

7 ▶ A booster is used if the network signal has a limited range (1).

8 ▶ Data is scrambled (1) using a key (1), meaning that it can only be accessed by other users with the key (1).

9 ▶ Any **three** from: logins/passwords (1); firewalls (1); encryption/VPN (1); file access rights (1).

10 ▶ Any **three** from: access to shared peripherals (1); access to shared storage and data (1); ability to use any device on the network (1); streaming media such as movies, music and games (1); ability to send messages and files to others on the network (1); shared access to the internet (1).

11 ▶ Several answers. Ask your teacher to check your diagram.

CHAPTER 6

1 ▶ **C** Firewall (1).

2 ▶ Characters cannot be read or interpreted (1) by an automated computer program (1).

3 ▶ To gain users' personal information without their permission (1).

4 ▶ Any **three** from: card number (1); expiry date (1); start date (1); name of the cardholder (1); CSC (1).

5 ▶ A differential backup saves a copy of all files that have changed since the last full backup (1). An incremental backup saves a copy of only the files that have changed since the last full **or incremental** backup (1).

6 ▶ Encryption ensures that unauthorised users cannot read data (1) without the key (1).

7 ▶ Any **two** from: passwords (1); PINs (1); biometrics (1).

8 ▶ Domain name spoofing (1) and redirecting traffic (for example, using malware) (1).

9 ▶ It can be slower to backup (1) because the connection to the internet provides less bandwidth than a local data connection (1).

CHAPTER 7

1 ▶ **C** Streaming (1).

2 ▶ Any two from: no need to travel to work (1); no stress caused by traffic or public transport delays and overcrowding (1); saves money (1); reduces impact on the environment (1); employees can spend more time working because they spend less time travelling to work (1); no need to wear uniform or business clothes, reducing employees' costs (1); employees can work at a time that suits them (1); employees can work on tasks for longer periods of time without distractions from colleagues or scheduled meetings (1); employees can work in a comfortable environment (1); employees can organise their work around social or family commitments (1).

3 ▶ Any **two** from: there may be concerns about data security (1); it can be more difficult to manage and support employees who are not in the office (1); employees working at home might not work as hard as employees in an office (1); it can be complicated to organise payments and permissions for employees in different countries (1).

4 ▶ Body language (1) is not always visible online (1) so people do not practise using and reading body language and other social and emotional cues (1).

5 ▶ Bullies can remain anonymous (1), making the bully feel as though they can behave more inappropriately (1).
OR:
Bullies can remain anonymous (1), which removes victims' ability to control the situation (1).

6 ▶ Working together (1).

7 ▶ Any **three** from: economy and infrastructure (1); location (1); politics (1); religion (1); disability (1); social factors such as age, gender, education and income (1).

8 ▶ Any **three** from: entertainment and leisure (1); shopping (1); education (1); banking (1); tax (1); applications for driving licences (1).

9 ▶ It has helped build strong communities (1) using social media (1).
It has increased access to the global society (1) at the expense of their local societies (1).

10 ▶ The gap has been made wider (1) because the internet has increased the amount of information available to the information rich (1).

11 ▶ Several answers. For example: The internet provides more opportunities for us to socialise by allowing us to connect with each other using global communication services such as instant messaging and social networks. We can communicate at any time of the day with friends from around the world and make use of the ability to connect data from different account profiles to create new connections with people we have never met. We use social features in many services, such as when we are watching television, using television as a 'back-channel' line of communication to comment upon, rate and discuss live television programmes and news. This allows us to access more than one point of view about the issues being shown on the news. We also use social features of the internet when shopping and learning in order to get more than one perspective, keep informed of new developments and gain a wider perspective on the world. However, some people's use of the internet means that they are not in touch with the real-world communities in their local geographical area, leading to the disintegration of those communities. Some people become so engrossed in online communication that they lose the skills that they need to communicate with people in the real world. Some people also argue that, despite the wide variety of social groups available to individuals, the ones you tend to join are those which share your views, as that is often how suggestions are made based on users' profiles. This means that individuals who think they are joining in with a wider community are simply reaffirming their own opinions, so they do not actually come to understand and integrate with the wider social communities available to them via the internet. In conclusion, there is a wide variety of social interaction available thanks to the internet, but people need to understand the ways in which they are connected to others to truly understand how to make the most of the opportunities that are available to them.

12 ▶ Keep personal information private (1) by being careful what is shared and by using privacy settings to control access to personal profiles (1); block people, especially strangers (1), who are offensive or whose behaviour is concerning (1); report (1) inappropriate behaviour to relevant authorities (1).

13 ▶ The use of the internet provides another method (1) of unauthorised access (1) to the data held by the organisation (1).

CHAPTER 8

1 ▶ **D** Acceptable use policies (1).

2 ▶ Tags are used to categorise (1) information so that it can be located more easily (1).

3 ▶ Sharing increases the reach of content (1) and encourages members to be more active users of the service (1). This means that they provide the service with more information (1), which the service can then use to sell marketing opportunities to advertisers (1).

4 ▶ Any **three** points from: Different levels of user responsibility can be set (1) so that people can be responsible for quality checking members and their posts (1) to ensure that the policies are being followed (1), block posts or enforce sanctions such as banning members from the community (1).

5 ▶ Any **three** from: biographical details such as name, gender, date of birth, location and language (1); an 'about you' or short description of the user (1); details about the user's work and education (1); travel history (1); family details such as relationship status, family members and pets (1); contact information such as telephone number, email address and website (1); profile and background images, colour schemes and designs (1).

6 ▶ To allow users to share URLs (1).

7 ▶ Any **three** points from: Because the organisation's workers will be located in different countries (1), which would make communicating and collaborating on work more difficult or expensive to organise and time consuming (1) due to differences in time zones and the costs and time associated with travelling (1). They would also benefit from having centralised resources such as virtual meeting spaces, shared documents and shared online calendars (1).

8 ▶ By matching (1) information shared by members (1).

9 ▶ By matching (1) information shared by members (1).

10 ▶ Any **four** from: students can access resources (1); students can interact with teachers (1); students can get notifications of assignments and grades (1); students can chat with classmates and share ideas and research (1); students can get immediate feedback from automatically marked quizzes (1); students can collaborate on assignments with other students and teachers (1).

11 ▶ Rate/like/upvote (1); share/repost (1); comment/quote (1).

12 ▶ Answers should discuss: cost of and need to protect their safety; companies sharing users' personal information; targeted marketing; cost to users' privacy.

CHAPTER 9

1 ▶ **C** Using an RCD (1).

2 ▶ They have reduced the cost of technology (1) so that more people can afford digital devices (1).

3 ▶ Location sharing has an impact upon their privacy (1) because their location could be shared with other people with whom they do not actually want to share their location (1).

4 ▶ Any **three** from: music (1), e-books (1), video (1), apps (1).

5 ▶ Several answers. For example: CCTV (1) can be used to watch people (1); ANPR (1) can trigger alerts for police (1); ID, travel or bank cards (1) can be tracked when scanned at terminals or used in transactions (1); IP or MAC addresses (1) can be identified on networks (1); GPS position (1) can be broadcast to apps (1).

6 ▶ To make them the only people who can legally use and distribute their work (1) and to prevent people from making a profit by using their work (1).

7 ▶ Several answers. For example: It can help parents keep their children safe (1); It can help friends to find each other (1).

8 ▶ Several answers. For example: It can help parents see what their children are saying online to keep them safe (1); It can help governments protect individuals by identifying potential criminals (1).

9 ▶ It reduces their privacy (1).

10 ▶ Any **three** from: ask people for consent (1); use data appropriately (1); use data only for the specified purpose (1); use data fairly and lawfully (1); use data for limited,

ANSWERS

specifically stated purposes (1); use data in a way that is adequate, relevant and not excessive (1); ensure that data is accurate (1); keep data for no longer than is absolutely necessary (1); handle data according to people's data protection rights (1); keep data safe and secure (1); if in the EU, not transferring data outside the European Economic Area without adequate protection (1).

11 ▶ Several answers. Should include up to four linked points from: online storage and apps are based in large data centres (1) which use lots of energy (1) to cool the servers (1) and power the servers (1). This energy could be created by using non-renewable energy (1), in order to avoid depleting the planet's natural resources and contributing to climate change (1).

12 ▶ Several answers. For example: Recycle their devices (1) so they do not leak toxins (1) which can cause health risks to plants, wildlife and people (1).

CHAPTER 10

1 ▶ **D** "" (1).

2 ▶ Any **two** from: size (1), colour (1), type (1), time and date (1), usage rights (1).

3 ▶ It might not represent the issue in full (1).

4 ▶ A search engine compares (1) words or phrases entered by a user (1) against a database of pages (1) and returns the URLs or descriptions of those that match (1).

5 ▶ You might infringe others' rights (1), leading to ethical and legal issues (1).

6 ▶ It shows that the student understands the meaning of the information (1).

7 ▶ AND (+) (1), NOT (-) (1), phrase matching ("") (1).

8 ▶ **Table 10.3** Identifying primary and secondary sources

Source	Primary or secondary?
A podcast that you have created	Primary (1)
A video of a discussion that you have with an expert	Primary (1)
Your own copy of a film	Secondary (1)
Notes that you take while visiting a museum	Primary (1)
A book that you borrow from someone	Secondary (1)
An image that you download from the internet	Secondary (1)
Your own recording of a radio broadcast	Secondary (1)

CHAPTER 11

1 ▶ **A** Paying in cheques (1).

2 ▶ Any **two** from: VLEs (1), online support (1), remote access to journals and books (1).

3 ▶ Several answers. For example: basket (1), product catalogue (1), checkout (1).

4 ▶ EITHER: It helps sellers know which buyers they can trust (1) to pay for items (1).
OR: It stops sellers having to relist (1) unpaid-for bids because they can restrict access to bidders with good ratings who are more likely to complete the purchase (1).

5 ▶ It uses encryption (1) which stops data, such as people's financial information, being read (1) by unauthorised users (1).

6 ▶ There is no need to check in at a check-in desk at the airport (1), which saves passengers time (1).

7 ▶ EITHER: Their use affects users' privacy (1).
OR: Users' experience is based on decisions made by computer code rather than on choices that they make (1).

8 ▶ Any **three** from: time and date of the transaction (1); IP addresses (1); referring website (1); the products and services previously viewed or bought (1); categories of products and services previously viewed or bought (1); items added to online shopping basket (1); buttons pressed (1); data entered into web forms, such as name and address (1); any other sensible response.

9 ▶ Session cookies are only stored while the browser has the site open or until the browser closes the site. Persistent cookies are stored after the browser closes the site.

10 ▶ The use of notifications or alerts (1).

11 ▶ Several answers. Relevant points include: Organisations use cookies to track the transactions that individuals carry out online, such as the websites that they visit. This browsing history can then be used by organisations to target their marketing and create a personalised experience for users. Although some people find this useful, other people do not like the fact that their online activity is tracked and monitored; as they believe this to be intrusive and to have a negative effect on their privacy. They do not like the ways in which these systems are used to decide the content people are shown and say that they would prefer to decide this themselves as it may limit or narrow their experience.

CHAPTER 12

1 ▶ **C** Server (1).

2 ▶ Any **three** from: automatic backup (1); greater scalability (1); enables sharing data (1); cheaper than local storage or even free (1); makes collaboration possible (1); reduces use of local storage making more space for locally installed software (1).

3 ▶ Any **three** from: shopping or auction sites (1); booking systems (1); banking services (1); education services such as VLEs and MOOCs (1); gaming (1); news and information (1); entertainment services such as on-demand television (1).

4 ▶ Online storage and/or applications that are hosted on online servers (1).

CHAPTER 13

1 ▶ **A** Image (1).

2 ▶ If there is not enough white space (1), the information could appear cramped (1).

3 ▶ Several answers. For example: number data (1) is turned into information through the creation of graphs or charts (1).

4 ▶ Spelling error because should be spelled 'supposed' (1); grammar error because the sentence should end with a question mark (?) (1); contextual error because 'two' should be given as 'to' (1).

5 ▶ A house style ensures that documents are consistent (1), which helps to create a brand or corporate identity (1).

6 ▶ A typeface that adds a short line, known as a serif, to the ends of some letters (1).

7 ▶ A low-resolution screen may not be able to display the serif details and make the text difficult to read (1).

8 ▶ Green (1).

9 ▶ **One** from: colour-blindness (1), partial-sightedness (1).

10 ▶ Spell checkers do not always pick up all errors (1).

CHAPTER 14

1 ▶ **C** School_Logo_v1.02 (1).

2 ▶ Any **three** marks from: To prevent data loss (1) if the computer crashes or loses power (1), because until data is saved in secondary storage (1) it is stored in RAM (1), which is volatile (1).

3 ▶ It enables you to go back to previous versions (1).

4 ▶ Several answers. For example: .pdf (1), .ppsx (1), .jpeg (1).

5 ▶ It allows the user to set the version (1), date (1) and build number for that date (1).

6 ▶ Add a password (1).

7 ▶ Exporting files saves them in a format that cannot be edited (1).

CHAPTER 15

1 ▶ **D** Newsletter (1).

2 ▶ If words are used out of context (1) but spelled correctly (1), they will not be highlighted by the spell checker.

3 ▶ Portrait (1) and landscape (1).

4 ▶ Any **three** from: Page title (1); Author's name (1); Page numbers (1); Date/time document created/modified (1); File name/location (1). Award one mark for 'document/file information' if no other mark awarded.

5 ▶ A data source is selected (1) and fields from it are placed into the document (1), which is then populated (1) from selected records (1).

6 ▶ Several answers. For example: Dear [Title Surname] (1).

7 ▶ Several answers. For example: Yours sincerely (1); Kind regards (1).

8 ▶ Any two from: Spreadsheet (1); Delimited file such as a .csv file (1); A table in a (word-processed) document (1); A contact list such as a mail application contact list (1).

CHAPTER 16

1 ▶ **B** Aspect ratio (1).

2 ▶ Because they are made up of co-ordinates and lines (1), which are recalculated (1) when the image is redrawn (1).

3 ▶ Layers allow elements to be placed (1) on top of or beneath each other on the z axis (1).

4 ▶ Pixels (1).

5 ▶ Vector graphics often look stylised or unnatural (1).

6 ▶ Any **two** from: Erase tool (1); Cropping (1); Recolouring or airbrushing (1).

CHAPTER 17

1 ▶ **D** High contrast between background and text (1).

2 ▶ The slide master layout is applied to all slides in the presentation (1).

3 ▶ **One** from: It may distract the audience (1); The audience might not listen to the speaker (1).

4 ▶ Bold (1), underline (1) and italic (1).

5 ▶ To emphasise the changes (1) between slides (1).

6 ▶ **One** from: Use images that represent the text (1); Summarise points into bullet points (1).

7 ▶ **One** from: To provide navigation (1) because some users who will not have access to keyboard and mouse (1); To provide navigation (1) because presentations are often published in kiosk mode for use with a touchscreen interface (1).

8 ▶ Any **two** from: URLs (1); Slides (1); Local files (1); Email addresses (1).

9 ▶ Handouts (1), full page slides (1) and notes pages (1).

10 ▶ Any **two** of: It can help a speaker to time their presentation (1) by displaying timings (1); Speakers can prepare for the next slide (1), which is displayed as a thumbnail (1); Notes for the slide are displayed (1), allowing the speaker to use them to introduce animations at the correct point (1).

CHAPTER 18

1 ▶ **A** <a> (1).

2 ▶ Image files are referenced, not embedded (1), so the web browser (1) will not be able to find them if their location is altered (1). This will result in a broken link and will make the browser display a placeholder image (1).

3 ▶ To provide the layout into which content can be added (1).

4 ▶ To draw attention to important information (1).

5 ▶ **A** index.html (1).

6 ▶ Any **three** from: Animation (1); Image (1); Text (1); Buttons (1); Video (1).

CHAPTER 19

1 ▶ **D** G1:J1 (1).

2 ▶ EITHER: As a way of documenting the spreadsheet (1) with meaningful names (1) that others/you can understand (1)
OR: You don't have to check the cell range every time you refer to it (1), saving time when referencing ranges in formulae or functions (1).

3 ▶ Unlike relative references, absolute references do not change (1) when copied to other cells (1), meaning that a

ANSWERS

cell reference can be fixed (1) and reducing the likelihood of errors and the work required to avoid errors (1).

4 ▶ **A** SUM (1).

5 ▶ Any **three** from: Pie chart (1); Bar chart (1); Column chart (1); Line chart (1); Scattergram (1).

6 ▶ It finds a given value (1) in the first column of a given array (1) and returns the corresponding value (1) from a given column (1).

7 ▶ Scattergram (1).

8 ▶ Pie chart (1).

9 ▶ Bar or column chart (1).

10 ▶ A trend line shows the general direction of data values or line of best fit (1), which can be extended beyond the range of the latest date (1).

11 ▶ The formulae will automatically update when values in referenced cells are changed (1).

12 ▶ **B** 9 = (5+4) (1).

CHAPTER 20

1 ▶ **B** Alphanumeric/text (1).

2 ▶ To ensure that each record is uniquely identifiable (1).

3 ▶ Any **two** from: To ensure that the data entered is acceptable (1); To reduce data entry errors (1); To enforce referential integrity (1).

4 ▶ Any **three** from: Title (1); ISBN (1); Number of pages (1); Author (1); Publisher (1); Published Date (1); Format (1).

5 ▶ Any **three** from: Referential integrity (1); Presence (1); Type (1); Length (1); Range (1).

6 ▶ The database will only allow data to be entered (1) from a foreign table (1) into a linked table (1) if the related record exists (1).

7 ▶ Range check (1).

8 ▶ 1,3,4,6,7 (1).

9 ▶ False (1).

10 ▶ **C** NOT Boy (1).

GLOSSARY

absolute reference in a spreadsheet, used to fix a cell reference in a formula so that does not change when it is copied from one cell to another

active cell the selected cell in a worksheet

ad server a web server that stores, delivers and often tracks banner advertisements

adware software that displays unwanted adverts

alphanumeric containing both letters and numbers

alt text alternative text that is displayed if an image cannot be loaded

analogue representing information with continuously variable electrical signals that digital signals approximate

analytics information that results from the analysis of data

application a program that allows a user to perform a task; applications are often called apps

application loading time how long it takes an application to load

application suite a collection of application software that share the same look and user interface; often, they can share data between each other and share some functionality

array a series of items

artificial intelligence (AI) the ability of a computer program to make decisions that would otherwise be made by humans

aspect ratio the ratio of an image's width and height

attribute something that provides additional information about an HTML element; in a database, a characteristic, feature, or quality of an entity

authenticate confirm that the user is who they say they are

authentication the process of confirming that a user is permitted to access certain files, hardware and software

autofill the automatic suggestion of a completed word or phrase that is provided as the user types

avatar a figure that represents a person in a computer game or other virtual environment

back up to make a copy of information stored on a computer in case the original is lost or damaged

backwards compatibility the ability to be used with older technology without having to be specially adapted

balance alert a service that automatically informs a customer, by text message or email, when the balance of their account reaches a specified amount

bandwidth the number of bits that can be carried by a connection in one second

banner advertisement an image, animation or video that displays an advertisement for a product or service in a section of a web page

barcode a pattern of lines and gaps that can be read by a device

big data the analysis of huge quantities of data collected from many sources (such as smartphones, online applications, social media and payment systems) in order to find patterns of behaviour and interactions

bit (**b**inary dig**it**) a single unit of information with a value of either 0 or 1; eight bits equal one byte

bitmap a computer image that is stored or printed as an arrangement of bits

blacklist a list of unacceptable URLs

blog (short for web log) a website or web page that is updated regularly, often written like a diary or a series of articles

blogger someone who creates or maintains a blog

Bluetooth wireless connectivity that allows devices to connect over short distances

boot start up

borders lines that surround the cells in a table

bot a computer program that can interact with systems or users

browsing history the URLs that an individual user has visited, which are stored in a file

buffer an area of memory used to temporarily store data, especially when streaming video

bugs errors in the program's source code

build date the date on which a file was created

build number the number within a series of versions from the build date

capacity the amount of data that can be stored on media

GLOSSARY

CAPTCHA a computer program or system that can identify whether a user is a human or a computer

cell padding the space *inside* cells in a table that determines how close to the edge of the cell the content will be placed

cell reference the name of a cell in a spreadsheet, created by combining a cell's column letter and its row number

cell spacing the space *between* cells

characters the letters and symbols used to write text

chat room a place on the internet where users can write messages to other people and receive messages back from them immediately

cipher a code

client a computer connected to a server

clip art images, photographs or pictures that you can copy and use in your own computer documents

clock cycles per second used to measure processor speed; the number of times per second the processor can carry out one or more instructions

closed circuit television (CCTV) a system of cameras placed in public buildings or in the street that are used to help prevent crime

cloud a term used to describe the internet when it is used to provide software or space for storing information, rather than relying on local storage

cloud storage storage provided by servers that are connected to the internet

colour value 6 hexadecimal characters which represent the amount of red, green and blue in the colour

compatibility ability of one device, system or application to work with other devices, systems and applications

connections people or accounts to whom a user is connected

connectivity a device's ability to connect to networks and other devices

contact list a virtual address book that allows users to access quickly the contact details of friends and colleagues

contactless users can use a contactless debit card or credit card to pay for things by waving it over a machine, without using a PIN number

convergence when the designs of devices change so that they become similar to one another

cookies information that a website leaves on a user's computer so that the website will recognise that user when they use it again

copper cable a cable that carries data as electrical signals, which are conducted through copper wires

cropping using a photo editor to remove the edges of an image

crowd-mapped data provided by many individuals, forming a 'crowd', which is then superimposed on a map using geolocation information from users' data submissions

cursor a movable point on a screen that identifies the point that the user's input will affect

cyberbullying using the internet to send text, images or multimedia in order to upset or embarrass someone

data access speed how quickly data can be read from or written to media

data values that represent information

database object an object in a database, such as a table, query or report

decompress extract data from a compressed file so that it can be read

deselect remove something from a list of choices on a computer

design characteristics properties of a database object

dialogue box a box that appears on your computer screen when the program needs to ask the user a question before it can continue to do something; the user clicks on one part of the box to give their answer

diaphragm a thin round object, especially in a telephone or loudspeaker, that is moved by sound or that moves when it produces sound

digital assets content used in a digital product such as digital images

digital divide the gap between people who have access to digital devices and the internet and people who do not

digital footprint all the data that a user creates online, which is recorded and stored

digital humanitarian movement a group of people working together using ICT to promote human welfare

digital zoom enlarging part of an image to produce the effect of zooming in

discharge remove the electrical charge from something

domain the name used to identify a web server

domain name server a computer connected to the internet that translates domain names, such as pearson.com, into IP addresses

dragging moving with the mouse

Dynamic Host Configuration Protocol (DHCP) server a networked computer that automatically assigns an IP address to other computers when they join the network

dynaset a dynamic set of data used to store the results of a query

eavesdropper an unauthorised person or piece of software that intercepts data from a private communication

element an individual component of a web page (for example, '<a> … </a>' is a hyperlink element)

embedded computing computing hardware that is fixed into position and carries out a specialist task

encrypt protect information by putting it into a special code that only some people can read

entity in a database, something that exists as a single and complete unit

entrance effect an animation effect that occurs when an object is brought onto a slide during a presentation

Ethernet a network connectivity standard that provides a way for computers to communicate

e-ticket an electronic version of a paper ticket

executable file a computer file that can be run as a program

exit effect an animation effect that occurs when an object leaves a slide during a presentation

experience points credits earned by a user for completing one part of a game

fibre optic cable a cable that sends data using light signals

file a collection of data that represents a document, image, database or similar

file extension the letters at the end of the name of a computer file, which show what type of file it is, such as .docx

file transfer protocol (FTP) a method of exchanging data and files across a network

filter a computer program that only allows certain types of information to pass through it

firewall a system (hardware or software) that protects a computer network from being used or looked at by people who do not have permission to do so

firmware a type of software that controls a hardware device

flash memory a form of storage that stores data as electrical charge held in tiny electrical cells

font the size and style of text

footer the area at the bottom of a page or slide that contains content to be repeated on every page or slide

foreign key in a database, a primary key from one table that is used in another table

formula (plural **formulae**) a mathematical operation or calculation

forum a web page, usually dedicated to a particular topic, where users can post comments and information and reply to other users' comments

free software software that can be modified or distributed by a user

freeware proprietary software provided free of charge to users

frequency the waveband at which a radio signal is transmitted

function in mathematics, an expression that represents a complex calculation or process

games console an electronic device that is used for playing computerised video games on a screen

Gbit/s the amount of data that can be transferred per second, measured in Gigabits (1 Gb = 1 000 000 000 bits)

geoblocking limiting access to internet content based on the user's geographical location (also known as geolocation rights management)

geolocation rights management the use of a user's location to block access to services online; for example, a television channel might only allow users in their own country to watch their shows online

geotag (verb) to add location data to a piece of content

GPS the Global Positioning System that uses radio signals from satellites to show your exact position on the Earth on a special piece of equipment

gradebook a virtual method of recording students' scores on assignments and tests

graphics card a device built into or added into a computer to allow it to display visual graphics

greyscale using a range of shades of grey

hacking accessing a system using malicious methods

HDMI (High-Definition Multimedia Interface) used to transmit video and audio data

header the area at the top of a page or slide that contains content to be repeated on every page or slide

GLOSSARY

hexadecimal a base-16 number system that uses the numbers 0–9 and the letters A–F

home page the introductory or main page of a website

hotspot a place in a public building where there is a computer system with an access point, which allows people in the building with a wireless computer or smartphone to connect to a network such as the internet

house style an organisation's preferred style of writing and layout of content

hover over use the mouse to position the cursor on an object on a computer screen without clicking on the object

hyperlink a link that can be clicked in order to go to another location (often a webpage on the internet)

Hypertext Markup Language (HTML) a computing language read by web browser software

Hypertext Transfer Protocol (HTTP) a set of standards that control how computer documents that are written in HTML connect to each other

Hypertext Transfer Protocol Secure (HTTPS) a secure form of HTTP

identifier a group of letters, numbers, or symbols that a computer has been programmed to recognise and uses to process information

indent marker a point at which text can be moved in from a margin, used to produce standardised spacing between text

information data that has been processed to be given context and meaning

information poor people with limited access to information provided by communication technologies

information rich people with good access to information provided by communication technologies

infra-red a type of electromagnetic radiation with a longer frequency than that of visible light

interactivity the ability of a computer to respond to input

Internet Service Provider (ISP) a company that provides customers with access to the internet

internet traffic data transferred between computers connected to the internet

intranet a computer network used for exchanging or seeing information within a company

in-video advertising advertisements that appear within online videos

IP address a unique address that networked devices use to send data to each other

keywords the words or search terms that a user types into a search engine in order to look for matching information

latency the amount of time it takes to send data between devices

layers individual sections of the image; each layer is positioned on a separate plane of the z axis and can contain one or more elements

layout the way in which text and/or images appear on a page

legitimate website a website that is operated legally

lock to make a device inactive, so that it requires a password or PIN to reactivate it

log a record of events

login user or account information, such as a user name or account name

macro a function that runs a set of instructions to perform a task

mainframe computer a large, powerful computer that can do a lot of complicated jobs quickly and can be used by a lot of people at the same time.

malware software that is created with the intention to do harm

mapped linked

markup the tags surrounding elements of text that indicate the purpose of the text and instruct the browser how to handle (display) them

masked hidden

Massive Open Online Course (MOOC) a course that is free of charge and available to large numbers of people over the internet

Massively Multiplayer Online Role-Playing Game (MMORPG) an online video game that allows large numbers of people to play together

Mbit/s the amount of data that can be transferred per second, measured in Megabits (1 Mb = 1 million bits)

media items such as memory cards and CD-ROMs that make information available to people and devices

media player an electronic device that can store and play digital music and videos and show digital photographs

member someone who is part of an online community

meme a photo, a piece of video, a joke or similar content that spreads quickly on the internet

Merge and Centre a spreadsheet tool that combines selected cells and centre-aligns the text in the new combined cell

microprocessor the device that controls what a computer does; it takes data as input, does something with it and provides output

minijack a plug and socket widely used for analogue audio signals in portable devices

moderate decide whether content is appropriate; moderators decide whether posts should be removed or posted at all

monochrome using a range of shades of one colour

multifunctional device a device that can perform a range of different functions

multimedia a combination of more than one medium, such as audio and video together

multiplayer games games that are played by more than one person, usually online

mute silence an audio track

navigate move around a piece of application software or a system, such as from one slide to the next

netbook a computer that does not have lots of storage or fast processors

network administrator a person who manages an organisation's network

normalisation increasing the average volume of a piece of audio to a defined maximum level

notification an alert that tells a user about a new interaction or new content within a social networking community

online community a group of people with a shared common interest who communicate online

open-source software software for which the source code is made available to users

operator a symbol that represents a mathematical action

optical zoom adjusting a lens in order to zoom in on an object

packet a unit of data packaged to travel across a network

page margin in a word processing application, where the white area of the ruler ends and the grey part begins

pair connect two devices (usually only with each other)

pathway the sequence of or route through a series of slides

payment processor a service that authorises financial transactions

payment server a computer that authorises financial transactions

peripheral device equipment that is connected to a computer and used with it

permissions authorisation settings that provide the ability for a user or users to access files, folders or drives

phishing the criminal activity of sending emails or having a website that is intended to trick someone into giving away personal information such as their bank account number or their computer password; this information is then used to get money or goods

physical computing interactive systems that can sense and respond to the world around them

pixel a small dot that helps to make up an image

pixelated an effect that creates an unclear image consisting of large individual pixels that are visible to the human eye

plain text text that is not specially formatted

platters circular plates

pointer an on-screen indicator used to select displayed objects

port a socket into which cables and devices can be plugged

post (noun) a message sent to an internet discussion group so that all members of the group can read it

post (verb) to put a message or computer document on the internet so that other people can see it

primary key field in a database, the field that holds the primary key, which is a unique attribute stored for each entity

print spooling the process of keeping pages queued so they are ready to be printed by a printer

privacy settings a method that allows users to control who can see information from their online profiles

processor cycle the process of fetching a program instruction from memory, decoding the actions required by the instruction and then executing those actions

processor one or more Central Processing Units (CPUs) that carry out software instructions

profile (noun) a collection of information about a user

profile (verb) to compile personal information about an individual

GLOSSARY

program a set of instructions that are carried out by the processor

proprietary software software that is marketed and distributed by its owner under a brand name

protocols rules that allow the exchange and transmission of data between devices

purpose what something (such as a digital product) is required to do

quarantine isolate a suspected virus in a protected area of storage where it cannot harm other files

query a request for data results

RAM Random Access Memory, which is the memory in a computer system that is used for running software

range a group of adjacent cells in a worksheet

reader a piece of electronic equipment that can read information that is stored or recorded somewhere, for example, on a card

read/write head the part of a disk drive that passes (or floats) across the platters on a very thin layer of gas above the platters

real time processing data within milliseconds of it being input and making the output available almost immediately

referential integrity the state of a database when any foreign key field in a table refers to a primary key in a related table

referring website the website previously visited, which linked the user to the website that they are currently visiting

required attribute an attribute that must be present for the element to work as intended

resize point a point at which an image can be dragged to be resized

resolution the number of pixels used by a screen to display an image

rotate point the pivot point around which an image can be rotated

seek time the time it takes for a read/write head to locate the area on the disk where the data to be read is stored

sensor an input peripheral that inputs data about the physical environment

service agreement contract

set-top box (STB) a device that sends video and audio received from a broadcaster to a television

shortcut a combination of key presses used to access common software commands quickly

single operator formula a formula that uses only one operator

single sign on (SSO) a system that allows users to log in once to access a number of related websites and systems

slide a single page of a presentation

slide master (or master slide) in a slide presentation, a template slide that specifies the layout and appearance of content slides

smart home a home equipped with devices that can connect to the internet and be controlled remotely by a computer or smartphone app

smart the ability of a device to use data from sensors to perform a programmed action independently; smart devices are often also able to connect to the internet

smartwatch a watch that provides data connectivity and often uses sensors to provide feedback to the device about its environment

snake case using underscores (underlines) to separate words in a filename

social bookmarking using tags to categorise web documents and URLs so that other people can find content by using the tags in a search

social network applications software that allows social interaction and the creation of links between users based on shared characteristics and interests

software licence a legal arrangement that gives a user the right to install and use software

solo only play one particular audio track

sort in a spreadsheet, arrange data in a particular order

sound card a device built into or added into a computer to allow it to playback and record audio

source code a collection of instructions that forms a piece of software

sprites on-screen graphics in a computer game, used to represent characters, vehicles and objects

spyware software that monitors and records data and user input

status update a message or post that a user adds to their own social media page to inform others of something that they consider important enough to share

stereo sound sound that comes from two sides (left and right)

stream play a file on your computer while it is being downloaded from the internet, rather than saving it as a file and then playing it

stylus a pen-shaped device

surround sound sound that comes from four or more sides, used so that sounds from a film or television programme come from all around the viewer as they would in real life

syntax the rules that describe how words and phrases are used in a language

tag a label that you can add to a post in order to categorise it

targeted marketing advertising that is matched to internet users based on their attributes, such as their age group or their gender, or their internet browsing history

telecommunications infrastructure the networks of hardware facilities, owned by private and public organisations, that are used to transfer data

tempo the speed at which a track is played

tethering connecting a host device that uses a mobile broadband connection with other devices so that they can use the host's broadband connection

third-party developer a software developer who is not the developer of the original application

third-party integration including features from an online service that do not belong to the original website and are not related to the user of the website

thread a series of messages concerning the same subject, written by members of an internet discussion group

toner a powder used by some printer types

toolbar a row of buttons or options at the top of a window that allow you to perform common actions within an application

track collect and analyse data

transaction the exchange of data

transactional data data that is sent between digital devices

transitions in a slide presentation, the effects that occur when a user moves from one slide to the next

transparency areas of an image that do not have a colour value, including white, are made see-through; if transparency is unavailable due to the file format, those areas are displayed as white

ungroup break apart the grouped components of an image

update (noun) a change or addition to a computer file so that it has the most recent information; (verb) to make a change or addition to a computer file so that it has the most recent information

upgrade to make a computer better and able to do more things

URL (uniform resource locator) a website address

usability the ease with which a device or application can be used

usage rights the way in which a piece of information is permitted to be used

USB (Universal Serial Bus) a standard for wired connectivity that can also supply electric power

user interface the system that allows a user to interact with a device

user the person who uses a computer system

user-generated created by the individuals who use the service

utility software (also known as utilities) system software that carries out configuration and maintenance tasks

validation the process of checking if something is acceptable when compared to given criteria

vector graphic a graphical image made up of points and lines

viral marketing a type of advertising used by internet companies in which computer users pass on advertising messages or images through email, sometimes without realising that they are doing so

viral something that is circulated widely by being shared through networks to large numbers of internet users

virtual keyboard a keyboard displayed on and used via a touchscreen

virtual learning environments (VLEs) websites that contain teaching and learning tools

virtual memory storage used by the processor once the space in RAM has run out

virus definitions sequences of code that are found in computer viruses

virus malware that uses networks to spread to connected devices

vlog (short for video log) a video blog

GLOSSARY

Voice over Internet Protocol (VoIP) the protocol that allows people to make telephone calls using the internet

voice recognition a system in which a computer obeys instructions spoken by a human voice

voucher code a code representing a specified amount of money that can be used on a shopping website to purchase goods or services

web server a computer that stores web pages and sends them to other devices that request them (often using web browser software)

webform a data entry form on a web page

white space the part of a page or digital product that is left blank

whitelist a list of acceptable URLs

Wi-Fi a way of connecting computers or other electronic machines to a network or the internet by using radio signals rather than wires

wiki a website or database that is developed by a number of collaborating users, all of whom can add and edit content

wipe to delete data from storage

WYSIWYG ('What You See Is What You Get') when something is presented on screen exactly as it will look when the finished product is output or published

z axis the dimension that provides an image's depth and allows elements to appear 'in front of' or 'behind' other elements

INDEX

A
absolute cell referencing 286–7
abuse, reporting of 117–18
accessibility 7–8, 26, 125–30, 179, 193
action buttons 254–6
active cells 277
actuators 37, 52
ad servers 174–5
adware 103
alignment 215–18, 220, 271
all-in-one computers 6
alphanumeric data 307, 308
alt text 269, 273
Alto 2 phone 7–8
analogous colours 191, 192
analogue radio/ television 73
analytics 138
AND logical operator 321
animation 183, 184, 256–7, 269–70
anonymity 144
anti-adware 103
anti-malware 102–3
anti-spyware 103
anti-virus software 102–3
application servers 86
applications (apps) 8, 11, 14, 46–7, 53–6, 93, 144
artificial intelligence 157
ascending order data 294, 317
aspect ratio 244
attributes 272–3, 308, 311
auction sites 171
authentication 46, 90, 107
authentication servers 86
autofill 162
automated checking tools 193–4
automatic number plate recognition cameras 151
avatars 12

B
back up files (backups) 19, 42, 57, 89, 93, 104–5
backspace function 210
backwards compatability 38, 274
balance alerts 170
bandwidth 66, 68, 75, 176–7
bank cards 106–7
banking 170, 172
banner advertisements 174–5, 266
bar charts 299
barcode scanners 24–5
big data 123, 173
biometric scanners 21, 27–9, 100
bitmap images 239–40

bits 40
blacklists 88
blogs 142
Blu-ray disks/players 11, 39
bluetooth 5
bold font 274
booking systems 169–70, 172
Boolean data 307, 308
boosters 86
boot (system) 61
borders 222, 281–2
botnets 97
bots 100–1
branding 189
broadband 76, 77
broadcast communication see radio; television
browsing history 162–3
buffers 67
bugs 57
build date 205
build number 205
bullet points 212–14

C
cables 68, 77, 83–4
Caesar cipher 90–1
camcorders 9–10, 69
cameras 9–10
capacitive touch screens 26–7
capacity 40–1
caps lock function 209
CAPTCHA tests 100–2
captions 245
card readers 29
Cat5e/Cat6e cables 83
CCTV 151
CDs 39
cell borders 222, 281–2
cell formats 278–9
cell merging 221, 263, 279–80
cell splitting 221, 279–80
cell padding 263
cell ranges 287–8
cell references 276, 277, 280, 285–7, 289
cell replication 285
cell shading 223, 281–2
cell spacing 263
cell text alignment 220
centre-aligned text 215, 216
charts 298–302
chat rooms 139, 140
chip and pin 29
ciphers 90–1
client-server networks 89–90, 177
clients 86, 104

clip art 250
clock cycles per second 62
closed circuit television 151
cloud storage 139, 178–9
collaborative working 113
colour-blindness 193, 299
colour choice 190–3, 217, 250–2, 265
Colour Picker tool 245–6
column charts 299
columns 219, 276–7, 283–4, 304–5
command line interface 16–17
communication see device-to-device communication; digital communication; email; instant messaging; military communications; multimedia messaging service (MMS); network communication; online conversations; satellite communication; short messaging service (SMS); social media; web browsers
communications monitoring 152–3
compatibility 38, 44, 55, 57, 206–7, 274
competition 125
complimentary closes 230–1
compression 44
computers (computing) 4, 5–7, 13, 15, 19, 69
conditional operators 291–3
connections 135–6
connectivity 16, 19, 64–93
contact lists 139
contactless cards 107
content 269–70
checking 193–4
user-generated 111, 129, 141–2
contrast colours 192
control devices 37, 52
control software 52–4
convergence 4, 15–16
cookies 174–5
copper cables 68, 77
copyright 149–50, 164
Creative Commons licences 149–50
cropping images 244
cross-sheet referencing 294
crowd-mapped data 130
currency data 307, 308
cursors 208–9
cyberbullying 114–15, 145

D
data 123–4, 130, 173–5, 178–9, 183–5, 277–8, 307–8

inputting 319
outputs 324
risks to 96–108
sorting 294–5, 317–19
data projectors 36
data protection laws 147–9
data source files 236–7
data transfer 66–8
data view 303
database management systems (DBMSs) 49, 183, 185, 307–33
datasheet view 309, 311, 320, 332–3
date data 307, 308
decompression 44
defragmentation 43
delete function 210
accidental deletion 98
descending order data 294, 317–18
design characteristics 330
design view 310, 330–2
desktop computers 5–6
desktop publishing (DTP) 48
device names 83–4
device-to-device communication 68–9
dialogue boxes 303
diaphragm 26
digital assets 187
digital audio broadcasting (DAB) 74
digital communication 66–78
digital devices 4–63
digital divide 125–30
digital footprint 118
digital humanitarian movement 129–30
digital product reviews 194–8
digital video broadcasting (DVB) 71–2
digital video broadcasting - terrestrial (DVB-T) 73–4
digital zoom 36
direct messages 137
discharge 34
disk formatting 44–5
disks 39, 40
documents 188, 227–8, 229–37
domain name servers 99
dot matrix printers 33, 34
drones 21
DVD disks/players 11, 39
dynamic host configuration protocol (DHCP) 81
dynasets 319

E
e-tickets 170
eavesdroppers 92
editing images 245–6
electric shocks 155
electrically erasable programmable read only memory (EEPROM) 61
elements (webpage) 272
emails 55, 104
embedded computing 7
employment 111–13
encryption 90–2, 100, 125, 174
energy consumption 20, 32
entity (database) 308, 311, 313
entrance effects 257
erasable programmable read only memory (EPROM) 61
ethernet 74
EU-US Privacy Shield Framework 148
evaluation 197–8
executable files 104
exit effects 257
expansion capability 20
experience points 138
eye health 155

F
Facebook 96, 114, 133, 134, 135, 139, 154
facial recognition 27, 151
fact sheets 235
fibre optic cables 84
file access rights (file permissions) 46, 90, 93, 103
file extensions 206
file formats 206–7
file management 202–7
    see also back up files (backups); data source files; executable files; file access rights (permissions); file names; file servers; file transfer protocol (FTP)
file names 204, 268
file servers 86
file transfer protocol 55
filter software 88
filtering (spreadsheets) 295–7
fingerprint recognition 27
fire hazards 155
firewalls 46, 90, 99, 125
firmware 61
flash media 40
flash memory storage 4, 13, 19, 62
flat file database 308
flexible working 113–14
folders 205–6
font 189–90, 217–18, 252–3, 270, 274
footers 226, 228, 250, 260, 304
formatting
    charts 302
    disks 44–5
    documents 212–13, 230–6
    spreadsheets 278–84
    web pages 270–1
formula view 303
formulae (spreadsheets) 284–8
forums 141
4G 76
frames 264
free software licences 56
freeware 57
frequency 68
full page print layout 260
functions (spreadsheet) 288–93

G
games consoles 8, 12–13, 69
gaming (gaming sites) 138, 171
gateways 85
Gbits 83
geoblocking 150
geolocation rights management 92, 150
gesture interface 19
gigabytes 41
governments 127
GPS (Global Positioning System) 14, 71, 151
gradebooks 140
grammar 211–12
graphical user interface 18
graphics 183, 185, 239–47, 302
graphics cards 46
graphics editors 50
graphics tablets 24
graphs 297
greyscale 190
gridlines 222, 282–3
grooming 117
groups (social networking) 135

H
hacking 125
handouts 258
hard disk drives 16, 38
hard disks 39, 40
harmonious colours 191
HD (high definition) televisions 10, 72, 73
HDMI (High-Definition Multimedia Interface) 69, 74
headers 226, 260, 304–5
headings 223–4, 271
health and safety 154–7
hexadecimal numbers 81
hidden columns/rows 283–4
home automation devices 14
home entertainment systems 10–13
home pages 268
home working 119–21
hosted applications software 176–8
hotspots 83
house style 187, 188–9, 224
HTML (hypertext markup language) 50, 262, 271–2, 273

HTTP (hypertext transfer protocol) 86, 104, 108, 110
HTTPS (hypertext transfer protocol secure) 104
hyperlinks 256, 264–5, 269, 272–3

I

I-beam (I-cursor) 208–9, 211
IBM 350 41
identifiers 82
IF function 290–1, 292
images 50–1, 184, 187, 239–47, 250–1, 253–4, 269, 273
impact printers 33, 34
in-video advertising 122
indent markers 210–11
information 117, 144–5, 159–65, 183–4
information bias 164
information (news) providers 171, 172
information rich/poor gap 129
information sheets 235
infra-red 76
injury at work 155
inkjet printers 33, 34
input peripheral devices 22–31
insert function 210
instant messaging 56, 98
interactivity 111
internet 69–70, 87–90, 109–31
internet protocol (IP) addresses 80–2, 85, 151
internet service providers (ISPs) 77, 85, 87, 153
intranet 50
Investigatory Powers Act (2016) 153
iris recognition 28
italic font 274

J

joysticks 24
justified text 216

K

keyboards 8, 22–3
keywords 161
kilobytes 41
kiosk displays 255
KompoZer 263, 268

L

landscape orientation (format) 227–8, 304
LANs (local area networks) 69, 85, 88–90, 92, 119
laptop computers 6, 15, 19, 69
laser printers 34
latency 67–8, 176–7

law enforcement 129
layers (images) 242–3
layout 186–8, 223–8
leaflets 234
learning tools 139–40, 170, 172
left-aligned text 215, 216
legitimate websites 104
LENGTH function 293
length validation 315
letters 230–1
LibreOffice Calc 303–4
LibreOffice Draw 239, 242
LibreOffice Impress 256
LibreOffice Writer 47, 209, 211–15, 217–19, 222, 224, 227–8
licensing, software 56–7
line charts 300
line graphs 297
linear barcodes 24
lines 216–17, 241–2
locks 20–1
logical functions 290–3
logical operators 321–3
logins 90, 124, 140
LOOKUP function 290

M

MAC addresses 82–3
macro function 256
magnetic strip readers 29
magnetic tape 40
mail merges 236–7, 329–30
main documents 236–7
main headings 223
mainframe computers 4, 5
malware 97, 102
marketing 122, 135, 174–5
massive online open courses 179
massively multiplayer online role-playing games 138
mathematical functions 288–9
matrix codes 24–5, 170
Mbits 83, 84
media 129
media players 11, 13
megabytes 41
memes 111
memory 16, 38, 59–62
see also flash memory storage; RAM (random access memory); ROM (read only memory)
memos 235–6
menu-driven interface 17
menus 267
microphones 26
microprocessors 4, 5
Microsoft Access 316, 324, 327
Microsoft Excel 277, 280, 282, 283, 286, 288, 293, 296, 304
Microsoft PowerPoint 248–61

military communications 73
minijacks 69
misrepresentation 144
mobile broadband 76, 77
mobile phones 7–8, 56, 70, 153
see also smartphones
moderators 129, 140, 141
monitoring technologies 150–3
monitors 32
mouse (keyboard) 23
multi-core processors 62
multifunctional devices 4, 15
multimedia 69, 74
multimedia messaging service (MMS) 56
multiple operator formulae 284–5
multiple worksheets 293–4

N

name boxes (cells) 277, 287–8
navigation aids 14
netbooks 179
network administrators 81
network communication 69–70
network operating systems 45, 80
networks 79–93, 97
see also LANs (local area networks); PANs (personal area networks); WPANs (wireless personal area networks)
news (information) providers 171, 172
newsletters 233
NFC (near field communication) 30, 76, 107
normalisation 52
NOT logical operator 321, 322–3
notes pages 259–60
notifications 137
numbers (numbering) 81, 184, 214–15, 228, 278–9
numeric data 307, 308

O

office productivity software 47–9
on-demand services 111
online communities 132–46
online conversations 136
online information 159–65
online safety 116–19, 143–5
online services 167–79
online work spaces 139
open-source software licences 56
operating systems 45–7
optical character recognition 24
optical disk drives 38
optical disks 39, 40
optical mark recognition 24
optical zoom 36
OR logical operator 321–2

INDEX

organisations
    and the internet 122–8
    and online services 173
output peripheral devices 32–7

P

page breaks 227
page layout 223–8
page numbering 228
PANs (personal area networks) 70
paragraph formatting 212–15
passwords 20, 100, 117
payment systems 105–8
peer-to-peer networks 88
peripheral devices 4, 5, 20, 21–37
persistent cookies 174
personal computers 5–7
personal data theft 98–9
personal information disclosure 117, 144–5
personal media players 13–14
personal video recorders 11
phablets 15
pharming 99
phishing 98
photo editors 51
photo-sharing 141–2
physical activity 116
physical computing 7
pie charts 298–9
PINs (personal identification numbers) 20–1, 100
pixels (pixelation) 9–10, 239–40
placeholders 250
plagiarism 164–5
plotters 35
pointing devices 23–4
portability 6, 16, 36
portrait orientation (format) 227–8, 304
posters 233–4
posts (status updates) 131, 134, 136, 137
presence validation 315
presentations 52, 183, 185, 248–61
Presenter View 260–1
primary information sources 159
primary key field (database) 311
print presentations 258–61
print ranges 303–4
print servers 86
print spooling 46
printers (printing) 33–5, 46, 303–5
privacy settings 117, 144
private messages 137
processor cycle 62
processors 16, 62–3
product catalogues 168–9
PRODUCT function 288, 289
product reviews 194–8
professional networks 133
profiles 133–4
project management software 54
PROM (programmable read only memory) 61
proofreading 194
proprietary software 57
protocols 110
public key encryption 91–2
published file formats 207
punctuation 211–12

Q

QR codes 24–5, 170
quarantine 102
queries (database) 319–21

R

radio 73, 74, 110
radio frequency identification (RFID) 30
RAM (Random Access Memory) 16, 38, 45, 59–60, 61
range 277
range validation 315
ransomware 97
Raspberry Pi Zero computer 7, 13
reactions (social networking) 136
reCAPTCHA tests 101–2
recordable/ write once (R) media 39
reference sites 129, 140–1
referential integrity 314, 315
referring website 174
relational databases 308, 313–15
relational operators 323–4
relative cell referencing 285–6
religion 127
repetitive strain injury (RSI) 155
reports 231–2, 324–8
required attributes 272, 273
resistive touch screens 26–7
resizing images 243–4
resolution 10, 32, 36, 239–40
return function 209, 211
rewritable (R/W) media 39
right-aligned text 215, 216
risks 96–108
ROM (read only memory) 38, 61
rotating images 243–4
routers 85
rows (spreadsheets) 277, 281, 283–4, 304–5

S

salutations 230–1
sans serif font 190, 218
satellite communication 71–3
saving files 202–3, 206–7
scanners 24
scattergrams 300–2
search engines 87–8, 160–3
search syntax 163
search tools 161–2
secondary information sources 159
secondary storage (storage) 38–41, 60
security 20–2, 46, 75, 90–3, 99–108, 124–5, 203
sensors 30–1, 69
serif font 189–90, 218
servers 86
session cookies 174
set-top boxes 11
share functionality 136
shift function 210
shopping sites 168–9, 172
shortcuts 22, 197, 202
SIM (subscriber identity module) 7, 9
single-board computers 7
single operator formulae 284
single sign on 140
single-user operating systems 45
skills requirements 112, 201–75
slide masters 249–53
smart homes 30
smart televisions 11, 13, 17
smartphones 8, 14–15, 21, 27, 53–4, 69, 107, 170
smartwatch 70, 107
SMS (short messaging service) 56, 98, 130
snake case 204
social bookmarking 143
social impact (internet) 114–16, 131
social network applications 55, 129, 132–8
    see also Facebook
software 42–58, 88, 90, 176–8, 182–99, 201–75
sound, editing of 51–2, 185
sound cards 26, 185
sound systems 11
source codes 56
space function 209
speakers 11, 36–7
specialist phones 7
specified fields (database) 330
spell checkers 193–4
spelling 211–12
split-complementary colours 192
spreadsheets 48–9, 183, 185, 276–306
sprites 24
spyware 103
SSDs (solid state drives) 38, 60, 62
statistical functions 288–9
status updates (posts) 131, 134, 136, 137
stereo sound 36
storage 16, 38–41, 60, 90, 139, 178–9
storage devices 38

storage media 19, 39–41
streaming 11, 67
stylus 24
sub-bullet points (sub-numbering) 213, 214
sub-headings 223
surround sound 36
sustainability 153–4
switches 84–5
symmetric key encryption 91
syntax 163, 184
system software 42–6

T

tab function 210
tables 220–3, 263–4, 297, 308
tablets 9, 15, 24, 42
tabs (indentation) 210–11, 216
tags 135
targeted marketing 135, 174–5
telecommunications 69, 84, 87
telephones 72
   see also mobile phones; smartphones
television 10–11, 13, 17, 71–2, 73–4, 110
templates 224–5, 248–9, 262–8
terabytes 41
tethering 70
text 184, 208–11, 215–17, 220, 245, 253–4, 269, 273
text boxes 219
text functions 293
text wrap 217, 280
third-party banners 266
third-party cookies 174–5
third-party integration 136–7, 140, 142, 143
third-party payment processors 106
threads 141
3D printers 34–5
3G 76
timeline 134
toolbars 279
touch screens 26–7
track pads 23
tracker balls 23
transaction logs 93
transactional data 174–5
transitions 257–8
transparency 207, 251, 252
trip hazards 155
type validation 315

U

ultra high definition televisions 10
unauthorised access 97, 125
underlining font 274
updates (software) 57, 60
upgrades 5

usability 26, 57
usage rights 162
USB (universal serial bus) 11, 20, 38, 62, 69, 74
user-generated content 111, 129, 141–2
user-generated reference sites 129, 140–1
user interface 16–19
users 186
utility software 42–5

V

validation (database) 315–17
vector graphics 240, 302
versioning 204–5
video-sharing 141–2
viral marketing 122
virtual keyboards 8
virtual memory 16, 38, 60
virtual private networks 92–3
virus definitions 102–3
VLEs (virtual learning environments) 139–40, 170
vlogs 142
VLOOKUP function 290
voice interface 18–19
voice recognition 28, 269
VoIP (voice over internet protocol) 26, 110
voucher codes 169

W

wall (social network applications) 134
WANs (wide area networks) 69–70, 85
web authoring 50, 55, 183, 185, 262–75
web browsers 55, 87, 162–3, 262
web links 104
web servers 86
webcams 25
webforms 99
webmail 55
websites 104, 174
white space 187
whitelists 88
Wi-Fi (wireless fidelity) 8, 9, 11, 15, 38, 75, 77, 84
Wi-Fi Protected Access 92
WIKIs 140
wired communication 71, 74, 77, 83–4, 86
wireless access points 84
wireless communication 71, 75–7, 84, 86
wireless encryption protocol (WEP) 92
word processing 47–8, 183, 185, 188, 208–38
workbooks see spreadsheets
working practices 113–14
WPANs (wireless personal area networks) 70
WYSIWYG (what you see is what you get) editors 50, 262–3

Z

z axis 242
zoom functionality 36